D1190939

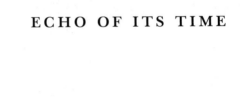

ECHO OF ITS TIME

ECHO OF ITS TIME

The History of the Federal District
Court of Nebraska, 1867–1933

John R. Wunder and Mark R. Scherer

UNIVERSITY OF NEBRASKA PRESS | LINCOLN AND LONDON

Portions of chapter 9 and 10 have been previously published
by Omaha attorney Nick Batter in "The Wayfaring Judge:
Woodrough and Organized Crime in the U.S. District
Court," *Nebraska History* 97, no. 2 (Summer 2016): 73–92.
The authors wish to thank Mr. Batter for his assistance and
cooperation in the research and preparation of this material.

Publication of this volume was assisted by the
Nebraska Branch of the Historical Society of the
United States Courts in the Eighth Circuit.

Library of Congress Cataloging-in-Publication Data

Names: Wunder, John R., author. | Scherer, Mark R., author.
Title: Echo of its time: the history of the Federal District Court
of Nebraska, 1867–1933 / John R. Wunder and Mark R. Scherer.
Description: Lincoln: University of Nebraska Press, 2019.
| Includes bibliographical references and index.
Identifiers: LCCN 2018041351
ISBN 9781496212146 (hardback)
ISBN 9781496213112 (epub)
ISBN 9781496213129 (mobi)
Subjects: LCSH: United States. District Court (Nebraska)—
History—19th century. | United States. District
Court (Nebraska)—History—20th century. | District
courts—Nebraska—History—19th century. | District courts—
Nebraska—History—20th century. | BISAC: HISTORY / United
States / State & Local / Midwest (IA, IL, IN, KS, MI, MN, MO,
ND, NE, OH, SD, WI). | LAW / Legal History. | LAW / Courts.
Classification: LCC KF8755.N35 W86 2019 |
DDC 347.73/220978209034—dc23
LC record available at https://lccn.loc.gov/2018041351

Set in New Baskerville ITC by E. Cuddy.
Designed by N. Putens.

CONTENTS

ILLUSTRATIONS

Following page 172

INTRODUCTION

In one of the more memorable passages from his classic *Democracy in America*, Alexis de Tocqueville noted, "There is hardly a political question in the United States which does not sooner or later turn into a judicial one."[1] The point to be drawn from Tocqueville's observation—the notion that a nation's history is revealed in its courts of law—has been echoed and restated by many subsequent scholars and commentators. Perhaps most notably, renowned jurist Oliver Wendell Holmes Jr., writing some sixty years after Tocqueville, characterized the American judicial system as a "magic mirror" that reflects the ebb and flow of the nation's social, political, and cultural history.[2]

That, in short, is the driving premise of this book. Throughout its 150 years of existence, the U.S. District Court of Nebraska has echoed the dynamics of its time, reflecting the concerns, interests, passions, and proclivities of the people who have made this place their home. The judges who have occupied the court's bench have dealt with a vast and diverse range of issues, controversies, and debates, all of which have shaped and defined the state's history and development—contests pitting laborers against management, homesteading farmers against free range cattlemen, progressive reformers against powerfully entrenched political and business interests, government regulators against free market capitalists, criminals against law enforcement officials, and Native Americans against the "mainstream" society that displaced them, to name just a few. At one time or another, and for better or worse, the aspirations of all of these groups and many more have made their way onto the docket of the Nebraska federal court. In their handling of those matters, the judges have indeed reflected the times in which they lived and worked. And in their stories, we are offered an instructive prism through which the state's political, cultural, and social evolution may be traced, analyzed, and assessed.

This project has been in the making for an inordinately long time, necessitating great patience and perseverance from all involved. The journey began more than seventeen years ago, when Dr. John R. Wunder, professor of history at the University of Nebraska–Lincoln, was named the official historian for the Nebraska branch of the Historical Society of the United States Courts in the Eighth Circuit, and he undertook the writing of a history of the court. Wunder made substantial progress on the research and drafting of the manuscript over the next several years, completing the first four chapters herein, before health issues and the press of other business began to slow the project's momentum. At that point, Wunder invited the participation of his former student, Dr. Mark R. Scherer, professor of history at the University of Nebraska–Omaha. Scherer picked up the project from there, working intermittently over the past decade to research and draft the final six chapters. As the process unfolded, it was determined that a full account of the court's history would ultimately require two volumes, with the first one, this book, tracing the court's operations up to the year 1933.

Through all the years of slow progress, the officers of the Nebraska branch of the Historical Society, most notably Jeanette Stull, Frank Mihulka, and John Sharp, have been steadfast—and remarkably tolerant—in their stewardship of the project, offering valuable direction, feedback, and encouragement as the process unfolded. So too, the current chief judge of the U.S. District Court of Nebraska, Laurie Smith Camp, has lent her abundant support and her own considerable skills as a writer and historian to the effort. Deep thanks are also owed to a number of research assistants who have participated in the project, from John Hussman in the early years through Katie Welchans and Nick Batter more recently. Their time and skills have made a vital contribution to the ultimate result. But as valuable as all of those individuals' participation has been, the sine qua non of this entire project has been Senior District Judge Richard Kopf, who has been its undisputed champion and indispensable guiding force from the outset. His sagacity, patience, serenity, and resolute determination to see the project to completion—often in the face of his own daunting medical challenges—have been an inspiration to everyone involved, and it is to him that this volume is dedicated.

This book is not intended to represent a "standard" institutional history, nor does it come even remotely close to offering an exhaustive account of all, or even most, of the court's significant decisions. For every case that is discussed, dozens more have been necessarily ignored. Our guiding principle has been to select and explore those stories from the court's annals that we feel best serve the dual goals of informing and entertaining the reader, seeking to provide accessible narrative as well as the occasional "history lesson" on the larger contextual milieu in which the court's actions are situated. It is, of course, for the reader to decide how well those goals have been accomplished.

In chapter 1, John Wunder provides an overview of the origins and evolution of the federal judicial system generally, and analyzes the political maneuvering that led to Nebraska statehood and the creation of Nebraska's new federal district court in 1867. Of particular note is Wunder's exploration of the complicated and still confusing overlap between the role and duties of nineteenth-century federal judges in their capacity as both "district" and "circuit" judges. Chapter 2 describes the biographical background, early legal career, and 1867 appointment of the first permanent judge of the Nebraska district court, Elmer S. Dundy. This chapter also explores many of the notable cases heard and decisions rendered by Dundy during his extremely influential twenty-eight-year tenure as Nebraska's first and only federal district judge and the often bitter partisan political environment in which he and the court operated.

Chapter 3 offers Wunder's specialized examination of some of the most notable Indian law cases handled by Dundy, with particular attention to his landmark opinions in *Standing Bear v. Crook* (1879) and *Elk v. Wilkins* (1880). Finally, in chapter 4, Wunder provides detailed discussion and analysis of Dundy's prominent and often controversial handling of numerous cases involving the railroads, which of course were among the most powerful corporate citizens of the state throughout the late nineteenth century.

Scherer takes the reins beginning with chapter 5, offering a relatively brief examination of the short-lived and ultimately unconfirmed nomination of William McHugh after Dundy's death in 1896. Chapter 6 explores the biographical background and 1897 appointment of William H. Munger as the next judge of the Nebraska district court and discusses the first decade of the court's operations under his leadership. Scherer places particular focus on Munger's handling of litigation arising out of the nationwide "Progressive" reform initiatives of the period, including volatile labor relations and allegations of political corruption. Chapter 7 is topically specialized, focusing on Munger's controversial handling of the federal prosecutions of wealthy and prominent Nebraska cattle ranchers for the illegal fencing of public lands and the filing of fraudulent homestead claims in the early twentieth century. Those cases brought nationwide notoriety to Munger and the Nebraska court, with results that infuriated President Theodore Roosevelt, who fired the U.S. district attorney and U.S. marshal in the aftermath of the proceedings.

Chapter 8 explores an important transitional era in the court's history, as Congress created a second Nebraska federal judicial seat in 1907. Remarkably, the man who would be appointed to that new judgeship was also named Munger (no relation to William), launching a period that we refer to as the "two Munger" court. During those years, the court presided over a number of prominent and colorful controversies, including more conflicts over railroad regulation and Thomas Munger's handling of the "Great Omaha Train Robbery" of 1909. This chapter also makes special use of Thomas Munger's personal correspondence during the period of his appointment and early service on the Nebraska federal bench. Those letters and memoranda offer intriguing glimpses into the inner workings of the court and the relationship between its two judges.

In chapter 9, Scherer explores the biographical background, prejudicial legal career, and appointment of the enigmatic Joseph W. Woodrough to replace William Munger in 1915. Special attention is given to the court's operations during the First World War and the 1920s, including matters related to free speech limitations and nativist/anti-German issues, as well as ongoing labor unrest and accompanying violence that led to the imposition of martial law in a portion of southeastern Nebraska in 1922. Finally, chapter 10 addresses Prohibition in the 1920s, a period that brought new burdens and challenges to the court, along with a rather sharp—and sometimes public—rift between Judges Munger and Woodrough over their contrasting attitudes and approaches to the overwhelming tide of Prohibition cases that engulfed their dockets during those years. Drawing from the previously published work of Chief Judge Laurie Smith Camp and attorney Nick Batter, this chapter concludes with an examination of Woodrough's handling of the massive 1933 conspiracy trial against notorious Omaha political boss and criminal kingpin Tom Dennison and Woodrough's subsequent appointment to the Eighth Circuit Court of Appeals by President Franklin Roosevelt.

Ultimately, our hope is that the stories we have chosen to tell will demonstrate both the instructive value and the enjoyably entertaining possibilities of judicial history as a medium for exploring the past and understanding the present. In its role as an "echo of its time," the U.S. District Court of Nebraska has played a dynamic role in both forging and revealing the history of this unique place and its people.

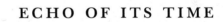

ECHO OF ITS TIME

1

In the Beginning

And such inferior Courts as the Congress may from time to time ordain
and establish.
—U.S. Constitution, Art. III, Section 1

Roscoe Pound, Nebraska's most prominent and profound legal thinker,
observed in 1922 that law and justice were dynamic concepts. For
Pound, the idea of law represented "a system of precepts discovered
by human experience whereby the individual human may realize the
most complete freedom possible consistently with the like freedom of
will of others." This system divided judges, Pound wrote. Some held to
the concept of enforcing law based exclusively on existing statutes and
past precedents while others believed that law evolved in some kind
of "inevitable way" by applying human experience in place and time.
This latter explanation seemed to appeal to Pound. An acknowledged
legal realist, he had had plenty of grounding in early Nebraska law
and practice. The judiciary presided over a process that "was determined by the unfolding of an idea of right and justice or an idea of
liberty which was realizing itself in [the] human administration of
justice, or by the operation of biological or psychological laws or of
race characters, whose necessary result was the system of law of the
time and people in question."[1]

A system of law "of the time and people in question" in essence denotes the history of Nebraska's first federal court. With the creation of a state came the vital umbilical connection to the federal judicial system, and for Nebraskans of 1867 this meant a new court and a new experience in justice. Other states had experienced this legal system, and it was a relatively new legal institution in process. Nebraskans had every reason to be confident that the U.S. District Court of Nebraska would accelerate the integration of Nebraskans into a shaken Union. It is important to remember context, and the most bloody and divisive experience for the relatively young nation had only just concluded. Nebraskans had done their part to preserve the nation. Unlike Kansas, a battleground on its own soil, Nebraskans had for the most part remained steadfast for the North, and the result of such loyalty meant passing from territorial status into statehood, from legal adolescence into lawful adulthood.

A gateway to the expanding American West, a centerpiece for the nearly completed transcontinental railroad, and a territory ready to host the tens of thousands of settlers who were poised to rush to the Great Plains and displace its indigenous inhabitants, Nebraska embodied a new frontier in time and in place. Less than eighty years previously, the first of several federal court frontiers expanded beyond the original thirteen states, and the state of Kentucky found itself confronting a new legal experiment. Kentucky, unlike Nebraska, endured no territorial period, and it acquired its first federal court more than two years before it gained statehood. This distinctive element in time did not seem to impede Kentucky's initial national legal experiences, for its district court functioned smoothly and quickly burrowed into the bluegrass social and political terrain. Blessed with well-qualified judges and court officers, Kentucky readily provided a model transition for potential states and the evolution of their connection to the federal legal system.

Mary K. Bonsteel Tachau, historian of Kentucky's early federal courts, characterized this first federal court frontier as "sophisticated" and reassuring for Kentucky's citizens. In her extensive culling of early legal records, Tachau concluded that "despite the primitive environment, the federal [district] court in Kentucky soon became very busy, in part because the law practiced there did not yield the crude justice generally associated with the frontier."[2] The reason for this positive assessment lay in the expectations of the settlers who were experienced with a legally trained bench and bar; a seasoned district judge, one Harry Innes, a man of extensive legal education and strong convictions, who served the first twenty-seven years of the court; and the loyal and efficient service of court officers who were also well trained.[3]

Tachau summarized the experience of this first federal district court. "This court and its immediate successors upheld the traditions of centuries of English experience, modified in the colonial period and now applied to a new political and judicial experiment." Tachau found that some "of that law was very old, developed in a different political and socioeconomic environment, but applicable in many of its forms and procedures to this sparsely settled and crudely surveyed land. Some of the law was an adaptation of familiar principles to the requirements of the new Constitution, which was founded on the unprecedented ideal of political and legal equality for all white men. Some of the law evolved in Kentucky in response to the competitiveness and land hunger of the population."[4] Thus Kentucky's federal court conformed to Roscoe Pound's observation of the judiciary. It had to balance the past—in fact, the not-too-distant past of the American Revolution—with the present and the future of the place and its peoples. So too would Nebraska's federal jurists, for they were also dealing with a new place, new peoples, and, some historians would argue, a new Constitution remade from the Civil War.

The Creation of the Federal District and Circuit Courts

Article III, Section 1 of the Constitution stipulates that the judiciary of the United States is to be composed of the Supreme Court and "such inferior Courts as the Congress may from time to time ordain and establish." Thus, unlike the U.S. Supreme Court, all other federal courts are creations of Congress. They owe their very existence to Congress. It is from Congress, then, that all federal district and circuit courts evolve.

All inferior federal courts began with the approval of the Judiciary Act of 1789. This law created two kinds of federal courts below the Supreme Court: district and circuit. Thirteen federal district courts were authorized in eleven states, with the northern detached portion of the state of Massachusetts named the Maine District, and the western portion of the state of Virginia designated as the Kentucky District. North Carolina and Rhode Island had yet to ratify the Constitution, so they were not initially included. They would later receive federal district court judges, again one per state.

The country as it was constituted in 1789 was divided into three circuits, and each circuit was authorized to host a court composed of two justices of the Supreme Court and a federal district judge from one of the states in the circuit. The Maine and Kentucky Districts were excluded from assignment in the circuit courts. Two judges of the three constituted a quorum and could conduct the business of the circuit court. No federal district court judge could vote on an appeal alleging an error in his own decision. He could, however, offer the reasons to the circuit court for his decision.

Federal district court judges were to hold four sessions per year, and Congress specifically established where and when these sessions were to be held. Circuit court judges were authorized to hold court twice a year in designated towns and cities on specific days in each of the states included in the circuit. Circuit courts could hold special sessions for particular criminal cases at their discretion or upon order of the Supreme Court. Judges did not have discretion over the temporal or spatial geography of their courts.

The jurisdiction of the federal district courts involved both exclusive and concurrent powers. All crimes against the laws of the United States committed within their particular district or upon the high seas where punishment did not exceed thirty whipping stripes, a fine over $100, or a term of imprisonment not exceeding six months, were exclusively heard in U.S. district courts. In addition, district courts had exclusive jurisdiction over all civil causes of admiralty and revenue including all seizures of vessels or trade in which a remedy at common law existed. Concurrent jurisdiction existed for the federal district courts with state courts and the federal circuit courts in all suits where the U.S. government sued for a value of $100 or less. All district court cases with the exception of admiralty disputes required a trial by jury, and the district courts were the only federal courts assigned a judge and a staff of a clerk and a marshal.[5]

Thus federal district court judges also served as judges in the first U.S. circuit courts. The circuit courts had specific original jurisdiction in both criminal and civil matters. Original jurisdiction covered all crimes committed against the United States that had penalties greater than those restricted to the district courts. Circuit courts heard civil cases where the dispute exceeded $500 in value and the U.S. government was a plaintiff and in cases involving an alien as either a defendant or a plaintiff or if one party was a citizen of a different state than the other party and in cases concerning title to land of a value over $500. These cases could originate in state courts, but upon petition by either party, they had to be moved to the circuit court or the district court in Maine and Kentucky. Circuit courts also had appellate jurisdiction from the district courts under certain restrictions. And no person could be arrested in one district for trial in another district, whether for an action applicable to either a circuit or a district court.

The Judiciary Act of 1789 gave all federal courts including the district and circuit courts certain powers. Each could issue writs of habeas corpus; they could compel parties to produce documents; and they could grant new trials and use the power of contempt of court against uncooperative parties.[6]

Thus the initial powers of the inferior federal courts were limited. District courts had very modest original jurisdiction. They could hear minor criminal cases, but their main function at first was the handling of admiralty matters. Congress assumed that state trial courts and the federal circuit courts would take care of the most important legal concerns. Over time federal district courts benefited from significant expansions of their original jurisdiction.

The first U.S. district court organized was that of New York State. It called itself to order on November 3, 1789. It is the precursor to the modern U.S. District Court for the Southern District of New York, and judges of the Southern District continue to call their court the "Mother Court."[7]

The role of the U.S. district court judge as an appellate court judge within the framework of the circuit courts would eventually be altered. There would be significant confusion over jurisdiction that would be complicated even further with the creation of separate U.S. courts of appeals in 1891. It was not until 1911 that the circuit courts were abolished, so for two decades two separate federal appellate courts existed side by side.[8] Nevertheless, the federal district court judge also assumed the mantle of a circuit court judge and made rulings accordingly. Such was the case for Nebraska's federal court judge.

The Judiciary Act of 1789 was immediately challenged, and the federal courts became embroiled in political machinations. This should not be seen as too surprising as the U.S. Constitution did not give the lower federal courts specific constitutional protection and instead left them to Congress and the political processes of the new nation to determine. The Judiciary Act of 1789 was the brainchild of the Federalists, and at that time political factions were in their nascent development. Once Jeffersonian Republicans challenged Federalist rule and eventually prevailed, they found Section 25 of the act objectionable. That section allowed federal courts to review the decisions of state courts that involved the U.S. Constitution or federal statutes.[9] It amounted to a direct attack by the Federalists on states' rights, so reasoned the Jeffersonians and their Jacksonian Democrat cousins several decades later. Section 34 cushioned this situation by stipulating that "the laws of the several states, except where the constitution, treaties or statutes of the United States shall otherwise require or provide, shall be regarded as rules of decision in trials at common law in the courts of the United States in cases where they apply."[10] In other words, on similar points of law district court judges had to regard decisions of state courts as prevailing. Nevertheless, the door was open for the federalization of the nation's judiciary that also included the curbing of the power of state courts.

The first judges were Federalists. Most Federalists were not what one might describe as "men of the people." They usually were from the towns, not the country, and they were relatively wealthy. Almost immediately they realized the implications of the Judiciary Act of 1789. District court judges were required to live in the districts they served. The time and place of their court sessions were circumscribed. Moreover, the circuit courts not only required the presence of the district court judges, but U.S. Supreme Court justices were mandated to come to the people as well. Legal historian Kermit Hall describes this act as making Supreme Court justices into "republican schoolmasters whose presence in the circuits symbolized the authority of the remote national government."[11] It also made for a debilitating judicial duty that no justice liked and most detested. Riding in uncomfortable stages or on horseback to distant parts of the new nation took its toll on the justices. Gouverneur Morris, an aspiring and often frustrated politician, criticized the circuit court arrangement. Few, he reflected, thought "riding rapidly from one end of this country to another is the best way to study law. . . . Knowledge may be more conveniently acquired in a closet than in the high road."[12] Not surprisingly, Federalist judges were more comfortable in an easy chair reading the law near their bedroom fireplace—their "closet"—than on horses in a rainstorm forging a swollen river.

Thus the Judiciary Act of 1789 created the lower federal courts. Both district courts and circuit courts were devised, and they linked the expanding nation together in a judicial mosaic that, while not perfect, offered a means of establishing the rule of law. It is well to remember that Congress, as observed by Stanford University law professor Lawrence M. Friedman, could have easily passed on creating inferior federal courts.[13] If it had, state courts would have had nearly complete original jurisdiction over almost all issues. A truly different kind of nation would have evolved.

Politics and Momentary Reform

In the first years of the United States, no institution proved more the subject of ideological tests than the federal courts. As such the federal district courts were in the thick of the disputes. The rhetoric rose as factions became hardened in American politics. Jeffersonians and Federalists alike saw the courts as threat and savior.

In 1794 when a federal excise tax was placed on whiskey, farmers in western Pennsylvania refused to pay the tax. The federal government responded by forcing the farmers under threat of land confiscation to travel to a federal circuit court in Philadelphia to stand trial, and the farmers threatened tax collectors and made plans to burn Pittsburgh. Federalists met this threat by calling up a larger national army than had fought in the Revolution to put down the farmers' revolt. Indictments were brought against more than thirty men, and at the trials Federalist judges used dubious interpretations of treason that only brought on greater contempt for the lower federal courts and the central government itself.

A similar situation arose four years later after the Federalists passed the Sedition Act of 1798, an attempt to curb the actions of sympathizers to the French Revolution, when Federalist judges of U.S. district courts invoked politics to obtain seditious libel convictions. For example, District Judge Richard Peters with Supreme Court Justice Samuel Chase forced a jury to convict one Thomas Cooper of libel for Cooper's accusation that President John Adams had borrowed money at too high an interest rate during peace and had interfered with the judiciary. The fact that President Adams may have done so was deemed irrelevant by the circuit court.

The results of the presidential election of 1800 stunned the Federalists. Thomas Jefferson's defeat of President Adams meant that the nation would now have an exchange of power based upon political parties. With the election results known in November and the Jeffersonians slated to take over the presidency in March, sufficient time existed for the Federalists to make appointments to government positions and pass legislation to reform the federal courts. Although the Federalists did not know it, this was to be their last political gasp.

Even with more than four months, the Federalists had difficulty making sure that all of their attempts to stave off the Jeffersonians were put in place. Numerous local officials were appointed, but as happened with one—William Marbury' s commission to be a District of Columbia justice of the peace—the process of appointment was not completely executed, and this failure eventually led to *Marbury v. Madison* (1803) and the Supreme Court's assumption of the power of judicial review.

Greater success was achieved with passage of the Judiciary Act of 1801. With President Adams's signature, the reforms became law. This act abolished the practice of circuit riding for Supreme Court justices who were the Federalists' last vestige of national power. The arduous task of meeting in the circuit courts with federal district judges was abolished so that the judges for life could lead long lives. At the same time sixteen circuit court judgeships were created. Another innovation of the act was the creation of five district courts, several within existing states (New Jersey, North Carolina, Maryland, and Virginia) and a new district court for the District of Columbia to be called the District of Potomac. The power of Congress also was expressed in the abolition of the district courts of Kentucky and Tennessee and turning over all of its cases to a circuit court for two districts in Tennessee and the entire state of Kentucky.[14]

Perhaps an admirable reform, the Judiciary Act of 1801 instead smacked of the exercise of rote political muscle as the Federalists hurriedly appointed their political cronies to these federal inferior courts. Jefferson tabbed the new jurists "midnight judges," and he viewed the appointments as a blatant political attempt by the Federalists to put up barriers to his legislative plans. The fact that Federalists may have legitimately meant to strengthen the national court system belied the evidence of the last-minute exercise of political might. Americans were not impressed.[15]

The Federalists' reform of the lower courts proved momentary. Once in power, Jeffersonians lost little time passing the third judiciary act in only thirteen years of national existence. Termed "An Act to amend the Judicial System of the United States," the Judiciary Act of 1802 has been generally regarded by legal scholars more as the repeal of the Judiciary Act of 1801 than as a statutory revision. The new Federalist circuit court judges were out of their jobs, and the Supreme Court's justices were literally back in the saddle again. Although the old circuit courts were restored, new federal district courts in North Carolina were retained.[16] The Jeffersonians, like the

Federalists, recognized that greater populations necessitated more district courts.

Thomas Jefferson himself, however, did not escape those Federalists who were safely secure in the federal judiciary, notably his cousin John Marshall, the new chief justice of the Supreme Court. He would find numerous ways to anchor into American law such Federalist concepts as a strong central government, the sanctity of contracts, and the supremacy of interstate commerce over state attempts to regulate it.

Some Federalist judges were targets of Jeffersonian political wrath, and this took the form of the first exercises of impeachment in American history. In fact, the very first federal official to be removed from office was John Pickering, a U.S. district judge in the state of New Hampshire. Pickering's is a complicated case that taxed the very core principles underpinning the newly formed federal judiciary system. Pickering was a dedicated Federalist. As "one of the most distinguished members of New Hampshire's revolutionary generation,"[17] he had drafted New Hampshire's constitution in 1784 and served as chief justice of the New Hampshire Supreme Court. While on the bench, Pickering started to forget his judicial duties, and he developed a nervous disorder. He also took to excessive drinking and by all accounts became an alcoholic. Many lawyers suspected that Judge Pickering had gone mad.

Pickering was almost removed by New Hampshire's legislature, but Federalists resolved to cut their state political losses by persuading President Washington to nominate Pickering as New Hampshire's federal district court judge. This was a serious mistake, although it certainly reflects the status of the new federal district courts within the legal community.

In one of Pickering's early cases before his court, he snapped. A ship, *Eliza*, was seized by the federal government for violating revenue laws, and the owner sought redress. *Eliza*'s owner and his lawyer knew Pickering well; they shared a close attachment to High Federalist political ideology. Politics seemed to surround the proceeding as the prosecuting attorney and U.S. marshal were Jeffersonian Republicans. Shortly after the opening of the court, Judge Pickering announced that he was finding for his Federalist friend. When the district attorney objected and complained that he had not even had a chance to call his witnesses for the prosecution, Pickering lambasted the lawyer: "You may bring forty thousand [witnesses] & they will not alter the decree."[18] The judge then shouted profanities as he left the bench. What should be done?

Clearly Pickering was a national embarrassment, and Federalists sought to have him retire. But he would have none of that, and he framed his notoriety as political persecution. The only provision covering removal of a federal judge was the Constitution's impeachment provisions, but they allowed for a removal trial based upon charges of committing treason, bribery, or other high crimes and misdemeanors. Incompetence and insanity were not covered by the Constitution. The two-week trial in March 1804 featured the Federalists trying to prove Judge Pickering was insane and therefore not impeachable and the Republicans attempting to show Pickering to be rational in order to be removed. It was not the republic's finest hour. Some of the Republicans deserted the president; even the president supposedly had doubts. But the trial was concluded with nineteen Senate votes for removal, just enough. The same day that Pickering was removed, Supreme Court justice Samuel Chase, an irascible, stalwart Federalist, was also impeached in the House. Chase would prevail, however, and the intimidation of the bench seemed to subside. The lower federal judiciary weathered the worst of the political storms surrounding the courts during the early nineteenth century.[19]

Congressional Legislation and the District Courts, 1803–1867

The next six decades in the history of the federal district courts was a time of relative calm, certainly when compared with the impeachments and the first three judiciary acts. After 1803, lower federal courts experienced a time of consolidation and statutory nuance. To be sure, there were firsts and legal experiments, but generally prior to the creation of Nebraska's federal district court, no major changes were heralded.

The primary business for the district courts involved admiralty jurisdiction. This is not too surprising given that water served as the nation's commercial lifeblood. Dating from as early as 1794, federal district courts were deemed the repository for actions having to do with the seizure of vessels.[20] It was, after all, the very type of cause of action that had led to the impeachment of Judge John Pickering in 1804. Of significance was a federal statute passed and signed by President Jefferson in 1800. This law, "An Act in addition to the act entitled 'An act to prohibit the carrying on the Slave Trade from the United States to any foreign place or country,'" prohibited American citizens from owning vessels involved in the slave trade or from working or even volunteering to travel on a slave ship.[21] Other American vessels if they suspected Americans on a slave ship or a slave ship owned by an American could seize that ship and divide among the sailors all things of value seized, with the exception of the slaves. They were to be legally treated as prizes discovered at sea. Jurisdiction over these actions was lodged in the federal district and circuit courts. When owners of ships, slave or other, felt they were not likely to be treated fairly in the federal courts, they tried to take their suits to state courts, but that tactic was thwarted in 1815 with passage of a law that allowed naval and customs officers and tax collectors to transfer any suit against them into the federal circuit courts.[22]

District courts were also relied upon to resolve issues that involved important diplomatic and financial ramifications. In 1818 Congress provided the district courts with specific jurisdiction to initiate action against American citizens who were employed as foreign agents. Not surprisingly, this power extended beyond the physical borders of the country into American waters. District courts, even where there were no circuit courts, were also given jurisdiction over the crime of piracy.[23] And when reforms were made in the Department of the Treasury, it fell to the district courts to provide a setting to assist anyone who was financially injured unknowingly by the changes. Here no specific dollar limitation was set on the causes of action, and the district court judge was given the power to issue an injunction to stay the proceedings and to prevent further damage to a plaintiff.[24] Gradually the district courts were accumulating important piecemeal jurisdiction within the federalized nation.

Confusion continued in the interrelationships between federal district courts and state courts and federal circuit courts. This was complicated by the growing nation. By 1807 a seventh circuit court was created for Ohio, Kentucky, and Tennessee, and more would be needed in the near future.[25] Also in 1807 it was necessary to give federal district court judges greater injunctive powers so that they could issue the same orders as Supreme Court justices acting as fellow circuit judges. To eliminate any confusion, these powers were made available to the district judges whether they were sitting as a district court or as a circuit court.[26]

By the 1820s another structural weakness became problematic. Appeals from district courts with exclusive federal jurisdiction in a few states were taken to circuit courts in another district. For example, from 1814 to 1826, some appeals were channeled by litigants from the District Court of the Northern District of New York to the Circuit Court of the Southern District of New York. Circuit shopping entered the lexicon of the federal practice of law. This became such a problem in Alabama that in 1842 all civil cases from the Northern District of Alabama were allowed to be appealed directly from the district courts to the U.S. Supreme Court. This created a legal oddity because it so happened that the same judge sat in both districts in Alabama. His jurisdiction in the Northern District became greater than in the Southern District because no such direct appeals were allowed in it. Similar anomalies existed in Pennsylvania as well.[27] All of these minute exceptions for individual federal district courts came with congressional tinkering.

Confusion continued over jurisdiction problems vis-à-vis the wearing of the district court/circuit court hat. When a district court judge was acting as a circuit court, a civil appeal could be taken to the U.S. Supreme Court only if the amount involved more than $2,000. A district court judge's opinion when acting as a circuit court was final if the amount was less than $2,000. If he was acting as a district court, his amount for an appellate review was $500. Thus new states that did not have circuit courts immediately were restrained in their abilities to appeal up the federal court system, and they noted that this was unequal treatment. Moreover, circuit courts attracted much more attention and incumbent legal business because of the attendance of a Supreme Court justice, that is, while they continued to ride circuit even though it was becoming less and less frequent.[28]

Although there were aspects of confusion over jurisdiction and a wide range of minor structural differences, the strength of the concept of a federal district and circuit court was tested in two ways. These tests went to the heart of the concept of a nation under law. One test was whether the district courts could successfully incorporate new lands that had serious problems of law and social order under the rule of law; the other met the challenge of the national breakup. With secession, the district courts managed to survive, perhaps better than might have been expected.

The United States, not unlike an abnormal cell that continues to reproduce at rapid speeds, proved to be an aggressive nation bent on postrevolutionary expansion. In 1803 it roughly doubled in size with the Louisiana Purchase from France. By 1820 the Floridas had been added to the national terrain by bullying and buying off Spain. After the Mexicans ended their colonial era, they found it increasingly difficult to restrain American movements, and the colonists who settled in Mexico's northernmost province, Texas, soon chafed under Mexico's democracy and revolted. The successful Texas Revolution of 1836 and its rather limpid nine years of international independence found annexation into the United States of mutual benefit to both parties in 1845. This helped precipitate the American war with Mexico the following year, which resulted in a further extension of U.S. sovereignty. Together with the Oregon Treaty with Britain signed in 1846, placing a large chunk of what is today the Pacific Northwest under American control, the United States increased its physical boundary by a third. Such incorporation of extensive lands and peoples required order and the extension of national law. That meant more U.S. district courts.

Innovation was needed, and the incorporation of Indian Territory under American law stretched the lower federal judiciary system as it was currently constituted. With the addition of Texas and California, and the frenzy from the gold rush beginning in 1849, western Arkansas became the closest settled outpost for departure to the new lands. Fort Smith swarmed with legal and often extralegal activity. In 1851 Congress divided Arkansas into two district courts, east and west, but it was in the West that innovation took hold. Attached to the Western District was "Indian Country," that part now known as Oklahoma. This is the first instance of providing jurisdiction to a federal district court beyond a state's boundary. It was necessary because of the chaos in both western Arkansas and the land beyond its western borders. Judge Daniel Ringo was appointed to this important post. Born in Kentucky around 1800, Ringo like so many Americans moved westward, first to Little Rock in 1820 and then upriver to Arkadelphia. He read law, became a court clerk for Clark County in 1825 at the age of twenty-five, and then became chief justice of Arkansas's supreme court six years later. In 1849 he was appointed judge of the single U.S. District Court of Arkansas, and when a second court was created, he also assumed that post.[29]

Judge Ringo was empowered with broad options to convict criminals and transfer them to eastern Arkansas, and on occasion he exercised that power. Historians and some local commentators have generally assessed Judge Ringo as somewhat soft on crime, particularly when compared with a more famous holder of this position from 1875 to 1896, Judge Isaac C. Parker, known affectionately in some circles as the "Hanging Judge." It would do well, however, to remember the context of the times. Judge Ringo's bench functioned during the 1850s, as the nation was splitting apart at its seams. Ringo, a Southerner and slaveholder, was sympathetic to the Confederate cause, and so he resigned his judgeship in 1860 just prior to the South's first wave of secessions and turned his records over to his clerk. Arkansas joined the rebellion on May 6, 1861, and shortly thereafter President Jefferson Davis appointed Ringo to be a district court judge for the Confederacy.[30] Although the records have been destroyed, it appears that Judge Ringo was able to provide some semblance of continuity.

Similarly, in Texas an amazingly smooth transition occurred in its federal district courts during the Civil War. The act creating Texas statehood in 1845 was unusual in many ways, including the new state's explicit ability to divide into up to five states and the creation of a single federal district court. That judge had to hold court in Galveston and any other place he deemed necessary. The district court judge was also a circuit court judge, and the first man named to the position after some political wrangling among Texas political factions was John C. Watrous. Born in Connecticut, Watrous settled first in Knoxville, Tennessee, in 1828, where he read law and supported a young Democrat congressman and protégé of Andrew Jackson, one James Knox Polk. A traveling man, Watrous practiced law next in Alabama and Mississippi and then in 1837 Watrous and his brother started over in Texas where they quickly became known for expertise in land title, a valued asset in the new state.

Watrous served as attorney general and district judge for the Independent District of Texas while it was a nation, but in 1846 his old friend, now President Polk, appointed him the first Texas federal district judge. By 1857 Texas had grown substantially, and it needed another district court. The Western District Court of Texas was created with Thomas Duval, a Virginian by birth, admitted to the bar in Tallahassee, Florida, and Texas secretary of state in 1853, appointed as its first judge.[31]

Both Watrous and Duval proved controversial, Watrous more so. Watrous was unfortunately confronted with making a number of unpopular land law determinations. Texas land titles were among the most confused in the nation, and it fell to federal district court judges to try to straighten them out. Watrous could not help but alienate powerful and wealthy Texans, and as a result he faced and survived no less than four impeachment attempts, including one formal vote in the House of Representatives in 1856. Nevertheless, both judges continued to hold court throughout the explosive pre–Civil War years, and when Texas seceded in 1861, the Northerner Watrous and the Southerner Duval both chose to remain loyal to the Union. They were the only southern federal judges to vacate their adopted states, spending the duration of the war in the North.

Watrous and Duval may have left their courtrooms, but their benches were soon occupied by replacements. The Confederacy quickly moved to create a supreme court and district courts in 1861, and in Texas Thomas Devine from San Antonio was chosen to replace Duval and William Pinckney Hill from Marshall took over for Watrous. Their courts were ready for business shortly after Watrous and Duval departed. Amazingly, most pending cases were heard, and the business of the federal courts, whether the Union's or the Confederacy's, did not seem to stop for a mere interruption of a civil war.[32]

In Texas and in most areas of the South, the structure of the federal district courts remained sufficiently anchored to minimize legal uncertainties. This would be true for areas of the North as well, areas such as those created by the Kansas-Nebraska Act of 1854, which had also undergone some serious disruptions as a result of the War of the Rebellion.

Statehood: Prelude to a U.S. District and Circuit Court for Nebraska

Democracy sometimes works in very mysterious ways, and that was certainly the case for Nebraska obtaining statehood and its federal courts. Out of the Kansas-Nebraska Act of 1854 (also known as the Nebraska Act) came not only a bloody Kansas but also a bruised Nebraska Territory that operated until 1867. Nebraskans began to push for statehood, but they were not all of one mind. In fact, there was considerable resistance to statehood. That resistance swirled around the major political divisions of the time and the age-old issue of taxes.

In 1860, on the eve of the Civil War, Nebraskans went to the polls to vote on whether to call a constitutional convention to write a state constitution and request statehood. The special election caught the interest of the electorate and both the Democrat and the nascent Republican Parties. Republicans who strongly favored a constitutional convention won forty of the fifty-two delegates at stake, but Nebraskans voted down holding a convention.

The next push for statehood occurred four years later, but it must have seemed that a century had intervened. The Civil War was now near its conclusion when, in January 1864, a majority of the Nebraska territorial legislature petitioned Congress to pass an authorization act allowing Nebraskans to create a state government. Republicans controlled Congress and now saw Nebraska as a safe haven for their political brothers, so the enabling legislation was passed permitting Nebraska Territory governor Alvin Saunders to call an election to choose delegates for a constitutional convention. Democrats who opposed statehood campaigned hard to choose delegates who would not write a state constitution. They argued that statehood would raise taxes because the funds currently supplied by the federal government would have to be made up by Nebraskans. This rather short-sighted view prevailed. The majority of delegates chosen were hostile to statehood, so when the convention convened, they immediately adjourned without taking any action.

It was now time for Republican political hardball. Governor Saunders secretly convened a select group of pro-statehood legislators and territorial officials who quickly crafted a state constitution. The constitution was submitted to a territorial Senate subcommittee that was stacked with pro-statehood representatives. The subcommittee took less than one day to approve the constitution and sent it on to the House, which quickly gave its ascent. Within nine days, Governor Saunders signed the bill approving a state constitution. Most legislators did not know what was in it, but they were very much aware of one provision. The Nebraska Territory House of Representatives voted 36–2 to restrict the eligibility to vote in Nebraska to free white males alone. This provision of the Nebraska constitution would raise eyebrows in the Radical Republican Congress in Washington DC.

Another unique development with the law passed to request statehood was the call for a special election that polled the voters not only on whether to approve a state constitution but also to select a state governor and a state legislature. Republicans favored statehood and nominated territorial legislator David Butler for governor. Democrats at first were divided evenly between those who opposed statehood or even running a candidate for governor and those who saw statehood as inevitable. Backed by Dr. George Miller, editor of the aggressive

Omaha Herald, J. Sterling Morton eventually decided to carry the Democrat gubernatorial banner. It was a very close election marked by blatant voting irregularities in Cass County, where wholesale precincts voting in favor of Morton were thrown out on technical grounds while dubious ballots from military absentees at Fort Kearny were counted. The state constitution was approved by exactly 100 votes out of nearly 7,000 votes cast, and Butler was chosen governor over Morton, 4,093 to 3,984. Recounts were not allowed, and no appeals went to the Nebrasksa Territory Supreme Court.

The state constitution was adopted on June 2, 1866. Governor Butler then called the first state legislature into session on July 4. The Republican-dominated solons selected two Republican senators, John M. Thayer and Andrew J. Poppleton. Congress, dominated by the Republican Party after the congressional elections of 1866, was divided between Radical Republicans and moderates. When Senator Benjamin Wade of Ohio, himself in the Radical camp, submitted a bill for Nebraska statehood, the Radicals forced an amendment that required Nebraskans to reconsider their racial suffrage restrictions. President Andrew Johnson vetoed the bill, but Congress overrode his veto, as they had been wont to do for a number of bills, and on February 9, 1867, Congress sent Nebraska's new constitutional "suit" back for alterations. Alvin Saunders, the territorial governor still in office, called both the territorial and state legislatures into session to revise the state constitution, and on February 22 the proposed state constitution was amended to meet the objections of Congress by excising the racial franchise restrictions. Acting as an intermediary and hoping to begin his Senate career, John Thayer then took a copy of the revised Nebraska constitution to Washington, where President Johnson, with misgivings, signed the act on March 1, making Nebraska the thirty-seventh state.[33]

In all of this tortured democratic exercise, no one had thought to do what had become standard practice. New states needed federal district and circuit courts. Nebraska's organic act had neglected this stabilizing and incorporating necessity. Enter Richard Yates, a one-term senator from Illinois.

Richard Yates was no stranger to Washington when he arrived just after the Civil War had concluded. His home state was still mourning the murder of its native-son president. Although Yates had been a Whig member of the U.S. House of Representatives, the war had transformed politics in most states including Illinois, and Yates became a Republican. Yates served a rather nondescript senatorial term from 1865 to 1871 and declined to stand for reappointment. Senators then were still chosen by state legislatures, so President Ulysses S. Grant appointed him to be a commissioner charged with inspecting railroad lands. Railroads and lands had long concerned Illinois congressmen.[34]

As a member of the Senate's Committee on Territories, it fell to Yates to introduce the corrective legislation needed to extend federal lower courts to the new state of Nebraska. He did so on March 13, 1867, asking for and receiving unanimous consent to introduce Senate Bill No. 61, "to provide for a district and a circuit court of the United States for the district of Nebraska, and for other purposes" and assign it to a committee. Standing close by was Nebraska's senator, John M. Thayer, who next took the podium, no doubt approvingly, to introduce legislation to reduce military lands at forts in Dakota Territory and Utah Territory.[35]

The official emergence of a bill from the Senate Committee on the Judiciary can be traced to March 16 when Senator George Edmunds, a Republican attorney and former member of the Vermont state legislature and the U.S. House, reported on Senate Bill No. 61. He read into the official record the proposed law, which he observed had had a few amendments made to it since it was received by the committee. Senator Edmunds was only in his second year in the Senate; he would serve twenty-seven more years, including four years in his political twilight as president pro tempore.[36]

The Nebraska federal lower court enabling act seemed uneventful. It provided for a federal district court to be officially called the District of Nebraska. A district judge would be appointed who would receive an annual salary of $3,500. A marshal and a district attorney were also authorized. The District of Nebraska was attached to the Eighth Judicial Circuit.[37] The district court and the circuit court would meet the first Monday of May and the first Monday of November each year in Omaha. The powers of the two courts were to be similar to all other federal district and circuit courts. A proper judicial transition was anticipated by requiring the U.S. Supreme Court to make sure all pending Nebraska cases having come to the justices from Nebraska's Territorial Supreme Court, no longer an entity, would be returned to the new federal district or circuit court or the new Nebraska Supreme Court, as the laws so dictated. Finally, until a new federal district judge was named, the federal district judge for Iowa was ordered to exercise jurisdiction over the state.

After introducing the legislation, Senator Edmunds then moved to amend it to make sure that the district judge, U.S. marshal, and district attorney were to be appointed "by the president, by and with the advice and consent of the Senate," language accidentally left out of the original bill. This was agreed to, and the entire bill was passed in one day.[38] No controversies here, unlike Nebraska's statehood ordeal. The action shifted to the U.S. House of Representatives, and debate would occur in this legislative body.

The House too lost little time in taking up the Nebraska courts matter. It received the Senate's legislation on March 18, and Iowa representative James Falconer Wilson moved to have it assigned to the House Committee on the Judiciary. This was approved unanimously. Wilson quite naturally was concerned about this matter, what with Nebraska being merged with Iowa's federal district court temporarily. Wilson, a Fairfield harness maker and Republican lawyer, served in the House from 1861 to 1869. President Grant wanted Wilson to be his secretary of state, but he decided instead to be a director of the Union Pacific Railroad. Wilson would return to politics, serving as Iowa's U.S. senator from 1882 to 1895. During his brief House term, Wilson not only shepherded the Nebraska federal lower courts bill in the House, but he served as one of the House managers of President Johnson's impeachment trial.[39]

On March 21, once again on the fast track, Representative Wilson reported back from the House Committee on the Judiciary that Senate Bill No. 61 had been approved and recommended in its entirety. Wilson explained to the House that the reason for the legislation was because Nebraska's statehood organic act had accidentally left this provision off. Then Wilson added that he had an amendment to offer on his own, not coming from the committee. Wilson proposed that the associate justice of the U.S. Supreme Court assigned to the Eighth Circuit be paid an additional $1,000 to defray his travel expenses. This provoked a debate.[40]

Representative George Boutwell rose and requested the floor. He reminded his colleagues that this amendment was not coming from the committee, because the rest of its members felt that no additional funds were necessary. The only exception for a Supreme Court justice receiving more travel funds was that person assigned to the Ninth Circuit composed of California, Oregon, and the western territories. Here it was the duty of the Eighth Circuit court judge to make ends meet. Boutwell's voice probably reached a new level of seriousness when he concluded that "to allow this species of compensation generally would, it seems to me, result in evil."[41]

George Boutwell, an enigmatic politician with a long resume, began his career as a Massachusetts schoolteacher. He then became a postmaster and entered politics as an antebellum Democrat. After serving briefly in the Massachusetts state legislature and then as Massachusetts governor from 1851 to 1852, Boutwell joined the Board of Overseers of Harvard University and then the State Board of Education (1855–61). The Civil War resulted in Boutwell's switch of parties, and in 1863 he was elected to the first of three terms in the U.S. House of Representatives as a Republican. Like Congressman Wilson, he was a manager for the Johnson impeachment trial. Later Boutwell would become secretary of the treasury (1869–73) and a Massachusetts U.S. senator (1873–77).[42]

Wilson testily responded, "I stated when I offered the amendment that it did not come from the committee; that I offered it simply on my own responsibility." Boutwell retorted, "I understood that; but I wished to state the [official] view of the committee on this question."

Countered Wilson, "I wish to state, in regard to this amendment, that the Eighth Circuit is the most extensive of the nine now existing." The facts were now changing.[43]

A representative from a neighboring Seventh Circuit state then offered his opinion. Charles Eldredge, a recently elected member of the House, a Democratic lawyer from Fond du Lac, and a man with Wisconsin state legislative experience, sought information. He wondered if this salary had not been raised in a bill passed during the last session of Congress. Wilson answered that it had not. Eldredge: "What is the salary of the judge?" Wilson: "Six thousand dollars. . . . There was no change made in the compensation of the members of the Supreme Court." Wilson could sense he was losing this point. He realized that the Ninth Circuit was unique, but he continued to argue that the Eighth was also special. Eldredge: "Allow me to suggest that the expenses which are allowed to the judge of the Ninth Circuit are for the purpose of paying for travel from California to Washington, and not on account of the extent of his district." Wilson reiterated his earlier argument that a judge in the Eighth Circuit traveled more than in the Ninth Circuit.

At this point, Representative Rufus Paine Spalding stepped in. A Republican lawyer and a former judge of the Ohio Supreme Court and a member of the House since 1863 who would only serve three terms, Spalding suggested that this was not the time to raise federal judicial salaries just because a new state was added to a circuit. Lashed out Spalding, "The argument is unsound." Wilson was hurt. He pleaded, "That is not the argument I make at all; it is not because we are adding Nebraska to the circuit."

Spalding moved in for the kill. "I do object at this closing hour of the session to raising the salary of one single judge." He was playing to the full House audience. "I think it is bad legislation, it is unprofitable legislation, it is dangerous legislation." Then Spalding stung Wilson. "I hope the gentleman will not take his own circuit and enlarge the salary of his justice and leave the other justices unprovided for." Wilson was reduced to whimpering, "I should be entirely willing to increase the salaries of all the judges of the Supreme Court." The House came to a vote and defeated the Wilson amendment. Wilson then moved to pass the bill, and the House approved Senate Bill No. 61.[44]

With the signature of the president *pro tempore* of the Senate and the Speaker of the House on March 22, the proposed law creating Nebraska's federal lower courts was sent to President Johnson. Who could accurately predict the outcome? Johnson had vetoed many bills only to have them passed by an angry Congress. Perhaps Johnson had grown weary of fighting his own party's insurgents, or maybe he felt Nebraska needed the stability, and so he ordered a U.S. district court brought to a region. We will not know his true feelings on this particular issue, but we do know he signed the bill on March 25 from a message he sent to the Congress. The U.S. District Court of Nebraska was now official for all to know.[45]

1867 Nebraska: The New State Prepares for a New Court

Nebraskans followed the statehood and federal court dramas from a distance. The month of March seemed relatively calm. A new conservative Democrat newspaper, the *Omaha Daily Herald*, seemed to be concentrating on Native American news that spring. It patronizingly editorialized that Gen. Ely Samuel Parker, a Seneca attorney, engineer, and tribal diplomat, was a tribute to his people.[46] "Gen. Parker is the representative man of what remains of the once powerful Six Nations. Great minds have preceded him to give that race a character which can never die. Only about 8,000 of the Tuscaroras, the Senecas, the Cayugas, the Onondagas, the Mohawks, and the Oneidas survive to recount the legendary history of their past glory. 'Passing away' is written upon them with a melancholy certainty." Subscribing to the generally believed myth that American Indians were dying out and would be a mere past remembrance within a generation, the *Herald* predicted: "We trust it may one day become a pleasing though sad duty with Gen. Parker, to trace the history, and give historical permanence and accuracy to the story of the rise and fall of that perishing people."[47] Parker had served as an adjutant and secretary to General Grant during the war, and two years later President Grant appointed him to be the first Indian to hold the office of commissioner of Indian affairs. Ironically, two months after the Parker article, the *Herald* proved prophetic when it editorialized in a story printed May 5, 1867, and headlined "Custar [*sic*] In Pursuit of Indians," that the colonel supposedly was pursuing 1,500 Indians, but he had not actually seen them yet. "Custar is a good soldier as a fighter for the Union, but this Indian business is an entirely different matter." Little Big Horn was nine years away.

On March 14, 1867, the *Omaha Daily Herald* recorded that Senator Yates had introduced a bill to provide for district and circuit courts for Nebraska. There were no editorials pro or con regarding this important development. The very day that the Nebraska courts bill passed and word of its presidential signature was received, the paper reported that "the aborigines of New Zealand are again giving trouble," the president of Panama had been shot by a drunk, and even though their movement was dying out, the Fenian Brotherhood continued to encourage Irish Americans to send supplies to Ireland for revolution.[48]

Two days later rumors were beginning to surface. Names of candidates for U.S. district attorney and district judge floated up, but the important political news featured the passing of power from Nebraska territorial governor Alvin Saunders to the governor-elect, David Butler. Almost immediately papers reported confusion over court referrals. Lawyers did not seem to know which court to use. State judge George B. Lake was quoted as blaming the new state constitution, which was silent on judicial transfers.[49]

On May 9 James M. Love, U.S. district judge from Iowa, arrived in Omaha to organize Nebraska's first district court. Love was a man of both law and letters. He had studied law in Ohio before moving to Iowa, where he joined in a law partnership with Samuel F. Miller, who would be appointed to the U.S. Supreme Court by President Lincoln in 1862. Love also read Shakespeare, giving speeches and writing on the subject. He published an essay, "Portia as a Lawyer," in the *American Law Review* and reportedly lectured on "A Lawyer's Standpoint on the Case of Shylock against Antonio." Another passion was pan-Slavic law. Love studied and "delved into the laws, domestic institutions, customs and condition of the common people of Russia."[50]

Active in the Democrat Party, Judge Love served first in the Iowa State Senate before he was appointed a district judge for Iowa in 1855.[51] Judge Love, perhaps seeking a middle ground in the uncertain terrain of the day's politics, reportedly had little sympathy for President Andrew Johnson or the Radical Republicans in Congress. He was termed a "bosom friend" of Thomas B. Cuming, former Democratic secretary and acting governor of Nebraska Territory and "founder" of Omaha. Perhaps influenced by his political affiliation, the Democratic *Daily Herald* praised Love, who reputedly possessed "unquestionable abilities, rare legal learning, and unsullied purity of personal character."[52] It was reported that he was praised by Republicans and Democrats alike and welcomed heartily.

On Wednesday, May 8, the first meeting of the federal district and circuit courts of Nebraska began in downtown Omaha at 2 p.m. Although federal law required the court to meet the first Monday in every May and the first Monday in every November, no one seemed to object. Acting Nebraska District Judge Love appointed E. B. Chandler clerk pro tem and admitted James M. Woolworth to the bar. He also adopted rules of court procedure. On May 10 Judge Love reconvened the federal courts to finish reading the rules, and he adjourned the courts at 10 a.m.[53] The first recorded decision of the Nebraska circuit court came six months later on November 13, 1867, when Judge Love was joined by his old law partner, Supreme Court Justice Miller, to rule on *Aaron Root v. James Test*. The unreported case ever so briefly described in the *Omaha Daily Herald* featured J. M. Woolworth arguing for the plaintiff who had sued the City of Omaha and other landholders over his preemption rights to land and certain boundary disputes. After several days of complex testimony, the court resolved the issue in a "lucid and conclusive opinion for plaintiff."[54]

Federal justice had arrived in frontier Nebraska. Justice, of course, had not been foreign to the peoples of the Platte. Nebraska's Native peoples had always resolved their differences with legal principles, and those decisions lived on in their histories and traditions. And the first Europeans to pass through the land of flat waters brought their own civil law traditions. Even the impressions left by the first citizens of the new republic seeking to trade and explore contained the fundamentals of criminal and commercial law. That was all codified and institutionalized with the creation of Nebraska Territory in 1854. The territorial legal system, however, proved more of a colonial relic than a useful Americanization technique, so it fell to the new federal court and statehood to anchor Nebraska to the American nation.

Historians have described the lower federal courts in their legal histories. Most have addressed the history of the functioning U.S. district and circuit courts as judiciaries presiding over a tension between local and national concerns. Judges were "torn between serving national priorities and local needs."[55] This dichotomy hearkened back to early modern heydays of the common law when England's kings and queens appointed justices of the peace to be the Crown's eyes and ears in Britain's villages and towns.

The more intellectually brave of these historical commentators have "Solomonized" this history and come down on which side they believe prevailed. Kermit Hall and to some extent Charles Zelden view local concerns as paramount, with federal judges dealing directly with the "divisive effects of federalism." Never underestimate the power of the local. Mary K. Bonsteel Tachau and Tony Freyer see national issues at the forefront of the court's activities. Freyer, in particular, connects these judges to a strong, budding national capitalism at work in the late nineteenth and early twentieth centuries. He found them literally to be doing the nation's business.[56]

Nebraska's first federal judges naturally had to deal with both of these dimensions, but initially they found themselves at the fulcrum of a national judiciary in crisis. The Civil War had overloaded the system. Wars have a tendency to generate many more disputes after they resolve, and those disputes are often related to both the national trauma and local destruction. Coupled with the natural tendency for the law's institutions to be imbued with institutional rigidity, change seemed to be slow. In fact, change was rapid though partial with Nebraska's lower federal courts at the cusp of that change. The 1860s and 1870s saw Congress increase dramatically the jurisdiction of its federal courts. This came within the increasingly confused appellate framework that cried out for reform. The circuit courts, on which the federal district judges served, became in essence a legal fiction. Congress eventually let the Supreme Court justices get off their horses and avoid the long stage and railroad rides in order to stay in Washington and ponder national legal issues, but the confusion remained until the creation of full-scale appellate judgeships in the twentieth century. In the beginning of its federal legal experience, though, Nebraska needed a judge.

2

The Dundy Years

He [Judge Elmer S. Dundy] is one of those smooth, slippery beings that glide into corruption and rascality as snakes into slimy matter; his head is so full of base scheme that hair already refused to hide its deformities; his very walk a sort of dodge-the-sheriff quickstep; his voice villainously vicious; his mean eye cast down; all of his features cadaverous and miserable; his face is endorsed "without recourse" by the hand of God himself.
—J. Sterling Morton in testimony before Congress, 1862

Judge Dundy has made an able, upright judge; has administered the law, as he has seen it, in a dignified and impartial way; and is one of the most pleasant and affable gentlemen to associate with there is within the boundaries of the State.
—James W. Savage, John T. Bell, and Consul W. Butterfield in their history of Omaha, 1894

For nearly the first three decades of the U.S. District Court of Nebraska, one man dominated that court. He dominated it completely. He came to symbolize the court. Even when the court met as a circuit court with other judges, he often issued the opinions that came to take on lives of their own. These ranged from basic political and social considerations inherent in the role of Native Americans within the United States to whether America's railroads could be economically restrained and their considerable political power brought to heel in the heartland.

Vexing questions faced the judges of Nebraska's lower federal judiciary as they attempted to solve the disputes of a frontier society undergoing significant population growth, urbanization, and industrialization. There were a number of fundamental issues addressing Indian rights within American culture. Was an Indian a person before the law? Could an Indian vote in federal or state elections? Could a member of a tribe be convicted of murder? There were cases involving the U.S. Army, a vestige of Nebraska's frontier past. Can the Army create an Indian reservation? Could an Army private who lied about his age in order to enlist obtain a writ of habeas corpus? There were cases concerning the railroad, that mighty juggernaut of the Plains. Can counties tax railroads? Might states tax railroads? Do citizens have the right to boycott railroads? Could one railroad whose workers are on strike force another railroad to carry its cargo? And there were the postal cases, the kidnapping cases, the bankruptcy cases, and many others.

Before these issues can be explored more fully, however, a consideration of the men who attempted to mediate and resolve these disputes is in order. One man first addressed these questions and established the U.S. district court as a powerful force in the lives of Nebraskans from 1868 to 1896. That man was Elmer Scipio Dundy. Who was Judge Dundy? And what did he bring to the bench?

Dundy's Early Life

Elmer S. Dundy was born March 5, 1830, in Trumbull County, Ohio, a part of the Western Reserve near the Pennsylvania border. Elmer was the son of eighteen-year old Polly Hummason and William Dundy, who had hurriedly married the previous July with the legally filed consent of William's father, Soloman Dundy. The Dundy family were German Protestants who initially settled in eastern Pennsylvania and Maryland before Soloman selected a farm and moved his family to northeastern Ohio.

As a child, it is recorded that young Elmer, the farm boy, took readily to hunting and fishing, and he was apprenticed to a local tanner where he excelled. He was also known as an entertaining fiddler. Elmer enjoyed learning sufficiently so that by his eighteenth birthday he had been certified to teach. At this point in his life, the Dundy family moved back to Pennsylvania, approximately 120 miles due east of Elmer's birthplace, to Clearfield County and the western Susquehanna River valley. It was time for Elmer to strike out on his own, but he was sufficiently tied to his family to join in their reverse migration. Once they resettled, however, Dundy rented a room from a blacksmith and started teaching in the county schools, and after a few years, he assumed the principalship of the school in the town of Clearfield. Still he was not content.

In Clearfield, Dundy met a young lawyer, William A. Wallace, and the town's favorite political son, William Bigler. Bigler would become governor of Pennsylvania in 1852 and a U.S. senator in 1856. They encouraged the affable Dundy to consider the study of law, and in 1853 at the age of twenty-three Elmer was admitted to the Pennsylvania bar by passing a courtroom examination before a judge. Forsaking a teaching career, Dundy practiced law in Clearfield for three years before he sought fame and fortune like so many young Americans in the 1850s. He did not move to California. It is almost certain he knew friends and perhaps even his own pupils who did. But Dundy chose to move to a new territory, just created, not the one that would have so much trouble, but Nebraska in the summer of 1857.[1]

Nebraska as Home

Dundy settled first in Nebraska City like many others who began their Nebraska experience in this frontier town. There he met Samuel W. Black, one of Nebraska Territory's relatively new Territorial Supreme Court justices. Seeking business, Dundy traveled with Judge Black to the southern part of his circuit, then the second judicial district, to Richardson County and the very small settlement of Archer. Here Dundy met John C. Miller, another judge and typical frontier local politician who fronted as a probate judge and justice of the peace. Miller was primarily engaged in land speculation and town boosterism.

Judge Miller allowed Dundy to practice law in his court, which was held in a log cabin tavern owned by the judge. Dundy decided to stay.

Dundy, Miller, and the Archerites had visions of grandeur for their community. They foresaw considerable population growth, increased numbers of businesses, and a county seat site, but those dreams were not meant to be. The problem was where Archer was located. Because of a surveying error, Archer was in fact located inside an Indian reservation on land disparagingly called the Half-Breed Tract.

In 1830 at a treaty signing at Prairie du Chien between the United States and the Sac and Foxes, Omahas, Iowas, Otoes, and Missouria and several Sioux bands, the federal government promised to create a reserve located between the Big Nemaha and the Little Nemaha rivers and west of the Missouri River for tribal mixed bloods, the children primarily of French fur traders, American soldiers, and Indian women. Land was to be allotted to mixed-blood families, and by 1833 between 150 and 200 mixed bloods had moved to the reserve, but the U.S. government moved slowly to survey the land. Considerable confusion occurred once white settlers began moving into the Half-Breed Tract. Congress was petitioned to get on with the surveying process, but no appropriations were made until July 1854. By that time, the Kansas-Nebraska Act had opened up areas west of the Missouri River to white settlement, and land title questions could not be resolved.

The Nebraska territorial legislature did not wait for the surveyors. It divided the eastern half of the territory into counties in 1855 and put the Half-Breed Tract adjacent to Richardson County. The town of Archer that grew up was thought to be outside of the Tract, and it was slated to be made a county seat, much to the delight of Dundy and his new entrepreneurial friends. But once it was discovered in 1857 that Archer was inside the Tract, vexing questions were raised about land title, problems in terms of voting, and the improbability that a county seat might be located there.[2]

Dundy was popular in the town, and he was hired by its citizens to go to Washington DC shortly after Christmas 1857 to lobby for a revision of the reservation boundary. He succeeded in persuading Nebraska's territorial delegate to Congress, Fenner Ferguson, to introduce a boundary revision statute for the Half-Breed Tract that was eventually approved, but the changes were too late. By summer of 1858 when Dundy returned to Archer, most residents had already abandoned the village, and Salem, a small settlement to the west, had been made county seat.

Not to be defeated in his bid to start a successful law practice in a community that would grow, Dundy moved to Falls City, another new settlement in Richardson County that in 1858 had but twenty-five residents. Falls City was known as a Republican enclave, sympathetic to those who would abolish slavery, and as an underground railroad stop.[3] While it is unknown up to this point what Elmer Dundy's political viewpoints were, it may be best to consider him a David Wilmot kind of Democrat. Wilmot was no doubt known to Dundy as the Pennsylvania congressman whose name is synonymous with the division in the nation over the extension of slavery to the Louisiana Purchase lands and the debate over the Wilmot Proviso.

An election to the Nebraska territorial council was about to take place, and Dundy decided to run against the incumbent, Charles McDonald, who had led the fight to put the county seat at Salem. The district included both Richardson County and Pawnee County. Dundy ran as a Democrat with sympathies for the abolitionist movement, the new Republican Party, and the fusionist tendencies already on the political table in Nebraska and surrounding regions. Dundy proved adept at negotiating the political terrain. Isham Reavis, a newcomer to Falls City that summer, later reminisced about the campaign: "Dundy was a crafty fellow and up to political snuff with the best of them, and so managed his cards as to get the support of all those antagonistic and warring elements in sufficient numbers to beat his two opponents with a very satisfactory majority."[4]

At the age of twenty-eight, Elmer Dundy was elected to the territorial council. His political rise in frontier Nebraska could only be described as meteoric. But there was a twist. Elections in early Nebraska never seemed what they were supposed to be. The results were always in doubt. And while Dundy appeared to be the winner, both he and McDonald were certified as having been elected, with McDonald given the seat on the first day of the new territorial legislative session. After an investigation by a legislative subcommittee, it was discovered that one of the precinct's votes that favored Dundy had not been counted. McDonald retreated and Dundy was declared the winner, but this event forecast the beginning of numerous political struggles that found Elmer Dundy often involved in the seamier side.[5]

Politics, Politics, Politics

Dundy cut his teeth on the divisive issues of territorial prewar politics. He made enemies and rewarded friends, and his first order of business upon assuming his seat in the territorial council was to wrestle the Richardson County government away from Salem and have it placed in Falls City. Several elections were called, and Dundy was involved in all of them.

These Richardson County elections were punctuated by fraud, bribery, vote selling for whiskey, and murder. Dundy's law office was a polling place in Falls City, and he was once nearly killed, sustaining a gunshot wound in his nose. Another competing community, Rulo, thought it had rightfully won the county seat only to have it taken back. Rulo residents threatened to lynch Dundy and to burn Falls City to the ground after a number of maneuverings that Dundy engineered resulted in Falls City being declared the county seat in 1860. Dundy's political biographer, David H. Price, concluded, "One must give Dundy the major credit for securing the county seat for Falls City. In doing so, he united the loyalty of that town behind him, but, at the same time, he made so many enemies throughout the county that he barely regained his seat on the Council."[6]

At the same time that Dundy was so engaged in Richardson County's volatile politics, he also was pursuing a secessionist movement of southeastern Nebraska from the territory to join Kansas in its quest for statehood. A secession convention was held in Brownville in January 1859. Dundy attended, and he authored the resolutions adopted at the convention to secede from Nebraska and join Kansas. Two weeks later the Kansas legislature passed a memorial that it sent to President James Buchanan urging these same sentiments. Lots of meetings were held in southeast Nebraska and Kansas, and when Kansas convened a constitutional convention, delegates from Nebraska attended with rights to participate but not to vote. Kansans, however, double-crossed the would-be Nebraska secessionists and voted down the attempt to add to their territory in July 1859, fearing it would muddy their statehood waters. The would-be Kansans went home furious, vowing to remain in Nebraska and work for their own political ends, including a new state.[7]

How did Dundy negotiate the politically explosive issues of slavery? Slavery in the territory became an issue in 1858 when a bill was introduced in the territorial house to abolish slavery in Nebraska Territory. Although Democrats in the House attempted to scuttle the bill, it passed and was referred to the Council. Here Democrats successfully moved to postpone consideration of the bill indefinitely, but Dundy voted against its postponement. He alone cast a vote to consider the measure.[8] The same issue returned in 1859, but this time Dundy had support for his position in the Council. The bill was passed, but former territorial justice and now governor Samuel W. Black, Dundy's first legalist acquaintance when he migrated to Nebraska, vetoed the measure. A vote to override was unsuccessful in 1860, but in 1861 Governor Black's second veto of the measure was overridden.[9] Dundy had by this point converted to Republicanism, and this would prove to be a wise expediency for him. When it came time for the new state of Nebraska to fill its first federal judgeship, Dundy would have the right political credentials.

On June 17, 1861, Elmer Dundy married Mary Robison, like himself an Ohio native. The ceremony was held in the home of the bride's parents in Omaha and was conducted by a Lutheran minister, the Rev. Henry W. Kuhns. Official witnesses were Eleazer Wakeley, William Pitt Kellogg, and William F. Lockwood, all Nebraska Territory Supreme Court former and current justices. Politics seemed to dominate Elmer Dundy's life, even in his most private moments. Mary and Elmer had four children: a son, Elmer Jr., born March 31, 1862, and three daughters, Mary Mae, Luna, and Enid Alva, the last born in 1866 but who only survived one year. The Dundy family located in Falls City where Elmer kept an eye on his political base, practiced law, and invested in real estate. In 1874 Dundy supervised the building of one of the largest and most beautiful homes in all of Richardson County. At one point, Elmer Dundy amassed considerable wealth, owning nearly half of the land within Falls City plus farms and even a quarry outside the city limits.[10]

Throughout the 1860s, Elmer Dundy actively pursued his local legal career and watched over his growing family, and he became bitterly entangled in numerous political fights in frontier Nebraska. He participated in many dubious activities that today would be seen as unbecoming, if not disqualifying, for a potential federal judge. He made mortal enemies, including J. Sterling Morton, the Nebraska Territory secretary and acting governor, another young politician anxious to make his own way and who would constantly engage in political combat with Dundy.

Dundy's own elections and those of many others seemed to require his behind-the-scenes maneuvering. In 1861, when Dundy was called upon to testify for the public record about contested elections, he was asked about his personal political philosophy. He replied, "I am a conservative republican; I am in favor of the Constitution as it is; opposed to any amendments; in favor of the preservation of the Union at any cost and at all hazards."[11] He was trying to straddle the divisions in Nebraska as he articulated both Northern Democrat and Republican ideology. By 1860 Elmer Dundy was identified by Democrat newspapers as a "Black Republican pimp" who was more than contemplating the switching of parties, and by 1862 he had firmly embraced Republicanism, serving as a delegate from Richardson County to the Republican territorial convention.[12] He had come full political circle.

Nebraska Territory Supreme Court Judge

Although Dundy's political survival seemed to require strongly held positions, whatever the situation, Dundy fortuitously found himself the beneficiary of a federal judgeship in June 1863. Judge Joseph Streeter, one of the Nebraska Territory Supreme Court justices only recently appointed by President Abraham Lincoln in October 1861, suddenly died in January 1862. He was replaced by Winthrop Welles Ketchum of Pennsylvania, but Ketchum resigned shortly after his nomination. Nebraska needed a judge, and one was potentially already in the territory. Elmer Dundy was nominated by the president and approved by Congress for the position.[13] By all accounts, it was a surprising judicial accession.

Perhaps Dundy had anticipated something might develop. He had strongly backed a friend, Samuel G. Daily, for territorial delegate in 1860. Dundy knew Daily from the territorial legislature where Daily, a member of the House from neighboring Nemaha County, had introduced the original antislavery bill. In the highly competitive territorial delegate election of 1860, Daily barely defeated J. Sterling Morton, who challenged the election results unsuccessfully in the House of Representatives. Morton used the occasion of an official investigation to bash Dundy in his House testimony. As a result, Dundy decided not to run for reelection to the territorial council in 1862, instead concentrating on the difficult renomination of Daily at the Republican territorial convention. Daily and Dundy prevailed, and Daily was elected easily in November 1862. Daily, therefore, owed Dundy in the most highly political sense, and he urged President Lincoln to appoint Dundy to a territorial office.[14]

Local Democrats and the more radical Republicans were not happy with this development. In particular, Oliver P. Mason of Nebraska City, a member of the territorial council, felt double-crossed. He thought he had made it clear that he desired this post.

Previously, Mason and Dundy had represented Falls City's quest for a county seat when the election squabbles had spilled over into court proceedings. Mason considered Dundy an ally. So when Dundy's friends urged the Otoe County Bar Association to forward an endorsement to the U.S. Senate to encourage Dundy's confirmation, Mason led a successful move that censured Dundy instead and urged retraction of the nomination. Mason went so far as to introduce a motion in the territorial council urging the Senate not to confirm Dundy. The motion was never brought to a vote. Meanwhile, Dundy received an endorsement from the Douglas County Bar Association and a successful Senate vote.[15]

At age thirty-three, Elmer Dundy was appointed to a four-year term on the Nebraska Territory Supreme Court. His appointment constituted only the second Nebraska resident out of fifteen state justices ever appointed, the other being William F. Lockwood. Dundy's political and judicial rise must have astounded him. He had not had a single day of advanced education, nor had he had the good fortune to attend a law school or even a law seminar. And yet he was now a member of the highest court of his home region, a true testament to his political acumen. Dundy's term, 1863–67, expired the same year that the Court died. Statehood terminated his territorial judicial career, but his judging ability would enter a new phase after his time on the territory's highest court.

On the court, Dundy served in the Second Judicial District, which included Falls City and half of the counties south of the Platte River. He held court in log cabins, office buildings, and dance halls. He worked with Justices Lockwood and William Pitt Kellogg, who were family friends. Paid $2,000 a year, the justices were required to live in their districts. Twice a year the three justices met in Omaha to form the Territorial Supreme Court, which heard appeals from their district court opinions and original jurisdictional disputes. There were few appeals to the Supreme Court because of the expense and the judicial double-dipping of the justices.[16]

Because the justices were not required to file written opinions, it is difficult to trace Judge Dundy's early jurisprudential trends. What we do have are indications. Records of the decisions of the justices of the Nebraska Territory Supreme Court include piecemeal surviving journals and docket books. From the journals it is estimated that from 1854 to 1867, justices of the First District, that of Douglas County, heard approximately 2,500 cases; dispute resolutions in the Third District, the region north of the Platte River, constituted 1,300 cases. Dundy's district has far fewer records. One docket constituting one month's schedule of cases in 1863 for Dundy's court briefly chronicles how Dundy heard a total of 103 cases. So he may have heard as many as 824 cases during his four years as a territorial justice. Clearly the court was busy.[17]

Dundy heard cases in three categories: those in which the United States was the plaintiff, those that involved territorial criminal actions, and those that concerned civil disputes among territorial residents. From his docket for the October 1863 term of the second district, Dundy heard thirty-six cases featuring the U.S. attorney as an adversary. Most of his judicial business concerned the selling of liquor to Native Americans. During that October term Dundy heard twenty-two cases charging various defendants with selling liquor on reservations, and they resulted in six indictments with no arrest, two indictments with an arrest, and nine indictments with an arrest and a plea of *nolle prosequi*, meaning Judge Dundy had accepted for the formal record that the prosecutor would not prosecute any further. Three liquor cases were taken to trial with the result of one not guilty jury verdict, another no verdict (presumably a hung jury), and one guilty on one count but not guilty on all other counts. Judge Dundy summarily reduced the penalty for one defendant previously found guilty by Judge Streeter of selling liquor to Indians. And Pe-toke-mah, also known as Hard Fish, was charged not with selling liquor but with introducing and attempting to introduce liquor into Indian country, with his case being continued for another term.[18]

It appears that Judge Dundy was not particularly harsh on those who were selling liquor to Indians. The sellers were white traders generally, although it is possible that there were mixed bloods involved in this business in southeastern Nebraska. Only one Indian is mentioned, and his case involved a different kind of nuance, that of the introduction of liquor rather than sales. Local juries were loath to convict, but on the one occasion when Judge Dundy allowed the case to go to trial and the jury did convict on one count, he refused to overturn the verdict and sentenced James Kough, also known as James Crow, to thirty days in jail and a fine of $250. The very next case also involved Kough, but Judge Dundy allowed for a nolle prosequi to be entered exonerating him.[19]

The rest of the docket considered three cases in which whites were indicted for unlawfully cutting and removing timber from public lands—most likely the reservation—but only one was actually arrested and held for trial. Judge Dundy also authorized indictments for rape, stealing horses, murder, and failure to obtain licenses to work as a photographer, peddler, and auctioneer for three different defendants in three different actions.[20]

Not too many cases were heard for violations of the territorial criminal code. Only eight causes of action were listed on Judge Dundy's docket that October term. George Boulware, William Schallinger, Nicholas Stubbs, and Reese Steel were indicted for rioting, but the prosecution entered a nolle prosequi request that was granted.[21] Other cases involved the unlawful selling of liquor, presumably to whites and not Indians; three separate hearings involving larceny; and assault and battery and plain assault. Of these eight cases, only two featured an arrest, one was dismissed, one was granted a release, and four were pled out nolle prosequi. Clearly Judge Dundy was not a "hanging" kind of criminal judge. His court had to have been known as reasonably lax for criminal prosecutions, at least after his 1863 first term.

The bulk of the judicial business featured civil actions involving numerous territorial residents suing each other. Judge Dundy heard fifty-nine civil cases the fall of 1863. On these, forty-nine were original cases in his court with the following results: fifteen verdicts for the plaintiff, nine verdicts for the defendants, twenty cases were continued for further consideration or time for the litigants to settle, and five were dismissed because two litigants died before trial and three disputes were settled in the interim. On one occasion J. Sterling Morton, the territorial citizen Judge Dundy no doubt most detested, sued former governor and judge Samuel W. Black for "confirmation of sale," presumably real estate, and Judge Dundy continued the case for another term giving the defendant time to prepare a defense and to consider making motions.[22] Six other civil cases were in Dundy's court on appeal from decisions made by justices of the peace, and four were on appeal from probate courts. Dundy reserved one justice of the peace decision and helped settle three others; one JP appeal was continued and another was dismissed. He dismissed all four of the probate court appeals. Judge Dundy appears to have acted with reason and care. There do not appear to have been any outcries in territorial newspapers about Dundy's court decisions, and the lack of criticism does not mean that the press was not following Dundy's court. It most certainly was watching closely.

The only records available for Nebraska Territory Supreme Court decisions are those published, and the only opinions published were selected by James Woolworth, a Democrat attorney with clear political issues in mind. He collected twenty-two territorial supreme court opinions from 1858 to 1866 and published them in 1871.[23] Two of them involved Dundy as the judge writing the opinion. One case, *Moffat v. Griswold* (1864), featured Woolworth as the attorney for the appellee, and he succeeded in gaining a reversal of the district court opinion.

The *Moffat* case originated out of the Second Judicial District and presumably had been decided by the late Judge Streeter. Judge Dundy overruled his predecessor's opinion. It appeared that on August 3, 1857, in the city of Kearney, Joseph Moffat loaned $150 in gold to C. W. Pierce and John Campbell, and they promised to repay Moffat within thirty days at 5 percent interest. Moffat then sold the note to H. C. Blackman on July 2, 1859. Although the opinion does not so state, it seems likely that this note somehow fell into the hands of the defendant in this appeal, one Griswold. Griswold sued Moffat when Griswold realized that he could not collect on the note. The district court judge ruled that Moffat was liable. Judge Dundy reversed this holding, ruling instead in favor of Moffat for a unanimous court because Griswold, nee Blackman, ignored normal rules of business by not attempting to obtain payment from Pierce and Campbell, particularly when the borrowers had property that could have been attached. The fact that they did not collect when the two Kearney partners had assets should not mean that Moffat was liable for the note holder's mistake. Basically, Judge Dundy was making a third-party purchaser live by reasonable standards of doing business. It is somewhat of a cold splash on the business of selling loans, but the opinion was sufficiently terse that third-party purchasers who were on top of their business could easily abide by the ruling.[24]

The second case featuring an opinion offered by Judge Dundy also involved a reversal. In *Aumock v. Jamison* (1865), Jamison sued Aumock in the First District Court in Omaha for the recovery of a debt. The suit began with the service of a summons on Aumock on August 4, 1862, and the summons was returned that same day. Aumock did not appear in court, so a default judgment was entered against him. The sheriff then levied the costs on lands owned by Aumock, who filed for an injunction to restrain the sheriff from selling Aumock's property, arguing that the First District Court had made a wrong decision because it did not have jurisdiction. Aumock prevailed at this point, and Jamison appealed the injunctive relief. The question on appeal was related to the service. The Nebraska Territory statute in question stated that service could be made by leaving a summons at a person's "usual place of residence at any time *before* the return day." In a one-sentence opinion Judge Dundy ruled that service on a return day was sufficient to require a defendant to appear; the injunction needed to be lifted so that Jamison could obtain what he was owed. Judge William Pitt Kellogg, First District judge, was recorded as dissenting. It was his opinion, after all, that Dundy was reversing.[25]

Dundy's opinions were brief and to the point. They were almost always based on "black letter" legal principles and rarely suggested any kind of legal nuance.[26] They suggest a judge who paid attention to detail and who would not be reluctant to assert his views upon even a divided court. The opinions of the Nebraska Territory Supreme Court in which Dundy was directly involved and the docket evidence for the 1863 term indicate a judge who was exposed to a variety of issues important to frontier Nebraskans and who was willing to assert his judicial powers. His nascent judicial philosophy portrays a judge who believed people who owed money should pay up, that procedural issues are not available to avoid one's legal responsibilities, that those with substantial wealth and power are not above their legal responsibilities, and that issues involving the clash of frontier cultures—while requiring restraint and careful attention—were presumed to be decided on the side of progress and settlement.

Moving On Up

Statehood brought an end to the Nebraska Territory Supreme Court and Elmer Dundy's judicial appointment. Dundy had to have anticipated this, and even so he was sufficiently confident about his political future that he favored statehood. During the statehood fight in Nebraska, which began in 1860, Dundy seems to have become less and less attached to his previous Democrat political constituency and more and more of a pro-war and pro-statehood Republican. While he did not take a leadership role, he clearly supported the statehood attempts of the Republicans, and he publicly criticized President Andrew Johnson's policies beginning in 1866, albeit mildly. While Dundy probably would have liked to have run for governor of the new state or to have been chosen by the new legislature as a new senator, he played a cautious role, and this served him well.

After Nebraska finally became a state in March 1867, Dundy's name was not initially mentioned as a possible federal judgeship appointee. Instead, newspapers suggested William Lockwood, a territorial supreme court justice, George Lake, a local judge in Omaha, and numerous others.[27] Even the state's Republican Party leaders were ignoring Dundy. He, however, was making his own plans. Dundy first had interim Nebraska district court judge James M. Love officially admit him to practice law before the new court in June 1867. Next Dundy traveled to Washington DC at what turned out to be the optimum moment. While the record is somewhat fuzzy on how this all came about, Dundy' s connections, going all the way back to his early Pennsylvania days including his friendship with Governor and then Senator Bigler, proved very helpful in solidifying President Johnson's support. Elmer Dundy, "with no support from press, party, or populace, had engineered another fantastic political coup. For lack of available evidence to the contrary, the just laurels must be awarded to him alone."[28] Elmer Dundy, age thirty-eight, secured his appointment as Nebraska's first federal district court judge.

Reaction was swift and sarcastic in Nebraska. The *Omaha Weekly Republican* was not enthusiastic about the appointment. It did editorialize that Copperheads, the Republican term for antiwar Democrats, would be distressed because Dundy was a stalwart Republican.[29] The *Nebraska City News* reminded its readers of Dundy's past brushes with political corruption,[30] and the *Omaha Weekly Herald* lambasted the appointment: "The ghost of the Richardson County reprobate affrights the souls of divers and sundry adversaries. It is a shell thrown into their [Republican] camp. . . . It is a delightful muddle."[31] The *Herald*'s print proved particularly vituperative.

Not only did Elmer Dundy become Nebraska's first U.S. district judge, but he presided over Nebraska's federal bench from May 1868, a few weeks after his appointment, until his death on October 28, 1896, a twenty-eight-year period that defined Nebraska's first era of its federal judiciary. His time on the bench carried Nebraska's district court nearly to the conclusion of the nineteenth century, and in many ways, it was definitive.

Nebraska's Circuit Court during the Dundy Years

Within a year of his assumption of his duties, Judge Dundy's powers were enhanced significantly when Congress revised the federal court system and gave greater powers to district court judges when they acted as circuit court judges. In 1869 Congress passed "An Act to amend the Judicial System of the United States."[32] This revision of the lower federal courts began the process of creating the modern appellate division, but it would take nearly forty years to straighten things out. Circuit riding was not a concept adaptable to an expanding, geographically challenging nation. Even with what many Reconstruction era Americans considered to be significant technological advancements in transportation—that is, railroads and steamboats which, when compared with horses and stages, truly represented improvements—riding the circuit was nevertheless debilitating. Supreme Court justices hated it; it literally sapped their health. With Reconstruction, it was important for courts to function in the West and the South, and that meant revision of the lower federal courts' structure and powers.

The act set the number of justices of the U.S. Supreme Court at nine with the possibility of a tenth being added as necessary. The tradition of appointing each justice to a circuit was retained, but significant change was adopted with reference to defining a circuit court. A circuit court was now constituted by a Supreme Court justice alone, a special circuit judge appointed acting alone, a sitting district court judge acting alone, or by a Supreme Court justice and a district court judge sitting together. Salaries were increased to $5,000 for circuit judges, and cases could be tried by each circuit judge sitting separately. Furthermore, justices of the Supreme Court needed to attend the circuit only once every two years.[33]

In practice, Supreme Court justices simply began to ignore their circuit responsibilities. They no longer believed, with the specific appointments of circuit judges, that U.S. Supreme Court justices were necessary for the application of federal laws at the local level. This was a great relief to them. Their actions set the stage for further appellate reforms in the early twentieth century that statutorily took them out of the circuit courts for good.

This new structural arrangement also meant that Elmer Dundy was now for all practical purposes both the district court judge and the circuit court judge for the state of Nebraska. He was fortunate to have appointed as Nebraska's circuit judge a personal friend, John F. Dillon from Iowa. Judge Dillon was greatly respected for his intelligence and knowledge of the law. Dillon's family moved to frontier Iowa during his early childhood. He was one of the first to attend the University of Iowa where he received a medical degree in 1850 at the age of nineteen. Dillon practiced medicine, but also began to study law. Unlike the patriot Benjamin Rush of revolutionary days, Dillon found greater challenge in his legal studies and gave up medicine.

In 1852 Dillon was admitted to the Iowa bar, and he served as a prosecuting attorney in Iowa, 1852–58; an Iowa district judge, 1858–63, and an Iowa Supreme Court judge, 1862–69, before being appointed to hold the new U.S. circuit judgeship for the Eighth Judicial Circuit. Judge Dillon joined Judge Dundy on the federal bench, and the two by all accounts enjoyed each other's company and worked easily together when the circuit court met. After ten years, John Dillon resigned and moved to New York City where he practiced law and accepted an appointment to teach real estate law and equity jurisprudence at the Columbia University School of Law.[34] Before Judge Dillon resigned, he and Judge Dundy held the first term of the U.S. district and circuit court in Lincoln, the new state's new capital city. In 1878 Congress authorized one term to be held in the city of Lincoln every first Monday in January.[35]

The circuit court's existence paralleled Dundy's lengthy federal judgeship, and for Nebraska the judges assigned proved to be learned men who went on to significant legal careers. After Dillon left the bench for Columbia's law school, he was replaced by Judge George McCrary, who served from 1879 to 1884. McCrary also had Iowa connections. A member of the Iowa bar as well as the Iowa House and Senate, he enjoyed a significant political career serving as an Iowa Republican in the U.S. House of Representatives from 1869 to 1877. While in the House, he investigated the Credit Mobilier financial scandal, authored the bill to create the Electoral Commission, and wrote a definitive legal text on election law at the time, *A Treatise on the American Law of Elections* (1875). McCrary was then nominated by President Rutherford Hayes and approved by Congress to be secretary of war. McCrary proved to be an activist leader of the nation's military and defense, withdrawing federal troops from the remaining Southern states of South Carolina and Louisiana and ordering federal troops to be used in a railroad strike in 1877 and to cross the Mexican border to pursue "invaders." After his five years as an Eighth Circuit court judge serving with Judge Dundy, McCrary moved to Kansas City, where he joined the law firm of Pratt, McCrary, Hagerman & Pratt in 1884.[36]

McCrary was succeeded by David J. Brewer. Judge Brewer experienced the world. He was born to Rev. Josiah and Emilia Field Brewer in Smyrna, Asia Minor, in 1837. He received an associate's degree from Yale University in 1856 and his LL.B from Albany Law School in 1858. He, like Elmer Dundy, then journeyed west but to Kansas, where in 1859 he began the practice of law in Leavenworth. In 1861 he was appointed a U.S. commissioner, and beginning in 1863 he held a series of state judgeships including probate judge, criminal court judge, district court judge, and finally as a justice on the Kansas Supreme Court. Perhaps the judiciary came naturally to him, as his mother was the sister of Supreme Court Justice Stephen J. Field. Judge Brewer served as an Eighth Circuit court judge with Judge

Dundy for five years, resigning in 1889 to follow his uncle and accept an appointment as an associate justice on the U.S. Supreme Court.[37]

After Judge Brewer's resignation, Henry C. Caldwell was appointed to the Eighth Circuit's pairing for Judge Dundy. Caldwell outlasted Dundy on the bench, serving until 1903. Once again, a member of the Iowa bar, Judge Caldwell brought to the Eighth Circuit experiences that had not been previously afforded Nebraska litigants. After serving in the Iowa legislature as well as in the Third Division of the Iowa Cavalry during the Civil War, Henry Caldwell accepted an appointment as a U.S. district court judge in Reconstruction Arkansas, where he served from 1864 to 1890. Over twenty years of U.S. district court judicial decision making were added to the Nebraska circuit court.[38]

These five judges—Dundy with Dillon, McCrary, Brewer, and Caldwell—during the first thirty years of the U.S. District Court of Nebraska provided the federal perspective for legal disputes in the Great Plains. They would grapple with important problems of legal significance.

Thus the lineup for Nebraska's early years of federal court history is an impressive one. Every judge brought useful baggage—extensive Republican Party connections, lengthy judgeship experience, impressive legal education, with the exception of Dundy—and considerable experience in the public sector from membership in state and territorial legislative bodies to holding previous judgeships. Two circuit judges even carried with them to Omaha and Lincoln impressive names—James Madison [Dillon] and George Washington [McCrary]. Think of the conversations as the judges met and decided the disputes that permeated Nebraska in its Reconstruction and Gilded Age years. With Judge Dundy—the savvy Nebraska politico who would accumulate political friends as quickly as political enemies, the former justice on the Nebraska Territory Supreme Court, and eventual twenty-eight-year veteran of the U.S. district court bench—would sit a future Columbia law professor, a secretary of war, an almost thirtyyear U.S. district court judge with Reconstruction stories to tell, and a future U.S. Supreme Court justice. Nebraskans did not have to suffer legal fools.

Together these judges addressed a number of disputes that emerged in late nineteenth-century Nebraska. Of particular national importance was the role of American Indians within U.S. legal, political, and social life. Similarly, of great economic significance was the emerging powerful corporate structure of American capitalism. Could railroads be restrained by citizens or by the courts? Nebraska provided both a setting and a perspective on these important concerns, and Judge Elmer Dundy had a great deal to say about them that would shape America's future in profound ways.

3

Native Americans and Judge Dundy

That hand is not the color of yours, but if I pierce it, I shall feel pain. If you pierce your hand, you also feel pain. The blood that will flow from mine will be of the same color as yours. I am a man. The same God made us both.

—Standing Bear, chief of the Poncas, in testimony before Nebraska district court judge Elmer S. Dundy, May 2, 1879, Omaha

With a stroke of his pen, Judge Dundy had done something unprecedented. He had not only granted the hearing, but had declared for the first time in the nation's history that an Indian was a person within the meaning of U.S. law. That the country's Native inhabitants were people who, if they obeyed the law, now had legal rights whites were bound to respect.

—Joe Starita, *"I Am a Man": Chief Standing Bear's Journey for Justice*

Judge Elmer Dundy and the early U.S. District Court for Nebraska are perhaps best known for Dundy's 1879 ruling in *Standing Bear v. Crook*, which reshaped federal Indian law. It is not that the judge set out to remake Indian law or to ratify his own personal views or even possible prejudices in his ruling. Prior to 1879, Dundy's eleven years as a federal district court judge and four years as a Nebraska Territory Supreme Court judge had not found him frequently addressing questions of law involving Indian individuals

49

or tribal nations, nor was he personally cognizant of much of the Native presence in Nebraska.[1]

Dundy and Indians in His Early Judicial Career

Although we do not have a diary or memoirs that reveal his personal views of Native Americans or specifically of Nebraska's Natives, Dundy did have dealings with Native peoples once he arrived in Nebraska. When he settled in extreme southeastern Nebraska, he and other settlers were distressed once they realized they owned property in what the U.S. government termed the Half-Breed Tract, which was created by a federal treaty for some Iowa Indians and mixed-blood Indians of the area. In legal terms, that meant that these settlers' property could never become a part of a county, and their community, Archer, could not become a county seat where the affairs of local governments were legally decided. Dundy would have to move off the Indian reservation if he wanted to advance his legal career. His neighbors personally enlisted Dundy to go to Washington DC in order to lobby Congress to change the boundaries of the Half-Breed Tract. He was successful, but it was too late to save the town. How that affected Dundy's attitudes toward Nebraska Natives is not known. He relocated to Nebraska City.[2]

This trip and subsequent political activities helped Dundy achieve an appointment to the Nebraska Territory Supreme Court, where he was called upon to make decisions involving Indians.[3] Obviously the practice of law did not represent for Dundy a strong desire. He wanted to make decisions, and the judiciary called to him. Dundy served the new territory from age thirty-three to thirty-seven. Those were perhaps formative years for a man who did not have much legal education or legal experience. The evidence we do have suggests Dundy performed his judicial duties efficiently, and he was involved in several cases that affected Native Nebraskans.

While Elmer Dundy was a justice, we know he decided thirty-six criminal cases, averaging nine cases per year. Twenty-two of those dealt with liquor sold on the Half-Breed Tract or directly to Indians. Only one conviction was actually litigated. White settlers were also involved in timber poaching on reservation land and stealing horses.

Violent crimes included a murder and a rape. No arrest was made of the murderer charged, while the rapist was arrested but not tried. Even when a defendant in a criminal case pleaded guilty, the fine or sentence was often lightened or dismissed.[4] Justice Dundy was most certainly not a "hanging judge." And judging from his record, he was not particularly helpful to Indians. The point is that there was nothing in Judge Dundy's legal experience that indicated he might make a significant decision favoring Indian legal rights.

Poncas

Several centuries ago, the Ponca nation settled near the mouth of the Niobrara River in what would become northeast Nebraska.[5] The Niobrara flows the entire length of northern Nebraska today, emptying into the Missouri after 535 miles. The Poncas, whose name means "sacred head," were one of several small indigenous tribes who were displaced from their original homes in the Ohio River valley.[6] With the movement of British and French settlers to what became Canada and the eastern United States and their subsequent rivalries and wars, major indigenous displacement occurred caused by the fur trade and the introduction of guns. Some tribes benefited briefly; many others did not.

The Haudenosaune, a five-nation confederation of Iroquoian-speaking Indian nations—Mohawks, Onondagas, Oneidas, Cayugas, and Senecas—was founded in 1142 near and north of today's Canada-U.S. border. The Indians acquired superior weapons from the Europeans and increased their spheres of influence, forcing other indigenous peoples from their homes in the Great Lakes region and the Ohio valley.[7] The Poncas, along with Osages, Otoes, Omahas, and several other Indian nations, were among those displaced. Poncas moved down the Ohio River and eventually up the Missouri River to a new location on the Niobrara in what would become Nebraska sometime during the late seventeenth and early eighteenth centuries. Poncas were farmers who, with the acquisition of horses, also hunted buffalo.[8]

Poncas soon found they were not alone in their new area. French and Spanish fur traders and explorers visited them, and Lakotas and other Siouan nations and Pawnees harassed and fought against them.

The European visitors brought trade goods and diseases. Smallpox was a scourge that attacked the Ponca people on numerous occasions, and the Lakotas forced the Poncas to seek refuge among their nearby friends and relatives, the Omahas, in 1804–5.[9] At the same time, the United States entered Poncaland with the Lewis and Clark Expedition, and the Poncas learned their home was a part of the Louisiana Purchase.

At first there was rapport between Poncas and Americans. On June 25, 1817, Poncas signed the first of four treaties with the United States. This was a treaty of perpetual peace and protection.[10] It was shortly followed by very difficult times for the Poncas in the 1820s as they discovered that American protection was meaningless. In 1824 the Lakotas ambushed a group of thirty Poncas. The next year Poncas agreed to a second treaty with the United States that sought to regulate trade in the Great Plains and prevent intertribal clashes.[11] Still many white traders continued to arrive on the Niobrara and brought more smallpox and other diseases. Sioux and Pawnees destroyed Ponca villages, and the American solution to this upheaval was to move the Poncas. The Poncas were not receptive to removal.[12]

In 1829 Standing Bear, the future Ponca chief, was born. Poncas during these early years of Standing Bear were able to retain their villages and increase in population despite being decimated by disease and attacks. By the 1850s Poncas numbered more than seven hundred.[13]

Because more and more pressure was building, the Poncas signed a third treaty with the United States in 1858. This agreement included the Poncas ceding claims to much of their homelands on the Niobrara in exchange for American promises of food, protection from tribal enemies, and a permanent reservation at the intersection of the Niobrara and the Missouri.[14] None of those treaty provisions were ultimately implemented.

This geopolitical situation on the Great Plains did not remain stable. Despite a fourth and final treaty made with the United States, Ponca lands were not going to be protected.[15] In 1865 Poncas ceded 30,000 more acres to the United States, but because Ponca farms were not protected and buffalo were scarce, a drought, grasshoppers, and American settlers brought suffering and starvation to Ponca country. Then in 1868 at Fort Laramie further west, the United States conducted a major treaty negotiation with a number of Indian nations. This gathering did not include the Poncas. This agreement with the Siouan peoples mistakenly placed the Ponca reservation lands on the Great Sioux Reservation. Lakotas now claimed they owned all American-recognized Ponca lands. By the time the government recognized the error, it was too late for the Poncas to assert their claims and have Congress recognize them. So Congress ordered that several tribes, including the Poncas, be removed to what was called Indian Territory in present-day Oklahoma in 1876.[16]

Standing Bear

Standing Bear was now the chief of the Poncas, and he attempted to stabilize their position. Omahas offered to sell part of their reservation to the Poncas in 1873, but Nebraska's U.S. senators prevented Congress from agreeing to it. Under Standing Bear's leadership, Poncas refused to move to Oklahoma, but Congress was adamant. A peace treaty was negotiated in 1876 between the Poncas and the Lakotas promising to let the Poncas stay where they had been for hundreds of years. No Ponca leaders, including Standing Bear, ever consented to leave the Niobrara, even though in several council meetings in 1877 the federal Indian inspector told them they must leave Nebraska.[17]

Finally Ponca leaders agreed to travel to Oklahoma to see the new lands proposed. Standing Bear and nine others left on February 2, 1877, and arrived in Oklahoma a week later. There Osages did not welcome them, and after members of the Ponca delegation were shown the proposed Ponca land, they agreed that the area was not farmable and quite rocky. Several members of the visiting Ponca group became sick, and they determined not to move. When the U.S. representatives threatened not to let them return to Nebraska, they left despite the threats. They arrived on the Omaha Reservation in late March suffering from near starvation and frostbite.[18]

To Oklahoma and Then Back to Nebraska

On April 2, 1877, federal officials told the Poncas they must move, and they were forced to do so, leaving their Nebraska villages on May

16. On July 9 Poncas arrived at the Quapaw Agency in northeastern Oklahoma after much suffering; they experienced many sicknesses, including malaria. It is likely that at least 200 died during the Ponca journey to Oklahoma; 523 Poncas were counted at the agency.[19] There were many Poncas who were very ill. Bear Shield, son of Standing Bear, arrived sick and died in December 1878. Before he died, he asked his father to take his bones back to Ponca country near the Niobrara, and Standing Bear promised his son he would. Thus began the series of events that would lead to the significant legal case of *Standing Bear v. Crook* in Judge Dundy's courtroom.[20]

On January 2, 1879, Standing Bear loaded four wagons with eight men and twenty-one women and children and his son's body to begin the trip back to Nebraska. Most Poncas did not want to return and stayed in Oklahoma. The first day the temperature was −19F degrees; the first three days averaged −22F degrees. At this time, in the depth of winter, it was −40F degrees in Fort Robinson.[21]

It took thirty-nine days for Standing Bear's party to reach the Platte River. Federal officials knew the Poncas were coming and likely headed to their old Ponca lands on the Niobrara. Gen. George Crook was commander of the Department of the Platte. He was quite cognizant of what had happened to the Poncas; he was sympathetic to their plight, and he began the process of anticipating becoming legally involved.[22]

By March 4 these Poncas were in northeast Nebraska camping west of the Omaha Reservation. Omahas visited the Poncas and were surprised by their plight. Most were starving, and they had little warm clothing. Omahas came back with food and blankets and promised to help the Poncas come to their reservation. Three weeks later, soldiers from Fort Omaha and General Crook's command arrived. They told Standing Bear that the commissioner of Indian affairs and the secretary of war had ordered Crook to arrest him and his group. Standing Bear and his people then walked to Fort Omaha where twenty-six Poncas were placed under arrest. Standing Bear told General Crook why he had come back to Nebraska—to bury his son.[23]

General Crook found Standing Bear to be an impressive leader and suggested that he apply for a writ of habeas corpus. Thomas Tibbles, a journalist with close connections to the Omahas, agreed to ask John Lee Webster, a prominent lawyer in Omaha, to be Standing Bear's attorney. Webster accepted. Omaha Jews took up donations for the costs of Standing Bear's representation. Willie Hamilton, who lived on the Omaha Reservation and was fluent in Ponca, acted as a translator.[24]

Standing Bear's Trial

The trial, *Ma-chu-nah-zha (Standing Bear) v. George Crook* officially began in the district court before Judge Dundy on the morning of April 30, 1879, in Omaha's federal courthouse. The next morning the first witness was General Crook, who arrived in his formal military uniform. Standing Bear came in traditional Ponca formal dress. Representing Standing Bear were two of Omaha's finest lawyers, John Lee Webster and his older compatriot, Andrew Jackson Poppleton, a lead attorney for the Union Pacific Railroad. Genio Lambertson represented the U.S. government and General Crook. It was Lambertson's first case as a U.S. attorney.[25]

Lambertson initially had Crook and witnesses describe Ponca dress and work habits. Judge Dundy was restless. Why, he wondered, was this being addressed by the government? Lambertson moved on to consider Ponca loyalty to Standing Bear and their chiefs. Again Judge Dundy seemed impatient, asking, "Why is that material?"[26] He recessed the trial for lunch.

At 2 p.m. the trial resumed, and the plaintiffs announced a new Indian witness for Standing Bear's side. The government objected, and Lambertson queried, "Does this court think an Indian is a competent witness?" Judge Dundy sternly responded, "They are competent in every purpose in both civil and criminal courts. The law makes no distinction on account of race, color, or previous condition."[27] That ruling may well have become the turning point in this legal matter.

The government chose not to call any further witnesses. Standing Bear's team then made the point in testimony that the lead question was whether Poncas were "civilized," a term that meant that they had become farmers with their own land and were no longer members of a tribe that would prevent them from achieving American citizenship. Attorney Poppleton then suggested to the judge that the newly approved Fourteenth Amendment should apply and the writ of habeas corpus granted. Then both sides moved to closing statements.[28]

Lambertson addressed the Fourteenth Amendment dilemma. He said that Poncas not only were not citizens but that they could not be "persons" under the law. He brought up the *Dred Scott* case where African Americans were found by the U.S. Supreme Court not to be citizens and might never be able to become citizens. They, Lambertson intoned, could not sue in federal court. He called the *Dred Scott* ruling a "guiding principle."[29]

Poppleton swiftly attacked the government's argument. He revisited the prior testimony about the death of Standing Bear's son, who had been nurtured and educated by the chief to become a "civilized man." Poppleton then asserted that the issue in the case was very narrow. This was, Poppleton reminded Judge Dundy, a contest over who might receive a writ of habeas corpus. Unlike the *Dred Scott* case, this dispute was not about citizenship. Any person or party might obtain such a writ from a court of law. Thus the crucial issue was simply whether or not Standing Bear was a person. The closing arguments were over, but the trial was not about to end.[30]

At this point, Standing Bear rose from his chair and asked Judge Dundy if he might address the court. Dundy allowed this irregular closing testimony. Standing Bear then approached the front of the room and turned toward the audience in the packed courtroom. He extended his right hand outward. There was a dramatic pause, and then the Ponca leader turned directly to address the judge. Standing Bear began his brief speech, which was translated from Ponca to English for the judge and the audience. "That hand," said Standing Bear, "is not the color of yours, but if I pierce it, I shall feel pain. If you pierce your hand, you also feel pain. The blood that will flow from mine will be of the same color as yours. I am a man. The same God made us both."[31] There was silence in the courtroom, except for several who were shedding tears. The bailiffs asked for order, and Judge Dundy adjourned the court and told everyone he would take the case under advisement and issue his opinion within a few days.[32]

Joe Starita, in his book *"I Am a Man": Chief Standing Bear's Journey to Justice*, offers succinctly what Judge Dundy faced. "In his office in the building that dominated the corner of Fifteenth and Dodge streets, one floor below the large courtroom, the judge would have much to ponder in the days ahead. He was aware that he was now in a position to bring some clarity to the long-muddled picture of exactly where the American Indian stood upon the nation's legal landscape."[33] Judge Dundy would take his time to sort out these important issues. He would not shirk his duty.

The Decision

Ten days later on May 12, Judge Dundy was ready to reveal his written opinion to everyone—the public, the attorneys, the army and its general, and the Poncas and their leader. The judge began by admitting that he had never before been so moved as he was by the testimony and issues in this case. He then outlined the district court's rendering of the law. As to jurisdiction, before this case was heard, it was taken as law that Indians could not sue the government; this, according to Dundy, was a legal non sequitur. The fact that no Indians had ever asked for a writ of habeas corpus didn't mean they could not do so. Second, as to a remedy, Poncas had been denied their liberty by a government that had violated their treaties. Such an action could only find a remedy in federal court. And third, although the government argued that only citizens could apply for a writ, the law says nothing about citizens. It says "persons" may apply for a writ, and Standing Bear was a person. Here the judge quoted a dictionary that proved his point. The jurisdiction of the court was thereby clarified.[34]

Next Judge Dundy established that Standing Bear and other Poncas could refuse tribal allegiance and adopt a civilized life that involved farming, love of the land, and some form of Christianity. If they did, then could the government remove the Poncas? Judge Dundy responded to this question firmly. No power exists, he stated, to force peaceful farmers from their land, and no treaty authorizes this power.[35]

Dundy then summarized his findings. An Indian was a person under American law; the Ponca prisoners were illegally held; no American military could force the Poncas from their treaty-guaranteed home-lands; and therefore Indians had a constitutional right to life, liberty, and the pursuit of happiness. Then Judge Dundy concluded that since the Poncas had been illegally held, they were immediately discharged from federal custody. The writ of habeas corpus had been granted.[36]

In terminology not used at the time, Judge Dundy was in essence a judicial "strict constructionist." To decide the Standing Bear case, he researched all of the applicable statutes. He found that the habeas corpus act involved persons, not citizens, and therefore he applied it because Standing Bear was indeed a person. Usually Judge Dundy did not allow context in a case to affect his decision making, but he nearly admitted as much as he reached his conclusion.

Based upon the Fourteenth Amendment and Judge Dundy's find-ings, General Crook freed Standing Bear and the Poncas, and the U.S. government chose not to appeal Judge Dundy's decision. Standing Bear had indeed been declared a human being under American law.

Joe Starita describes the "big picture" significance : "Dundy's ruling had caught the wave of energy created by East Coast reformers and would trigger far-reaching changes in federal Indian policy." Writes Starita, "The right of blacks, women, Indians, and other minorities to vote, to own property, to live where they wanted, to engage in the full democracy . . . would next confront the American nation."[37] And Judge Dundy was not done weighing these issues. Indian voting rights soon became a part of the U.S. District Court of Nebraska's agenda.

Let us not forget that Judge Dundy was politically connected in Nebraska and interested in politics and public office. By May 1879 he was worried about reactions to his *Standing Bear* decision. He did not want the case to be misinterpreted or be a reason to cause personal political repercussions. Several out-of-state newspapers were critical, stating that he had gone too far by giving the Poncas certain rights, and some Nebraska papers were expressing a kind of puzzled neu-trality about the decision.[38]

Nebraska's legislature would be choosing a new U.S. senator in 1880, and Judge Dundy wanted that position. So, in preparation for his political campaign, he wrote an op-ed article for the *New York Times*.

He worried about his image. In this May 20, 1879, essay, Dundy sought to clarify and restrict the meaning of his *Standing Bear* decision.[39]

"There is no law of the United States or treaty stipulation," wrote Dundy, "setting apart a reservation in the Indian Territory for the Indians, nor for removing them thereto, or keeping them thereon. They cannot be removed and kept there by force, for the one reason that no law or treaty authorizes this to be done, and the decision [in the *Standing Bear* case] is based on that idea alone. It is not claimed in this opinion that Congress might not authorize this, nor that a treaty could not be made which would justify a resort to force, but simply that no such authority has ever been conferred so far as these particular Ponca Indians are concerned." Dundy provided a caveat: "Of course, it is not claimed that the same rules would apply to Indian tribes having reservations to which their treaties require them to remove and remain thereon."[40]

The judge was slipping. An act passed by Congress in 1871 forbid future treaty making, so the treaty solution intimated in his essay was not legally available.[41] His statement that the written decision was very narrowly based did not seem accurate. True, if Congress wanted to authorize specific tribal moves to Oklahoma, it could do that by statute, but it had yet to do so. Moreover, he seemed to imply that force might be a remedy to use if authorized by Congress.

It is not certain how Dundy's retreat on Indian civil rights was received, particularly in the Nebraska legislature. But the Senate race was in full bloom when the new year arrived. The session to elect a senator was scheduled for January 1880. The term of Senator Algernon S. Paddock, Nebraska's sitting senator, was expiring, and he sought reelection. He was vulnerable as a number of candidates came forward, including Dundy. Nebraska's Democrats did not think they had an opportunity in this political event, so the candidates were all Republicans. On the first ballot, Paddock had thirty-nine votes, Dundy twelve, and other candidates split forty-seven votes. After two days of balloting, a dark horse candidate emerged, and Charles Van Wyck became Nebraska's new senator. Dundy was crushed.[42]

Elk v. Wilkins (1884)

Dundy must have felt that it was his *Standing Bear* opinion that cost him the Senate seat, and within that context a new case involving Indian rights came before him: *John Elk v. Charles Wilkins.*[43] On April 5, 1880, John Elk sought to register to vote, and Wilkins, an Omaha voting registrar, denied his request. Elk had been born on the Winnebago Reservation, but he had severed his tribal ties and moved to Omaha where he worked as a taxi driver. After he was denied what he considered his right to vote, the same attorneys who had represented Standing Bear, Andrew J. Poppleton and John L. Webster, filed suit against Wilkins asking for $6,000 damages and requiring that Elk be added to the voting rolls. Formed in 1879, the "Ponca Committee," chaired by *Omaha Herald* editor Tom Tibbles, provided finances and advice for Elk as it had for Standing Bear. The case was heard before the circuit court that included Judge Dundy and George Washington McCrary. Once again Poppleton and Webster faced off against District Attorney Genio Lambertson, who represented Wilkins.[44]

The circuit courts were a relatively new innovation. McCrary was appointed in 1879 and served with Judge Dundy until 1884 when McCrary resigned to become general counsel of the Atchison, Topeka & Santa Fe Railway. Prior to his circuit court appointment, he had served in the U.S. House of Representatives from 1869 to 1877. He was secretary of war from 1877 to 1879 for the Rutherford B. Hayes administration.[45]

The *Elk v. Wilkins* trial was heard before Judge Dundy in Omaha. Dundy kept McCrary, who remained in Iowa, posted on developments. After establishing the facts, Webster and Poppleton argued that John Elk was a U.S. citizen under the Fourteenth and Fifteenth Amendments, having been born in the United States and having given up his tribal affiliation. Lambertson had filed a demurrer stating that Elk's petition did not state the necessary facts for a cause of action. Since Elk was not a citizen, he argued, the court had no jurisdiction. Dundy accepted the government's demurrer, and McCrary agreed.

John Elk lost his suit, and his lawyers filed an appeal, a writ of error to the U.S. Supreme Court.[46]

In a 7–2 opinion, the Supreme Court ruled against Elk. In the majority opinion written by Justice Horace Gray, the court noted that Elk could not be a citizen unless by congressional act. It recognized that Judge Dundy's ruling in the *Standing Bear* case was settled law for the proposition that Indians were "persons" eligible to apply for a writ of habeas corpus, but noted that the ruling did not apply to Elk's situation. Justice John Harlan wrote in a dissent that because Elk was subject to Nebraska taxes and could be in the Nebraska militia, he had citizenship that included voting rights. It remained for Indians to obtain voting rights by act of Congress in 1924.[47]

There was little national attention to *Elk v. Wilkins*, as the Supreme Court announced the ruling a day before the contentious and very close presidential election of 1884 between Benjamin Harrison and Grover Cleveland. Judge Dundy's opinion denying Indian voting rights was upheld, and his letter-of-the-law opinion in the *Standing Bear* case was given judicial sanction.

One last Indian case that came before Judge Dundy in 1888 and also went to the U.S. Supreme Court was *Felix v. Patrick*. Briefly, this situation involved land of substantial value in Omaha that was claimed by the heirs of Sophia Felix, a Dakota Indian woman from Minnesota. Felix had received 480 acres of land scrip because of an 1854 act of Congress, and a real estate broker named Patrick had committed a fraud upon her by using 120 acres of the scrip to obtain land within the city of Omaha valued in 1888 at more than $1 million.[48]

When the case began, Judge Dundy withdrew from it because Patrick had sold land to a member of his family whom Dundy termed "inexperienced." Ironically, John L. Webster represented Patrick, and he filed a demurrer attacking the time lapse of twenty-eight years that rendered the claim beyond the statute of limitations. The Felix heirs stated that they had had to wait until they had gained citizenship to sue. Judge David J. Brewer then heard the case alone, and he quickly accepted the demurrer and found for the plaintiffs. In a somewhat unseemly action, Judge Dundy publicly commented that he agreed with Judge Brewer. The plaintiffs then appealed to the U.S. Supreme Court and lost.

In a rare moment of candidness, Justice Henry Billings Brown wrote that the defendant had committed an unlawful act. But Brown admitted he was afraid that "if the court ruled for the plaintiff it would offer sanction to similar actions throughout the West, placing innumerable titles and claims in question."[49] So the Felix family lost their lands in Omaha because the Supreme Court worried it would destabilize land titles elsewhere. And Judge Dundy was comfortable with this result.

The 1880s brought important Indian cases before Judge Dundy and the Nebraska federal courts and also witnessed many legal issues that involved railroads. "As iron rails extended over Nebraska during the eighties and the state government groped at a means to regulate them, the federal court again became a focal point."[50] Many of those disputes would join the Indian cases on Judge Elmer Dundy's court docket.

4

Railroads and the Ermine of the Bench

From the end of the Civil War until the beginning of the First World War, the railroad was a central, if not the major, element in the political, economic, and social development of the United States.

—Gabriel Kolko, *Railroads and Regulation, 1877–1916* (1965)

But the company [Union Pacific Railroad] has not yet done all that is required of it, and the result is, the United States still retains a pecuniary interest in the land, as well as the legal title to it. So long as that pecuniary interest exists, the right to enjoy it, and the remedy to protect and secure it, cannot in any way be abridged or embarrassed by the action of individuals or of states.

—Judge Elmer S. Dundy, *Union Pac. R. Co. v. McShane* (1873)

There is a story in Alabama legal lore, and it goes something like this. Judge W. T. Blackford called his court to order in early 1870. He knew he had the power in his hands. Hale County Court had to certify certain railroad bonds approved by the county's supervisors as a subsidy for the Selma, Marion & Memphis Railroad. There is no doubt that when he appeared before the court in Greensboro, attorney Nathan B. Forrest, the general of Civil War infamy, was thinking this a mere formality. Perhaps he could be back in the capital city by dinnertime. Judge Blackford, however, had something else in mind.

Forrest presented some legal documents. They needed the judge's signature. When the judge questioned the validity of the documents, the general began to utter a number of legal arguments. "Sir," the judge admonished Forrest, "I don't care a damn about your *nunc pro tuncs,* your *nolens volens* or your *amicus curia:* I am not going to sign them bonds." Forrest was furious. He was so angry with the judge that he charged the bench. The shocked judge stood up and pulled out a pistol he had under his robes for just such an occasion. He pointed it directly at Forrest, and everyone in the courtroom thought the general's days were numbered. Irony surely smiled: Forrest had managed to survive the bloody war, only to die in an Alabama courtroom at the hand of a county judge!

Fortunately for Forrest, he managed to grab the gun and yank it from the judge's hand. "Wal, Judge," General Forrest hissed, "I don't care a damn whether you sign them bonds *nunc pro tunc, nolens volens* or *amicus curia;* you are going to sign 'em." With that, Forrest dragged Judge Blackford into a back room, the judge's chambers.[1]

Those present to record this judicial proceeding may have known or quickly learned that *nunc pro tunc* was a Latin term from the common law meaning "now for then," a phrase used to apply to documents that should have been signed before but could legally be signed in the present while still retaining a retroactive effect. The railroad needed its money, and General Forrest was going to see to it that his company obtained its subsidy. Perhaps he was guilty of overpreparation. The railroad's lawyer had decided that if he ran into problems with the judge and Blackford did not grant his *nunc pro tunc* signature, Forrest could present a *nolens volens* argument, again Latin in the common law meaning whether willing or unwilling, consenting or not. General Forrest argued that whether Judge Blackford signed it or not, the documents had the force of law. The judge did not find this argument persuasive; instead, he found it offensive. Nor it seemed was *amicus curiae* needed.

Whatever the case, Blackford and Forrest reentered the courtroom laughing and joking, no longer threatening or manhandling each other. The gun was gone, and the judge had changed his mind. Indeed, the law itself had changed in that brief interlude. With a swish of the pen, Judge Blackford signed all of the documents. General Forrest was on his way, and the railroad prevailed. Of course, the Hale County incident has nothing to do with Nebraska. Or does it?

In Reconstruction America, whether it was in the devastated South or the developing West, railroads were set to become "king." Prior to the Civil War, the South and North could not agree on a railroad investment strategy. Southern senators and representatives were extremely sensitive and deeply retrenched on slavery issues; they also worried about any kind of change that somehow might disturb their increasingly petrified society. Thus when the South seceded and its members walked out of Congress, it took just a year to pass the first of two important laws that would become the subject of significant litigation and interpretation in Nebraska's federal lower courts. Even the U.S. Supreme Court would be called upon to intervene. Nebraska's federal district court judge, Elmer Dundy, and his circuit court colleagues spent a great deal of their time deciding issues that affected railroads throughout the heartland. Those legal issues revolved around complex questions primarily concerning taxation and labor relations. In addition to the pathbreaking decisions that Nebraska's lower federal courts rendered with reference to the state's indigenous peoples, railroad disputes certainly proved seminal during the Dundy years.

Transcontinental Railroads and Land Grants

In 1862 Congress approved and President Abraham Lincoln signed a bill authorizing the first of several initiatives that would provide federal support for the creation of a transcontinental railroad. The law, known as the Pacific Railroad Act, put in motion forces that would transform Nebraska and the American West in the coming decades.

The Pacific Railroad Act created the Union Pacific Railroad Company. The law's purpose was to build a railroad from the 100th meridian between the Republican and Platte River valleys west to the western boundary of Nevada Territory. The Union Pacific was granted several rights, including the right to sue and be sued in all courts of law in the

United States. To assist the company and provide it with incentives, the federal government allowed the company to issue bonds that required a 10 percent cash return annually and to sell capital stock of up to 100,000 shares at $1,000 each, with no more than 200 shares purchasable per person. Similar provisions were made for the Central Pacific Railroad Company, already functioning in California, and the Kansas Pacific Railroad, operating in Missouri and Kansas.

It was the land, however, that the backers of the companies eyed. The Union Pacific and subsequent Pacific railroads were guaranteed right-of-ways through all public lands. These right-of-ways included two hundred feet on each side of the railroad and all lands necessary for stations, buildings, depots, machine shops, switches, sidetracks, water towers, and turntables. In addition, the railroad companies could take whatever earth, stone, and timber nearby that was needed for construction. To assist in making the public domain more available to the railroads, the U.S. government pledged to extinguish Indian land titles as rapidly as possible.

Land grants were also bestowed upon the Union Pacific Railroad Company. These lands included alternate sections on each side of the constructed railroad on which no preemption or homestead claims were attached. Mineral lands were also exempted. These land grants were to be disposed of within three years, either sold to individuals or retained by the railroad company. If they were not sold, then the U.S. government could step in and authorize the sale of the lands under its public domain land acts at $1.25 per acre, the proceeds to be provided to the railroad company.

A process was set up to certify the allocation of lands to the railroads. Whenever forty miles of track were completed and deemed passable, and located adjacent to a working telegraph line that had been constructed, a commission appointed by the president was to examine the road. The commissioners then reported to the president, and if they certified the suitability of the forty-mile stretch of completed railroad and telegraph lines, then patents for land were issued to the company. In addition, after certification, the U.S. Treasury Department was required to issue thirty-year bonds to the Union Pacific at a rate of sixteen bonds per completed mile that would yield a 6 percent annual interest. The bonds amounted to a generous first mortgage. In return, the law required the railroads to provide for the safe and speedy transportation of the mails, the public, and the military.[2]

Within two years, Congress already needed to amend the act. The provided incentives had not yet spurred the Union Pacific into active operation, and modifications were required to protect the interests of the nation. In an 1864 amendment, other railroad companies were cut in on the deal, and the Burlington and Missouri River Railroad was authorized to build through Nebraska Territory to intersect with the Union Pacific Railroad. It too was given land, but the Burlington was not issued government bonds.[3]

Section 21 of this amendment proved significant. Some historians consider it a mere congressional afterthought, but whatever its original intent, its language soon came to occupy the thoughts of many in railroad boardrooms, Senate and House hearing rooms, and western courtrooms.[4] The section provided that "before any land granted by this act shall be conveyed to any company or party entitled thereto under this act, there shall first be paid into the treasury of the United States, the cost of surveying, selecting, and conveying the same, by the said company or party in interest."[5]

Thus the Pacific Railroad Act and its amendment provided railroads with three restrictions on their land grants that were to have a major impact on western landholding and distribution patterns for decades to come. First, title to land that was provided to railroads could be contingent upon the rights of preemption. If the railroads' lands were not sold within three years of the original grant, the lands were deemed open to settlement without railroad control. Second, the U.S. government allowed railroads to sell the first mortgage of bonds to subscribers while holding the second mortgage. That gave subscribers' rights priority in any bankruptcy action, and this right would have a serious bearing on subsequent disputes over taxation. And third, railroads had to pay the cost of surveying and conveying the land *before* they received a government patent to the land. In effect, the laws provided for three types of liens or reserved rights on the land grants: those of the preemptors, the mortgagors, and the U.S. government.[6] Who then owned the land, and when did they own it?

This question proved central to the settlement of the American West. It was important because of the amount of land involved. Railroads gained more than 240 million acres of land, of which 170 million acres were west of the Mississippi River and more than 8 million acres were in Nebraska—a "princely estate."[7] Each level of government gave much and gave often during the first three-quarters of the nineteenth century. States, counties, and local communities, it has been estimated, provided roughly 28 percent of the lands granted to railroads, whereas the U.S. government supplied nearly 72 percent of the free land. The federal handout began in the 1850s when it started distributing the public domain to the states to encourage the building of railroads. But beginning with the Pacific Railroad Act in 1862, federal land gifts went directly to railroad companies.

Of the land grants themselves, 77 percent were held by transcontinental railroads; 15 percent were taken by Midwest regional railroads that began as branch lines, the largest such railroad being the Burlington; and 8 percent were provided by the South's Reconstruction governments to railroads such as the Selma, Marion & Memphis in Alabama. The total acreage awarded amounted to almost 10 percent of the entire continental United States. Moreover, because of delays by railroads in making selections of land and surveying land, over 30 percent of the public domain eligible for settlement was restricted, slowing the migration of farmers and ranchers. Federal railroad land grants ended in 1871, and local railroad subsidies concluded in the late 1870s.[8]

The railroad land grants became the subject of public debate and legal tugs-of-war because of the time lag between the occupation of the land by an individual who wanted to own it and the actual transfer of the title. By law, railroads were supposed to move toward what amounted to a divestiture of lands within three years. So too, Congress required preemption claims to take one year to transfer a fee simple title. Conveyance times varied under other government programs. The time for conveyance of land titles to colleges under the Morrill Act of 1862 and military land warrants to veterans was less than one year.

Homestead Act acreages took up to five years to patent; fee simple titles conveyed under the Kinkaid Act in 1904 in Nebraska's Sandhills also took five years; and land obtained under the Timber Culture Act of 1873 took eight years. Railroads, however, took more than twenty years on average to perfect title to their lands. Clearly, the conveyance of land to the railroads was a *process* and not an event.[9]

The Public Beware

Railroads seemed obsessed with their lands. They wanted the exclusive use of the public domain without the attendant responsibilities. At least that's what late nineteenth-century America came to believe. At first, the public supported railroads with words and deeds, but by the 1870s John and Margaret Q. Public began to suspect that the railroads were not all that they thought. Twenty years later, citizen support for the railroads was so low that they nearly took the railroads away from private companies and nationalized them.

Public opinion regarding the railroads and their land grants moved through various stages of political consciousness, from ignorance and permissiveness, to reform and restructuring, and ultimately toward punitive attitudes. In the 1860s railroads asked for privileges, which by and large were granted by governments with public ratification; by the 1870s railroads perceived what were previously requested privileges as rights to be demanded; and by the 1890s when the privileges/rights began to come under local, state, and federal restrictions, railroads portrayed themselves as victims of oppression. Critics called this development the evolution of "commercial feudalism."[10]

Railroads interpreted rising public concern as commercial interference, and the companies resisted at all levels. They sought control over the economic landscape, and that meant financial and legal control over lands and labor. After all, as longtime railroad manager Charles Delano Hine advised his son who was learning the business, "Commercialism, like patriotism, rests on certain fundamental principles. The application of these principles may be as uniform as a train of system cars; it may be as diverse as cars in a train of a connecting line." Warned Hine, "Orthodoxy is usually my doxy."[11]

Whether it was Major Hine or railroad speculator Jay Gould or the attorneys and advance men of the Union Pacific, railroad officials typically had trouble perceiving of a public interest in their business. The more reasonable sought a dialogue, such as Henry S. Haines, a civil engineer who published a reformist call-to-arms, *Restrictive Railway Legislation,* in 1905, a book he dedicated to Melville Bigelow, dean of the Boston University School of Law. Wrote Haines, "The residuum which represents the investments from public funds raised by taxation and of grants from the public domain is certainly large enough to entitle the citizens of the United States to a voice in the management of the lines of transportation which have been built over their private estates by the exercise of their own sovereign power, roads constructed largely from the taxation of their own property and income."[12] Haines and the majority of Americans concluded that railroads owed their existence to the contributions of the public, and therefore it was time to put a stop to abusive actions. Others saw railroad companies as motivated exclusively by greed. "To the capitalists who furnished the directive impulse," wrote historians Charles and Mary Beard, "the outlook was especially pleasing because they were called upon to contribute so little money relatively and yet were assured handsome profits from the construction of the roadbed and tracks and from the land endowments accompanying the long mileage."[13]

When frustrations boiled over, a political movement emerged in the form of Populism. Angry farmers felt the injustices most. Heckled as land grabbers, political overlords, and economic masters, the companies were vilified. Railroads, once they had established their transportation monopolies in local regions, jacked up their rates. They indulged in speculative purchases of Indian reservations and public lands, their critics charged, and then when they sold their massive lands, they did so to "insiders"—bonanza farmers, big business cattlemen, lumber magnates, and mining barons.

While the rhetoric was extreme, some of it was justified. There were problems, and the railroads chose to either ignore them or exacerbate them. Railroad debts were, in fact, large, and to make payments they demanded and received cut-rate government loans. Hauling rates were irregular and hurt small farmers. Railroads seemed reluctant to divest themselves of the bulk of their land grants. They delayed surveying and selecting lands and challenged the right of counties and states to tax the lands they controlled. Those who worked for the railroads were not treated well. In particular, those who were injured were unceremoniously cast in a scrap heap of human costs on the company's ledgers. Railroads fiercely fought wrongful death and negligence lawsuits, and they attempted to prevent any union organizing. When things got out of control, railroads hired their own armies to maintain order or, if necessary, they requested and received federal support to run the trains.[14]

Perhaps most galling to the average voter was the involvement of railroads in the political and legal processes. Clearly the railroads played for keeps in the political arena. They bought and sold politicians from the lowest of levels to the highest. They had friends in Congress. For example, when the Burlington and Union Pacific Railroads became worried that feeder lines were going to compete against them with lower freight rates, they got Representative George McCrary, Republican from Iowa and a future Nebraska circuit court judge, to introduce legislation to prorate the system of charges so that branch lines and the main lines had the same rates. Such a blatant attempt at systematic favoritism was surprisingly defeated in Congress. And if senators introduced legislation that was viewed as hostile, railroads such as the Union Pacific openly worked to defeat their renomination, as was the case in the defeat of Nebraska's senator Charles Van Wyck.[15]

Railroads became so adept at politicking that they welcomed regulation when it came. They argued that federal intervention would stabilize economic forces they could not control. But if politics failed, railroad companies turned to mergers, pooling, and secret cross-company agreements to reduce or eliminate costly cutthroat competition. These pools standardized rates and divided up the business. The most successful was the Omaha Pool begun in 1870, which took control of the lucrative Omaha-to-Chicago route. Pools, however, were vulnerable to speculators such as Jay Gould, who bought into railroad companies, ignored pool agreements, and tried to control large lines by monopolizing the feeders. Even with the backdoor arrangements, a war of attrition eventually gripped the railroads. Monopolies emerged so that by the new century, four groups of magnates controlled the nation's rail transportation networks. There were the Jay Gould roads, the Rock Island group that put together the Santa Fe empire, the James G. Hill roads of the Great Northern across the northern ridge of the country, and the Edward C. Harriman lines, a merger of the transcontinentals, the Union Pacific and the Southern Pacific. Railroads had become "creatures of eastern investment bankers," so historians observed.[16]

To preserve their power and presence, railroads resorted to manipulation of legislative bodies and the courts. They frequently bought the votes of elected officials. It was a crude and expensive ad hoc bribery. In Nebraska, John Thurston, legal counsel for the Union Pacific, very successfully operated a political machine that involved Republicans and Democrats alike. It thrived on the free pass system beginning in 1872. The system was set up to reward friends and punish enemies. The Union Pacific maintained in every county in Nebraska a local pass committee that decided who got free train trips. The committee in turn reported to a traveling pass superintendent who moved about the state providing free passes and gathering political information for headquarters back in Omaha. If a county board of supervisors looked like they might pass an unfavorable local regulation, the free passes might be revoked. Lobbyists for the Union Pacific who were dispatched to enlighten the decision makers made it clear to the local recipients what to do.[17]

Entire state political convention delegations enjoyed receiving free passes to Lincoln and Omaha, and judges were particularly vulnerable to free pass abuses. After all, they had to hold court outside of their local communities, and they became dependent on the services provided. Even jurors received passes, which tended to cause some concern about their impartiality. In the 1890s, judges' receipt of free train passes became so controversial that it split the relatively young Lancaster County Bar Association when its members met to discuss whether to chastise judges for taking railroad company gifts. They did not meet again for a quarter of a century.[18]

Thus as railroads were protected, whether in the halls of Congress or on dingy stairwells of Nebraska county courthouses or by bought-off local newspaper editors or even within courtrooms big and small, the increasingly attentive public began to react. They organized and sometimes defeated politicians with a political alliance that became particularly fierce on the Great Plains. The rhetoric electrified and inspired—and divided. One Populist farmer in 1890 wrote to the editor of the *Hayes County Republican* that the editor and those locals who supported the railroad would not prevail. "We're going to have a [new] paper here before long and then things will pop," he threatened. "We'll have an Alliance Store too, at Hayes Center and back these merchants off the track. You just wait till we control things and we'll make you town fellers hump yourselves."[19] But it was labor activist Ignatius Donnelly's preamble to the Populist Party platform, approved on July 4, 1892, in Omaha, that is most remembered. "We meet in the midst of a nation brought to the verge of moral, political, and material ruin," intoned the pugnacious Donnelly. "Corruption dominates the ballot-box, the Legislatures, the Congress, and touches even the ermine of the bench."[20]

Railroads in Nebraska

In its early years, Nebraska was a railroad state. After all, the Union Pacific began in Nebraska. Track laying officially started for the new congressionally created railroad company on July 10, 1865, and by the spring of 1867, more than three hundred miles of track had been completed so that daily trains traversed between Omaha and the new settlement of North Platte. By November 1867, the Union Pacific had laid tracks beyond Nebraska, reaching Cheyenne, Wyoming Territory. Within twenty years, the Union Pacific grew to include no fewer than forty-seven other railroad companies. The Plains of Nebraska had spawned a conglomerate.[21]

The topography, availability of timber, and water resources shaped railroad and subsequent settlement patterns in Nebraska. Leslie E. Decker describes the coming of railroads to Nebraska as creating a "moving right triangle." With the base of the triangle attached to the Kansas border and the perpendicular leg planted at the Missouri River, the hypotenuse gradually extended westward with settlement and tracks throughout the last forty years of the nineteenth century.[22] The Sandhills waited for twentieth-century developments.

Five railroads, of which only four actually laid tracks in Nebraska, received federal land grants from Nebraska's domain. The lands of four of the train companies were restricted to eastern Nebraska. The Sioux City & Pacific Railroad, which built west and north of the Platte River in eastern Nebraska, obtained 38,000 acres; the St. Joseph & Denver City Railroad, which entered Nebraska from Kansas and extended northwestward eventually to Grand Island, received 380,000 acres; and the Kansas Pacific Railroad, which became part of the Union Pacific after 1880, did not even build in Nebraska but claimed 2,500 acres in the southeast tip of Nebraska. These three land grants were relatively small, certainly when compared with the more "princely estates" accrued by Nebraska's big two, the Burlington and the Union Pacific.

The Burlington Railroad's original line crossed Nebraska's borders at Plattsmouth and followed south along the Platte River, eventually joining the Union Pacific. Although not a transcontinental railroad, the Burlington provided valuable feeder services to the Union Pacific and became its strong competitor. The Burlington received 2,225,000 acres, but because the road was in such proximity to the Union Pacific, half of its lands were taken in northeast Nebraska, north of the Platte. The Union Pacific garnered the majority of its land grant acres in Nebraska. Running the entire length of the state in the Platte valley, it received more than 4,225,000 acres, much of it selected from the forty-mile strip in alternate sections. All totaled, including a number of small feeder railroad grants, close to 8 million acres of Nebraska, with over half of it in the early eastern triangle, were made available to railroad companies.[23]

What did these railroads mean for Nebraska and the Great Plains? Sociologist Karl Kraenzel explains that these transportation businesses quickly became the major means of hauling people and manufactured products throughout the region. At the same time, given the land grants, the railroads became colonizers. Because of the timing of its development, the 1860s–1890s, railroads saved remnants of the severely stressed cattle industry by encouraging ranchers to purchase railroad land.[24] Historian Richard White goes further. For White, "The modern western extractive economy began with the railroads." He credits the development of commercial agriculture, mining, cattle raising, and timber production to the introduction of steel-based transportation. It created the basic infrastructure so necessary for the profitability of those industries.[25]

There was, however, a downside to Nebraska's railroads. Because they preceded settlement, townsites were often chosen arbitrarily, while unhealthy speculations occurred in town locations and a ruinous competition soon affected all company decisions. Because the national focus was on a Pacific railroad, the emphasis on east-west transportation split the natural north-south environmental unity of the Plains and Nebraska. Moreover, the Plains became a hinterland, a place whose resources were used to subsidize and finance national priorities. This state of dependency held back and rankled new immigrants into the area. Many settlers perceived of their relationship to the railroads and the national government as that of the colonized to the colonizer.

Some settlers also became increasingly alarmed at the railroads' environmental impacts, as the companies seemed to be exclusively concerned with development of the land whatever the effect. Railroads promoted and subsidized the drainage of prairie wetlands, creating the modern-day stresses that characterize Plains ecosystems. Railroads also used their lands to encourage farming whether or not farming was compatible with the environment. Mixed grass ecosystems declined by up to 70 percent. Even the routes chosen were not always the best or most efficient routes available. Railroad surveys were billed as scientific trips, but all too often the surveyors were required to choose potential road locations because of politics.[26] The primary confrontations between society and the railroads, however, centered around two issues, both of which would ultimately require Nebraska's federal courts to render important landmark decisions. Those cases were complex, and the judges involved did not always agree on the results. The issues involved taxation and strikes.

"The Great Railroad Tax Swindle"

From their very beginning, Nebraska's railroads avoided paying taxes on their property. The companies' officers and attorneys knew that the railroads would have to pay taxes, but they continuously sought to lessen the amount or avoid them altogether. Three kinds of taxes were placed on railroads, primarily by counties and local communities: an *ad valorum* tax on the road bed and what was termed the rolling stock; a property tax on patented land that the railroads held in fee simple; and a property tax on the massive amounts of land provided through land grants.

Two kinds of strategies were adopted by Nebraska's railroads. Basically the Union Pacific avoided the courts and concentrated on manipulating political bodies. They sought to prevent being taxed by county governments and school boards or to lessen the tax. For example, in 1872 some school districts in Adams County taxed individual landholders at 76 cents per acre, but the Union Pacific paid 25 cents per acre. When they were taxed, Burlington's unimproved lands in the 1870s were assessed from 3 to 15 cents per acre south of the Platte and on average 10 cents per acre north of the Platte. Lobbying and influencing county supervisors and school boards paid handsomely for the railroads. If the Union Pacific thought it could not avoid a difficult tax, it would ultimately go to court, usually seeking injunctions. The Burlington Railroad, on the other hand, generally placed most of its energy into challenging tax laws in the lower federal courts or state courts.[27] Both companies, especially the Union Pacific, achieved significant success in the courtroom.

The first major dispute to find its way into Nebraska's lower federal courts involved Lincoln County and the Union Pacific. In 1869 Lincoln County treasurer William S. Peniston attempted to assess property taxes on the Union Pacific. He ruled that the railroad owed taxes on real property and personal property in the amount of $45,264 for that year. Rather than pay the taxes, the railroad went to Nebraska's federal district court, where Judge Elmer S. Dundy granted them an injunction allowing the company to avoid the payment of any taxes until the Nebraska circuit court could hear the dispute.[28]

The Union Pacific challenged the taxing power not only of Lincoln County but of the state of Nebraska and all of Nebraska's communities. It argued that it should not have to pay taxes because, as a corporation that had been created by federal statute, the Pacific Railroad Act, it was an extension of the U.S. government under the Nebraska constitution and the Supreme Court's landmark 1819 decision in *McCulloch v. Maryland*. Moreover, the railroad challenged the ability of Lincoln County to tax lands to the west that were in unorganized territory yet attached to the county for administrative purposes, and it disputed the amount of rail track mileage that the county treasurer used for calculating the tax.

At the Nebraska circuit court hearing, Judges Dundy and John F. Dillon sat while attorneys for the Union Pacific and Lincoln County made their arguments. Judge Dillon wrote the sole and unanimous opinion of the court. Within *Union Pacific Railroad Company v. Lincoln County* (1871)[29] were the seeds for the end of taxation on the unpatented lands in the hands of the railroads, but few recognized the potentially dramatic effects of the decision at the time.

Dillon began his opinion with a typical statement of the facts, and he moved immediately to a discussion of the issues and questions raised by Union Pacific's counsel. First, was the Union Pacific a part of the federal government? No, he reasoned, even though a federal statute had created the company, and it was the federal government that gave the company certain powers, such as the power to sell bonds, and certain benefits, such as low interest loans and free land. Sufficient control of the company was not vested in the U.S. government for the railroad to be deemed an appendage of the federal government.

Judge Dillon gratuitously praised the Supreme Court justice assigned to his circuit, Samuel Freeman Miller, a close Iowa friend, when he quoted his definition of the doctrine of "implied exemption." This doctrine applied to "federal instrumentalities," and its proper application could not prevent railroads from being taxed. Miller had held, however, that this doctrine had limits that were dictated by the entity that sought to impose a tax. In this case, Lincoln County had to be asserting "a principle in its nature antagonistic to the federal instrumentality, and which may be exercised to destroy it."[30] In other words, for *McCulloch* to apply, Lincoln County had to be capable of destroying the Union Pacific Railroad, and that simply was not the case.

Judge Dillon could have left everyone at this point, but he went further. He explained with *Marbury v. Madison*–like reasoning how the federal government did maintain a strong interest in the railroad company, an interest so strong that it could not be defeated even if the company went bankrupt. He explained in detail how Congress's grant of bonding ability to the railroad and loans gave the government a clear second mortgage and that interest in the company was not lessened even by a sale. If Union Pacific was forced to sell its stock, "the purchaser must take his title subject to all the conditions of the original grant," thereby recognizing the permanent interest of the U.S. government. After all, the Pacific Railroad was created expressly to provide for postal, military, and public purposes, and those circumstances had not been changed by Congress.[31] It was not a far walk, perhaps just one simple step, to reach the conclusion that if the U.S. government retained an interest in Union Pacific's solvency through the loans and bonds bestowed, it also retained an interest in the land grants until title was quieted and the lands were sold.

Thus Judges Dillon and Dundy held that the Union Pacific was not an instrument of the U.S. government so as to justify a blanket exemption from taxation by a state or its subordinate entities, but they also ruled that the federal government did retain certain interests in the company through the incorporation act, and those interests were fully reserved and secured. Although Lincoln County could tax the Union Pacific, the amount had not been proven. Thus the injunction was retained until agreement was reached on the mileage of passably constructed track within the county. Two openings then remained. Everyone was still in court, and a loophole—large enough for a locomotive to burst through—was available.

Of course, the Union Pacific was not going to pay its taxes, and Lincoln County had to come back to court in 1872. By that time, the Lincoln County treasurer had adjusted the taxes, and when Union Pacific still refused to pay, he ordered three locomotives seized to sell for the UP's tax arrears. The Union Pacific then went back to the Nebraska circuit court seeking another injunction, and this time Judges Dillon and Dundy did not look kindly on the railroad. Writing for the court, Dillon observed that "courts of equity, and particularly the *federal courts* sitting in equity in the states, will exercise great caution in interfering with the collection of revenues by the states, or their public or municipal agencies."[32] That was cause enough for ruling against the railroad, but Judge Dillon also noted that since the property in question was personal property, this was an appropriate seizure for tax sale. Precisely what Judge Dillon had in mind is not revealed. Had Treasurer Peniston attempted to seize the Union Pacific's land, however, a different result might have occurred.

Given the hardball that the Lincoln County treasurer seemed to be playing, the Union Pacific decided to become obstructionist. The very next year, Lincoln County issued $30,000 in bonds in order to borrow money to pay for erecting a courthouse. Issuance of the bonds required an election, and on May 25, 1873, voters in Lincoln County approved the proposition. The bonds were to be paid off within twenty years.

Because the Union Pacific believed it was going to have to pay increased taxes for this public improvement, and because other counties were doing or about to do the same thing as Lincoln County, the UP attorneys went to court to prevent the issuing of the bonds. It seems like a rather trivial matter, a mean-spirited public action, and in the long term it was. Omaha attorney A. J. Poppleton trotted out Section 23 of an 1869 Nebraska statute that required counties to pay off debts within ten years. Lincoln County probably was not aware of this section of Nebraska's new statutes, or if it was it may have been trying to lessen the rate of taxation by spreading the pain out over an additional ten years. Dillon and Dundy felt they had no choice but to honor the state statute and grant an injunction preventing the expenditures.[33]

The Union Pacific attorneys were very busy in 1873. Poppleton and William M. Evarts, a national practice attorney who at that time was being considered for a U.S. Supreme Court appointment, appeared in the nation's highest courtroom arguing the first of the lower federal court Lincoln County disputes, and on December 15, the U.S. Supreme Court handed down its decision in *Union Pacific Railroad Company v. William S. Peniston, Treasurer of Lincoln County, Nebraska.*[34]

It seemed the Union Pacific adopted a legal strategy of going after the entire loaf. Half a loaf might have been more prudent, but this early tendency to seek a greedy resolution of the issue caused the company to overplay its legal hand. It argued, as it had in Dillon and Dundy's court, that the company was a creature of the federal government and therefore was not subject to any taxation. A plurality of the Supreme Court found this line of reasoning spurious.

The Supreme Court was in a state of flux. It had been called upon to handle a number of controversial and arguably very significant Reconstruction disputes, and the Congress and presidency seemed to be in general disarray. The recent assassination of President Lincoln, the impeachment of President Johnson, the polarization of the Congress over Reconstruction policies, and the weak and corrupt presidency of national hero Ulysses S. Grant all haunted the court. In May 1873 Chief Justice Salmon P. Chase died, and President Grant had gone through no fewer than seven announced candidates without success by the time the court had to decide the *Peniston* case.

On the court were Lincoln appointees David Davis, a former Illinois circuit court judge; Samuel Miller, a learned Iowa Republican attorney destined to become a Supreme Court heavyweight; and Noah Swayne, an Ohio Republican lawyer with strong ties to the business community. Lincoln had also appointed Stephen Field, a pro-Union California Democrat and personal friend of California governor Leland Stanford. Stanford, co-owner of the Central Pacific Railroad, had lobbied Lincoln to appoint Field. The sole holdover from the pre-Lincoln Democrat presidencies was Nathan Clifford, former attorney general during the Polk administration and an appointee of President James Buchanan.[35] Already President Grant had elevated William Strong, a Pennsylvania lawyer; Ward Hunt, a New York Supreme Court justice with ties to the business community and the railroads; and Joseph Bradley, a New Jersey attorney, to seats on the court. Bradley had no previous judicial experience, but "he had practiced a variety of law for many years, obtaining considerable prominence as one of the foremost railroad attorneys in the nation."[36] Bradley was not going to disappoint the Union Pacific.

So the 1873 court contained eight justices. Four sided with Lincoln County. The majority opinion written by Justice Strong echoed the decision of Judge Dillon. Joining Strong were Justices Clifford, Miller, and Davis. Justice Strong concluded that the Union Pacific was a private corporation with public duties. Moreover, states by their very nature have a strong presumption in favor of their taxing authority. To overcome it, one must look to the purpose of the tax and its impact. Addressing the impact first, Strong concluded that to deny the state the ability to tax railroad property would cause a grievous harm to the states. After all, he reasoned, the tax itself was on property, not on services, unlike the situation in the *McCulloch* decision, so it was not too injurious to the railroad per se. The test, according to Strong, was that a state tax on a federally created corporation "must not be so used as to burden or embarrass the operations of the National Government."[37] Moreover, according to Strong, nothing in the U.S. Constitution could overcome this presumption, so the railroads were not free to go to Congress to restrain the state's right to tax them. Though hanging by a single thread, the Strong opinion was devastating to the railroad position.

Justice Swayne's concurrence tipped the balance. Without it, Lincoln County might have lost the case. His opinion was brief and to the point. Swayne reasoned that if Congress had intended to prevent states from taxing railroads, it could have done so explicitly. Moreover, he agreed with Strong's holding that Congress had within its power the ability to protect the Union Pacific from state taxation anytime it so chose. Thus the railroad's remedy, to Swayne, was political.[38]

Justice Bradley dissented and was joined by Justices Field and Hunt. Bradley declared that if the Union Pacific walks like a federal agency and quacks like a federal agency, it was a federal agency, and as such it was not subject to state taxation. But it was Bradley who carried this logic further with a careful examination of the options available. Bradley noted railroad property subject to taxation came from three different sources: the roadbed, rolling stock, and real estate. Railroad real estate consisted of three kinds of lands: that of the right-of-ways, patented lands, and unpatented lands. The power to tax, argued Bradley, required that one must be able to seize the property if the tax is not paid. Could the state lawfully seize the Union Pacific's property? Bradley argued that it could not, because if it took the roadbed or the rolling stock or the right-of-ways, it prevented the company from completing its public purpose. That left the patented and unpatented lands. Here were two opportunities.

There was no question as to who owned the patented land—the railroad, and it could be taxed only if the railroad was declared a private corporation, something Bradley had already discussed. But who owned the unpatented land? Clearly the railroad had the right to use the land, but it did not have title. Lincoln County, therefore, could not seize land not owned by the Union Pacific.[39] So there for all to see was the crucial loophole.

Although the Union Pacific did not prevail in its first Nebraska challenge, it had cause for optimism. That optimism resulted in further challenges in Nebraska's lower courts. The same year as the U.S. Supreme Court was grappling with Lincoln County's attempts to tax the Union Pacific, the railroad brought suit for yet another injunction, this time against Edward C. McShane, treasurer of Douglas County, and the treasurers of several other counties to prevent them from taxing railroad land grants. The Union Pacific had quickly learned its legal lesson from its judicial teachers, Judge Dillon and Justice Bradley. They now appeared before district court judge Dundy, who had read the law as it was so recently developing and rewarded the Union Pacific for its diligence.

In *Union Pacific Railroad Company v. McShane* (1873), Dundy held that the Union Pacific was entitled to its injunction against the collection of taxes on unpatented lands.[40] He also declared that the Union Pacific could not be forced to select lands or pay for the surveying by the levying of taxes. Certainly going against the spirit of the construction of the Union Pacific's tax obligations as held by the U.S. Supreme Court, he referred to the state's "naked right to tax" and expressed his view that the right to tax could not accrue for just any purpose.[41] Dundy held as a matter of law that the land grants were neither absolute nor unconditional. Railroads had to complete the railroad, make the selection of lands, and pay for the surveys. At each step, conditions had to be honored, not compelled.

Moreover, Judge Dundy latched onto Bradley's argument that would be important in future judicial considerations. He wrote that "the right to tax the lands would necessarily carry with it the right to enforce the payment of the tax."[42] If recognized, the right to tax includes the right to sell the land for nonpayment. That requires the perfection of title, and such was not the situation with unpatented lands. Therefore, those lands of the Union Pacific could not be taxed.

Not to be outdone, Nebraska county treasurers initiated the process to seize Union Pacific lands, advertise them, and sell them to satisfy county and school taxes. Back to court went the railroad, and this time Judge Dillon heard them out.[43] The treasurers were buttressed and emboldened by a recent Nebraska Supreme Court opinion, *Hagenbuck v. Reed, Treasurer of Washington County* (1873), where Nebraska's learned justices ruled that school lands given to the State of Nebraska by the federal government that the state sold to individuals on credit were subject to taxation from the individual before title to the land was transferred from the state.[44] Judge Dillon paid no attention to Nebraska's highest court.

Union Pacific argued before the Nebraska circuit court that Nebraska's counties had no right to tax either patented or unpatented railroad lands. The railroad's reasoning was based on timing: that is, that all of the lands had been assessed for taxes before they were patented and before the company paid for some of the surveying. Moreover, Union Pacific was now advertising and selling patented lands at their own prices, which they had a right to do under the Pacific Railroad Act. Judge Dillon stepped into the legal quagmire. He ruled that the Union Pacific was handling its grants within the framework of existing law and that they had every right to treat the lands as "absolute property."[45] However, once land was patented, but before it was sold, the Union Pacific could be assessed for property taxes. It was a legal threshold, however narrow, into which counties and schools could enter. But before the patenting process had been completed, the lands could not be taxed, and after they were sold to a third party, that party was liable for the tax. Judge Dillon dissolved the injunction for all patented lands, but left it in place for those lands that remained unpatented.

On to the U.S. Supreme Court went the parties once again. Several of the *McShane* cases were joined when the court heard arguments on December 15, 1874, and then quickly rendered an opinion in January.[46] By that time, the pro-tax position had extremely able representation, perhaps the best it had had throughout all of the litigation. Clinton Briggs appeared for Nebraska's counties and argued that all of the land grants should be declared taxable because the Union Pacific had treated the land as if it owned it. After all, Briggs informed the court, the railroad had mortgaged the lands, raising money to help construct the road. The bondholders had to believe that the company owned the land. Briggs even hinted at some illicit railroad action when he asked, if the company did not honor its bonds, could the purchaser simply convey the land back to the railroad without suing? Would everything then be settled? Might the railroad be thinking along those lines? For the counties, mortgaging the lands defeated any federal right in the lands that still existed, whether the land was patented or unpatented. According to Briggs, the Union Pacific, once receiving its land grant, had withdrawn the land from the marketplace. It had accepted the grant, completed the road, received patents on part of the grant, paid for some surveying, mortgaged the grant, and received the money. In essence, the Union Pacific "exercised exclusive acts of ownership, by selecting, classifying, advertising for sale, and selling portions of its grant."[47]

The time for powerful arguments, however, had passed. The court had moved on. A new chief justice was now installed, Morrison Waite, a known expert on real estate and land titles. He tipped the balance on the court toward the railroads' position, even though some on the court, notably Justice Field, did not think highly of "His Accidency," as Justice Waite was dubbed. Wrote Field, the new chief justice was a "man that would never have been thought of for the position by any person except President Grant . . . an experiment which no President has a right to make with our Court."[48] Field, however, would find himself more often than not in agreement with Waite, particularly on railroad cases.

Waite assigned Justice Samuel Miller the task of writing the *McShane* decision for a unanimous court. Unpatented lands held by land grant railroads were not taxable. Miller adopted Judge Dundy's reasoning from the first *McShane* case. The U.S. government retains an interest in unpatented lands because of the three-year requirement for disposal of lands and because of the stipulation that surveying and selection costs must be paid by the railroad before lands are patented. But what about the brilliant argument raised by the counties' counsel? What about the fact that the railroads had mortgaged the unpatented land? Justice Miller proved to be a jurisprudential coward: "It is not necessary to go into the merely technical question whether the legal title passed from the United States by virtue of that mortgage, and the Act of Congress which authorized it, nor whether, if it ever becomes necessary to foreclose that mortgage, the rights of the United States in the land would be divested by the proceeding, because we are satisfied that the United States, until she conveys them by patent or otherwise, has an interest, whether it be legal or equitable, which the State of Nebraska is not at liberty to divest by the exercise of the right of taxation."[49] He pretended that it would never happen, but if it did, he did not care because federal rights were still alive. This decision could not have sat well with independent, non-railroad-connected bondholders. According to the court, they really did not own the bonds they had purchased free and clear after all.

There was substantial fallout from the *McShane* decision. When Judge Dundy granted the injunction so that the Union Pacific could avoid paying taxes, Nebraska's newspapers went berserk. The *Omaha Bee* forecast rampant bankruptcy for counties and even the state. Public improvements required public debt, and if railroad lands were exempt from taxation, there were simply no other resources available.[50] The *Beatrice Express*, a conservative Republican newspaper, accused the railroads of stirring up "the hostility of the people." Its editor labeled the Union Pacific's successful attempt to avoid paying taxes as "the railroad tax swindle."[51] The *Grand Island Times* added, "Of all the impositions that the railroad monopolies have tried to perpetrate upon the people of this country, the resistance to taxation of the UPRR [Union Pacific Railroad] and B&MRR [Burlington and Missouri River Railroad] is by far ahead of anything in that line that has come under our observation."[52]

Nebraska congressman Lorenzo Crounse, reflecting the fears and frustrations of his constituents, attacked the railroads on the floor of the House of Representatives. Crounse was appalled that the courts had not "put the railroad companies on the same footing as the struggling settler, who has to deprive himself of the very necessities of life to meet the taxation which inexorably comes around with every recurring year." The congressman reminded his colleagues, "Every day [the railroads'] lands are being enhanced in value by the sweat and toil of the settlers upon the alternate sections. The alternate sections are sold for $2.50 per acre, and the settler strains himself to pay that amount, and by industry labors to meet taxation; and by his building up schoolhouses, bridges, and courthouses, and in all the various ways that men improve and advance settlements, the lands of the railroad company are also advanced in value."[53]

The die had been cast for the railroads. Obviously no friend of theirs, the Union Pacific and Burlington targeted Representative Crounse for defeat in the next election, and they were successful. The railroad had its defenders outside of the judiciary and members of Congress. Ironically, J. Sterling Morton, who found homesteaders more problematic than railroads, crawled into bed with Judge Dundy for the first and only time in his long political career.[54]

And the Union Pacific, because it had not won complete tax exemptions for all of its lands, notified preemptors on land they claimed that the railroad would treat them as trespassers and go after them in the courts. The railroads now saw the homesteader as enemy number one, and to test their concerns, they challenged the preemption priorities in court. Union Pacific employee William Platt was "encouraged" to file a preemption claim on one of the Union Pacific's mortgaged sections in Hall County by UP attorney Andrew Poppleton. Platt settled on the property in 1874 and filed his claim in 1878. Who was to prevail: the settler or the mortgage holder? After the usual injunction was granted by Judge Dundy, the U.S. Supreme Court ruled in a split decision that the settler prevailed over the mortgage holder. It was a temporary reprieve.[55]

There would be numerous other railroad suits in Nebraska's lower federal courts during the Dundy years. For example, when Merrick County, a picturesque landscape nestled around the Loup and Platte Rivers in central Nebraska, decided to submit bonds to its voters to provide $125,000 to the Midland Pacific Railway Company to construct a railroad to Lone Tree, the Union Pacific sought an injunction to prevent the vote because the UP owned a significant amount of patented land in the county. First, the railroad challenged the legality of the election because the flyer detailing the language of the referendum was nailed to the county courthouse door rather than inside next to the ballot box, but Judge Dillon rejected that argument. Then the Union Pacific claimed that the referendum covered too many subjects, including construction of a railroad, establishment of a depot, and construction of a wagon bridge. Dillon also rejected that contention, and the Nebraska circuit court saw no legal reason to void the election.[56]

On another occasion, Union Pacific successfully prevented a homesteader from claiming lands the UP preferred. This dispute involved a patent in a land grant dispute. It seems four individuals filed homesteads that abutted each other and constructed a four-sided house at their intersection to perfect title. One of the claimants was Peter Hugus, but the railroad persuaded Hugus to testify that he had never intended to settle on the land, but rather had only done the filing. Moreover, he claimed that he had no intention of homesteading. Thus the defendant, James R. Watts, who had claimed the Hugus homestead, was unable to do so, ruled Judge Dillon, because no valid homestead claim had ever been made. One is left to read between the lines about the relationship between the Union Pacific and the bogus homesteader.[57]

The Burlington was also heavily involved in litigation in the 1870s.

Their attempts to prevent taxation of their lands seemed inept when compared with the Union Pacific's legal arsenal, although they often tried to curry judicial favor. In 1874 one Horatio H. Hunnewell, an attorney for the Burlington who owned some of its stock and resided in Massachusetts, sued the railroad—in essence he sued himself as a stockholder—seeking to prevent the payment of taxes on Burlington lands to Cass County and others. The Burlington had been so efficient that it had perfected title to much more of its land than the Union Pacific had done, and once it saw how the UP was avoiding taxation, it wanted in on the loopholes. The same arguments that had been made in the *McShane* case were presented by Burlington's attorneys, but to no avail. Judge Dillon ruled that because there were no government bonds involved, the Burlington would have to pay taxes. Moreover, although the Burlington delayed paying certain small fees and registered title to their lands beyond the deadline, it could not use the lapse to avoid taxation. Dillon dismissed the Burlington assertions and their cause of action.[58]

This decision was appealed by the railroad to the U.S. Supreme Court, and Justice Miller made short shrift of the Burlington argument. He almost asserted they were wasting the court's time with a contrived dispute by a stockholder providing diversity of jurisdiction. Justice Miller used the term "embarrassing" on at least two occasions to describe the Burlington argument for nonpayment of taxes. The remedy the railroad sought was termed "extraordinary" and dismissed. The Burlington had simply gone too far.[59]

Finally, after all was said and done, the Union Pacific tried to reclaim taxes previously paid on unpatented land. It had paid its tax bill in full too soon—prior to *McShane*—and now the company wanted its money back. To make its point, the railroad sued Dodge County and took its citizens all the way to the U.S. Supreme Court. Arguing for Dodge County was its local resident attorney, William H. Munger from Fremont, a man who would become the next Nebraska district court judge. And Munger would prevail for his clients.

Chief Justice Morrison Waite delivered a concise opinion, one of his first decisions as a member of the court, in February 1879. Waite carefully outlined the payments made by Union Pacific to Dodge County. He held that at no time was the Union Pacific forced to pay the taxes against its will and that even though the UP did file a formal challenge, it did so without major objections. If the court had decided that the Union Pacific had paid taxes under compulsion, then it had a remedy, but here no such remedy was available.[60] Waite told the railroads they had gotten a partial tax write-off, and it was time to move on.

How well had the railroads done? From 1862 to 1886, the Union Pacific paid a total of $1,120,526.30 in taxes on its land, averaging $62,251.46 a year at an annual tax rate of $.0058 per acre. The Burlington paid $1,131,072.61 in taxes, averaging annually $66,533.68 at a tax rate of $.0272 per acre. The Burlington railroad got its land patents immediately and consequently paid more, but still at a considerably lower rate than Nebraska's farmers and ranchers. By 1886 the Union Pacific had patented only 2 million acres out of 12 million land grant acres. If the company had been taxed on all of its land at the average rate, it would have paid $326,000 in taxes per year instead of $62,000. While the UP was saving nearly $264,000 per year on taxes, the Burlington was saving $63,000. Obviously, the savings to the railroads were huge, and the loss to the state, counties, and school districts was equally huge.

It is significant that the railroads obtained a substantial partial tax exemption not through the action of the Nebraska legislature or the Congress but through judicial opinion. Because of the initial interpretations of Dundy and Dillon, and their subsequent ratification by the U.S. Supreme Court, Nebraska's lower federal court became the fulcrum for railroad legal maneuvering and citizen complaint. The railroads sought to use every possible means to prevent their contributions to the public. They delayed quieting title to the land grants, even in the face of the Nebraska legislature, which in 1872 memorialized Congress to seek laws that would compel the railroads to take title to their lands, and they went to Nebraska's district court often.

By the end of the Dundy years, most of the tax issues seemed to be settled law, and even though political upheaval in Nebraska and the surrounding states had tried to reverse the railroad's legal successes, most of those efforts had been unsuccessful. Still the residue remained. Take the editorial in the *Lincoln Evening News* on December 11, 1905: "The chief criticism that has been leveled at the railroads has been that they have very often acted as though they regarded themselves as superior to the law and as picked out for other things than obedience to whatever does not suit them. An instance in point is that afforded by the Burlington and Union Pacific going again into federal court to restrain the collection by the various counties of the state of the taxes assessed against the corporations." Observed the editors, "And so they [the railroads] attempt what amounts to anarchy while accusing the people generally of being anarchists because they favor making corporations toe the mark." Perhaps the people working for the railroads needed to speak up. Judge Dundy would hear from them as well.

The Burlington Strike of 1888

Taking a ride on the Q in late nineteenth-century Nebraska meant booking tickets on a flyer from Omaha east or a slower passenger train from Broken Bow to Alliance or even a freight from McCook to Lincoln on the Burlington & Missouri River Railroad (B&M). The Q actually referred to the Chicago, Burlington, and Quincy Railroad [CB&Q], a railroad owned by the B&M that was a primary partner of the Burlington system. The Burlington included seven separate railroads composed of five companies that together controlled nearly 6,000 miles of track. The B&M with the CB&Q maintained approximately 4,800 miles of track and served more than 1,500 cities and towns in eight states, including Nebraska, thus making it a mainstay of the Burlington system. Within Nebraska, the B&M traversed 2,120 miles of track, its engines entering the state from the east at four sites: Omaha, Plattsmouth, Nebraska City, and Rulo. Burlington track and trains covered southeastern Nebraska. Two main lines extended west, one north of the Platte to Alliance with branches to Blaine and Loup Counties in the Sandhills, and a second south of the Platte that amalgamated thirteen branch lines. Along with the Union Pacific, the Q dominated transportation in Nebraska.[61]

It thus came as a shock to many when on February 27, 1888, 1,600 members of the Brotherhood of Locomotive Engineers and Brotherhood of Locomotive Firemen struck the B&M, crippling Nebraska's lifeline. Five hundred daily trains stopped. Negotiations with the Burlington by representatives of the enginemen, including eight Nebraskans, four engineers and four firemen, had been frustrating for everyone.[62] Labor relations had generally been good up to this point. While the B&M and other companies in the Burlington system had not paid top dollar, they had not paid bottom dollar either. The engineers and their compatriots, the firemen, mostly wanted an increase in the average rate of pay, but they also felt constrained by a classification system that offered rewards irrationally and pay based on miles traveled rather than days worked. Known as conservative unions, the two Brotherhood memberships as well as Burlington management thought a strike unlikely.[63]

The negotiations conducted by the Burlington Railroad involved three men primarily. Burlington president Charles Perkins, a Harvard man who had gained his railroad experience on assignment in the West, opposed all regulation and treated labor with stern paternalism. He believed the workplace was no place for philanthropy, and those who provided workers with insurance or responded positively to union demands committed "errors of sentimentalists."[64] He also took a hands-off approach to labor negotiations, placing two other Harvard men—Henry Stone and George Holdrege—in charge.

These two men anchored the Burlington holdings west of Chicago. Stone held the position of general manager of the CB&Q, while Holdrege's portfolio placed him as general manager of the B&M. Holdrege also served as director of the Lincoln Land Company, the B&M's primary town site speculation company. Characterized as austere, unbending, and secretive, Holdrege built a potent political machine in Nebraska. As for labor, a strike to Holdrege equaled an act of company disloyalty. He preferred to crush strikes using all means possible. Although the B&M owned the CB&Q, Stone assumed leadership for Burlington's labor negotiations. Another company official remembered today on Lincoln's street grid, the general superintendent of the B&M, T. E. Calvert, actively assisted Holdrege in planning the Nebraska strategy.[65]

Burlington's leaders did not agree to any of the union's requests. Management had many concerns, including a downturn in profits generally, a new attempt by the U.S. government to regulate railroads through the Interstate Commerce Act of 1887, and the end of railroad pools. It seemed to company officials that a new business climate required steadiness and few changes. Moreover, because of a lack of communications and a decentralized strategy of corporate decision making that unnerved the Harvard-trained managers in the field, confusion and delay abounded. The Brotherhoods also had plenty of miscommunication. The members had no idea a strike was at hand until their leaders decided that a walkout was the only alternative. When the company refused to even consider a scaled-down labor suggestion, the union called for a limited strike, one that involved only Burlington engineers and firemen. Historian Donald McMurry summarized the feelings of the time: "The strongest labor union in the country was at war with the largest, wealthiest, and best managed railroad corporation in the West." [66]

During the first days of the strike, order prevailed and public opinion seemed sympathetic to the engineers and firemen. Rallies for the strikers featured merchants, a former senator and governor, community religious and political leaders, and other railroad company engineers and firemen. Of those newspapers that commented on the strike, the *Omaha Bee*, the *Grand Island Independent*, the *Falls City Journal*, and the *Wymore Democrat* backed the workers. Papers from Nebraska's largest cities tilted toward the Burlington. Lincoln's newspapers, the *Journal* and the *News*, favored the railroad along with the *Omaha Daily Herald* and the *Omaha Republican*.[67]

The initial relative peace provided the company with time to implement its plan to break the strike. Stone and Holdrege opted to hire replacement labor from three sources immediately: any current employees with an interest in or limited experience as engineers or firemen, former employees or local labor, and eastern engineers from other railroad lines. Those with any kind of engineering experience got bonuses for signing on, along with easy terms on Sandhills railroad lands. G. M. Moore from York, for example, had some engineering experience, but was not currently employed, so he began his extensive railroad career at this moment with a bonus and a down payment on his own land in the Sandhills. Eastern engineers, called "wise men" by the strikers, as well as scabs, got a 20 percent pay increase, but it took some time to transport them to the Burlington lines. In addition, B&M hired two hundred men for security, including nearly one hundred Pinkerton agents. In Nebraska, the Pinkertons were stationed in Omaha, McCook, Hastings, and Plattsmouth, and they proved controversial with the public and excited the strikers.[68]

Within a week, some trains were running again. By the third day of the strike, the "wise men" had begun to arrive. By March 1 more than half of the strikers had been replaced. Passenger trains and freight engines reclaimed Burlington's roads. The flyers had yet to be rescheduled; those engineers needed to be the best trained and most experienced of the new employees, but by August the fast trains also took to the tracks. The union decided to meet this new challenge with a boycott. In part, the Burlington's Brotherhoods had tremendous sympathy from other railroad employees, especially engineers, who refused to move Burlington cars. A formal boycott among engineers and firemen began with virtually all of the rival lines, and their railroad ownership winked at this action. Union Pacific and other railway management did so in part to avoid the very real possibility of their own strikes given the engineers' high feelings and because they thought Burlington management to be haughty and deserving of a labor defeat.[69]

The boycott hurt the Q. What had been a confident management soon resorted to court action. Stone and Holdrege believed the strike would be prolonged without court intervention. Their team of company attorneys first asked for temporary injunctions to stem the boycott, and Nebraska's Judge Dundy suddenly found himself in the legal spotlight when the Burlington came to him asking for an injunction to force the Union Pacific to transport Burlington cars.

In Nebraska political circles, politicians and judges sometimes found themselves typecast. In part because of previous political stops and starts and his own Omaha friends and acquaintances, Judge Dundy had been placed in the Union Pacific Railroad camp. Perhaps his old political nemesis, J. Sterling Morton, who was under the employ of the Burlington as a kind of public relations specialist, made certain press, and politicos perceived Dundy this way. So when this case suddenly appeared on the docket of Nebraska's circuit court, Burlington engineers and firemen and Burlington management shared their anxiety with those who kept up with developments in Nebraska's political culture. But Judge Dundy would leave no uncertainty. He would never be a Union Pacific dupe.

The history of labor injunctions in American law in 1888 was extremely sparse. Most lawyers and judges did not deem it a proper legal remedy for a strike. Beginning in the 1870s, state and federal jurists first began considerations of invoking injunctions for railroad labor disputes, but only for lines that were in receivership and were being run by the courts. In those circumstances, judges reasoned that injunctions constituted proper remedies because a strike constituted a threat to the public peace and the public's mail, the possible destruction of property, and even more important a direct slap in the face of the courts who were running the railroads. Judges wrote that workers, if they had a concern, should come talk to the judges rather than stop working or start conspiring to obtain some kind of edge over management. But that judicial reasoning had little connection to the reality of work on the railroad. "In effect," wrote historian Gerald G. Eggert, "the receivership became a device by which managers of insolvent railroads, with the courts' assistance, escaped from control by the rightful owners of the company, from harassment by the unpaid creditors of the line and, as it turned out, even from such pressures as employee strikes and boycotts."[70] But by 1888 no judge, federal or state, had ever granted a temporary or permanent injunction in a railway labor dispute over a railroad company that was not under receivership. Moreover, no judge had used an injunction to prevent a boycott by one railroad of another railroad's cars, whether the line was under receivership or not. To use injunctions in such a manner constituted an unheard-of legal development, but Judge Dundy proved up to creating new law.

On March 5, 1888, Dundy marked his fiftieth birthday. Two months later, he would begin his twentieth year on the federal bench. Although his legal career had been lengthy, he had not prepared for the public pressures surrounding his court just four days after his birthday celebration, when the Q requested a temporary injunction against the UP. Nevertheless, he granted the temporary injunction, and the *Omaha Daily Herald* reported his opinion verbatim.

Dundy used what some called rather extravagant language. He ordered the Union Pacific management along with twenty-three named UP engineers and "their unknown confederates" to "receive, handle, haul, and deliver any and all traffic" from the Burlington to their assigned destinations. The UP was to do so because it was their duty as a common carrier, and the Interstate Commerce Act required UP not to discriminate among the cars it hauled. But Dundy did not stop with his general order. He observed that the engineers and their "confederates," a loaded postwar term, had "unlawfully, unjustly and *wickedly* combined, organized, connived, confederated, and conspired, and are still organizing, combining, conniving, confederating, and conspiring" to force the Burlington to fire new employees hired to replace striking workers as well as "injuring, destroying, and annihilating its [the Burlington's] business and property."[71]

As if these accusations were not sufficient, Dundy accused the Union Pacific engineers of conspiring to unite into a general strike that would cause "great and immeasurable loss, injury, and destruction of property and business" to the CB&Q, the UP, and the general public. Such a labor action, Dundy pontificated, would be disastrous for the country, and because the Burlington is "wholly without any adequate remedy at law," an injunction became justifiable. The injunction prohibited Union Pacific engineers, whom Dundy accused of attempting to act in a "wicked combination," from striking as well as "meddling or interfering with the Chicago, Burlington & Quincy railroad company's employees." Those who failed to honor the judge's command were subject to a "penalty of __ dollars" to be levied on their individual lands or goods. As if to place a legal stamp of approval on his extraordinary order, Dundy concluded by invoking "Witness the Hon. Morrison R. Waite, Chief Justice of the Supreme Court of the United States."[72]

The decision was a stunner. The Burlington legal team had invited Judge Dundy to make new law because all American business, they argued, now completely depended upon unimpeded rail traffic. In their brief, they asserted that the Brotherhoods were members of secret societies who sought to monopolize skilled labor in the United States and to control all railroads in order to "cripple and paralyze all social, commercial, industrial, and political forces of the entire nation and thereby entail upon the people thereof an immeasurable and irreparable injury and destruction of property, rights, and happiness."[73] Evidently this incendiary language persuaded Judge Dundy to issue the temporary injunction in order to save the nation.

Immediate reaction in and outside the courtroom ranged from looking like "a cat swallowing a canary" to being stunned or expressing outrage. George Holdrege, who had anticipated something "big," publicly evaluated Judge Dundy's opinion as "an exceedingly strong clear document" with "strong possibilities."[74] Burlington president Perkins presciently deemed Dundy's order a strikebreaker. Everyone agreed that this action constituted a "far-reaching injunction."[75]

Newspapers sympathetic to the engineers and firemen mocked the court when copies of the order increased into the hundreds, and court officers had to carry them in baskets in order to serve them. The *Omaha Daily Bee* editorialized the next day noting the gravity of the temporary injunction for labor: "This is probably the first instance of the power of the court being invoked to restrain men from striking." UP workers received the news with disbelief. Two engineers told the *Bee* that the injunction "would carry but little weight as they believed that no court on earth could compel them to remain on their engines if they were not so disposed."[76] National media picked up the story. In the *New York Times*, a Brotherhood official bluntly summarized Dundy's opinion: "I think it is nonsense for any court to order a lot of men not to quit work. It might do well enough to talk to the men as a brotherhood and issue legal mandates against them, but as individuals how can any court compel the engineers on the Union Pacific to haul Burlington freight if they don't want to? How can a court prevent them from quitting rather than pull Burlington cars if they want?"[77]

Pressure arose almost immediately to force Judge Dundy to rescind, modify, or make permanent his temporary injunction. He absorbed a number of hits in Nebraska papers.[78] Dundy probably took a gulp and decided to wait, albeit briefly, to see what another judge might do. It's not easy being out front on something so contentious as a labor dispute.

At the same time the Q sent its lawyers to Nebraska's circuit court, it petitioned Illinois circuit judge Walter Q. Gresham. Judge Gresham, a man with significant political connections in the national Republican Party, so much so that he was rumored to be the party's next presidential nominee, had served as a major general in the Civil War and held such offices as secretary of the Treasury and postmaster general until his appointment as circuit judge of the Seventh U.S. Judicial District in 1884. He broke with the Republican Party over the McKinley tariff and supported Grover Cleveland for president in 1892 before becoming Cleveland's secretary of state.[79] Gresham also happened in 1888 to be administering the receivership of the Wabash, St. Louis and Pacific Railway Company, a competitor of the Burlington.

Judge Gresham's court in Chicago took judicial notice that the court-appointed receiver of the Wabash had rescinded his order not to move Burlington cars, and Wabash engineers had promised to move the freight, so there was little need to offer a lecture to workers and management. He issued the temporary injunction only to put it on file, and he did not schedule a hearing to make it permanent. Although this represented a receivership case, Gresham based his decision on the notion that common carriers had obligations to move all cars alike.[80] Ironically, the Burlington, which might have anticipated a ringing endorsement from Judge Gresham against a receivership railroad, barely achieved a temporary injunction while the Q obtained much more than they might have realistically anticipated from Judge Dundy. According to the *Omaha Daily Bee*, "Judge Gresham does not issue hand-me-down injunctions on application of railroad managers. This is an exclusive monopoly of the federal judge of this district."[81]

Even though Judge Gresham did not afford Judge Dundy with backup precedent, Nebraska's federal jurist moved ahead and issued a permanent injunction against the Union Pacific. His opinion, again not reported officially but printed in the *Omaha Republican* on March 18, reinforced his previous reasoning. Dundy offered his own jurisprudential philosophy to justify his decision. "I apply the law as I find it," he stated. "It is my duty, when a proper case is made to enforce it. I propose to discharge my duty in the premises regardless of consequences. If I could, like the old Athenian, suspend the operation of the laws for a day or two, I might do so. But the power to do so is wanting. If the laws are not satisfactory, the only remedy in sight is repeal. Until then, it seems to me the duties of the court are clear."

Dundy reiterated much of his previous temporary injunctive rhetoric. He referred to the common law, provisions in the Interstate Commerce Act, and Congress's charter of the Union Pacific. Taken together, he determined, those acts required the UP to handle traffic on its roads in a reasonable, nondiscriminatory manner.[82] Backing off somewhat from his previous conspiratorial theories, Dundy said, "There is no law, human or divine, so far as I know, to compel these defendants, or any one of them, to remain in the service of the defendant [rail]road against their or his will. Certainly, however much I might regret a determination on their part to leave the road, I shall not undertake to prevent it by injunction or otherwise." Having given ground, he then took some back. "At the same time, it must be understood that in so doing [quitting one's railroad job], it is with the qualifications and limitations before stated. That sort of liberty must not be abused nor be accompanied with wrongful and injurious acts to the prejudice of the property rights of others." Exercising his flair for the dramatic, Dundy then concluded: "If otherwise, it is liable, if not certain, to prove in the end, that the 'velvet glove of liberty encases the merciless hand of the law.'"

By this point, both an exhausted Burlington management team and the unions offered predictable reactions. An outbreak of "Q flu" proved of epidemic proportion for several days, but within a week UP engineers agreed to move Burlington cars, and UP management pledged that their railway would not forsake the law and the judge's order. And while the strike lasted officially until April 1889, for all practical purposes it was a lost cause for the engineers and firemen. Assessed Gerald Eggert, "Judge Dundy's order quite clearly outlawed secondary boycotts. Less certain was the right of men to strike under the order, even giving 'strike' its most conservative and narrow definition: men quitting their jobs en masse. Was it lawful, under Dundy's order, for men to leave their jobs peacefully in a group, so long as they did not interfere with the company, its nonstriking employees, or the men hired to replace them if the result was injurious to the company? By implication at least, the action would be conspiratorial and hence enjoinable."[83] Thus Dundy's decision truly contained far-reaching ramifications.

Meanwhile, Dundy became the object of much derision as well as concomitant defense. Unrelenting, the *Omaha Daily Bee* lambasted the judge: "Judge Dundy's bull against the comet has had some effect at last. A car load of whisky that had been standing in the Union Pacific yards at Lincoln for several days has been switched by the rebellious engine men and forwarded to points where the armed mercenaries recently imported into Nebraska by the Burlington need bracing up."[84] Wrote the *New York Times*, "What he said upon the subject [of the UP engineers striking] recalls the advice of the old Judge to the young Judge—always to give his decisions without giving his reasons. . . . Telling a railroad company to sue its engineers for damages and calling that process a 'remedy' is more suitable to a Western humorist than for a Western Judge."[85]

In his defense, the *Omaha Republican* offered reasoned judgment and fair justice as the hallmarks of Judge Dundy. "He was on the bench. Did anyone expect he could be a partisan? He had the law and the facts, and it was upon these that he had to pass. He had nothing to do with railroads or labor organizations." This last statement seemed somewhat debatable, but the *Republican* moved ahead. "There could be no introduction of sentiment. The issue was before him, the statute books were behind him, and it was in this atmosphere that he decided. Both sides presented their cases. It is a matter of record that the Burlington attorney made a case and that the attorney for the strikers did not."[86]

Dundy defended himself, but rather poorly. In an interview with the sympathetic *Omaha Daily Herald,* Dundy revealed the toll this case had taken on him personally:

> "I find that there are several persons who, in the exercise of what they claim to be their right, and perhaps it is admissible for them, take it upon themselves to criticise me rather harshly. Officious persons and intermeddlers existed always; they exist now, and they hover about this case." Dundy, the scorned.

> "No one is safe from their vituperation and malice—not even the bench." Dundy, the victim.

> "I find that my judicial action in this case has been harshly spoken of in some papers, and one paper in this state went so far as to say that I had been bribed into my action by the Q road. The press formerly had me on the list as the judge for the Union Pacific, and now, it seems, I have changed my employers." Dundy, the slandered.

> "The press may make all the comments they choose, and charge me with what they please. I have no motives in being bribed. I have no office to ask, am not looking for one, and in fact *am tired of the one I possess.* Whatever I do is done from a conviction of official duties, and the consequences have nothing to do with me." Dundy, the brave and the dutiful.[87]

Dundy's target, of course, the *Omaha Bee,* offered a response in a subsequent editorial entitled "He Doth Protest Too Much." The *Bee* quoted an old adage that "He who excuses himself, accuses himself," referring to Dundy' s own defense. The editorial then went for the jugular: "What a pitiable spectacle the judge presents before the whole country when he invents criminal charges against himself and winds up with a declaration that he does not want the office which he now holds." In an allusion to the Burlington opinions, the *Bee* chided Dundy: "Every schoolboy in the land knows that nobody can be compelled to hold on to an office which he does not wish to fill." The editorial concluded with an implied quid pro quo: "A judge who goes out hunting and junketing in railroad palace cars, and dines and wines with railroad managers and attorneys may be endowed with a high moral sense and spotless integrity, but if he has any gratitude in his makeup he will reciprocate favors."[88]

Dundy no doubt came to near physical exhaustion over the Burlington strike decisions. He had made law, and many people would not let him forget it. As one historian summarized, Dundy's Burlington injunctive orders combined with "a series of other injunctions and decisions which were to make his name anathema to organized labor."[89] Still, more railroad issues beckoned Dundy.

More Railroad Fireworks

In the years immediately after Judge Dundy's far-reaching Burlington strike opinions, he confronted even more vexing railroad problems. They not only caused him great personal stress, but also ruined his relationship with Nebraska's circuit judge, Henry Clay Caldwell. Throughout the period, Dundy remained steadfast in his legal views that favored railroad management.

Like other western and midwestern states, Nebraska had become hostile to railroad company interests by the 1890s. The Populist influence in the legislature and governor's office resulted in the passage of the Newberry Act in April 1893. This statute essentially gave the state the ability to set freight rates that railroad companies had to accept. Aghast at their possible losses, the railroads ran to the courts for help, and that of course meant engaging Nebraska's federal judge. The Burlington estimated that it might lose more than $1 million annually because of the Newberry Act. Three railways brought their concerns to Judge Dundy in July, and he issued yet another temporary injunction to prevent the state from enforcing the Newberry Act.[90]

The following June, Justice David Brewer of the U.S. Supreme Court, acting in his seldom-invoked capacity as a circuit judge, upheld Dundy's injunction. Brewer declared that the Newberry Act "deprives these property owners of all chances to make profit which result from private control of business, and compels them to pay out of their pockets all the losses which result in the enforcement of an absolute system."[91] Thus Justice Brewer, with Judge Dundy's help, in essence rendered Nebraska's reform unconstitutional. Proceedings then followed that Judge Dundy did not live to see—a significant judicial victory for the railroads when the Supreme Court ruled in *Smyth v. Ames* (1898) that state legislatures could fix rates only so far that they are reasonable as determined by judicial scrutiny.[92]

In the meantime, the Union Pacific Railway became insolvent. On October 13, 1893, Judge Dundy acting as a circuit judge placed the Union Pacific under the receivership of the court. Dundy appointed S. H. H. Clark, the president of the UP; Oliver W. Mink, the UP's comptroller; and E. Ellery Anderson, a government director on the UP board and one of three members of a commission that had investigated the UP's finances in 1887 and had recommended a receivership. It must have been a cozy group. At the request of the U.S. attorney general, who was watching this situation closely, two more receivers were appointed: John W. Doane and Frederick R. Coudert, who had financial and railroad expertise but not direct UP connections.[93] Railroad receivers naturally related operational efficiencies to cost cutting, and excessive costs inevitably meant reducing the number of employees and their wages. For the Union Pacific, its receivers recommended immediate and significant wage reductions, and they requested that Judge Dundy enforce their decision with the barring of a possible strike. There remained, however, procedural problems. Union Pacific labor contracts required thirty days' notice to all workers before changing the wage schedule, plus hearings so that labor could raise any objections or requests for information.

The UP receivers ignored these procedures when they petitioned Judge Dundy on January 27, 1894, for an order enforcing the reduced wage schedule. Acting in his capacity as a circuit judge, Dundy considered the problematic contract provisions, but he decided they no longer were binding on the receivers for the company. He did provide within his order that workers could petition the court to challenge the new wage rules, but Dundy also held that "the new rules and schedules were prima facie reasonable and just."[94] The new wage schedules went into effect. Moreover, Dundy barred any strike activity or any individual or collective actions that would obstruct business or damage property.

Judge Dundy's actions struck even general supporters of the railroads as irrational. The *Omaha World Herald* carried an interview with a well-informed, articulate railroad worker who allowed, "True, we have the right to go in and ask the court to reconsider, but it is plain that a court will not be inclined to overrule itself without an extremity of showing. The showing which we might have won on, had the court not committed itself, will not be adequate to carry our case through now." The employee continued, "It seems to me that the employees should have had notice of the pendency of the action, so that they might have gone in and made a proper representation." The newspaper revealed that Judge Dundy had ignored what the receivers wanted which had been an order barring any activities that would "embarrass" the receivers. "Whew!" exclaimed a quoted employee upon being told this. "Embarrass? That sounds pretty broad. There would have been nothing worth living for had that been allowed. It is plain that the receivers' love for the employees is not so great that it can be heard when it breathes hard."[95]

Although they must have felt hopeless, the UP labor unions followed Judge Dundy's order and prepared petitions to the circuit court asking for the order to be overturned. In his original order, Dundy requested that the receivers file similar requests in circuit courts in Wyoming and Colorado, but those judges refused to endorse them and instead advised the receivers to first hold hearings, and in Nebraska the labor petitions came not before Dundy but before Henry C. Caldwell.[96] Judge Caldwell had a different view of the matter.

On April 5, 1894, after holding hearings that in essence served as an appeal of Judge Dundy's order, Caldwell ruled that the railroad's unilateral wage reductions had not been imposed in accordance with proper contractual procedures, and that therefore the original wage schedules had to remain in force. Caldwell had changed the ground rules. Instead of assuming the newly proposed wage schedule was "prima facie just and reasonable," he found that "the burden was cast upon the receivers to show that the wages received by the employees under the existing regulations were in excess of a fair, just, and reasonable compensation for the service performed, taking into consideration all the circumstances and in view of the existing conditions."[97]

Caldwell excoriated Judge Dundy. He ordered that the wages would not be reduced because the court could not undermine a competent and experienced workforce without convincing reasons. Such reasons, he concluded, had never been provided by the receivers, and most of the receivers were "not practical railroad men" who were familiar with the subject, thereby rejecting the testimony of one of the receivers who had claimed that the wage schedules needed only modest modifications. Without holding a hearing beforehand, Caldwell chided Dundy: "This was very much like first hanging a man, and trying him afterwards. It is small consolation to the victim of the mob to be told he shall have a trial after he is hanged." And as to the order barring a strike, Caldwell sarcastically concluded, "In this country it is not unlawful for employees to associate, consult, and confer together with a view to maintain or increase their wages, by lawful and peaceful means, any more than it is unlawful for the receivers to counsel and confer together for the purpose of reducing their wages." To Judge Caldwell, no "court of equity will act in that manner, or approve the action of its receivers who have acted in that manner."[98]

As he had after the Burlington Strike, Judge Dundy lashed out at his critics, this time using the occasion of a further hearing to take swipes at Judge Caldwell. According to the *Omaha World Herald*'s inflammatory report of the officially unreported opinion by Judge Dundy entitled "He's a Liar," the beleaguered judge had a severe cold when he called the parties into his chambers at 11:20 p.m. on April 13. Dundy partially rolled back Caldwell's opinion, but he laced his diatribe with personal attacks on Caldwell. His claim that "this is the first order and notice to men, so far as I know, ever made in a court, where the right of the employees to go into court was recognized and provided for" appeared callous and empty after the printed ruling of Judge Caldwell. The *Omaha Bee*, normally not prone to understatement, particularly with reference to Judge Dundy, mildly commented that the damage to the longtime judge had already been self-inflicted. "Judge Dundy has a perfect right to resent any lack of courtesy or ill treatment which he may have suffered at the hands of the circuit judge," wrote the *Bee* editor. "But he can scarcely expect to improve matters by attributing this to malice, or by referring his grievance to the public for sympathy. The many, to whom he alludes, who have questioned the good taste and decency of the manner in which the wage schedule hearing was had and the opinions therein prepared, must also question the propriety of incorporating a retaliatory attack into the decision."[99]

The End of the Dundy Years

Judge Elmer Scipio Dundy served as Nebraska's first federal district court judge for twenty-eight years. During his time on the bench, he proved to be a leader in Nebraska politics and law who had a profound effect upon the development of his adopted state. As his career was winding down, however, his ability to function at the highest levels seemed unfortunately to be increasingly compromised. It well may have been the contentiousness of the railroad litigation that assisted in this deterioration.

In an 1890 child custody case, for example, Judge Dundy may have acted precipitously, if not above the law. A father tried to regain custody of his daughter from her grandparents who had taken the child after the sudden death of the man's wife. In the courtroom, Judge Dundy correctly interpreted the law, giving the father custody, but the emotional trauma for the child overcame Dundy. In his reminiscences decades after the event, local writer and historian David Reavis wrote that when the train left for Iowa with the father and daughter on it, several passengers who had been in court stopped the train, took the child from the father, and passed her through an open window to her grandparents. According to Reavis, Dundy may well have organized the kidnapping.[100] In another case of significant public notoriety, a Lincoln banker, Charles Mosher, presided over the collapse of his bank, resulting in the loss of more than $1 million to bank stockholders.

Charged with embezzlement and falsification of records, Mosher pleaded for mercy. Judge Dundy sentenced him to only a five-year prison sentence, "just because he [Judge Dundy] liked the man, and had trained with him in politics."[101] Judge Dundy's eccentricities and autocratic behavior increased in his final years. As a jurist, he proved to be a curious combination of compassion and autocracy, vacillating between demonstrations of courageous legal creativity and dogmatic defense of hierarchy and wealth.

On October 28, 1896, at the age of sixty-six, Judge Dundy died at his home in Omaha. The death certificate stated he died of apoplexy. His passing was not a sudden surprise, as his health had deteriorated. But with his passing, a new era began for the U.S. District Court of Nebraska. Finding a successor proved complicated.

5

The Politics of Transition

If he is so easily swayed by the political winds, how can he be trusted with the most important position in the state?

—*Omaha World-Herald*, December 4, 1896

Having served for more than thirty years as Nebraska's first and only federal district judge, Elmer Dundy cast a long shadow over the state's legal landscape. Not surprisingly, his death in the fall of 1896 and the selection of his successor attracted considerable public and political interest. Then as now, political considerations played a significant role in the appointment of federal judges, and the process of seating Dundy's replacement became a textbook illustration of that ongoing reality. Moreover, the story of the selection of Nebraska's next federal judge provides another vivid example of the way in which the district court's history reflects and illuminates many of the broadest patterns in the nation's history. The political dynamics of the late Gilded Age were particularly turbulent, characterized by the familiar imagery of corrupt urban "machines" controlled by unelected political bosses operating out of smoke-filled backrooms. The era also spawned bitter partisan struggles that blurred traditional party boundaries, as an assortment of third parties seeking to advance wide-ranging social, economic, regional, and occupational interests destabilized the mainstream

Democratic and Republican coalitions.[1] That political upheaval, in turn, significantly affected the process of selecting the man who would become Nebraska's next federal district judge.

The most influential new political movement was the People's Party of America, better known as the Populists. The group originated in the early 1890s as a merger of the Farmers Alliance and the Knights of Labor, organizations that had vigorously advocated the interests of small farmers and urban industrial workers, respectively.[2] Nebraska played a uniquely prominent role in the emergence and development of the Populists, as the state's largest city would become synonymous with the group's most significant legacy, while the state capital provided the man who became the party's most legendary voice. In July 1892 the Populists held their first national party convention in Omaha, drawing more than thirteen hundred delegates from across the nation. The meeting produced the "Omaha Platform," an agenda for reform that became one of the most significant political manifestos in American history. Condemning the nationwide corruption that "dominates the ballot box, the Legislatures, the Congress, and touches even the ermine of the bench," the party called for sweeping changes in American social, economic, and political dynamics, including public ownership of railroads and utilities, a graduated income tax, direct election of senators, secret ballots, and the eight-hour workday for industrial laborers.[3]

Of all the reforms demanded by the Populists, however, the one that would prove to have the most immediate political impact was their call for an end to the "gold standard" for American currency. While the issue still defies easy explanation, the Populists essentially contended that the country needed more currency in circulation. The issuance of additional coinage and paper money, they believed, would produce mild inflation, allowing the nation's "debtor classes" (the Populists' constituency) to repay their obligations to creditors with money that was less valuable than the funds they originally received. To achieve that result, the Populists called for the minting of coins and currency that were backed not only by a fixed quantity of gold in the federal treasury (the "gold standard") but also by silver, to be minted at a ratio of sixteen ounces of silver to one ounce of gold. In 1890 Congress had succumbed to the arguments of the "free silver" proponents by passing the Sherman Silver Purchase Act, legislation that, in essence, took the country off the gold standard.[4] Almost immediately, "sound money" opponents of the statute began urging a return to the gold standard, a campaign that came to fruition just three years later with the repeal of the Sherman Act. Nevertheless, the silver question remained the hottest political controversy in the country for the rest of the decade, pitting the Populists and certain factions of both the Democrats and Republicans against sound money conservative forces that also transcended traditional party lines.

As the silver debate raged, the 1892 Populist convention in Omaha nominated James Weaver of Iowa as the party's first presidential candidate. He ran well in the fall election, attracting more than one million popular votes and carrying four states in the Electoral College. Just as significantly, the Populists' strong initial showing in presidential politics caught the attention of the traditional parties' leadership and confirmed the importance of the free silver issue in the political dynamics of the period. Liberal factions of Democrats and, to a lesser extent, Republicans not only continued the drumbeat for free silver but also began to absorb other elements of the Populists' agenda into their own.

The Populists' selection of Omaha as the launching point for their first foray into national politics provides a clear indication of Nebraska's pivotal place in the escalating political turbulence. The state's prominence grew even more pronounced after the 1892 campaign, as the crusade for "free silver" found its greatest champion in William Jennings Bryan. Just four months before Elmer Dundy's death in the fall of 1896, Bryan, a former Nebraska Democratic congressman from Lincoln, who was then serving as the editor of the *Omaha World-Herald*, delivered a speech at the Democratic national convention in Chicago that would become one of the most memorable in American history. Exhorting the party to prevent what he called the "crucifixion" of mankind on a "cross of gold," Bryan's passionate rhetoric propelled him to the Democratic presidential nomination and marked his ascendance to the leadership of that party's "silver wing."[5] Meeting several weeks later in St. Louis, the Populists also selected Bryan as their presidential nominee. Thus as the 1896 campaign unfolded, Bryan's "fusion" ticket representing both the Silver Democrats and the Populists found itself battling not only the Republicans, who had nominated Ohio governor William McKinley, but also the conservative wing of Bryan's own party (the Gold Democrats), led by outgoing president Grover Cleveland. Bryan lost that 1896 race to McKinley by about 600,000 votes, but he emerged from the campaign as a rising political star. Celebrated by his admirers as the "Boy Orator of the Platte" and the "Great Commoner," Bryan entered the last years of the century firmly positioned as the leader of an increasingly liberal Democratic Party that was well on its way to absorbing much of the Populist agenda into its own platform.[6]

Meanwhile, in the midst of that memorable 1896 presidential campaign and the bitter partisan debates over the free silver issue, the selection of a new judge for the U.S. District Court for the District of Nebraska moved forward. The process was complicated not only by the Cleveland administration's lame duck status but also by the fact that Nebraska's state Democratic organization was just as deeply divided as the national party. At the time of Dundy's death, the leading Gold Democrat in the state was one of its most renowned citizens, J. Sterling Morton of Nebraska City, who was then serving as Cleveland's secretary of agriculture. As the "free silver" controversy escalated during the early 1890s, Morton and Bryan, once Democratic political allies, became bitter rivals. From his insider position within the Cleveland White House, Morton naturally played a key role in the selection of Dundy's successor, and perhaps just as naturally, tensions over that selection between the Morton and Bryan factions of the state party quickly emerged. The journey toward the appointment of a new Nebraska federal judge became quite a bumpy ride.

The Emergence of William McHugh

In the immediate aftermath of Dundy's death, and until a new judge assumed the Nebraska seat, Judges John J. Woolson and Oliver P.

Shiras of Iowa presided over the court's November term.[7] The court's business proceeded without notable disruption as they dealt with a variety of routine matters. On November 17, for example, Shiras handled the sentencing of nine men who had pled guilty to charges of cutting timber from government land, fining each of the defendants ten dollars plus court costs.[8] The following week, he sentenced a man from Homer, Nebraska, to sixty days' imprisonment for selling liquor to Indians, and he presided over the trial of an alleged counterfeiter accused of "passing a bogus silver dollar at Hill's saloon in South Omaha."[9]

On November 20, 1896, Cleveland nominated Omaha attorney William Douglas McHugh to fill the Nebraska judicial seat. Because Congress was not in session at the time, McHugh's selection was a "recess appointment," meaning that he held the position, at least nominally, until the Senate voted to confirm or reject his appointment, or until that session of Congress expired on March 4, 1897, with the arrival of the new McKinley administration.[10] McHugh formally took the oath on November 30, becoming, at thirty-seven, the youngest federal district judge in the country.[11] By all outward appearances, he seemed to be a qualified, if rather undistinguished, choice. Born in Galena, Illinois, in 1859, McHugh apprenticed as a shoemaker during his teenage years and then attended Illinois State Normal College. He later taught school by day and studied law by night and was admitted to the Illinois bar at age twenty-two. He practiced in Galena for five years before moving to Nebraska in 1888. In Omaha he entered into a partnership with John C. Cowin, with offices at 15th and Farnam Streets, and they quickly developed an impressive clientele that included the Omaha Commercial Club, the predecessor to the modern Chamber of Commerce. At the time, the Commercial Club was engaged in numerous proceedings before the Interstate Commerce Commission and other state and federal regulatory agencies seeking, among other results, the adjustment of railroad freight rates and the reduction or elimination of bridge tolls for the benefit of the city's business interests.[12] McHugh's representation of the Commercial Club in those and other matters elevated his profile considerably within the city's legal, business, and political communities, and he soon acquired notable prominence within local Democratic Party circles.

Whatever his legal reputation or credentials, however, McHugh's nomination to the federal bench in late 1896 was almost certainly attributable far more to his close association with J. Sterling Morton and his standing as a Gold Democrat than any other factor. As the friction between the Morton and Bryan factions of the state Democratic Party over the silver question had escalated during the previous years, McHugh ultimately came down firmly in Morton's sound money camp. The pivotal moment on that issue for McHugh came in 1893, when Bryan threatened to leave the party unless it adopted free silver principles. Although he had previously expressed support for Bryan, McHugh now reversed course and supported the repeal of the Sherman Act and a return to the gold standard. McHugh's connections to Morton and the Gold Democrats grew stronger during that period, and when the sound money interests succeeded in obtaining the repeal of the Sherman Act later that year, McHugh sent Morton a telegram celebrating the accomplishment.[13] Three years later, his commitment to Morton and sound money principles was rewarded with his nomination to the federal bench.

McHugh's selection drew mixed and politically predictable reviews in the Nebraska press. As the leading "silver organ" in the region (and the newspaper that Bryan himself had recently led), the *Omaha World-Herald* expressed the most stridently critical reaction, lambasting McHugh for his early vacillation on the silver issue and generally portraying him as an opportunist who was willing to sacrifice his principles in order to advance his personal ambitions. In its first reports of the nomination, the *World-Herald* referred to McHugh as an "administration democrat" who "owes his appointment to the fact that the administration desired to pay tribute to a consistent and persistent bolter from the Democratic Party."[14] Over the ensuing weeks, the paper's opposition to McHugh grew harsher. A November 29 article suggested that the nomination had resulted from railroad interests' influence on the Cleveland administration, claiming that McHugh had been the choice of "some very important attaches of the Chicago, Burlington, and

Quincy [railroad] system."[15] A few days later, the paper unleashed more venom, claiming that "the selection was due to the desire of the administration to reward those who have been treacherous to the democratic party." The story noted that McHugh had been "conspicuous" among a group of local politicians who had been aboard a "tagger train" that followed Bryan throughout Nebraska on the day before the previous month's presidential election, denouncing the candidate to the crowds. With dripping sarcasm, the writer suggested that "it may be that a man who would stoop to such cheap methods is the proper man to be given a life appointment to the federal bench— but many will be inclined to seriously doubt such a claim." The paper also reminded readers of McHugh's frequent changes in position on the silver question and his shifting attitudes toward Bryan and his wing of the party. In early 1894, it reported, McHugh had attended a reception held for Bryan and had "presented the most pathetic sight . . . when he exerted every effort to fondle the hand of the man [Bryan] whom he had previously assailed." Within six months, the story claimed, McHugh "had shifted his devotions once more, and become one of the most vindictive critics of the man whom he had adored and despised at intervals." If McHugh were so easily swayed by the political winds, the paper concluded, how could he be expected to stand firm in "the most important position in the state"?[16]

Many of the state's other newspapers offered considerably more restrained or even favorable perspectives. The *Pawnee City Republican*, for example, seemed bemused by the *World-Herald's* histrionics, dryly noting that the Omaha paper "is tearing its hair and doesn't want McHugh confirmed, because he is a Grover Cleveland Democrat." The *Columbus Telegram* offered a reaction that was even more lighthearted, as it playfully punned that McHugh "was a shoemaker in his early manhood, but while he pegged away he studied law and waxed in legal learning until he fairly bristled with judicial acumen, and now he has reached a higher bench. As a judge he will prove no cobbler and his decisions ought to last for awl time."[17] The *Central City Nonpareil* described the nominee as "highly intelligent," while the *North Bend Republican* called him "the best man for the job."[18] In

Fremont, Nebraska, the *Dodge Criterion* claimed that it had no particular grievance against McHugh, but in a suggestion that presaged coming events, it expressed a preference for its own "favorite son" candidate, local attorney William H. Munger.

The *Nebraska State Journal* in Lincoln, generally Republican in its editorial leanings, provided extensive and relatively evenhanded coverage throughout the McHugh nomination process. In its earliest reports, the *Journal* noted merely that McHugh was "a warm friend" of J. Sterling Morton and went on to describe his background and legal credentials in rather dispassionate terms.[19] The paper also suggested that other "influential connections" in the Omaha legal and political community may have played a role in the selection, placing particular emphasis on McHugh's relationship with prominent Omaha attorney James M. Woolworth, who was then serving as president of the powerful American Bar Association, as well as the "flattering indorsement" of McHugh by former Nebraska senator Charles Manderson. Those men's support for McHugh, the *Journal* suggested, was probably at least as significant as Morton's in shaping the president's thinking on the matter. The paper also noted that the president's former law partner, Francis Lynde Stetson of New York City, had recently offered McHugh a partnership and that Stetson's apparent high regard for the nominee certainly "did not operate against him."[20]

The Opposition

Ultimately, of course, McHugh's fate would be determined not by the florid rhetoric of Nebraska newspaper editors but by the cold realities of Washington politics. And in that process, Nebraska senator John Thurston, a sound money Republican with a seat on the powerful Senate Judiciary Committee, would play the decisive role. Immediately following the announcement of Cleveland's choice, Thurston offered no public comment on the matter, but his opposition to McHugh soon began to trickle into the public record. On December 11 he was reported as saying that Cleveland should have deferred to incoming Republican president-elect McKinley to fill the Nebraska judicial opening. Alternatively, Thurston suggested, Cleveland should have appointed a Republican himself, citing the example of former president Benjamin Harrison, who, in the waning days of his lame duck Republican administration four years earlier, had nominated a Democrat to the U.S. Supreme Court in deference to the incoming Cleveland administration and a new Senate controlled by the Democrats. Thurston acknowledged the nominee's sound money credentials, but contended that the Gold Democrats like McHugh who had supported McKinley in the just-concluded election were only "temporary allies" of the Republicans at best and could not be trusted on matters other than the free silver issue.[21]

When the Judiciary Committee convened on December 15, Thurston's position on the McHugh appointment and his strategy for blocking it became even more apparent. He asked his committee colleagues to table their consideration of McHugh's nomination until after the impending holiday recess, allowing Thurston time to consult with McKinley and other members of the incoming Republican administration.[22] As those deliberations proceeded, it became increasingly clear that Thurston's preferred choice for the federal bench was his friend and law partner, Richard S. Hall. In contrast to McHugh's past political inconsistency, Thurston contended, Hall had always exhibited steadfast "Republican values." Ominously and prophetically, the *Nebraska State Journal* reported these developments on December 27 under the headline "McHugh Cannot Win." In early January, as the next judicial committee meeting to consider the Nebraska seat approached, any lingering doubt about Thurston's intentions dissolved. He announced that the committee would once again defer action on the nomination and that both he and Nebraska's other senator, Populist William Allen, would formally oppose McHugh's confirmation.[23]

Having remained quiet on the issue until that time, Allen now confirmed Thurston's indication of his position. Indeed, Allen's opposition to McHugh proved to be just as vigorous as Thurston's, if not more so. While acknowledging that he had no qualms about the nominee's "competency or honesty," Allen expressed his disgust at the notion that McHugh could get away with "betraying the Democratic Party . . . and being awarded for his treachery." Given McHugh's dubious political loyalties, Allen concluded, he would "prefer a Republican to a renegade Democrat."[24]

Despite the mounting opposition to McHugh's appointment, his supporters pressed on. Woolworth and Manderson traveled to Washington in mid-January to lobby on the nominee's behalf, and they impressed at least one prominent senator with their arguments. On January 20 Senator Henry Teller of Colorado told the *Nebraska State Journal* that it was "not at all impossible" that the Senate would confirm McHugh despite the objections of both of the state's senators. Teller declared that, if it became apparent that Thurston and Allen's resistance was based on "nothing more than political grounds," he believed that "the appointment will be confirmed." Teller concluded the interview by acknowledging the influential reputations of McHugh's supporters, saying, "From what I have learned . . . McHugh is a good man. [Former Senator] Manderson seems to feel that way about it, and you know we all think a great deal of him."[25]

Despite such sentiment, by late January McHugh's appointment teetered on the brink of complete collapse. Long-standing senatorial protocol and tradition made it almost certain that, without the support of either of the Nebraska senators, McHugh would not be confirmed. Again, the *Nebraska State Journal* offered an accurate assessment of the political dynamics of the situation on January 25, reporting that "even if the judiciary committee should report [on the McHugh nomination] tomorrow . . . , the absence of either [Nebraska] senator from subsequent executive sessions [would be cause] for delay, which is what senators Thurston and Allen are fighting for."

On February 1, 1897, Cleveland bowed to the inevitable and withdrew McHugh's name from consideration for the Nebraska judicial seat. His recess appointment had lasted a little more than two months. At the same time, Cleveland announced his new choice, prominent Fremont attorney William H. Munger. During the preceding weeks, Munger's name had emerged as a likely replacement for McHugh, and the proposal had been met with generalized approval from almost all of the competing interests involved in the matter, despite the fact that Munger, like McHugh, was a Gold Democrat. Most significantly, both Thurston and Allen were reported to have quietly indicated to Cleveland that they would have no objection to Munger's nomination.[26] If Thurston did in fact give such an impression to Cleveland, however, his actions in the aftermath of Munger's nomination offered no hint of that acquiescence. While he freely acknowledged that Munger was a "personal friend," he offered no public support for his nomination, claiming that he wanted "to hear from the bar of Nebraska as to their wishes before any definite action is taken."[27] What Thurston really wanted, most observers believed, was to stall the Judiciary Committee's consideration of the Munger nomination, as he had done with McHugh's, until the congressional session expired in early March. At that point, Munger's unconfirmed nomination would be dead, allowing the incoming McKinley administration to fill the Nebraska seat. Thurston, it seemed, was still holding out for the appointment of his law partner and fellow Republican, Richard Hall.[28]

Allen, on the other hand, quickly and openly expressed his support for Munger's confirmation. Although the new nominee shared McHugh's anti-silver views, Allen regarded him as far less brazenly treacherous toward Bryan and the rest of his Democratic brethren in the recent election than McHugh had been. In a news report published on the day after Munger's nomination was announced, Allen explained, "He [Munger] is a gold man, but his position was different from that of McHugh. While the latter made himself an active factor in the fight against the democratic nominee [Bryan], and his appointment could be regarded in no other light than a reward for his political service, Munger observed a dignified course throughout the campaign and I shall not oppose his confirmation."[29]

On February 15 the Judiciary Committee refused to further sanction Thurston's delaying tactics and moved ahead on the Munger nomination, sending a favorable report to the full Senate for its consideration.[30] It seemed clear that Thurston had overplayed his hand, as the Nebraska papers reported that his foot-dragging had alienated his colleagues, especially the Gold Democrats on the committee who had supported McHugh. The *World-Herald* reported that "the majority of the judiciary committee of the senate was not very well pleased at the turning down of McHugh and [indicated] that it would have been very difficult for Thurston to get the committee to acquiesce in holding up Munger's name."[31]

On February 19 the full Senate confirmed Munger's appointment as U.S. district judge for Nebraska. That conclusion to the saga generated an outpouring of bipartisan positive reaction that reflected the high standing that the new judge had attained in the local legal and political community over thirty years, illustrated perhaps most memorably by a letter sent from sound money stalwart Manderson to Senator Allen several days after Munger was confirmed. Manderson wrote, "Now that the smoke of battle has cleared away, I wish to congratulate you upon the happy issue of the fight on the Federal Judgeship. The appointment and confirmation of Judge Munger gives very general satisfaction throughout the State. He is an honest, conscientious man, with the ability and experience to make an excellent Judge."[32] A new era in the history of the U.S. District Court of Nebraska had begun.

6

The "One Munger" Court

Labor unions, when lawfully conducted to promote the welfare of the individual members, are not only commendable, but should be encouraged.
—Judge William Munger, *Union Pacific R. Co. v. Ruef* (1902)

What about the boy, Judge Munger? . . . If it is merely a question of mercy, . . . let it not be merely for the man who is surrounded by rich and influential friends. . . . Let it be that mercy that encircles both friend and foe, both great and small, both powerful and helpless.
—*Omaha World-Herald,* January 17, 1904

Born in 1845, William Munger grew up on a small family farm near the town of Bergen in Genesee County, New York.[1] In 1865 he moved to Cleveland, Ohio, where he worked in his uncle's dry goods store and began reading law in his spare hours. Munger eventually became a clerk in a Cleveland law firm and in 1868 gained admission to the Ohio bar. Later that same year, the young lawyer moved west in search of new opportunities. By October he had arrived in Fremont, Nebraska, with just $2.50 in his pocket.[2] He went to work in a local lumberyard, while building a law practice in his off hours. From 1871 until 1873, he practiced in partnership with local attorney W. C. Ghost, until Ghost won election to state judgeship. Munger continued the practice alone until 1877 and thereafter entered into partnerships with a number of other leading attorneys in the region, including W. A. Marlow, W. J. Cartwright, and nationally prominent Omaha attorney James M. Woolworth.[3] During those years Munger earned a reputation as an honest, capable, and thoroughly professional litigator.

He also emerged as an active participant in local and state politics, becoming a prominent figure within the "sound money" wing of the Democratic Party, led by J. Sterling Morton.[4] In 1875 he served as a delegate to the state constitutional convention, and in 1882 he narrowly lost a race to become Nebraska's first congressman from the newly created Third District. In 1887 and 1888 he served as the secretary of the State Board of Transportation, a post that was particularly visible in light of the contentious debates over railroad freight-rate regulation. Munger also gained prominence among the area's social elite through his active leadership in the Fremont Masonic lodge and his marriage in 1871 to Jennie M. Fowler, daughter of one of Nebraska's early entrepreneurs in the freighting industry, Samuel Fowler.[5] Thus by the time he assumed the federal bench in 1897, Munger had been practicing law in eastern Nebraska for almost thirty years. He was fifty-two years old, a widely respected attorney with deep roots in the region and strong connections to many of the most powerful and influential interests in the area. Notwithstanding his impressive credentials and lofty reputation, however, his seventeen years on the federal bench would not be free of controversy.

Progressivism Comes to Court

Munger's judicial career coincided with the Progressive Era in U.S. history, generally defined as the period of the late nineteenth century through the conclusion of World War I and broadly characterized by efforts to utilize the power of government in new and innovative ways to improve the quality of life for all Americans. Progressivism was not a unified movement, nor did it evolve into a single identifiable political party. Rather, it encompassed a wide range of disparate groups with differing—sometimes even contradictory—agendas and goals. Some

Progressives focused their efforts on attacking monopolistic, unfair, or fraudulent business practices through antitrust legislation and other forms of commercial regulation; others sought to advance the cause of social justice by advocating for women's suffrage, prohibition of alcohol, prison reform, zoning regulations aimed at cleaning up squalid inner-city tenements, and enhanced educational programming and occupational training for children and newly arriving immigrants. Progressive political reformers of the era took aim at widespread patterns of corruption dictated by old-style party or "boss" rule in many municipal governments, while other Progressives sought to level the field of labor-management relations through governmental regulation of wages, hours, and conditions of work, elimination of child labor, and enhanced protection for unionization and collective bargaining. Conservation of natural resources was another pervasive Progressive concern, reflected most notably by new governmental efforts to control access to and exploitation of the millions of acres of public domain lands in the Trans-Mississippi West.[6] As the Progressives' initiatives reverberated throughout the country, the resulting tensions with the status quo of the late nineteenth century spawned a host of new issues that would ultimately arrive in the federal courts to be addressed and resolved.

This then was the contextual environment that enveloped William Munger as he took his seat on the Nebraska federal bench in 1897. To be sure, many if not most of the cases that made their way into the federal court during Munger's tenure involved relatively mundane legal issues with little direct connection to the Progressive trends of the period, and they generated little publicity or notoriety.[7] Nevertheless, the pervasive progressivism of the era did manifest itself on the court's docket with considerable frequency, and that "Progressive litigation" often produced some of the most conspicuous and controversial decisions of Munger's judicial career. That was particularly the case in matters involving labor-management conflict, political and civil service reforms, and public land use issues. And as was the case in other federal courts, Munger's handling of the complex issues involved in those cases rarely satisfied everyone.

Labor Wars

Intense labor-management conflict was one of the most prevalent and disturbing features of American society during the Progressive Era. As the nation's industrial productivity skyrocketed, issues related to workers' wages, hours, and safety became increasingly prominent and polarizing. By the mid-1870s, violent clashes between the owners and managers of the nation's businesses and fledgling unions seeking to protect the interests of the laboring classes had become tragically commonplace. Many Americans, particularly those in positions of power and influence, perceived unionization, collective bargaining, and governmental regulation of the employer-employee relationship as sinister ideas that smacked of socialism and violated some deeply entrenched national values and ideals: the romanticized ethos of rugged individualism and individual liberty, the then-influential doctrine of social Darwinism, and the always powerful allure of the free marketplace. Those sentiments, along with the prevailing laissez-faire economic philosophy of the day, combined to produce an environment in which the initial unionizing efforts of the late nineteenth century enjoyed little favor with government officials, including federal judges. To be sure, as Kermit Hall and other legal historians have pointed out, the federal courts' reaction to reform legislation generally, and labor activism specifically, was not as stereotypically rigid, reactionary, and doctrinaire as textbook treatments often suggest. There was a good deal of nuance and complexity in the judicial response to all of the dynamics of progressivism, including labor relations issues.[8] But it is nevertheless accurate to note that business owners of the late nineteenth and early twentieth centuries frequently invoked the equitable powers of the federal courts by seeking injunctions to end strikes or otherwise restrict the activities of strikers and union organizers. It is also true that, more often than not, federal judges complied with those requests. As this environment, often characterized as "government by injunction," saturated the country, labor unions found, as legal historian Jeffrey Brandon Morris has observed, that they "had few friends in the federal courts."[9]

Nebraska enjoyed no immunity from the often nasty labor-management dynamics of the day. Indeed, in light of the state's pivotal role in two extremely important industries of the period, railroading and meatpacking, confrontations between labor and capital were regular occurrences. Not surprisingly, those controversies often made their way into Judge Munger's courtroom. One of the first began in the summer of 1902, when boiler operators in the machine shops at the Union Pacific Railroad headquarters in Omaha went on strike for higher wages.[10] Machinists and blacksmiths in the railroad's shops soon joined the boilermakers, and within weeks more than 1,300 UP workers across Nebraska and the Great Plains were taking part in the work stoppage.[11] As the impasse continued, railroad officials began importing strikebreaking replacements from all over the country. In response, the strikers created picket lines around the Omaha shops and began harassing the replacement workers as well as other railroad employees, customers, and suppliers who sought to cross the lines. Railroad officials, in turn, hired armed security forces to protect the replacement workers and intimidate the strikers.[12] Newspaper coverage and other sources suggest that public opinion was generally sympathetic to the strikers. A Nebraska "Guidebook" published in 1947, for example, recounted that during the initial months of the strike, "merchants would not sell to strike-breakers, barbers would not shave them, and landlords refused to rent to them."[13] So the company converted some of the buildings in its sprawling shops area north of downtown Omaha into barracks for the replacement workers. As the summer turned to fall, an ominous atmosphere thick with threats of violence from both sides permeated the area.

In the early morning hours of Sunday, September 14, the tension along the picket lines took a tragic turn when half a dozen strikers and strike supporters beat a replacement machinist named Earl Caldwell to death.[14] The ugly incident proved to be a tipping point in the escalating conflict. Within thirty-six hours of Caldwell's death, a team of attorneys for the UP, led by the company's assistant general counsel, John N. Baldwin, appeared in federal district court seeking a temporary restraining order to rein in the picketers. The railroad's petition was heard by Judge Smith McPherson of the Southern District of Iowa, sitting in for Judge Munger, who was presiding over a trial in Minneapolis in the court of Judge William Lochren.[15] McPherson listened to the *ex parte* arguments of the railroad attorneys and quickly granted their request for a restraining order. The temporary order he signed had been drafted by the railroad's attorneys and was quite sweeping in its scope and effect. Directed against 145 named union officials and individual striking workers, it purported to prohibit them from engaging in eleven broadly categorized and ambiguously defined types of activities, including "congregating, assembling, or loitering . . . in the neighborhood of Union Pacific Railway company . . . and from interfering with or terrorizing or intimidating the employees of said company with the intent to cause them to leave the service of said company." Other sections of the order prohibited the strikers from "congregating or assembling at or near the gates or entrances of said Union Pacific Railway company" and from "following the employees, servants, or agents of said railway company in the streets of the city of Omaha, or to their homes or residences, or any other place in said city of Omaha." The ninth categorical prohibition in the restraining order was particularly expansive in its effect, commanding strikers to refrain "from publishing orders, statements, rules, or directions . . . which in any way tends to agitate, create or engender feelings or sentiments, which in any way tend to provoke assaults or violent acts of any kind or description."[16]

McPherson's temporary order, issued on September 15, remained in place until an evidentiary hearing commenced several weeks later. Munger had returned to Nebraska by then, and both he and McPherson presided over the hearing, which proceeded over several days in late September. More than twenty witnesses testified, offering predictably contradictory accounts of the activities of the opposing forces along the picket lines. The railroad's witnesses generally depicted the strikers as depraved beasts who engaged in unchecked acts of shameful intimidation and violence against the strikebreakers and their families. A wife of one of the replacement workers poignantly read from a letter she had purportedly received from a union officer, urging her to "induce her husband to quit his work as a scab" because he was "doing an unmanly act that would leave a stain upon his character by taking the place of a striker." The letter warned the woman that if her husband did not stop his "scabbing," his photograph and description would be distributed throughout the country, and it suggested that it would "naturally be unpleasant for her to appear in public with a husband against whom the public would point its finger in scorn."[17] Union witnesses, in contrast, contended that the railroad's accounts of violence along the picket lines were grossly overstated and that the few inappropriate acts that had occurred were the work of just a handful of strikers or their supporters. Union officials claimed that they repeatedly sought to control their members' actions so as to prevent violence, while other witnesses testified that the security forces hired by the company had been just as aggressive in their tactics throughout the strike as any of the union men had been.

On October 13 and 14 Munger and McPherson heard final arguments from the parties' counsel.[18] These were impassioned and elaborate summations that went on for more than ten hours combined, presented by three of the most prominent attorneys in the region: Baldwin for the railroad and Edward P. Smith and C. J. Smyth for the strikers.[19] Baldwin recapped the testimony of witnesses who had described dozens of assaults, in addition to the murder of Earl Caldwell, and the endless threats and "vile epithets" heaped upon the company's employees and customers. All of those actions, he argued, proved that the picket line was "a menace to law and order and the safe transaction of the business of the company and its employees in the shops."[20] He urged the court to make the temporary order of September 15 into a permanent injunction against the strikers. In response, Smith pointed out that only 8 of the more than 140 named defendants had been even minimally implicated in any of the alleged acts of violence that had occurred. As for the rest of the defendants, there was "not a syllable of evidence to ever show that they even worked for the Union Pacific railroad company, or were strikers." Thus, Smith maintained, the evidence proved that the picketing had been overwhelmingly peaceful and orderly. If and when acts of violence might occur, the company had "ample remedies through the police and the local courts to seek the suppression of disorder." It would be a great injustice, Smith concluded, to cast a stigma on the hundreds of men engaged in the strike who were "honored citizens of the community, taxpayers and homeowners, and who have worked in the shops [for as much as] thirty-five years of honest and continuous service."[21]

At the conclusion of the arguments, Munger and McPherson took the matter under advisement and indicated that they would have a decision soon. In the meantime, the original temporary order entered a month earlier by McPherson remained in effect.[22] Three weeks later, on November 8, the two judges announced their decision, issuing a permanent injunction against the striking workers, but modifying or eliminating entirely some of the most sweeping restrictions on the strikers' activities contained in McPherson's original restraining order.[23] Both Munger and McPherson wrote opinions in the case, and although they agreed on the final outcome, the tone of their respective writings was markedly different.

McPherson's long opinion was laced with anti-union sentiment, some of which seemed to have been adopted, almost verbatim, from portions of Baldwin's arguments for the railroad. He began with a recitation of dozens of recent labor cases in which an injunction had been issued to prevent violent or intimidating picketing by striking workers. He then scoffed at the concerns of those who worried about the perils of "government by injunction," noting that "courts of equity from time immemorial [have] restrained the doing of wrongful acts; and the fair and conservative and great state of Iowa [McPherson's home state] has been 'governed by injunction' to the dismay of no one but law-breakers." McPherson repeatedly expressed his revulsion with the abusive and profane language used by some of the strikers, at one point writing that "much of the intimidation was by language so low and coarse and brutal and vulgar and obscene" that he would not repeat it in writing. Based on his analysis of the evidence before him, McPherson would have banned all picketing of any kind by the strikers, as he ultimately concluded as a matter of law that "picketing, as evidenced by the facts in this case, is wrong, and cannot be countenanced by law-abiding men, and such picketing cannot but be condemned by any court."[24]

Though Munger agreed with McPherson that a permanent injunction limiting the strikers' activities should be issued, his opinion was considerably more nuanced than his colleague's. Indeed, Munger's written decision in the case would prove to be one of the lengthiest and most insightful of his entire career, revealing a man who seemed to be genuinely torn on the equities of the matter. While he echoed McPherson's disgust at the violent atmosphere that the strike had spawned, Munger also expressed an apparently sincere respect for unionism in general, stating that "labor unions, when lawfully conducted to promote the welfare of the individual members, are not only commendable, but should be encouraged." Similarly, he rejected McPherson's blanket conclusion that picketing was unlawful per se, writing at one point that "picketing, in and of itself, when properly conducted, is not unlawful" and later repeating the point that "if picketing is only done to obtain information, to reason with and peacefully persuade a fellow being to cease his employment, it is not unlawful."[25] But, Munger concluded, in this case some of the picketers and their supporters had disregarded the instructions of their leaders to maintain their ranks in a peaceful and orderly manner, and therefore the court could and would intervene.

Ultimately then, Munger's opinion, which became the court's operative decree in the case, imposed a permanent injunction against the striking shop workers, but modified the terms of McPherson's existing temporary order in several significant ways. First, it dismissed from the proceedings 56 of the original 145 named respondents, finding that there was no evidence linking any of them to any specific violent acts. As to the remaining 89 respondents, the new injunction was quite broad in its terms, prohibiting them from engaging in activities that might interfere with the railroad's use of its premises or the ingress or egress of its employees or agents from its premises. Picketing was permitted, but the strikers were prohibited from engaging in acts of violence or intimidation. McPherson's original prohibitions against strikers "following" replacement workers and the provision barring them from "publishing" items that might stir up violence were removed completely from the new order.

Munger's ruling allowed both sides to claim a legal victory. Baldwin reacted to the decision by observing, "The decision is certainly a victory for the Union Pacific. . . . In unmistakable terms the opinion excoriates the pickets who have violated the law, condemns their method and restrains them in the future." But Smith viewed the decision as a judicial vindication of the strikers, inasmuch as they "had never for a moment claimed that violence or intimidation were legal or right." A union officer echoed Smith's interpretation, claiming that the court's decision was "simply a warning to pickets to refrain from violence or intimidation under penalty of punishment by the federal court, a provision to which we must heartily agree as right."[26] On the matter of future enforcement of the court's decree, Munger acknowledged the ambiguity of some of the order's language, but closed his opinion with the observation that "it is impossible, as well as impracticable, for the court in advance to specify all the acts and things which shall or may constitute intimidation or coercion. This must be left to the wisdom and intelligence of [the strikers]. Any violation of the order will, however, be done at the party's peril."[27]

Events would soon put Munger's warning to the test. Within weeks of the issuance of the permanent injunction, the railroad's attorneys were back in court seeking contempt proceedings against twenty-seven strikers who, they claimed, had acted in violation of the injunction. Munger held evidentiary hearings on the charges over several days in December, with both parties producing numerous witnesses who again offered varying accounts of the activities around the picket lines in the time since the injunction had gone into effect. On December 15 Munger ruled in favor of the strikers, finding them not guilty of the contempt charges raised by the railroad. He held that the company officials had failed to show that there had been a violation of "the spirit of the injunction," and he dismissed all further proceedings against the named defendants.[28] Union officials expressed their elation with the judge's ruling and vowed to continue with their picketing "wherever and whenever they [saw] fit," as long as they remained within the parameters of the injunction.[29]

The UP shop workers' strike dragged on for another five months with no further court intervention before ending in late May 1903 when company officials finally gave in to almost all of the workers' demands.[30] But for Judge Munger, the railroad strike of 1902–3 was just one of the earliest and most visible of many occasions when he would be required to intervene in the heated labor-management conflicts of the Progressive Era. For example, even as the railroad impasse was ending, Munger was drawn into another ugly labor dispute, this one involving teamsters unions who were on strike against various local freighting, transport, and delivery companies. As the strikers' activities became increasingly aggressive, the employers appeared in Munger's court seeking an injunction to restrict the strikers' actions. Just as the railroad attorneys had done the previous September before Judge McPherson, the management lawyers brought Munger a preprinted restraining order that contained an array of prohibitions. Unlike McPherson, however, Munger refused to sign the "blank check" the companies were offering, opting instead to impose a more limited and carefully worded order that allowed the strikers to continue with many of their tactics but prohibited any further violence or disturbance of the public peace.[31] Munger's relatively moderate judicial posture on labor issues revealed itself again the following year, when South Omaha meatpackers went on strike and their employers rushed into court to restrict them. Again Munger enjoined the strikers from engaging in violence, threatening behavior, or acts of intimidation, but he refused to accede to the employers' demand for a complete ban on all picketing of any kind. At a hearing on July 25, 1904, he specifically invoked the position he had taken during the Union Pacific strike two years earlier, saying, "Picketing without violence, intimidation, or coercion is not unlawful." That result was perfectly acceptable to the strikers' attorneys, one of whom was quoted as saying that Munger's allowance of orderly picketing and peaceful persuasion was "exactly what we were contending for."[32]

The takeaway point here is that, while William Munger was in many ways an archetypical conservative Republican of the early twentieth century, he was also—like all human beings—a man with the capacity for flexibility and nuance, whose attitudes and actions defy simplistic stereotypical characterization. He was not wholly unsympathetic to the fledgling union movement of his era, nor was he insensitive to the workplace conditions that galvanized that movement, but he would not allow the legitimate concerns of organized labor to run roughshod over the public peace. By the words he used in his opinions, and by his actions when called upon for equitable relief, he sought to find the appropriate balance point—a reasonable middle ground in an arena bounded by polarized extremes.

The Skip Dundy Controversy

Another key element of the Progressive agenda was the effort to root out the perceived evils of the "spoils" system of political patronage through civil service reform and regulation of government hiring practices. Like the labor disputes of the day, the controversies spawned by these types of political reforms appeared on Judge Munger's docket early and often. In fact, he had only been on the bench a few months when he found himself in the delicate position of having to pass judgment on the propriety of a personnel decision made by his well-known predecessor, Elmer Dundy. In 1882 Judge Dundy had appointed his son, Elmer S. "Skip" Dundy Jr., to be the clerk of the district court, a position that Dundy Jr. still held in 1897, when Munger assumed the elder Dundy's position. In 1886 Judge Dundy had also appointed Skip to be a "master in chancery" for the court. Court masters were authorized to perform certain administrative functions on an ad hoc basis, subject to the control and direction of the court. Typical masters' duties included inventorying and taking possession of real or personal property involved in litigation and conducting sales of foreclosed property.

Several years after Skip Dundy's appointment as both clerk and master of the court, Congress passed a number of Progressive statutes aimed at reforming the civil service system and eliminating rampant nepotism within the federal bureaucracy. Those laws included provisions that prohibited any person related to a sitting judge from being appointed to "any office or duty in any courts of which such judge may be a member." They also prohibited the clerk of a federal district court from acting simultaneously in the role of master in chancery. During Judge Dundy's tenure, no one had questioned his son's service in those dual capacities, but in the aftermath of Dundy's death and with a new judge on the bench, some litigants felt emboldened to raise such a challenge, and it fell to Munger to rule on the question.

In *Northwestern Mut. Life Ins. Co. v. Seaman*, debtors whose property had been foreclosed upon challenged Dundy Jr.'s actions in obtaining an appraisal of their property and proceeding with its sale, claiming that his actions were invalid under the recently enacted reform statutes. In an opinion that became his first to be published in the *Federal Reports*, Munger rejected the debtors' arguments. After first acknowledging that the appointment of Dundy Jr. to the positions of both clerk and master may have been "irregular," Munger went on to note that the statutes prohibiting his appointments to those positions had been passed several years after the appointments were made. Therefore, applying the long-standing principle that statutes will not operate retroactively unless the legislature specifically so provides, Munger affirmed the appraisal and sale of the property, holding that Dundy Jr.'s actions in the foreclosure proceeding were "at least those of a de facto officer [of the court]" and were thus lawful and binding.[33] The U.S. Court of Appeals for the Eighth Circuit affirmed Munger's ruling the following year.[34]

Despite the judicial validation of his dual roles, the adverse publicity generated by the litigation prompted Dundy to step down from his position as clerk of the court in April 1897.[35] Several months later, Munger filled the district court clerk's position with the appointment of Oscar B. Hillis, who was then also serving as the clerk of the federal circuit court. Munger justified the consolidation of the two offices as an efficiency measure, stating that it would be "more convenient for the attorneys who have business in both courts and more convenient for the court itself."[36] At the same time, Munger appointed H. C. Hoyt of Beatrice, a distant relative of former president Grover Cleveland, to serve as Hillis's deputy.[37]

Meanwhile, Skip Dundy retained his position as a court master for several more years. During Omaha's famed Trans-Mississippi and International Exposition in 1898, Dundy became enamored with the world of amusement park thrill rides, and in 1900 he stepped down from his position with the court to pursue that interest full time. He left Omaha and embarked upon a colorful second career during which he became a major entertainment impresario in New York City. Among other accomplishments, Dundy built and managed the successful Hippodrome Theatre in Midtown Manhattan and developed a first-of-its-kind amusement center called Luna Park at Coney Island in Brooklyn.[38]

The Charles Dietrich Scandal

The Progressive Era effort to purge corruption from the political system—and the intense political infighting that often accompanied those reform efforts—was also reflected in another high-profile case that made its way onto Munger's docket early in his tenure. In November 1903 a federal grand jury in Omaha indicted Nebraska senator Charles H. Dietrich and Hastings postmaster Jacob Fisher for conspiracy to engage in bribery. Dietrich was a Republican who had served as Nebraska's governor for five months in early 1901 before being appointed to a vacant Senate seat later that year. The indictment accused him of accepting a bribe of $1,300 from Fisher in exchange for appointing him to the postmaster position.[39] Several weeks later, the grand jury issued another indictment against Dietrich, this one charging him with the violation of a federal statute that prohibited a member of Congress from enjoying the benefit of a contract with the government, as a result of the lease of a building Dietrich owned in Hastings for use as the city's post office.[40]

The filing of federal criminal charges against a sitting U.S. senator was a novelty that attracted nationwide press coverage.[41] Closer to home, it also aroused the chronic and highly partisan animosity between the two primary newspapers in Omaha at the time, the Democratic-leaning *Omaha World-Herald*, edited by Progressive reformer/newspaperman/politician Gilbert Hitchcock (who was at that time serving in Congress as the representative of Nebraska's Second District), and the usually Republican-leaning *Omaha Daily Bee*, published by the influential and notoriously mercurial Edward Rosewater. Throughout the Dietrich affair, the *World-Herald*'s coverage of the case was extensive and full-throated, while the *Bee* downplayed the story, seeking to portray the indictments as a politically motivated vendetta against Dietrich by one of his chief political rivals, U.S. Attorney Williamson S. Summers, a Democrat. For example, the *World-Herald*'s November 17 headline announcing Dietrich's initial indictment spanned the paper's entire width, and stories detailing the scandalous allegations against the senator filled almost the entire front page. A subheadline even revealed the purported details of the grand jury's balloting, declaring, "Twenty to One Is the Vote on Each Indictment." In contrast, that same day's *Bee* reported the indictments in a mere one-column story that mentioned Dietrich's name only in small print, accompanied by a story in the immediately adjacent column headlined "Summers May Be Suspended; Actions in Dietrich Matter Stirs Things Up in the National Capitol." The two papers' sniping at one another quickly escalated. The next day, Rosewater accused the *World-Herald* in print of having already "convicted, sentenced, drawn, and quartered Dietrich before the case had even been docketed for trial."[42] In response, the *World-Herald* declared that it had "simply printed the news, keeping its readers informed at every stage of the proceedings [while] the *Bee* failed to keep its readers informed and did not print the news until it was forced to do so by the formal return of the indictment."[43] Coverage in other newspapers across the state similarly followed partisan lines. For example, renowned Progressive activist William Jennings Bryan's weekly, the *Commoner*, usually mirrored the *World-Herald*'s aggressive reporting on the case, while the *Columbus Leader*, a generally Republican organ, adopted the *Bee*'s pro-Dietrich stance and dismissed the matter as merely "an outgrowth of a personal and political feud between District Attorney Summers, who has been seeking reappointment, and Senator Dietrich, who has refused to endorse Summers."[44]

The intense media scrutiny of the case and the heated political dimensions of the controversy were not lost on Judge Munger. Under the procedural statutes of the day, he was empowered to transfer to the circuit court any pending indictment that involved "difficult and important questions of law."[45] No doubt eager to have some assistance in handling the volatile matter, Munger remitted the case to the circuit court and requested the appointment of an additional circuit judge to join him in hearing the case. On December 30 he received a letter notifying him that circuit judge (and future U.S. Supreme Court justice) Willis Van Devanter of Wyoming was on his way to Omaha to sit with him on the case.[46]

When the Dietrich trial commenced on Monday, January 4, 1904, the senator's attorney, John C. Cowin, immediately offered a demurrer to the conspiracy charges against the defendants. He argued that the indictment was improperly constructed, in that it charged both of the defendants, Dietrich and Fisher, with distinct and separable offenses under a single joint indictment. Later that day, Munger and Van Devanter agreed with Cowin and dismissed the conspiracy indictment.[47] The trial of both men on the remaining charges resumed the following morning, with jury selection and additional pretrial maneuvering consuming most of the next two days. On Thursday Summers delivered a detailed opening statement to the court and jury. When he concluded, Cowin immediately moved for a directed verdict in the defense's favor, arguing that his client had not yet officially assumed his senatorial duties at the time the alleged bribery occurred, and therefore he did not fall within the coverage of the statute under which he was charged.[48] Munger and Van Devanter recessed the trial for the remainder of the day to deliberate on Cowin's motion.

On Friday morning, Munger and Van Devanter took the bench to announce their rulings on the pending defense motion. Coincidentally, the annual meeting of the state bar association was taking place that same weekend, bringing many of the state's most renowned attorneys, judges, and public officials into Omaha. The enticing spectacle of a U.S. senator facing criminal charges drew many of the bar's dignitaries to watch the proceedings, resulting in a courtroom that was described as "crowded to suffocation." As the judges read their rulings to the packed gallery, it soon became apparent that the defense had carried the day. Just as Cowin had urged, Van Devanter and Munger held that Dietrich's appointment to the Senate had not taken effect until he formally took the oath of office on December 2, 1901. Because Summers had acknowledged in his opening statement that all of the actions that constituted the alleged bribery occurred prior to that date, Dietrich was not a member of Congress at the time the alleged bribery occurred, and so he could not be charged under the statute in question. Accordingly, Van Devanter and Munger ordered the jury to enter a verdict in Dietrich's favor. In light of the court's ruling on that dispositive issue of when Dietrich officially became a senator, Summers concluded that he could not possibly prevail on the remaining charges against Fisher, nor could he effectively proceed on the accusations against Dietrich regarding the allegedly illegal lease agreement. He therefore entered a *nolle prosequi* on those indictments, and both Dietrich and Fisher walked out of the courthouse as free men.[49]

From a purely legal perspective, Munger and Van Devanter's interpretation of the statutory language involved in the Dietrich indictments was at least arguably correct; certainly their ruling represented a plausible reading of the applicable law. Even the state's most famous Progressive, William Jennings Bryan, acknowledged in the *Commoner* that many Nebraska lawyers thought that Van Devanter and Munger's resolution of the case "was good law."[50] And whatever the legal propriety of the decision, the senator's supporters certainly viewed the abrupt conclusion of the trial as a complete vindication of their man and reported it accordingly. Rosewater's *Bee* announced the acquittals with the bold headline "Dietrich Is Clear," while simultaneously heaping additional scorn on District Attorney Summers with the subheading "Summers Utterly Fails to Prove Accusations Included in His Indictments; Makes Poorer Showing than Expected."[51]

Among most Democrats and Progressives, however, the dismissal of the charges against the two men on what seemed to be superficial and overly legalistic grounds smacked of judicial favoritism toward the powerful and well connected. The *World-Herald* left little doubt about its disgust with the result, splashing the large headline "Dietrich Escapes Trial through Technicality" across its January 8 front page along with prominent sidebar headings such as "Dietrich Not Senator When Deal Was Made" and "Court Sustains Technical Objection to Trial on Charge of Bribery."[52] A large photo of Judges Munger and Van Devanter occupied the top center of the page, positioned just above an article that contrasted their ruling that day with the actions of a New York federal court that had just convicted New York congressman Edmund Driggs of bribery on facts that were similar to those involved in the Dietrich prosecution.

Even the normally moderate editor of the *Alliance Herald,* Thomas J. O'Keefe, expressed dismay at the results of the trial, caustically noting in an editorial that Dietrich had been acquitted on "the slightest technicality" while going on to declare, "With this flimsy technicality, Senator Dietrich finds himself a vindicated character—so far as law is interpreted, but before the people of Nebraska he must explain further the charge preferred against him."[53] In the same column in which he had acknowledged that many attorneys in the state agreed with the ruling as a matter of law, William Jennings Bryan similarly lamented Dietrich's "resort to technicalities" and observed that "newspaper opinion throughout the country generally condemns Senator Dietrich and in Nebraska public opinion is very generally against him."[54]

As the public debate over the Dietrich scandal continued, a *World-Herald* article published the day following the dismissal of the case offers intriguing insight into the legal culture of the state and at the same time provides a glimpse of the sociopolitical philosophy of future Supreme Court justice Van Devanter. The story described the annual banquet of the state bar association held on the evening of January 8, 1904. As previously noted, many of the state's most illustrious legal personalities had been in the courtroom when the judges' opinions were delivered earlier that same day, and no doubt the attendees' opinions on the case varied a good deal depending on the political leanings of the observer. But, the article noted, any potential rancor over the Dietrich scandal was set aside for the evening's festivities. In fact, the paper reported that "owing to the intense interest aroused among the members of the association by the just-concluded Dietrich cases," Munger and Van Devanter were showered with attention as "lions of the hour," and the future Supreme Court jurist was urged to deliver some remarks to the gathering. In his brief speech, Van Devanter himself made reference to the Dietrich proceedings, wryly noting that when he was asked to speak, he first had demurred, "just as my friend [Dietrich's attorney] Cowin" had in the trial, but that his own demurrer "didn't seem to meet with the same success that [Cowin] has experienced." Tellingly, Van Devanter then went on to offer his thoughts on some of the leading issues of the day, including what he called the "labor problem." He proceeded to articulate the classic conservative argument in opposition to union activism, declaring, "The individual should stand foremost. The time should never come when anyone willing to solicit employment will not be permitted to ask it of anyone willing to pay his price. When labor unions undertake to take away that inherent right . . . they have gone further than they should be permitted to go. . . . It should ever be remembered that the individual ought to be permitted to sell his services and use his capital freely."[55]

Dietrich was no doubt aware that the court's actions had not fully cleared him in the minds of many Nebraskans. The lingering stain on his reputation compelled him to seek an unqualified exoneration from his congressional colleagues. In early March he asked the Senate leadership to appoint a select committee to investigate the charges that had been brought against him. Chaired by Massachusetts senator George Hoar, a prominent Progressive Republican, the committee conducted hearings over several weeks, calling to Washington many of the witnesses who would have testified in Omaha had the case proceeded to a full trial on the merits.[56] On April 14 Hoar's committee issued a 219-page report that ultimately concluded that Dietrich had "not been guilty of any violation of the statutes of the United States or of any corrupt or unworthy conduct relating either to the appointment of Jacob Fisher as postmaster at Hastings, Nebraska, or the leasing of the building in question to the United States for the purposes of a post-office."[57] In another intriguing postlude to the case, Dietrich and his supporters exacted political vengeance on his nemesis Summers by engineering his termination as the U.S.

district attorney for Nebraska.[58] But despite all of those results favoring Dietrich, many Nebraskans, including of course the majority of the state's Democrats and Progressives, continued to regard him with considerable suspicion, if not outright disdain. Recognizing that his political credibility had been irreparably damaged, state Republican leaders pushed Dietrich aside when his term expired in 1905. He left politics and returned to Hastings, where he lived in retirement until his death in 1924.

"What About the Boy, Judge Munger?"

One final postscript to the Dietrich case is instructive on at least two levels: first, it offers a glimpse into some aspects of Judge Munger's judicial philosophy; second, it helps to illuminate the way in which— then as now, and correctly or not—opinions about judicial decisions are often filtered through the lens of political partisanship.

While none of the newspaper coverage of the Dietrich trial had directly and explicitly criticized Munger or Van Devanter for the dismissal of the charges against the senator, the implicit message embedded in much of the Progressive newspapers' reporting was clear: the two judges had adopted a strained interpretation of the applicable statutes in order to free a powerful Republican politician and his crony, on the basis of a legalistic technicality rather than the merits of the charges against them. Given that generalized perception, it could not have been coincidental that, just one week after the conclusion of the Dietrich trial, the *World-Herald* took an open swipe at Judge Munger for what the paper perceived to be his "flexible" standards of judicial discretion. In an editorial titled "There Are Others, Merciful Judge," the paper scolded Munger, directly and by name, for the apparent inconsistency of his sentencing decisions in three criminal cases that he had recently handled.[59] In the first case, Munger had sentenced a "poor, unemployed, and friendless young boy" named James Davis to two years' imprisonment in the federal penitentiary at Sioux Falls for breaking into a post office and stealing thirty pennies and $9.60 worth of stamps. In the second case, Munger sentenced a former clerk in the Lincoln Post Office, J. H. Diefendorf, to one year in the

Dodge County jail for stealing $2.25 from a letter that passed through his hands during processing.

The paper then compared the sentences imposed on Davis and Diefendorf with the one that Munger handed down to Alfred M. Oleson, a former stamp clerk in Omaha, who had pled guilty to stealing $2,029 from the post office.[60] The judge fined Oleson $2,000 but imposed no prison time for his crime. Rome Miller, a prominent Omaha hotel owner and local Republican Party official, was present in the courtroom and immediately guaranteed the payment of Oleson's fine. Other newspaper stories noted that part of the money was paid "by the fraternal order of which Oleson was a prominent member."[61] The *World-Herald* also reported that Oleson's attorney, John T. Cathers, had urged Munger not to imprison his client, telling the judge that Oleson had a wife and daughter who were dependent on him for support and assuring Munger that Oleson did not have a "criminal heart." His client's mistake, Cathers argued, would "make a man" out of him. Munger was apparently swayed by the attorney's appeal. In passing sentence on Oleson, the judge reportedly said to the man, "I have given this case very much thought and reflection. It is not the severity of the punishment, but its certainty, that is the deterrent of crime. . . . I do not believe that you have a criminal heart, but that you overstepped the bounds of propriety and discretion. I am inclined to give you one more chance to become a good citizen."

The *World-Herald* columnist pointed out that Diefendorf, the clerk who had stolen a mere $2.25, also had a family to support; in fact, he had seven children under the age of fifteen depending on him. The writer then caustically suggested that "the one child in Oleson's case seemed to touch Judge Munger's heart" while the "wife and seven children in the Diefendorf case failed to elicit the mercy of the court." Therefore, he continued, "It is difficult to avoid the conclusion that Oleson, the man who stole $2,029, was permitted to escape with a mere fine because he had powerful friends, while Diefendorf, the man who stole $2.25, is now doing service in the Dodge county jail, because he was without the power and influence which Oleson was able to summon to his assistance."[62] The editorialist's rhetorical flourishes then soared to even greater heights as he lamented the plight of the boy whom Munger had sentenced even more harshly than either of the two adults:

And the boy who, for stealing $9.60 in stamps and thirty pennies, was sentenced to two years at Sioux Falls—what about the boy? Is there not as great an opportunity for making a man out of this boy as there is for making a man out of the Omaha stamp clerk? Will the work of making a man out of this boy be simplified by his incarceration in Sioux Falls prison, among the hardened inmates of that institution? To be sure, he has no influential friends to raise a voice on his behalf, but . . . What about the boy, Judge Munger? . . . If it is merely a question of mercy, . . . let it not be merely for the man who is surrounded by rich and influential friends. . . . Let it be that mercy that encircles both friend and foe, both great and small, both powerful and helpless.[63]

The Dietrich and Oleson cases would not be the last times that Munger would be criticized for being too lenient on well-connected criminal defendants. In fact, he would soon be assailed on that issue by a far more prominent and powerful voice than the *Omaha World-Herald*. Judge Munger was about to draw the wrath of President Theodore Roosevelt.

7

The Cattle Barons Cases

The existing fences are all illegal. . . . All these fences, those that are hurtful and those that are beneficial, are alike illegal and must come down. . . . The unlawful fencing of public lands for private grazing must be stopped.

—President Theodore Roosevelt, 1907

There is no moral turpitude connected with the offense with which the defendants are charged, the offense being merely a statutory one. . . . The defendants shall be imprisoned in the custody of the United States marshal for six hours.

—Judge William Munger, *U.S. v. Bartlett Richards et al.*, 1905

The occasional controversies sparked by Munger's handling of labor disputes and political corruption cases during his first eight years on the bench paled in comparison to the notoriety he attained as a result of the "cattle barons" litigation that came before his court starting in 1905. That chapter in the court's history emerged from a mingling of some of the most iconic elements of American history: the rise of the great cattle empires that have become so romanticized in the popular imagery of the American West; the hardscrabble lives of homesteading farmers trying to eke out a living on the semiarid Great Plains; the privilege and influence wielded by the wealthy tycoons of the late

Gilded Age; and finally the bluster and dynamism that accompanied the arrival of an energetic and charismatic young president determined to rein in those business titans of the day. In the cattle barons' cases, Munger found himself placed squarely and uncomfortably at the confluence of all those powerful forces. He would not emerge unscathed.

Ranchers vs. Nesters

The story begins during the Civil War, when Congress passed the Homestead Act of 1862 as a means to encourage the settlement and development of the vast public domain in the western half of the nation and reap the potentially enormous agricultural bounty of the Midwest and Great Plains. The fundamentals of the homesteading process have become familiar to most Americans: any adult head of household could claim 160 acres of the public domain by paying a nominal administrative fee and promising to live on and improve the land for at least five years. At the end of that period, and after complying with a cursory "proving up" process, the claimant obtained clear title to the land through a patent deed from the government. If the homesteader wished to acquire title more quickly, he or she could commute the claim by paying $1.25 per acre. Notably and significantly, this opportunity for landownership was available not only to white males but also to unmarried or widowed women, former slaves, and even newly arriving immigrants who had not yet become naturalized citizens. While many homesteaders' efforts to wring a living from their 160-acre claims would fail, the impact of the act cannot be overstated. Through its provisions, millions of acres of federal land were claimed and brought into agricultural production, including about 9.6 million acres in Nebraska alone.[1]

In the late 1860s and throughout the 1870s, another powerful catalytic force combined with, and often competed with, the homesteaders for preeminence on the Great Plains: the massive cattle herds driven north out of Texas to railroad terminals in Kansas and Nebraska. By the mid-1870s, towns throughout the region, exemplified most notably by Dodge City, Kansas, and Ogallala, Nebraska, had sprung to life to service the cowboys on their drives, evolving into the colorful and rowdy "cow towns" that would become so familiar in the traditional, though not wholly accurate, popular imagery of the historic "Wild West."[2] The cattle drives ultimately gave way to the establishment and growth of large livestock grazing operations throughout the Plains, and no region was better suited or more attractive for that booming industry than the rich grasslands of central and western Nebraska, particularly the famous Sandhills region encompassing all or parts of more than thirty Nebraska counties. By the early 1900s, "cattle barons" dominated the area's social, political, and legal landscape, operating enormous ranches.

The profitability of those ranching enterprises was dependent on many factors, none more important than the operators' ability to graze their herds on the vast stretches of unclaimed public land without paying rent or taxes for that usage. Conversely, as homesteading farmers moved into the Sandhills and other portions of central and western Nebraska, they naturally sought to file their claims on parcels of land that were near or adjacent to water sources, which the ranchers needed for their livestock as well. Conflicts inevitably arose. The ranchers developed the practice of constructing fences on the public lands to protect the water sources and prime grazing areas from settlement by homesteaders, whom they disdainfully referred to as "nesters," and they sometimes turned to harassment and intimidation to keep the settlers out of their areas of operation. Farmers, in turn, struck back against the ranchers, sometimes by cutting cattlemen's fences and occasionally by shooting cattle that wandered onto their claims. The result was a period of intense rivalry and sporadic "fence cutter" violence between cattlemen and homesteaders during the 1870s and 1880s.[3]

Congress took action on the fencing issue in 1885, when Nebraska senator Charles Van Wyck spearheaded the enactment of "An Act to Prevent Unlawful Occupancy of the Public Lands." The statute, which became known as the Van Wyck law, made the fencing of any portion of the public domain a federal criminal offense, and it specifically prohibited the use of "force, threats, intimidation, or any fencing or inclosing . . . to prevent or obstruct any person from peaceably entering upon or establishing a residence on any tract of public land subject to entry under the public land laws of the United States." Upon conviction, violators were subject to a fine of up to $1,000 and imprisonment up to one year for each offense.[4] Despite the unambiguous letter and spirit of the new law, federal authorities made little effort to enforce its provisions, and the fencing of public lands by the cattle interests continued largely unimpeded for the rest of the century.

The Roosevelt Effect

Then came Theodore Roosevelt. Ascending to the presidency after the assassination of William McKinley in 1901, Roosevelt took the country by storm, launching a transformative era in presidential history that would be marked by vigorous executive leadership to advance a host of Progressive causes. Among many other goals, his "Square Deal" agenda for reforms in American society called for the elimination of special privileges for the wealthy and a commitment to the protection and efficient management of the public lands for the benefit of all. Though he had himself been a rancher in the Dakota Badlands in the 1880s, Roosevelt had little sympathy for the cattlemen's position on the issue of fencing the public domain. In his Annual Message to Congress in 1907, Roosevelt recognized the complexity of the competing interests at stake, but left no doubt that his primary concern was for the welfare of the small farmer rather than the cattle barons:

> As the West settles, the range becomes more and more overgrazed. Much of it cannot be used to advantage unless it is fenced, for fencing is the only way by which to keep in check the owners of nomad flocks which run hither and thither, utterly destroying the pastures and leaving a waste behind so that their presence is incompatible with the presence of homemakers. The existing fences are all illegal. . . . All these fences, those that are hurtful and those that are beneficial, are alike illegal and must come down. . . . The unlawful fencing of public lands for private grazing must be stopped, but the necessity which occasioned it must be provided for. . . . Our prime object is to secure the rights and guard the interests of the

small ranchman, the man who ploughs and pitches hay for himself. It is this small ranchman, this actual settler and homemaker, who in the long run is most hurt by permitting thefts of public land in whatever form.[5]

By the time he delivered that message, Roosevelt had already been working for more than five years to bring down illegal fences all across the Great Plains. Indeed, from the outset of his presidency he had called for the vigorous enforcement of the 1885 antifencing law, and officials responded to the pressure with an aggressive assault on illegal fences. In early 1902 Secretary of the Interior Ethan Allen Hitchcock formally ordered the removal of all privately constructed fences on the public domain. In Nebraska, as elsewhere, cattlemen responded by asking federal authorities to defer immediate action on the removal of fences while they worked to secure the enactment of legislation that would allow them to lease grazing lands from the government.[6] Meeting at Alliance in the heart of western Nebraska cattle country on February 18, the Nebraska Stockgrowers' Association adopted a proclamation that clearly articulated their position:

WHEREAS, That portion of Nebraska west of the 100th Meridian and known as the Sand Hills, is adapted to stock raising only, and is fit for no other purpose, and which section at this time is almost wholly engaged in said industry, and

WHEREAS, The success of the stockgrowers in said section depends largely on the maintenance of pastures which have been fenced, at enormous expense, and

WHEREAS, It is now imminent, that the Government intends the removal of all fences from the public domain.

Now, therefore, we the members of the Nebraska Stockgrowers' association, in convention now assembled, do most emphatically petition Theodore Roosevelt, the president of the United States, to immediately stay further proceedings in the Interior department which are now, or may be, directed toward the removal of fences from the public domain, until we have time to pass appropriate legislation pertaining to the disposal of the lands of this section.

RESOLVED, that it is the sense of this meeting, that in view of the probable removal of fences on government domain, we are in favor of the leasing of the public lands in such a manner, and under such restrictions, as will protect the small stockgrower, as well as the larger owner.[7]

Roosevelt temporarily yielded to the cattlemen's resistance, granting extensions that ultimately stretched out for about a year. By the following spring, however, Congress had still not passed a leasing law, and the president would wait no longer. He ordered the Interior Department to renew its enforcement of the fence removal order, and western Nebraska soon became ground zero for that federal campaign. Special agents, led by the famed former Confederate cavalryman John Mosby, were dispatched onto the Plains to inventory and record the locations of illegal fences. Their findings prompted Secretary Hitchcock to report that western Nebraska was home to more illegal enclosures than any other part of the country. He went on to indicate that the worst offenders were often prominent cattlemen who appeared to operate under the assumption that they could maintain their fences with impunity, inasmuch as prosecutors and judges seemed reluctant to punish any specific individual for such a routine and pervasive practice.[8]

The Fencing Trials Begin

That long-standing pattern of noncompliance and lax enforcement finally ended in May 1905, when Nebraska's U.S. district attorney, Irving F. Baxter, announced his intention to "proceed at once" with the prosecution of almost two dozen western Nebraska cattlemen who had been previously indicted for the illegal fencing of government land.[9] Baxter vowed, "There will be no further parleying in the matter. Promises do not go. The fences have got to come down. The cattlemen have been given all the immunity they are entitled to, and now the government will take a hand and see that its mandates are strictly and impartially enforced."[10] He appointed former assistant district attorney Sylvester R. Rush to serve as his special assistant for prosecuting the cases and vowed that he and Rush would "push the cases vigorously."[11]

The first of the indicted ranchers to be tried were John and Herman Krause, who were charged with enclosing more than 7,500 acres of public land for their cattle grazing operations in Sheridan and Box Butte Counties. With Munger presiding, the case was tried to a jury in Omaha in early June. During eight days of testimony, the often violent dimensions of the fencing battles between ranchers and homesteaders became readily apparent. Settlers Theodore and Bessie Osborn, whose homestead claim fell within some of the public range enclosed by the Krause brothers' fences, described to the jury the numerous confrontations and threats they experienced in their dealings with the cattlemen. The incidents included several fistfights and at least one episode in which one of the defendants tried to "ride them down" with his horse.[12] In an even more dramatic exchange during Rush's cross-examination of John Krause, the cattleman admitted that he had shot and killed another homesteader seven years earlier over another fencing dispute, but asserted that the shooting had been in self-defense. The unexpected disclosure, to which Krause's attorneys quickly objected, was reported to have "created quite a stir in the court room."[13]

As the trial proceeded, there was no shortage of published opinion on both sides of the controversy. At least one area newspaper weighed in on the merits of the case and came down squarely on the side of the homesteaders. In an editorial published in its June 6 edition, the *Kearney Daily Hub* opined:

It is well that the government has [begun prosecuting] the land stealing business with the determination to break it up, and to give the homesteader a chance, for the time is very near at hand when nearly every acre of the former arid belt will be adapted to agriculture, and especially to alfalfa growing and small stock farming and dairying. It is estimated that in the past fifteen years 15,000,000 acres of government land have been illegally taken by the cattlemen.[14]

On the other hand, the hatred of the nesters by the cattlemen and their supporters was starkly expressed by at least one courtroom observer, when a reporter heard him tell District Attorney Baxter during a break in the trial that "the homesteaders up there are nothing but a set of scoundrels and blackmailers and they ought to be made to suffer for it. They are always trying to blackmail the cattlemen."[15] Even Judge Munger apparently felt compelled to comment on the equities of the case. At one point during the trial, he was quoted in several newspapers as stating from the bench that "a man with one cow has the same right to the public range as the man with 2,000 steers. The man with 2,000 steers has no more right to enclose the public lands than a man with one cow. A man may, however, enclose his own land, but not the public land."[16]

On June 9 the jury returned convictions against the Krause brothers, finding them guilty of illegally enclosing more than 4,500 acres of public land. John Krause was also convicted of trying to prevent the Osborns and other settlers from freely entering into that same public domain. The defense immediately informed Munger that they intended to file a motion for rehearing, and he agreed to defer sentencing during the pendency of the post-trial proceedings. After several more months of procedural skirmishing, Munger overruled the Krauses' motion for a new trial, and at a hearing on September 28 he entertained final arguments from counsel on sentencing. Defense attorney C. C. Barker asked the judge for leniency, arguing that the offenses his clients were convicted of were "purely statutory in nature" and did not involve "any moral turpitude." He analogized their actions to that of a mere hunting violation and went on to argue that his men were not rich or well connected. Rather, Barker suggested, "They are poor men. They are not cattle barons. . . . They went into that inhospitable section and stayed there, while others passed on. They work with their own hands and by that means support themselves. . . . I ask that the court look into the equity of the case and ask for the mercy of the court and expect justice." In response, Baxter contended that the case was "highly important" and asked for the law to be "rigidly enforced." He aimed his most vehement rhetoric at John Krause, arguing that his acts of intimidation toward his neighboring settlers were "heinous" and that he was "an intimidator of the worst sort" for whom "the limit of the law is none too little punishment." He concluded with a ringing demand for the court to make an example of the Krause brothers, "whereby the public may be notified that this thing cannot continue with impunity and that the intimidation of settlers on the public domain must cease."[17]

Munger's own statements at the hearing seemed to reflect a Solomonic desire to assuage both sides. He agreed with the defense assertion that the Krauses' actions were "statutory offenses per se and not immoral ones," and he went on to acknowledge that "for many years large and wealthy corporations have been tacitly permitted to do this thing in violation of the law." In the next breath, however, he seemed to attach a significant moral dimension to the case, as he piously noted that "the purpose of the law is to preserve the public domain for the use of actual settlers. No one has the right to arrogate to himself the right of dominion and control over the public lands. . . . The humblest citizen has the same right as the corporation." Munger also purported to agree with the government's desire to set an example with the case, expressing the hope that his punishment of the Krause brothers would help to ensure that "further prosecutions may be avoided, and in passing sentence it will show to offenders . . . that it will not be profitable to continue paying fines for the privilege of keeping their illegal fences up."[18]

Ultimately, the sentences that Munger delivered seemed to reflect his apparent ambivalence about the seriousness of the Krause brothers' offenses. While he could have imposed fines of up to $1,000 and jail sentences of up to one year, he opted to fine John Krause $800 and his brother Herman $500, and he assessed court costs against them both in the amount of $1,175. Those relatively heavy monetary fines were mitigated, however, by the token nature of the rest of the sentence, as he ordered the two men to be retained in the custody of the U.S. marshal for just twenty-four hours. Munger's leniency toward the cattlemen on the incarceration issue presaged a far more controversial result in a more notorious fencing case that loomed on the horizon.

Bartlett Richards and the Spade Ranch

In the aftermath of the Krause convictions, many observers, including the federal prosecutors themselves, expressed optimism that no further trials would prove to be necessary. Shortly after the guilty verdicts were announced, Baxter predicted to a reporter that "the effect of the conviction in the Krause brothers' case will be to compel the [other indicted] cattlemen to comply with the law in reference to taking down their unlawful fences. Any one of them who shows a willingness to take down their fences will be given a reasonable amount of time to do it, but the government will not permit any [further] dallying."[19] Echoing Baxter's statement, the *Kearney Daily Hub* anticipated that the government's victory over the Krauses would "undoubtedly [be] the beginning of the end in dispossessing the cattlemen entirely of their stolen grazing lands."[20] A few weeks later, Special Assistant District Attorney Sylvester R. Rush indicated that no new cases would be tried immediately, as he hoped that "the moral effect of the conviction of John and Herman Krause of illegal fencing will have a deterrent influence upon other cattlemen, . . . and that [their] fences will be taken down."[21] That optimism proved unfounded, however, as little progress in the voluntary removal of fences occurred throughout the rest of that summer. By November 1905 the patience of Roosevelt and his prosecutors had finally run out, and they brought the biggest of their targets, renowned cattleman Bartlett Richards and his partner Will Comstock, into court to face Judge Munger.

Bartlett Richards's story provides a quintessential example of the immense wealth and power that could be amassed in the open range cattle business by individuals who possessed the right combination of sharp business skills, sufficient capital, tenacity, luck, and a willingness to disregard public land laws. Heading west from his native Vermont at age seventeen, Richards arrived in Wyoming in 1879 and quickly entered the booming cattle business of the era. Within a year he had purchased his first thousand head of cattle and grazed them in the Belle Fourche River valley about three hundred miles northeast of Cheyenne. In the aftermath of the devastating winter of 1886–87, Richards moved his cattle operations several hundred miles to the east, into the more sheltered and fertile Nebraska Sandhills region, which he found to be "the best grazing land on the continent."[22] During those same years, he also partnered with one of his brothers and other investors to launch or acquire several banks in the northwestern section of the state. In 1888 he purchased fellow cattleman Bennett Irwin's grazing operation southeast of Chadron and renamed it the Spade Ranch. Within a few years, Richards had persuaded his friend John Cairnes to invest in the Spade, and during the 1890s the two men skillfully and steadily built the ranch into the biggest and most lucrative cattle operation in the state. Among his many other activities and accomplishments, Richards introduced Hereford cattle to the region and, through careful breeding and management, refined the Spade Hereford line into award-winning stock; drilled wells and built dozens of windmills and reservoirs for watering his herds; built a house, barn, bunkhouse, and other structures on the ranch; installed telephone lines and rudimentary roads throughout the area; and ultimately established the village of Ellsworth twenty miles southwest of the ranch as a "company town" to serve as a supply depot and railhead for the shipment of Spade cattle to midwestern feedlots and eastern markets. At Ellsworth, Richards built a store, hotel, and ranch office and eventually a sprawling frame house where he lived with his family during the summer months. As his wealth mounted, he also built a luxurious winter residence in Coronado, California.

In 1899 Cairnes sold out of his partnership with Richards and was replaced by another of Richards's friends and business associates, William G. Comstock. Later that year, the two men joined with other investors to incorporate the Spade as the Nebraska Land and Feeding Company, with Richards and Comstock as president and vice president, respectively. By that time, the company's operations encompassed some 500,000 acres in Sheridan, Box Butte, and Cherry Counties, grazing more than 15,000 head of cattle.

As was the case with most other large cattle operations in the West, however, much of the land controlled by the Spade was, in fact, public domain and thus open to homesteading claims.[23] As his operations expanded, Richards, like his fellow cattlemen throughout the region, began erecting fences to keep cattle from straying, protect watering sites and breeding purity, and inhibit homesteaders from filing claims within the bounds of "his" grazing operations. Many of those fences, of course, were in direct violation of the 1885 Van Wyck law, and during the years since the law's passage, Richards had been at the forefront of the Nebraska cattlemen's efforts to delay or thwart federal enforcement of the statute. They sincerely believed that the government's policies regarding land distribution and usage in the vast and largely arid public lands west of the 100th meridian were unrealistic and foolishly misguided. They believed that, through their cattle operations, they were making improvements and adding value to land that was wholly unsuited for any other use, including grain agriculture. In such areas, they contended, the government ought to lease lands to cattle ranchers, so that they could amass enough acreage to sustain the profitability of their operations through legitimate, rather than technically illegal, means. The government, in return, would reap the benefit of the lease payments as well as the enhanced value of the land thus improved. Testifying at a 1902 hearing on a leasing bill then under consideration by the House Committee on Public Lands, Richards articulated the cattlemen's position quite effectively:

> Here the United States has immense properties that are not improving, which we [cattlemen] have grown up with and have improved, and we ask you that while you have no better use for this land, that you will lease it to us at a reasonable rental, and that the moment you have any better use for it, for irrigation, for mineral entries, for storage reservoirs, for agricultural purposes, for forest reserves, for anything else which may come up and be the sense of Congress that it wants, that land shall be lifted out of the lease, and no recompense shall be made to the former leaseholder.[24]

Others, of course, viewed the matter quite differently, believing that widespread leasing of government land for cattle grazing would ultimately benefit only the largest and wealthiest of the stockmen and would lead to overgrazing and despoliation of the public domain. Given the intensity of the debate among the interested parties, and perhaps in light of the prevailing Progressive dynamics of the period that mitigated against any apparent favoritism toward "moneyed" interests, Congress did not enact the ranchers' requested leasing legislation. Thus the Roosevelt administration moved forward with its prosecutions.

At the time of their indictments, Richards and Comstock had pled not guilty to the fencing charges against them, and they maintained that position throughout the Krause prosecution and during the months leading up to their scheduled court appearance in early November. On the eve of their trial, however, they reconsidered their plea after their attorney, Richard S. Hall, reached an agreement with prosecutors Baxter and Rush. The government agreed to drop several counts of the indictment relating to fences on land that the ranchers claimed to hold legitimately, in return for a guilty plea on the remaining counts and a promise from the cattlemen to bring down all their remaining illegal fences immediately. At the sentencing hearing before Judge Munger on November 13, Hall asked the court for leniency toward his clients. He told Munger that the ranchers intended to comply with the law and that their employees were in the process of removing the fences as rapidly as they could. "Wherever the government shows us that we have an unlawful fence," Hall promised, "we will bring it down." Speaking for the government, Baxter expressed his willingness to accept the defendants' promises and offered no specific resistance to Hall's request for judicial leniency, telling Munger, "I believe the defendants will do all they have said they will do. They appear to be acting in good faith. If there is any further dispute as to any particular fence that will be a matter for further action."[25]

Sentencing and Reaction

Judge Munger accepted the plea agreement and proceeded to pass sentence on the two renowned cattlemen. It would prove to be arguably the most famous, and certainly one of the most controversial, sentencing decisions in the history of the Nebraska federal court. Munger ordered Richards and Comstock to each pay a $300 fine and court costs totaling $339. Much more notably, he also sentenced the two men to "be imprisoned in the custody of the United States marshal for six hours." As he announced those penalties, Munger was reported to have said, "There is no moral turpitude connected with the offense with which the defendants are charged, the offense being merely a statutory one."[26]

The events that immediately followed the imposition of this six-hour sentence on Richards and Comstock have been described with considerable inconsistency in the historical record, based no doubt on a good deal of speculative and perhaps exaggerated reporting in the contemporary accounts. The hearing in Munger's courtroom had begun in the late afternoon of November 13, leaving about six hours until Richards and Comstock were scheduled to depart Omaha on a westbound Burlington train at 11:00 p.m. Indeed, it seems almost certain that Munger must have had that timetable in mind when he came up with the odd six-hour period for their sentence. At some point shortly after the hearing, U.S. Marshal Trevanyon Matthews turned Richards and Comstock over to the supervision and control of their attorney, Richard Hall. By 5:00, Richards had returned from the courthouse to his room at the Iler Grand Hotel some four blocks away, where he began to write a letter to his wife in California inform-ing her of the afternoon's events. He was in a euphoric mood, telling her that he was heading home "with a light heart" and expressing great satisfaction at the case's outcome, saying, "Nothing ever went off more quietly, decently, and properly."[27] He went on to indicate that the court had treated him with great courtesy, saying that "Judge Munger did everything but apologize, for he stated, 'I want it to be understood that this case shows no moral turpitude but under the statutes as required I must impose a fine' etc." With respect to the six-hour sentence, Richards told her that he had not yet even met Marshal Matthews, inasmuch as the marshal had "directed Mr. Hall to look after us" for the duration of the sentence that Munger had imposed. Tellingly and accurately, Richards also predicted that gov-ernment officials in Washington would not be pleased with the day's results, writing, "It [Munger's disposition of the case] will paralyze old Hitchcock [the secretary of the interior] and I am so glad." Mid-way through his writing of the letter, Richards interrupted himself to complete some shopping errands and to meet Hall and several others at the Omaha Club for dinner at 6:45. After dinner, he returned to the hotel, finished his letter to his wife, checked out, and headed to the train station eleven blocks away, mailing the letter along the way.

While some newspaper accounts of Comstock and Richards's activities after their sentencing suggested that the dinner at the Omaha Club had taken the form of a boisterous victory celebration, there is little, if any, evidence to support that characterization. Indeed, as Richards's son defensively but compellingly pointed out in his 1980 biography of his father, the sequence and timing of the evening's events suggested that the dinner at the Omaha Club "could hardly have been the gala affair it was reported to be in news accounts. Considering that errands, letter writing, and riding or walking time between destinations occupied much of the time during the evening, it is unlikely that there was time for a soiree." Moreover, if his father had been inclined toward extensive or demonstrative gloating over Munger's leniency, he likely would have sent an "exultant telegram" to his wife, as was his habit on other unusual or significant occasions, "rather than a letter which would not reach her in California for several days."[28] Whatever uncertainty about the specific events of that evening may remain, it is indisputable that the six-hour sentence that Munger imposed on Richards and Comstock was nothing more than a token slap on the wrist that had little if any impact on the ranchers' freedom of movement. When news of the case's outcome reached Washington, that reality was not lost on President Roosevelt and his men. And, as Richards himself had anticipated, they were not amused.

Almost immediately after he first received word of the sentencing, Secretary Hitchcock publicly expressed his deep displeasure with Baxter and Munger's handling of the case. On November 16, he told newspaper reporters:

> You can say that I am surprised and indignant. The punishment is utterly inadequate. The indictment was the result of four years of determined effort and the expenditure of thousands of dollars by the government. We had selected the large operators in the hope that the result would be a warning to those engaged on a smaller scale. That the case was a strong one is evident by the fact that the

men pleaded guilty. The result is discouraging, but we will not cease our efforts. . . . If [Richards and Comstock] do not keep their promises, they will be indicted again and again until they learn that laws are made to be obeyed. We will not let up.[29]

At almost the same time, and in sharp contrast to Hitchcock's indignation, Baxter was expressing his great satisfaction with the outcome of the case, telling reporters that he was "naturally gratified" that the plea agreement with the ranchers had allowed the government to avoid the time, expense, and uncertain result of a lengthy and hard fought trial. Baxter went on to offer his optimistic prediction that the Richards and Comstock case would have a "most salutary effect" in accomplishing the government's primary objective—the removal of all illegal fences. "The government has not sought to persecute these men or any of the cattlemen," Baxter stated, "but simply to secure the public domain to the equal rights and privileges of all. We look now for the general removal of the fences on the public lands and [we believe] that the outcome of the Richards and Comstock cases will be the stimulus to a speedy removal of the fences."[30]

Baxter's sanguine outlook notwithstanding, government officials' wrath escalated rather than abated over the ensuing days, accompanied by a steady outpouring of scornful headlines and heated commentary in local, regional, and national newspapers. On November 17 the *Lincoln Evening News* splashed a large headline across its front page, predicting that the "Head of Mr. Baxter May Fall into Basket" as a result of what it called the "Farcical Prosecution of Cattle Barons in Land Fencing Cases." The accompanying story reported that Hitchcock had dispatched a message to Attorney General William H. Moody, asking the Department of Justice to launch an immediate investigation into Baxter's handling of the case. Even more ominously, the article went on to note that "President Roosevelt is said to share the indignation of Hitchcock."[31] Similarly, in a story headlined "Penalty Too Light," the *Omaha Daily Bee* reported that Hitchcock was especially outraged at Baxter's statements to the court about the ranchers' "good faith" in the fencing litigation and his failure to challenge Judge Munger's comments about the lack of "moral turpitude" in the defendants' offenses. Contrary to those assertions, the secretary fumed, Richards and Comstock had repeatedly promised to take down their fences "and no sooner were our backs turned than they went and replaced the fences which they had torn down, or, if they agreed to tear down fences, they failed to do so." If those were not acts of moral turpitude, Hitchcock asked rhetorically, "What is moral turpitude?"[32]

In a story that reflected the growing national attention to the Nebraska fencing controversy, the *Washington Times* revealed additional details about Hitchcock's complaint to the Justice Department regarding Baxter's conduct. The article noted that "officials freely declare that if Mr. Baxter had explained the great expense in time and trouble that the Government had [devoted to] apprehending and indicting these cattlemen, the court would not have let the men off with the slight punishment of six hours in the custody of the marshal."[33] On a more philosophical level, the general reaction to the fencing case among many of the progressive newspapers of the era is reflected in a December 9 editorial in the *Labor World*, a pro-union paper published in Duluth, Minnesota. Hearkening back to the controversies sparked by some of Munger's previous criminal sentences (see chapter 6), an article titled "Here Is a Reason Why Workingmen Have a Growing Contempt for the Courts" lambasted Munger for his apparently preferential treatment of Richards and Comstock. Drawing a sharp contrast between the harsh sentences that Munger had imposed on some petty thieves, including a purported "life sentence" for a man who had stolen just two cents from a mail carrier, and sentencing Richards and Comstock to merely "visit with the United States Marshall for six hours," the writer concluded by asking his readers, "Do you understand now why the workingmen of the country believe that there is one law for the rich and another for the poor? Does this explain the growing contempt for the courts?"

As the furor intensified, neither Baxter nor Munger proved willing to remain silent in the face of the growing chorus of criticism. The district attorney initially deflected Hitchcock's criticism by suggesting that the secretary simply did not yet understand all the circumstances of the case and was thus reacting prematurely. Over the ensuing days, however, Baxter became more strident in his own defense, denying that there was anything inappropriate or inadequate about his handling of the case and ultimately claiming that, as the mere prosecutor, he had no control whatsoever over Judge Munger's decision on the matter of sentencing.[34] No doubt emboldened by his lifetime tenure as a federal judge, Munger was a good deal more pointed in his response. Asked by a reporter for his reaction to Hitchcock's criticism, he sarcastically replied, "Oh, he is surprised and indignant, is he? Well, the secretary of the interior has a perfect right to be surprised and indignant if he wants to be. One would naturally think that he had enough to look after with the affairs pertaining to his office without seeking to saddle himself with additional responsibilities."[35] The judge said he believed that the "sentence passed upon [the defendants] was sufficient to meet the situation" and expressed his confidence that the "result which the government sought to attain has been effected."

While most of the initial outcry over the case was directed toward the judge and the prosecutor, the first head to fall belonged to the man who had been rather ambiguously instructed by the court to take custody of Richards and Comstock during their six-hour sentence, Marshal Matthews. On November 28 Matthews received a notice from the attorney general asking him for an explanation of his handling of the case. In his reply Matthews first vehemently denounced newspaper stories reporting that he and the two ranchers had "dined sumptuously," "spent part of the evening at the theater," or "languished in a saloon." Calling such stories "straight up and down lies," he proceeded to acknowledge that he had turned the two men over to the custody of their attorney, a practice that he claimed was not at all unusual or exceptional among marshals and sheriffs in similar situations. Matthews went on to explain to Moody: "My understanding was, and is, that the sentence 'the custody of the marshal' for a few hours was a formality which did not contemplate or mean severe treatment, and I did not think that the court intended it otherwise. My understanding of the order was that they were to be restrained of their liberty for six hours and that was done, under a reliable man and in a reputable place, known to me, and where I could find them at any minute during that period."[36]

Matthews concluded by saying that if he had "misapprehended my duties in the matter," he hoped for the attorney general's understanding and indulgence. Moody, however, was not in a forgiving mood. Interpreting the marshal's letter as an admission of his official misconduct, the attorney general recommended that the president should remove Matthews from his office, and on December 8 Roosevelt did just that.

Both Munger and Baxter declined to comment on the marshal's firing, but reaction from others was quick and intense. The Nebraska congressional delegation expressed surprise and dismay at both the firing and the fact that they had not been consulted by the president before he made up his mind on Matthews's fate. They asked for and obtained a meeting on December 10 with Attorney General Moody to seek the marshal's reinstatement, arguing that the termination was not deserved and that he should have at least been given a hearing before being removed from office. Moody listened courteously but offered no concessions, stating that the firing was based on "a great offense and not a [mere] misunderstanding of the law." As to the delegates' complaints that they had not been previously informed or consulted in the matter, he replied that there was no need for congressional consultation "when persons in the service were found derelict in duty," and he pointed out that "it has never been the custom of the Department of Justice to advise the delegation when one of their appointees was found incompetent to perform the duties of his office."[37] Meanwhile, another defender of the marshal, his brother-in-law R. B. Schneider, was taking his appeal directly to the president. As the Nebraska representative on the executive committee of the national Republican Party, Schneider knew Roosevelt well. He visited the White House on December 14 and asked the president to reconsider his decision, but to no avail.[38] Four days later, Schneider returned to the White House, this time accompanied by Matthews himself. The fired marshal made a direct appeal to the president for reinstatement, but again Roosevelt would not be swayed. "Gentlemen, the case is closed. I must stand by the recommendations of the attorney general in this matter."[39] Matthews had little choice but to accept his fate and fade away.

No sooner had Matthews's dismissal been finalized than Roosevelt's displeasure found its second target. On the afternoon of December 19, just hours after his meeting with Matthews and Schneider, the president asked District Attorney Baxter for his resignation, citing his "perfunctory prosecution" of the Richards and Comstock case. Baxter expressed shock and dismay at the news, telling reporters, "Perfunctory prosecution? Why, there was no prosecution at all. How could there be when the two men voluntarily pleaded guilty?" He went on to shift the blame solely toward Judge Munger, asking, "Can I be held responsible for the sentence that was passed upon them? Surely I had nothing to do with that. I wasn't the court. I didn't have jurisdiction."[40]

As always, the volume and tone of editorial reaction to the firing was colored by politics, with Republican papers generally treating the news with considerably more restraint than their Democratic or Progressive counterparts. Among the latter, the *Omaha World-Herald* was particularly boisterous in its coverage, devoting the entire top half of its December 20 front page to the news, with a large headline announcing, "Baxter's Head Drops under the Big Stick," accompanied by a cartoon image of Baxter's head being smashed by Roosevelt's proverbial big stick, with blood squirting into the eyes of Republican senator Joseph Millard and *Omaha Daily Bee* publisher Edward Rosewater, who was a bitter rival of the *World-Herald*.

As word of the president's action spread, it was reported to have "created a great sensation among the Nebraska senators and representatives," who were said to be still reeling from the president's unexpected and precipitous firing of Marshal Matthews.[41] The Nebraska delegation made a token effort to dissuade Roosevelt, but in light of his refusal to budge on the Matthews firing, it quickly became apparent to even Baxter's most ardent supporters that there was no hope of changing the president's mind. Roosevelt let it be known that if Baxter did not resign, he would fire him, and that's precisely how the event played out. Baxter refused to step down, and on December 24 the president formally relieved him of his office. Baxter, like Matthews before him, accepted the decision without further resistance and announced that he would return to private practice in Omaha. Shortly thereafter, the president replaced him with Charles A. Goss, an Omaha attorney who would go on to become chief justice of the Nebraska Supreme Court.

The Land Fraud Trials

As heated as the fencing trials and their aftermath had been, those events were only the first stage of the government's multipronged assault on the power of Nebraska's open range cattlemen. Larger and more complex litigation would soon follow. As the fencing prosecutions were under way during the summer and fall of 1905, more than two dozen Interior Department investigators were once again scrutinizing land office records throughout western Nebraska searching for irregularities in the filing and processing of homestead claims. At the heart of the issue was the long-standing practice among western ranchers of using "dummy" or "widow" filings to circumvent the spirit and the letter of the homestead law. Briefly summarized, the scheme typically involved the solicitation of Civil War veterans, widows, and orphans to file homestead claims on lands they had no intention of actually settling upon. The cattlemen would pay their recruits a fee, "lend" them the funds for the required administrative costs, and assist them in making the necessary "improvements" to the property, which usually amounted to nothing more than rough lean-tos or shacks. Typically, the claims would be filed on lands that encircled the ranchers' preferred grazing areas—a process sometimes referred to as "donuting." At some point thereafter, the ostensible claimants would lease or sell the land to their benefactor at a previously agreed-upon price. The net result of the scheme was to allow the cattlemen to accumulate massive landholdings far in excess of the intended 160-acre homestead parcels, while protecting their grazing ranges, watering sites, and illegal fence lines from the claims of legitimate homesteaders.

In 1904 the ranchers' incentive to engage in those shady tactics was greatly enhanced by the enactment of the Kinkaid Act. Sponsored and pushed through Congress by western Nebraska congressman Moses Kinkaid, the new law amended the original homestead provisions by allowing applicants to enter claims on 640-acre parcels rather than the standard 160-acre homestead unit. Kinkaid's bill specifically applied to thirty-seven counties in the northwestern two-thirds of Nebraska—essentially the Sandhills region—and reflected a legislative acknowledgment that the arid climate and sandy soils of the area would not support mere 160-acre farms. Ranchers quickly recognized the opportunity provided by the new law and accelerated their efforts to recruit "dummy" claimants for these vastly larger tracts. As historian Arthur R. Reynolds has observed, the passage of the Kinkaid law in 1904 marked a "transition from the custom of illegal fencing, which was [beginning to be] severely prosecuted by the Interior Department, to a policy of obtaining fraudulent filings on 640-acre tracts in order to secure title to the lands that formerly had been illegally fenced. Under the 160-acre homestead law the process of securing enough dishonest filings to cover the vast empires that the cattlemen used for grazing purposes would have taken too long and would have been too expensive."[42]

But even as the Nebraska cattlemen sought to expand their control of the public domain through those techniques, the Justice and Interior Departments, exhorted by their boss in the White House, moved just as quickly to curtail their activities. And as that legal drama unfolded, once again Judge Munger and his court would take center stage.

Based upon the evidence gathered by federal investigators in late 1905, prosecutors launched a series of cases in 1906 and 1907 against many of the same ranchers who had previously been charged with illegal fencing, including Richards and Comstock. Those proceedings, often collectively referred to as the "conspiracy cases," typically charged the defendants with conspiring to defraud the government of title to the public domain by the use of spurious or fictitious homestead or Kinkaid claims and entries. The first of the big Nebraska cattlemen prosecuted on those types of charges was the Reverend George Ware, an Episcopal minister who served as the rector of churches in Deadwood and Lead, South Dakota, while simultaneously operating the

200,000-acre UBI cattle ranch in Hooker County, Nebraska. Beginning in 1902, agents employed by Ware made repeated trips to old soldiers homes in Grand Island, Nebraska, and several Iowa towns, soliciting veterans or widows to make fraudulent filings for land within or encircling the UBI's grazing ranges. After the Kinkaid Act went into effect, those recruiting efforts accelerated, and by the time of his indictment in late 1905, Ware stood accused of inducing the entry of about thirty such claims totaling nearly 20,000 acres.[43]

The UBI conspiracy trial commenced in Judge Munger's court in January 1906. Special Assistant District Attorney Sylvester Rush, who had retained the approval of Roosevelt and the rest of the administration during the furor following the Richards and Comstock sentencing, remained in his position under the new district attorney, Charles Goss, and led the prosecution. Because the two "recruiters" used by Ware had agreed to a plea bargain whereby they agreed to testify for the government in exchange for the promise of reduced sentences, Rush's case was relatively easy to make. The two men testified that, at Ware's expense, they transported dozens of "dummy" claimants to Broken Bow to sign and file the necessary claim forms, using descriptions of the desired land that Ware had provided. All the filing fees and other administrative costs were paid by Ware, and as soon as the necessary papers had been filed, the agents paid each of the purported homesteaders a small fee for a ninety-nine-year lease on the claimed land. Most important, each recruited claimant also signed an agreement to sell the land to Ware at the rate of $100 to $150 per quarter section as soon as final title was obtained. In the case of military veterans or their widows, the wait for that transfer and payment could be quite short, inasmuch as they were entitled to credit against the five-year "proving up" period for each year of military service. To put the finishing touches on the scheme, Ware constructed crude shacks on the claims, at an average cost of $7 apiece, to ostensibly comply with the requirement that entrants make "improvements" to the property during the homestead period.

The trial proceeded over two weeks. Ware offered little in the way of defense, other than challenging the credibility of the government's witnesses and claiming that he had always tried to avoid violating any land laws. The jury, made up entirely of eastern Nebraska residents, most of them farmers, took only a few hours to find Ware guilty on all counts. Perhaps having learned his lesson from Roosevelt's reaction to his sentencing of Richards and Comstock two months earlier, or perhaps finding that Ware's offenses reflected considerably greater "moral turpitude" than the Spade ranchers' fencing practices had entailed, Munger delivered a relatively stiff penalty on the erstwhile minister: a fine of $1,000 and confinement for one year in the Douglas County jail. Ware remained free on bond while he appealed his conviction to the Eighth Circuit, where he lost a 2–1 decision delivered in July 1907.[44] Several months later, the U.S. Supreme Court denied his petition for certiorari, and Ware began serving his sentence in October 1907.[45]

Meanwhile, in May 1906 a federal grand jury indicted Richards, Comstock, and seven other Spade Ranch officials on charges identical to those that Ware had just faced. Specifically, the first thirty counts of the 550-page indictment alleged that the defendants had conspired to defraud the government of title to large tracts of land in Sheridan, Box Butte, and Cherry Counties by inducing sixty-three men and women to file fictitious and illegal claims to those lands under the terms of the Kinkaid Act. An additional eight counts charged the men with conspiring to induce those purported claimants to perjure themselves in the swearing and signing of the papers required for Kinkaid claims.

The Richards-Comstock "conspiracy case" was called for trial before Judge Munger on November 12, 1906. Given the prominence of the defendants, the serious nature of the charges against them, and the still-lingering notoriety of the six-hour sentence they had received the previous fall, it was one of the best publicized and most closely followed trials in the court's history. Preliminary maneuvering among the attorneys resulted in the division of the nine defendants into two groups for trial. First to be tried were Richards, Comstock, ranch secretary-treasurer Charles G. Jameson, Aquilla Triplett, who was alleged to be one of the Spade's recruiting agents or "locaters," and Valentine attorney and former state judge F. M. Walcott, who had served as legal advisor to the Spade Ranch. By November 21 the pretrial skirmishing was concluded, a twelve-man jury was empaneled, and Rush began his presentation of the government's case.

Over the next four weeks (including Saturday court sessions), the prosecution called more than 130 witnesses to the stand, including dozens of elderly soldiers and military widows, most of whom told the same basic story: they had been approached by agents of the Spade Ranch, who offered them various inducements to file homestead or Kinkaid claims on lands in the area of the Spade; they had filed the claims with no intention of actually residing on the land or making permanent improvements thereto; the Spade representatives had induced them to lie about those intentions in signing the sworn paperwork required for the claims; and the true purpose of the transactions was to give control of the land to the operators of the Spade Ranch by lease during the proving period and by outright sale to Spade at a prearranged price following the acquisition of full title by the fraudulent claimant. Using records and maps derived from Land Office Tract Books, prosecutors showed the way in which many of the fraudulent "widow entries" had been lined up sequentially so as to coincide with the already existing (or, in some cases, recently removed) illegal Spade fence lines.

Rush also offered into evidence scores of letters and other documents subpoenaed from the Nebraska Land and Feeding Company files, which the government claimed provided additional evidence of the alleged conspiracy.[46] Defense attorneys A. W. Crites of Chadron and Richard S. Hall and Harry C. Brome of Omaha vehemently challenged the admissibility of much of the evidence introduced by the prosecution, but opted not to put their clients on the witness stand in their own defense. Hall was particularly critical of the corporate documents admitted into the record, arguing that they "were of no incriminating character whatsoever" and "contained no evidence of collusion for the commission of any offense." In almost all of the many such evidentiary objections that arose during the long trial, Judge Munger ruled in favor of the prosecution.

While most of the trial featured far more tedium and repetition than drama, counsel on both sides employed some of their deepest passion and eloquence in their closing arguments to the jury. Crites, who had served for many years as both a land agent and a state judge in northwestern Nebraska during the free range era, was particularly forceful in his arguments for the defense, telling the jury that the cattlemen's actions were completely legitimate and wholly consistent with longtime practice in the area:

> Richards and Comstock wanted good men to settle up there; they wanted to use the land for grazing purposes; and if the homesteaders were willing to allow this use of the land that was their affair and not the affair of the government. . . . The land locating business is as legitimate a business as the grocery business or the law. It is to make money, just as is any other business. On the question of the lease of the lands, the entrymen had a perfect right to lease them. They could not sell the land [until they obtained clear title] but they could do anything else they wanted to do with it.[47]

Crites also bitterly denounced the tactics employed by the government agents who had investigated the case:

> I never saw a greater wrong perpetrated on innocent men. . . . These old soldier witnesses were scared to death by special agents. . . . Some of [them] were so weak and feeble they had to be assisted to the witness stand. It was a travesty of justice to have these men testify. These government agents, spies, detectives, and informers went to [one of the witnesses] when he was on the brink of the grave, to compel him by threats to give up correspondence, when he was physically unable to object.[48]

Brome followed Crites with more attacks on the government's investigators, asserting that "each of those government detectives has his hand in the public treasury and wants to keep it there."[49] He went on to compare the prosecution of the Spade ranchers to the Salem witchcraft trials of the late 1600s and implored the jury to remain untouched by the public clamor over the case and to be guided solely by the actual evidence rather than by prejudice and hysteria. Finally

Richard Hall weighed in with a powerful assault on the very nature of the "conspiracy" charges, arguing:

Conspiracy means cunning, secret methods of accomplishing an unlawful thing, and it is so hard to prove it. And as in the case at bar, it [often] cannot be proved at all. Conspiracy is simply a dragnet, but then after all you cannot find a man guilty on probabilities. In all of this great array of witnesses, there was not one—not a single one—to testify that there was any illegal agreement. . . . When you get to the question of conspiracy you will find that there is absolutely nothing to base that charge upon. . . . [The government is] merely relying upon what you may conjecture. They are leaving it solely to your speculation.[50]

In his closing argument for the prosecution, Rush strongly denied that the Spade men had been singled out for prosecution because of their wealth or prominence, saying, "Counsel for the defense have sought to influence this jury with the belief that this prosecution of a crime by these defendants is [a matter of] personal malice on the part of the government attorneys. . . . The government has no interest in this case other than the punishment of the guilty. . . . The evidence speaks for itself. You have heard it as well as I or counsel for the defense."[51] Likewise, Rush emphatically denied the defense claims that witnesses had been coerced and intimidated, pointing out to the jury: "There has not been the slightest particle of evidence to substantiate this baseless charge. On the other hand every witness who told that he had been visited by a special agent said all the agent asked him to do was tell the truth."[52]

The case went to the jury on the afternoon of December 20, almost one year to the day after former district attorney Baxter had been fired in the aftermath of the fencing case. Despite the massive amount of evidence presented and the complexity of the legal issues involved, which Judge Munger sought to explain to the jurors in a charge that took some forty-five minutes to read, it took just two hours for the panel to reach its verdict.[53] Richards, Comstock, Jameson, and Triplett were each found guilty on thirty-six counts of the indictment. (Munger had directed a verdict of not guilty for the fifth defendant, Spade attorney Walcott.) Sentencing was deferred while defense counsel prepared and filed a motion for a new trial. That motion was heard and over-ruled on March 18, at which time Munger imposed his sentences on the four defendants. Richards and Comstock took the heaviest hit, as each was fined $1,500 and sentenced to serve one year in the Douglas County jail. Jameson and Triplett received $500 fines and eight months in jail. All four were released on bond during their ensuing appeals.

For the better part of the next four years, the Spade men doggedly pursued the reversal of their convictions on appeal. In December 1909 the same Eighth Circuit panel that had upheld Reverend Ware's conviction did likewise in the *Spade* case, by the same 2–1 vote.[54] In his dissenting opinion, Judge John Philips was even more vehement than he had been in *Ware*, asserting that Richards and the other defendants had been convicted for acts that "courts of authority had held to be permissible." Echoing the arguments that the Spade attorneys had been making throughout the litigation (and which defenders of the cattlemen's position have clung to ever since), Philips contended that it was perfectly permissible for the ranchers to have loaned money to Kinkaiders to assist them in making their claims and to then lease the land from the homesteaders as a means of repaying those loans. Moreover, he wrote, the defendants had "violated no law" merely by asking for a right of first refusal to purchase the land once the home-steader acquired full title. Combining that legal reasoning with the many erroneous evidentiary rulings and misguided jury instructions that he believed Munger had issued during the trial, Philips concluded that the Spade defendants "were not accorded the fair and impartial trial guaranteed them by the Constitution, and, therefore, the judg-ment should be reversed."[55]

Imprisonment and Demise

Whatever the merits of Philips's views, his was a lonely judicial voice, and when the U.S. Supreme Court denied the ranchers' petition for certiorari on October 17, 1910, there was nothing left for the Spade defendants to do but to turn themselves in to face their long-delayed prison sentence. And therein lies a final intriguing—and often misunderstood—piece of this colorful chapter in the court's history. Munger's 1907 sentencing order had specified that the cattlemen were to be imprisoned in the Douglas County jail. When the four defendants were finally set to begin serving their time in late 1910, however, they asked the government to permit them to be confined in a jail closer to their homes in northwestern Nebraska. U.S. Attorney General George Wickersham agreed to the request, and after consideration of many possible destinations, the defendants were transferred to the Adams County jail in Hastings to serve their sentences. Not surprisingly, the notion of convicted criminals being able to "shop around" for the most favorable places to be confined provided ample fodder for newspapers throughout the state to publish derisive stories about what appeared to be continuing preferential treatment for the wealthy cattle barons. Once the ranchers arrived in Hastings, the media furor intensified, as stories circulated about the supposedly luxurious special accommodations for the men in what became known as the "millionaire flats" in the Adams County jail. Typical of the coverage was a story in the *North Platte Semi-Weekly Tribune* reporting that the Hastings jail had been "thoroughly renovated and specially furnished" for the comfort of the wealthy prisoners, whose meals would be prepared and delivered "steaming hot to their cells" by a specially retained "Jap chef."[56] Other reported refinements included oriental rugs, elaborate light fixtures, and luxurious new mattresses and bed linens.

Just as in the aftermath of the "six-hour sentence" five years earlier, the press reports of opulent living conditions drew the attention of government officials. On December 7 new Nebraska district attorney Frank Howell, accompanied by a special envoy from Attorney General Wickersham's office, visited the Hastings jail to investigate the newspaper accounts. In his ensuing report to both the attorney general and Judge Munger, Howell concluded that the press reports of special accommodations for the cattlemen were "wholly unfounded." Rather, he found that they were "receiving exactly the same treatment as other prisoners" in the Hastings facility.[57] Over time, the rabid press coverage gradually dissipated, but the legend of the luxurious amenities supposedly enjoyed by Richards and Comstock during their incarceration never fully died, and it flared up once again the following summer, when Richards began to experience serious medical problems.

Richards had long suffered from a variety of infirmities, and his imprisonment apparently exacerbated his condition. By June 1911 he had become so incapacitated by pain and weakness that he asked to be allowed to seek treatment at the Mayo Brothers' clinic in Rochester, Minnesota, for what was believed to be an acute attack of gallstones. Government officials agreed to the request, and when the press learned that the famed cattleman had been transferred out of Nebraska, another flurry of sarcastic news stories emerged, breathlessly reporting that he was once again enjoying "special treatment" as he whiled away "the hot summer days among the cool pines" of a "resort" in Minnesota.[58] Richards underwent two operations for gallstones at the Mayo facility, which were apparently only partially successful. Federal marshals returned him to the Hastings jail on August 10, where his condition continued to deteriorate over the ensuing weeks. He died on September 4, 1911, with the official cause of death recorded as "ileitis: inflammation of the ileum, or lower section of the small intestine."[59] Much of the press coverage of Richards's death was relatively restrained, and some was even sympathetic, but vestiges of the old sneering accusations of favoritism—and backhanded swipes at the court's treatment of the famous rancher—remained. Perhaps most notably, the *New York Times* report on Richards's death illustrated the lingering and often outrageous inaccuracies that continued to swirl, as the paper referred to the "palatial quarters" and "frequent banquets" that Richards and his partners had enjoyed during their imprisonment at Hastings. The *Times* also resurrected the furor over Judge Munger's notorious six-hour sentence imposed on Richards and Comstock in 1905, erroneously describing it as a "two-hour" sentence and perpetuating some of the most common historical perceptions of the event with references to a "fine banquet with large quantities of wine for everyone in the house" hosted by Richards at the Omaha Club that evening.[60]

While there would be many more prosecutions of cattlemen for homestead fraud and illegal fencing during the ensuing years, the convictions of the Spade men along with Richards's subsequent death in prison are generally perceived as the seminal events that signaled the end of the free range era in western Nebraska. In the aftermath of Richards's death, Comstock received a commutation of the remaining weeks of his sentence from President William Howard Taft in order to arrange and attend the funeral of his friend and partner. He then attempted to rebuild the now-struggling Spade operation. But Comstock himself died of cancer in 1916, and as the fraudulent homestead entries that had fueled the rise of the cattle kingdoms were eliminated and Kinkaiders claimed much of the ranch's former grazing territory, the Spade's fortunes continued to decline. In 1923 banks foreclosed on what was left of the company's landholdings and other assets, and the original Spade ranch was gone.

As the iconic free range era in American western history came to a close, once again the Nebraska district court had played a central role in both shaping and reflecting the history of its region. Moreover, just as the prosecutions of the cattle barons marked an important transitional period in western history, the court was undergoing a major transition in its own existence as well. The era of the "two Munger" court was about to begin.

1. Judge Elmer S. Dundy. U.S. District Court, District of Nebraska, Judicial Archive.

2. Judge William D. McHugh. U.S. District Court, District of Nebraska, Judicial Archive.

3. Judge William H. Munger. U.S. District Court, District of Nebraska, Judicial Archive.

FEDERAL BLDG., AND POST OFFICE, OMAHA, NEB.   6550

4. Postcard image of the Omaha Post Office and Federal Building at 16th and Capitol, which served as the U.S. District Courthouse during most of the period covered in this volume. Nebraska State Historical Society, RG2341.PH-1513.

Judge Munger.   Judge Van Devanter.

DIETRICH GOES FREE AND DRIGGS IS CONVICTED

5. Judge Munger and future Supreme Court justice Willis Van Devanter at the time of the Dietrich trial and acquittal. *Omaha World-Herald,* January 8, 1904.

6. Staged photo of masked farmers cutting portions of the Brighton Ranch
fence line along the South Loup River in Custer County, 1885. Nebraska State
Historical Society, Solomon Butcher collection, RG2608.PH-2430.

7. Cartoon depicting Theodore Roosevelt's reaction to Munger's sentencing of Richards and Comstock. *Omaha World-Herald*, December 20, 1905.

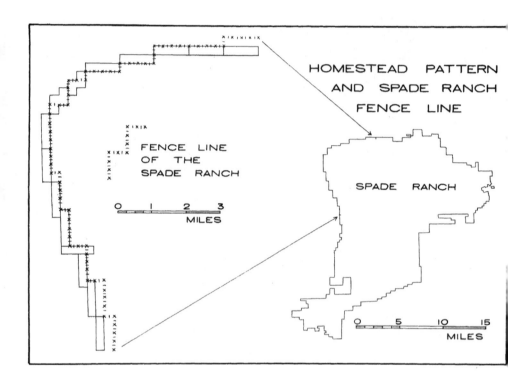

8. Map depicting fraudulent homestead patterns and Spade Ranch line. From C. Barron McIntosh, "Patterns from Land Alienation Maps," *Annals of the Association of American Geographers* 66, no. 4 (December 1976): 570–82, reprinted by permission of the Association of American Geographers.

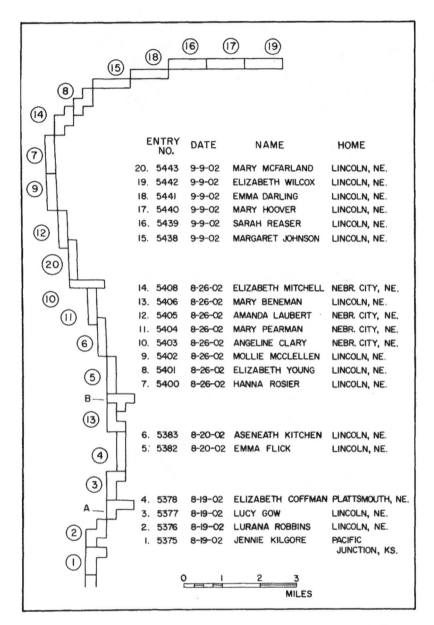

ENTRY NO.	DATE	NAME	HOME
20. 5443	9-9-02	MARY MCFARLAND	LINCOLN, NE.
19. 5442	9-9-02	ELIZABETH WILCOX	LINCOLN, NE.
18. 5441	9-9-02	EMMA DARLING	LINCOLN, NE.
17. 5440	9-9-02	MARY HOOVER	LINCOLN, NE.
16. 5439	9-9-02	SARAH REASER	LINCOLN, NE.
15. 5438	9-9-02	MARGARET JOHNSON	LINCOLN, NE.
14. 5408	8-26-02	ELIZABETH MITCHELL	NEBR. CITY, NE.
13. 5406	8-26-02	MARY BENEMAN	LINCOLN, NE.
12. 5405	8-26-02	AMANDA LAUBERT	NEBR. CITY, NE.
11. 5404	8-26-02	MARY PEARMAN	NEBR. CITY, NE.
10. 5403	8-26-02	ANGELINE CLARY	NEBR. CITY, NE.
9. 5402	8-26-02	MOLLIE MCCLELLEN	LINCOLN, NE.
8. 5401	8-26-02	ELIZABETH YOUNG	LINCOLN, NE.
7. 5400	8-26-02	HANNA ROSIER	LINCOLN, NE.
6. 5383	8-20-02	ASENEATH KITCHEN	LINCOLN, NE.
5. 5382	8-20-02	EMMA FLICK	LINCOLN, NE.
4. 5378	8-19-02	ELIZABETH COFFMAN	PLATTSMOUTH, NE.
3. 5377	8-19-02	LUCY GOW	LINCOLN, NE.
2. 5376	8-19-02	LURANA ROBBINS	LINCOLN, NE.
1. 5375	8-19-02	JENNIE KILGORE	PACIFIC JUNCTION, KS.

0 1 2 3
MILES

9. Map depicting sequential "widow" homestead filings. From C. Barron McIntosh, "Patterns from Land Alienation Maps," *Annals of the Association of American Geographers* 66, no. 4 (December 1976): 570–82, reprinted by permission of the Association of American Geographers.

10. Judge Thomas C. Munger. U.S. District Court, District of Nebraska, Judicial Archive, http://www.ned.uscourts.gov/public/judicial-archive/munger-t-c.

A Tale of Woe and a Tale of Wealth.

11. Cartoon lampooning the railroads' claims of poverty. *Omaha World-Herald,* September 4, 1907.

12. Cartoon commenting on the railroads' reaction to a proposed two-cent fare law. *Omaha World-Herald,* September 10, 1907.

13. Cartoon lamenting the federal court's issuance of injunctions to shelter railroads from state regulation. *Omaha World-Herald*, September 12, 1907.

14. *Omaha World-Herald* feature story on Woodrough at the time of his appointment, presaging what would prove to be the paper's long-term infatuation with the judge. *Omaha World-Herald*, March 26, 1916.

15. Judge Joseph W. Woodrough. U.S. District Court, District of Nebraska, Judicial Archive, http://www.ned.uscourts.gov/public/judicial-archive /woodrough-j-w.

PROCLAMATION

HEADQUARTERS

NEBRASKA NATIONAL GUARD

Nebraska City, Jan. 28, 1922.

Four Mile precinct, in Otoe county, Nebraska, including the city of Nebraska City and all of its subdivisions, having been declared by the Governor, of the state of Nebraska to be in a state of insurrection and rebellion, and the military forces of the state having been ordered by the Governor and Commander-in-Chief to assume charge and restore order in said Four Mile precinct and city of Nebraska City and all of its subdivisions, the commanding officer of said military forces hereby proclaims the following rules and regulations which will be in force until further orders:

1. All pool halls, whether run in connection with other business or not, and all soft drink parlors, with card table accomodations, will immediately close and remain closed until further orders.

2. All persons in the possession of arms, equipment and munitions of war are required to surrender the same on or before Sunday, January 29, 1922, at six o'clock, p. m. to the commanding officer of the military forces, taking receipt for the same at the Court House.

3. All persons who have heretofore given aid to or otherwise supported the lawlessness hitherto existing in the above named district who shall return to peaceful occupations, holding no communication of any kind with the lawless persons or persons, will not be disturbed.

4. All rights of property of whatever kind will be held inviolate and will not be disturbed, except as the exigencies of the public welfare may necessitate, by direct command of the commanding officer of the district.

5. All shops and places, except as heretofore provided, will be kept open as usual in times of peace, and all persons are enjoined to continue their customary peaceful occupation.

6. Excepting as herein provided or where the existence of martial law implies the contrary the usual laws of the community will be in force; crimes will be subject to proper authority; civil causes will await the ordinary tribunals. Causes in violation of military proclamations will be tried by a military court.

7. No publication, either by newspaper, pamphlet, hand bill or otherwise, reflecting in any way upon the United States or the state of Nebraska or their officers, or tending to influence the public mind against the United States or the State of Nebraska or their officers, and no article commenting in any way on the work or action of the military authorities will be permitted.

8. All assemblages in the streets, either by day or night, are prohibited.

9. All persons found on the streets who appear to be habitually idle and without visible means of support, will be placed under arrest.

10. While it is the desire of the authorities to exercise the powers of martial law mildly, it must not be supposed that they will not be vigorously and firmly enforced as occasion arises.

By Command of

LT. COL. ROBERT G. DOUGLAS.

CAPT. VIRGIL J. HAGGART,
Adjutant Four Mile Precinct, Military District.

16. Martial law proclamation of Nebraska National Guard, January 28, 1922. *Nebraska Daily Press,* January 29, 1922.

PROCLAMATION

Whereas, Four Mile Precinct, in Otoe County, Nebraska, including the City of Nebraska City, Nebraska, and all of its subdivisions, has been declared and ordered by me, under and subject to martial law, and

Whereas, the National Guard of the State of Nebraska has been ordered to, and has assumed charge and control of said District, and

Whereas, a state of lawlessness, violence and disorder still exists and continues in said district now under martial law, and

Whereas, there have been infractions and violations of the laws of the state of Nebraska, and of the rules and regulations prescribed for said district, now under martial law, now

Therefore, I, Samuel R. McKelvie, Governor of the State of Nebraska, by virtue of my office, and of the authority vested in me by the Constitution and laws of the State of Nebraska, do hereby order, authorize and empower the Commanding Officer of said district of Four Mile Precinct, including the City of Nebraska City and all of its subdivisions, now under and subject to martial law to create and appoint a Military Commission, or Provost Court, or both, to take cognizance and jurisdiction of offenses against the public peace, and of violations of military rules and regulations, now in force, and as may be hereafter promulgated, for the preservation of law and order, and the public safety in said district; and also, to take cognizance and jurisdiction of such violations of the civil law and the ordinances in force in said district as the Commanding Officer in his discretion may prescribe, as necessary for the public safety and the restoration of law and order in said district; and such Commission and Provost Court shall have full power and authority to issue all necessary process for the conduct of its proceedings, with like powers to compel the attendance of witnesses therein, as are exercised by the civil courts of the State of Nebraska.

Given under my hand, and the great seal of the State of Nebraska, this 30th day of January, A. D., 1922.

SAMUEL R. M'KELVIE,
Governor of Nebraska.

Attest:
DARIUS M. AMSBERRY,
Secretary of State.

17. Proclamation of Governor Samuel McKelvie establishing military courts in Nebraska City. *Nebraska Daily Press*, January 30, 1922.

Dry's Son Sworn In

Edson Smith, son of Robert Smith, clerk of the district court and well-known dry leader, has a job as rum crusader. He was sworn in Friday as assistant United States district attorney, and is shown here looking at the evidence in his first case.

18. Federal prosecutor Edson Smith at the time of his appointment in 1929. *Omaha Evening Bee-News,* June 21, 1929.

Scene in Judge Woodrough's Courtroo m at the Federal Building Where the L iquor Syndicate Trial Is in Progress

Above is a general view of the south courtroom at the federal building as the liquor syndicate case started Monday afternoon, showing many of their 50 defendants and their attorneys. No. 1, arrow pointing to Tom Dennison; No. 2, E. K. Murray; No. 3, Frank Dinuzzo; No. 4, Johnny Ford, (behind hat); No- 5, Bill Maher; No. 6, Paul Sutton; No. 7, Carlyle Donahue; No. 8, Frank Calamia; No. 9, Joe Patach; No. 10, Roscoe Rawley; No. 11, Joe Hendricks; No. 12, Attorney Edward Shafton; No. 13, Attorney W. C. Dorsey; No. 14, Attorney Harold Cald-well; No. 15, Attorney Paul Garrotto; No. 16, Attorney Daniel J. Gross; No. 17, Attorney John O. Yeiser; No- 18, Attorney A. W. Jefferis; No. 19, Attorney John Berger; No. 20, Attorney John Wear; No. 21, Attorney Howard Marx. Standing in the center towards the rear is Deputy United States Marshal Earl Young, in charge of court attaches during the trial.

19. Judge Woodrough's courtroom during the Dennison conspiracy trial. *Omaha World-Herald,* October 11, 1932.

8

The "Two Munger" Court

I hope that the people in Nebraska will put you out of business as Supreme
Judge when your term expires.

—Citizen's letter to Judge Thomas C. Munger, September 12, 1907

A Second Judge Arrives

When William Munger took his seat on the Nebraska federal court
bench in 1897, there were more than 330 cases pending on the court's
docket.[1] Over the ensuing decade, that already staggering number
steadily increased. By 1906, more than 460 cases clogged the court's
calendar, stretching Munger's energies and physical capacity nearly
to the breaking point.[2] As delays in the handling and disposition of
cases produced an ever-mounting backlog, it became apparent to all
observers that help was needed. In response, the state's congressional
delegation, led by Senator Elmer Burkett and Representative George
Norris, launched an aggressive and unified effort to create a second
judicial seat for the Nebraska court. Citing the "pressure of business"
that had created a "serious demand for relief," Burkett guided a bill
through the Senate Judiciary Committee in 1906 designed to achieve
that result.[3] Meanwhile, Norris and Nebraska's five other congressmen were shepherding an identical bill through the House.[4] Those

combined efforts were rewarded with the passage of Public Law 59-133, signed into law by President Theodore Roosevelt on February 27, 1907.

The law created an additional judicial seat for the Nebraska district court and authorized the new appointee to "possess the same powers, perform the same duties, and receive the same salary as the present judge of said district." The legislation also made key changes in the administrative operations of the newly expanded court. Most notably, the Nebraska court—while remaining a single district—would be divided into eight geographic units designated as the Omaha, Norfolk, Grand Island, North Platte, Chadron, Lincoln, Hastings, and McCook divisions. Generally, for purposes of both civil and criminal jurisdiction as well as the selection of trial court juries, the divisional structure would dictate the location where any particular case would be processed and tried, while grand juries would continue to sit only in the Omaha and Lincoln divisions of the court.[5]

Naturally, the selection of a nominee to the new second seat drew substantial interest within the state's legal and political community. Indeed, a good deal of posturing and speculation was already under way well before the position was formally authorized. Names of more than a dozen prominent Nebraska lawyers and political figures circulated on the rumor mill, including attorney Frank Hall of Omaha, Dean Roscoe Pound of the University of Nebraska Law School, and Congressman Norris himself, who had previous judicial experience as a state district judge. While the speculative candidates carried varying degrees of support throughout the state, eventually a loose consensus seemed to emerge around a relatively obscure Lincoln attorney named Thomas C. Munger. Although he had a solid record of success as a practicing lawyer in and around Lincoln and an unblemished reputation for integrity, Munger's most obvious qualification for the job was his close affiliation with Senator Burkett, having served as the manager of Burkett's recent successful campaign for appointment to the Senate seat. It quickly became apparent that, as far as Burkett was concerned, Munger was the man for the job, and that view was ultimately supported by other groups and individuals who endorsed Munger, including many district court judges across the state and the bar associations of Kearney, Lincoln, Dodge, and Lancaster Counties. But a number of groups and individuals continued to press for other candidates. Representatives of the Nebraska State Bar Association made a rather tepid effort to derail the Munger nomination, sending letters to the Nebraska congressional delegation and to U.S. Attorney General Charles Bonaparte complaining that Munger did not possess the requisite experience and gravitas for such an important position and pointing out that he had not even been admitted to practice in the federal circuit courts.[6]

But Burkett would not be denied. Eager to win approval of Munger's nomination before the 59th Congress adjourned on March 4, he convened a meeting of the entire Nebraska congressional delegation on the morning of February 27. While no formal transcript of that closed-door meeting exists, newspaper reports indicated that some fifteen ballots were taken before Munger finally won the support of the majority of the Nebraska caucus.[7] Immediately following that meeting, Burkett went to the White House to notify the president, and by then any remaining resistance to Munger's appointment had withered away, replaced by completely unified and ostensibly enthusiastic support for the nominee. Burkett brought the president a bundle of letters and telegrams from Nebraska constituencies enthusiastically endorsing Munger. Roosevelt was duly impressed, saying, "It is seldom that a candidate for high office is brought before me for appointment so universally endorsed as Munger. Therefore, I will take great pleasure in appointing him."[8]

Munger received word of his nomination on the evening of February 27 and promptly left Nebraska for Washington. Several days later, he enjoyed a brief but memorable meeting with the president. As Munger later recalled, he found the president to be "very human, working in his office, shirt sleeves rolled." Roosevelt reiterated his satisfaction with Munger's selection, telling him, "You look and talk to me like a man who will make a good judge."[9] Within days of his formal nomination, Munger's appointment was confirmed by the Senate, and on March 13, 1907, he took the oath of office and embarked upon his new duties. For the next eight years, Nebraska would have a "two Munger" court.[10]

Whatever doubts his political rivals may have harbored about Munger's qualifications, by any objective standards his background and credentials seemed entirely acceptable for the position. Born in 1861, the new Judge Munger grew up in rural Fletcher, Ohio, the elder of two sons of Mary and Samuel Munger.[11] His father farmed and taught school and passed on to his son a love of nature that would be reflected in the judge's lifelong affinity for fishing, hunting, ornithology, golf, and other outdoor pursuits. His mother was a highly educated teacher, administrator, and social reform activist who became known for her decades of "effective and courageous temperance work."[12] Munger would later credit his mother and the devout Presbyterian environment that she created in the family home for instilling in him the self-discipline to refrain from using alcohol or tobacco throughout his long life. Many years later, Munger's grandson, billionaire businessman and philanthropist Charles Thomas Munger, a close friend and business partner of renowned Omaha investor Warren Buffett, would confirm his grandfather's unyielding personal rectitude. In an interview with Buffett biographer Alice Schroeder, Charlie remembered his grandfather as a stern but compassionate patriarch and an "iron disciplinarian" who "liked to lecture his relatives on the virtue of saving and the vices of gambling and saloons" and required his children to "read *Robinson Crusoe* to absorb the book's portrayal of the conquest of nature through discipline."[13]

In 1877 Munger and his family left Ohio for New Sharon, Iowa, where both of his parents accepted teaching positions. One year later, he graduated from the local high school and the family moved again, this time to Nebraska City, where his parents took positions as the principal and vice principal of the local high school. In Nebraska City, Munger attended Nebraska (now Peru State) College for two years and then enrolled at Iowa (now Grinnell) College for the fall 1881 semester. Although a lack of funds prevented Munger from completing his degree program at Grinnell, he did meet and begin a courtship there with Carrie A. Case from Cedar Rapids, Iowa, who would become his wife seven years later.

Munger worked for several summers as a railroad surveyor in South Dakota and Oregon before returning to Nebraska in 1883, where he began reading law under the tutelage of several attorneys in Nebraska City and Lincoln. In the fall he enrolled in Union College of Law in Chicago. He excelled in his coursework until a lack of funds once again necessitated his return to Nebraska, where he taught school and continued his legal studies under the sponsorship of attorney A. R. Talbot. In February 1885 Munger passed the Nebraska bar exam and opened his own office in Benkelman, Dundy County. Elected Dundy County attorney that fall, Munger served in that position for one year before moving to the larger market of Lincoln in the fall of 1886. He practiced with various attorneys until, in 1893, he settled into a stable and very successful partnership with John M. Stewart, which would continue until his appointment to the federal bench some fourteen years later.

Throughout these early years, Munger also emerged as an active participant in local and state politics, becoming a prominent figure within the progressive wing of the Republican Party. In 1894 he was elected to the Nebraska legislature, where he chaired the house judiciary committee and played a pivotal role in securing an appropriation earmarked for the building of the main library on the University of Nebraska's campus. After one term in the legislature, Munger was elected Lancaster County attorney. During his four years in that position, he gained a reputation as a reform-minded prosecutor who placed particular emphasis on rooting out and destroying gambling dens and other pockets of vice and corruption that permeated the capital city around the turn of the century. As one Republican newspaper admiringly reported at the time of Munger's judicial appointment: "One of the things accomplished during his term was the breaking up of public gambling, which had up to that time been common in the city of Lincoln. A grand jury was called and many indictments against the gamblers returned. Two were sentenced to the penitentiary; others were given long jail sentences, and the rest driven from the city. The old public resorts of gambling were closed, and have never since been opened."[14]After one term as county prosecutor, Munger returned to his private practice but remained active in Republican political affairs, culminating in his management of Elmer Burkett's successful campaign for appointment to the U.S. Senate in 1905.

By the time he assumed the new second seat on the Nebraska federal bench, Tom Munger had been practicing law in eastern Nebraska for more than twenty years and had been elected to public office three times. He was forty-six, a respected if relatively low-profile figure in the state's legal community, and he enjoyed a strong political relationship with the man who would be best positioned to influence the appointment of the new Nebraska judge. Though both Munger and Burkett sought to disavow any hint of political favoritism in the senator's support for his friend's nomination, the whispers about Munger as "Burkett's judge" would reverberate—especially in partisan Democratic circles—for many years. In fact, a slip of the tongue by Burkett himself at a Memorial Day event in 1910 provided a humorous reminder of that ongoing perception. According to press accounts, the senator was delivering a speech in which he gently chided the federal courts for failing to "keep abreast with the times" in their constitutional interpretations. Because Judge Munger was present, Burkett turned to him and quipped that he was offering his critique "with due deference to my judge." When some members of the crowd began to laugh at the unintended insinuation embedded in his choice of words, Burkett realized his mistake and amended his phrasing to "With due deference to my friend, the judge" and then proceeded with his speech. The reporter pointedly noted that "Judge Munger did not smile when the slip was made."[15] Despite the lingering innuendo reflected in Burkett's "my judge" gaffe, there can be little objective doubt that Munger was qualified, widely approved, and completely acceptable in the new position. And despite the inevitable controversies that his rulings would occasionally produce, he would amply prove his suitability for the job over the next thirty-five years.

The New Munger Settles In

With Tom Munger officially on the job, the two judges jointly adopted and announced significant new procedural rules for the division and administration of the court's business. Utilizing the newly codified geographic regional divisions of the state, they declared that all new judicial matters arising in the Lincoln, Hastings, Grand Island, and McCook divisions would be presented to Tom Munger and heard primarily in Lincoln, while cases arising in the Omaha, Norfolk, Chadron, and North Platte divisions would be handled by William Munger, operating out of Omaha. The matter of dividing up the court's *existing* caseload was a more ambiguous issue, however. Ultimately—and as the statute itself provided—it fell to the two judges to "agree between themselves" on how those cases would be handled. Fortunately, they proved willing and able to sort out those potentially thorny particulars without any apparent disagreement or rancor. Indeed, surviving correspondence from Tom Munger's files suggests that the two men quickly developed a warm and effective relationship.[16] For example, in an early exchange of brief notes, they agreed on the manner in which they would interpret and apply a recent Supreme Court procedural decision related to the adjournment of court sessions. In a reflection of their shared affinity for hunting, Tom Munger told his senior colleague that he had hesitated to bother him about the matter earlier, since he was "thinking that you would be shooting ducks until the end of the week."[17] Such references to hunting and fishing were commonplace in the judges' correspondence throughout their eight years together on the federal bench, as were good-natured commiserations over such topics as tediously complex litigation, personal health issues, and the oppressive summer heat and humidity. In a February 1909 letter to his colleague, Tom touched on several of those topics, describing recent cases he had handled by saying, "I have about reached the conclusion that I would rather have an operation for gall stones than to have to go through those cases again, but would prefer the cases to typhoid fever, such as [circuit court clerk George] Thummel has."[18] Later that year, when he was assigned to sit as a visiting judge in Salt Lake City, he sought the advice of his more experienced colleague on the intricacies of government expense accounting: "Judge Sanborn says that it may be necessary for me to stay through April and May at Salt Lake. I am at a loss to know how much money to take with me. Do you make a certificate to the marshal for a portion of your expenses after you have incurred them, and then an additional certificate later on, or do you wait until the entire service is finished, and make one certificate?"[19]

Other items from Munger's files reflect the crush of administrative details that accompanied his appointment, from endless importuning by applicants for clerk, stenographer, bailiff, and messenger positions, to mundane requisitions for office supplies. In a very early indication of his personal integrity and sense of judicial propriety, Tom turned down a book of "franked" (prepaid) telegrams from Western Union, saying, "I thank you for your courtesy but as I view the matter I think it would be improper for me to accept or use them and I therefore return them to you."[20] Other bureaucratic frustrations that must have accompanied the establishment of the new judicial seat may be seen in an exchange of letters between the new judge and the U.S. attorney general's office early in Munger's tenure. A week after he was sworn in, Munger sent a detailed listing of items that he desired for his new office in Lincoln, including such basic necessities as a set of the *U.S. Reports,* federal *Digests, Statutes at Large, Attorney Generals' Opinions,* and even blank requisition forms for future minor supply requests.[21] The outfitting of the court's new divisional offices seemed to have become a particularly troublesome issue. In May he asked for permission to purchase bookcases to hold law books at the court's new divisional offices in McCook. Despite the seemingly innocuous nature of the request, the Department of Justice denied it. Explaining the decision with rationale that might most charitably be interpreted as a reflection of the Roosevelt administration's concern for efficient use of public resources, the acting attorney general told Munger that "the purchase of expensive cases for these reports is considered impracticable, and it is suggested that the deputy clerk of the court ascertain and advise the Department as to the cost of putting up such shelving as may be necessary."[22]

Munger's luck in obtaining resources for his offices did not improve. Just a few months after his bid for bookcases was denied, he received a letter from the assistant secretary of the Interior telling him that his request for a set of *U.S. Digests* could not be fulfilled because "the

Digest is now out of print and the plates were destroyed in the late San Francisco fire. It is therefore impossible to comply with your request."[23] The parsimony of his superiors in Washington, especially with respect to the need for enhanced "creature comforts" to mitigate the harshness of the judges' working conditions, seemed a matter of ongoing concern for the new judge. Even more than two years into his tenure, he rather wistfully queried his senior colleague on the best way to obtain a fan for his courtroom, writing, "I am interested in your statement that the government has provided you with an electric fan, and wish to inquire whether you obtained it through the Department of Justice, or through the Custodian of the building."[24]

As distracting as such administrative burdens may have been, the new judge's most pressing role, of course, was to be a jurist: to wade in and begin to relieve some of the backlog of cases that plagued the court's docket. For example, he took the bench just as his colleague was pronouncing sentence on Bartlett Richards, Will Comstock, and the other two leading defendants in the notorious Spade Ranch land fraud conspiracy case. (see chapter 7). But several additional indicted Spade defendants, led by former ranch manager Thomas M. Huntington, remained to be tried. In what must have been a great relief to the beleaguered William Munger, Tom immediately assumed responsibility for presiding over that second Spade trial, which commenced on April 8, less than a month after he had taken his seat on the bench. Because most of the factual background and legal issues were identical to those involved in the Richards and Comstock trial, the attorneys stipulated to the admission of most of the evidence presented in that previous trial, supplemented by the testimony of about a dozen new witnesses.[25] On April 18 Munger submitted the case to the jury, which quickly returned guilty verdicts against three of the defendants. No doubt well aware of the backlash that had attended his colleague's earlier handling of the cattlemen cases, Tom Munger pulled no punches in his sentencing. Despite defense attorneys' pleas for clemency on the basis of their clients' age and various medical ailments, Munger ordered two of the defendants to serve three months in jail and pay $1,000 fines, while the third man received the same fine but no jail time. In announcing the sentences, Munger stated that he intended to impose "both a punishment and a warning," adding that the defendants' professed ignorance of the illegality of their actions was no excuse.[26]

Although William Munger retained jurisdiction over Richards and Comstock while their appeals dragged on over the next several years, Tom Munger would handle most of the additional land fraud and "cattlemen vs. homesteader" cases that came to the court. For example, in October 1907 Munger was presiding over the trial of western Nebraska ranchers accused of securing fraudulent claims to government land when one of the defendants, G. T. H. Babcock, suffered a nervous seizure in the courtroom and was subsequently hospitalized.[27] Munger suspended the trial until a later court session, and Babcock and his fellow defendants were ultimately convicted and sentenced to short jail terms.[28]

In an even more dramatic case several years later, nine prominent western Nebraska ranchers, led by Perry A. Yeast, were indicted by the grand jury sitting in Omaha for crimes similar to those charged in the Richards and Comstock cases.[29] Indeed, the Yeast indictment alleged acts of harassment and intimidation against homesteaders that were even more brutal than the tactics for which the Spade defendants had been convicted. Yeast's gang was accused of destroying homesteaders' yokes and harnesses for their draft animals, tearing to shreds many of the settlers' tents and other rudimentary shelters, and even managing to arrange for a stubborn Kinkaider to be fraudulently committed to the local mental asylum until he agreed to give up his claim to prime land in the middle of the rancher's grazing operation. Munger presided over the trial of the Yeast defendants, but this time the case was tried in the court's new divisional office in North Platte. Perhaps not surprisingly, a local jury sympathetic to the ranchers' position quickly acquitted all the defendants, and the result produced virtually no reaction whatsoever back east in the Omaha or Lincoln papers.[30] As that example indicates, by the 1910s Nebraska's "open range" era was gradually fading into history, and public attention had shifted to other issues and concerns. But the turbulence produced by other progressive reforms of that period continued to ripple throughout the region and, as always, the court's operations continued to both reflect and shape many of those issues.

Continuing Railroad Controversies

Throughout the late nineteenth and early twentieth centuries, government regulation of railroads and other public transportation and communication enterprises remained hallmarks of the Progressive reform agenda. Nebraska's state government first entered the arena of railroad regulation in 1893 with the enactment of the Newberry Bill, a law that sought to reduce railroad shipping rates within the state by almost one-third, bringing them into rough parity with rates charged in neighboring Iowa.[31] Various railroads operating in the state joined forces to challenge the constitutionality of the legislation, arguing that it deprived them of their property rights without due process of law. Ultimately, the U.S. Supreme Court agreed, declaring in *Smyth v. Ames* (1895) that the Nebraska law did in fact impermissibly interfere with the railroads' constitutionally protected property interests.[32] Writing for the court, Justice David Brewer held that only regulation of freight rates that was "reasonable," as determined by a federal court on a case-by-case basis, could pass constitutional muster.

In many ways, no case better epitomizes the head-to-head conflict between established business interests and the Progressive reform agenda than *Smyth v. Ames.* Nor was it coincidental that the decision emerged out of Nebraska, because perhaps no state lay more squarely at the intersection of those two competing interests. That is, the state was not only one of the most significant points of origin for the agrarian protest movement that spawned the Populists and their Progressive successors. It also was home to one of the most influential corporate giants of the day, the Union Pacific Railroad. Not surprisingly, then, the battle over railroad regulation in Nebraska did not end with *Smyth v. Ames*; in some ways, it was only getting started. And the federal district court would soon be pulled back into the fray.

From 1903 through 1908, progressivism dominated Nebraska politics. Supported by Progressive Republican governors John Mickey and George Sheldon, the state legislature passed laws that regulated railroad freight rates, limited fares for passenger traffic, prohibited the traditional free railroad passes for state officials, and raised state fees, taxes, and surcharges on various aspects of the railroads' operations.[33] Perhaps even more notably, in 1906 the state constitution was amended so as to allow the creation of a permanent state railway commission authorized to oversee the setting of freight rates and investigate public complaints regarding railroad operations and services. Predictably, the railroads complained bitterly about all of those measures, and just as predictably, they would soon head to the courts for relief from what they perceived to be this unwarranted and unconstitutional legislative interference with their business interests. By the early summer of 1907, the local press had already begun to speculate on the impending drama. In a June 3 column, the reliably progressive *Omaha World-Herald* castigated the railroads for planning a judicial "war" against the state: "Judging from indications and events, it is to be war. The great railroad corporations are to resist, all along the line, the authority of the state to regulate their business, fix their taxes, and control their rates. . . . If it is war with Nebraska these gentry are seeking, we predict now they will get all they want of it."[34]

That anticipated legal warfare would soon commence. In early September a consortium of railroads led by the Union Pacific filed an application with Judge Tom Munger in Lincoln seeking a temporary restraining order and, after another hearing, a permanent injunction against the state railway commission to stop it from proceeding with hearings that would presumably lower the rates the railroads could charge for the transport of grain and other commodities within the state.

With that filing, the Nebraska district court once again found itself in the crucible, required to find a viable path through the treacherous eddies produced by the clash of big business interests and the perceived needs of the "common man." On September 10 Munger announced the most controversial decision of his young judicial career. He granted the railroads' request, issuing a temporary restraining order that prohibited the state commission from continuing its hearings or imposing reduced freight rates on the railroads, pending the results of a full evidentiary hearing that he scheduled for September 23, less than two weeks later.[35]

Despite the obvious fact that Munger's restraining order, by its own terms, would only be in effect for a short time, its "temporary" status did little to mute the immediate—and loud—public reaction to his decision. Not since the furor over the elder Munger's notorious "six-hour sentence" of cattle barons Bartlett Richards and Will Comstock two years earlier had the court been the subject of such widespread and strident criticism. Governor George Sheldon wasted no time in attacking Munger's order, announcing on September 11 that he would consider calling a special session of the legislature to ensure that the "expressed will of the people" would not be thwarted by federal intervention. Echoing the prediction made by the *World-Herald* several months earlier, Sheldon vowed that "inasmuch as the railroads have indicated a desire to fight the state by enjoining the state railroad commission from reducing rates, they will be accommodated with all the fighting that they want." He concluded his diatribe with a call for congressional action "to curtail the power of the federal court in granting injunctions of this character." Attorney General William Thompson was equally incensed at the railroads' rush for relief in the federal court, calling the tactic "a move for time to give [them] an opportunity to move the fall crop under the old schedule of rates."[36] Influential Progressive Republican state senator and future governor Chester Aldrich agreed with Thompson's assessment, declaring that Munger should have allowed the commission to proceed with its rate-setting hearings. Only after the commission acted, he argued, might the railroads have sought injunctive relief to try to prevent the new rates from taking effect.

As always, press reaction to the matter varied according to the particular paper's political orientation, but the clear majority of media commentary, led by the *Omaha World-Herald*, was caustically critical of Munger's order. In an editorial titled "Face to Face with the Issue," the paper denounced the new judge by name for having "tied the hands of Nebraska's state railway commission" at a particularly critical time of the year, allowing the railroads to transport the fall harvest under the existing rate structure:

> Should it finally be shown that the new rate the commission was to establish is a just rate and should have prevailed, it will be too late. Great and irreparable injury will have been done Nebraska farmers in the moving of this year's crops. And farmers who have paid the exorbitant rate will have Judge Munger to thank for it—with no recourse. . . . Meanwhile, it is clear that the railroads, which today are punishing Nebraska with execrable service, have declared and are inviting war. They have made the federal courts their shield, and behind that shield propose to fight state regulation in any form. . . . Nebraska, being called upon to meet this issue squarely, should meet it with such force and ability and determination as will attest that the west, as well as the south, is firmly wedded to local self-government.[37]

The *World-Herald* backed its words of outrage with illustrations. Three times during the two weeks following the entry of Munger's restraining order, the paper's front page featured a large editorial cartoon ridiculing the railroads or the federal court. The first, published on September 4, mocked the railroads for masquerading as a destitute pauper, beleaguered by excessive regulation, two-cent fares, and reduced freight rates, crying, "I'm almost ruined! Starvation and bankruptcy stare me in the face!" In a second frame, the artist then showed a satchel behind the railroad figure overflowing with an assortment of goodies that belied the railroads' claim of near-ruin, including "increased earnings, increased dividends, increased mileage, and increased capitalization." On September 10 another cartoon depicted a spiteful Union Pacific railcar speeding past a waiting passenger labeled "Nebraska," while a top-hatted figure at the back of the car thumbed his nose at the forlorn consumer, vindictively saying, "You *will* pass a 2 cent fare law, will you?" Two days later a third cartoon appeared. It depicted a small figure labeled "Federal Court" holding a huge umbrella labeled "Injunction" over the head of a fat-cat tycoon representing the railroads, protecting them from the deluge of "freight rate regulation" being poured upon them from a watering can labeled "Nebraska Railroad Commission." The collective message of the cartoons could not have been clearer: from the *World-Herald*'s perspective, Munger's order represented nothing less than a complete judicial sellout to the power and influence of big business.

The *World-Herald*'s attacks on the railroads and the federal court did not go completely unchallenged. In a September 13 editorial, the traditionally pro-railroad *Lincoln Journal* poked fun at its rival's histrionics over the temporary restraining order:

> With its usual genius for blundering the *Omaha World-Herald* is caricaturing and scolding the federal court for "issuing an injunction favoring the railroads." In truth, the injunction prayed for by the corporations was denied by Judge T. C. Munger. The restraining order which he did issue was of a temporary and harmless character, inasmuch as the commission can go ahead in the meantime with its preparations for promulgating new rates.[38]

Predictably, the *World-Herald* fired back, lambasting its Lincoln rival for its "talent for mendacity" and pointing out that the state's farmers, governor, and railway commissioners certainly did not view the restraining order as "harmless," since it allowed the railroads to continue to collect the old higher rates while the litigation proceeded. The paper concluded its outburst with another direct attack on Munger's judicial legitimacy:

> It is easy to see where the shoe pinches the *Journal*. This restraining order was issued by "Tom" Munger, formerly a Burlington machine politician at Lincoln but now, thanks to [Senator] Elmer Jacob Burkett and [Republican congressman] Norris Brown, a federal judge, with the power to set at naught the will of the people as crystallized into law. And the *Journal*, out of loyalty to Burkett and Brown, must defend Tom Munger, however ridiculous such defense makes the *Journal* appear.[39]

Similarly, at least one member of the general public expressed his opinion on the issue directly to the judge himself. In a letter dated

September 12 addressed to "Supreme Judge T. C. Munger," a live-stock and grain dealer in Marion, Nebraska, made his disgust with the judge's action—if not his understanding of the lifetime tenure of federal judges—quite apparent:

Dear Sir,

I see by the [news reports] that you have favored the Rail Road with an injunction against the Rail Road Commissioners. I do not think you had any business doing that as the Rail Road Commissioners are working for the interests of the people, you also are supposed to be working for the people. The rates in Nebraska are twice as high as in Iowa, and it is no more than right that they should be reduced, and I hope that the people in Nebraska will put you out of business as Supreme Judge when [your] term expires."[40]

Two weeks after the entry of the restraining order, both Mungers presided over a hearing in Omaha to determine whether an injunction should be issued to continue the court's temporary curtailment of the state commission's pending rate reductions. It was an intense, closely watched, and lengthy proceeding, extending well into the evening hours of September 23. For all the rhetoric spilled out by the attorneys, there was little that was novel in the issues that were framed or the arguments that were advanced. Relying on the precedent in *Smyth v. Ames* and similar cases, railroad attorney William D. McHugh (who ten years earlier had been denied Senate confirmation for the judicial seat now occupied by W. H. Munger; see chapter 5) argued that a state administrative agency could not be vested with the power to set rates that were confiscatory in nature, as the Nebraska railway commission was threatening to do. McHugh noted that the state had already lowered passenger rates by more than a third and freight rates by almost the same amount and that the railroads had complied with those restrictions. Further reductions, he argued, would clearly be punitive, excessive, and confiscatory in nature, and therefore must be enjoined. Arguing for the state, Attorney General Thompson and State Senator Aldrich contended that neither the common law of injunctive relief nor the *Smyth* precedent supported the result urged by the railroads. The time had not yet arrived for the court to rule on the "reasonableness" of any newly imposed freight rates, because Munger had restrained the commission from even beginning its proposed investigatory hearings that *might* have resulted in rate reductions. Since there were no new rates yet in place, they insisted, there was nothing that the court could lawfully enjoin. Besides, the fixing of freight rates was inherently within the discretion of the state legislature, and the recently enacted state constitutional amendment had lawfully vested that legislative discretion with the state railway commission.[41]

The two Mungers deliberated for several days. Then, on the evening of September 26, Tom issued the court's opinion, with his colleague concurring. He dissolved his existing restraining order and ruled that the commission could proceed with its hearings to set and impose new freight rates on the railroads operating within the state. The opinion directly rejected the railroads' challenge to the authority of the commission to act in a quasi-legislative capacity, holding:

> If the legislature of the state were hearing such a proposed reduction of rates it would not be contended that a court of equity might restrain the hearing or enactment of a statute embodying the conclusion reached. The railway commission of this state has been clothed with the authority to hear and determine these questions and to make orders embodying the result of their judgment. In this case the power of the railway commission to fix and regulate rates is plainly given by the constitutional amendment and the acts of the legislature.

Munger went on to specifically agree with the state's contention that the time for possible judicial intervention had not yet arrived:

> As yet the commissioners have done nothing. There is certainly much they may do in regulating charges within the state which will not be in conflict with the constitution of the United States. It is to be presumed that they will always act within the limits of

their constitutional authority. It will be time enough to consider what can be done to prevent it when they attempt to go beyond.[42]

Accordingly, Munger dissolved his two-week-old restraining order and denied the railroads' request for further injunctive relief.

Thus a final assessment of this round in the seemingly endless "railroad wars" of the late nineteenth and early twentieth centuries necessarily leads to two somewhat contradictory, but equally plausible, conclusions. On the one hand, it could be argued that a good deal of the furor arising out of Tom Munger's restraining order was overwrought—much ado about very little—inasmuch as the order remained in effect for only sixteen days. Although it is impossible to now determine how much of the state's 1907 grain harvest the railroads were able to move under the old higher rates during that short window of time, it seems safe to conclude that the financial benefit accruing to the railroads during those sixteen days was relatively small, especially since much of the year's crop was likely still unharvested when the restraining order was lifted. Yet if that is the case, then it seems equally reasonable to conclude that the brief but intense burst of public outrage that followed the issuance of the restraining order was perhaps not at all excessive or overstated. Rather, the furor may have had precisely the desired effect on the minds of the two Mungers. No one will ever be able to determine with certainty whether Tom Munger was swayed in any way by the harsh public backlash that descended upon him in the days following his September 10 restraining order. But as a new judge whose appointment to his position remained at least mildly tainted by the scent of political opportunism, it would only have been natural for him to wonder just how much worse the public reaction might be and how much more his credibility might be diminished, if he extended his order indefinitely. Whatever the case, the Nebraska court's decision to lift its restraining order and allow the state commission to proceed with its rate-reduction hearings reflected an incremental but significant step away from the laissez-faire, business-as-usual ideology that had characterized so much of the federal judiciary's response to progressive efforts to regulate big business during the late nineteenth century. To be sure, *Smyth v. Ames* remained the law of the land, but the judicial pendulum was beginning to swing in the opposite direction—toward a greater judicial tolerance for increased governmental intrusion into business practices.

The Great "Mud Cut" Train Robbery

In the aftermath of the injunction litigation, the freight rate controversies generally faded into the more obscure realm of legislative wrangling between the railroads and the state railway commission. Then a dramatically different type of railroad case arose that would once again put Tom Munger squarely into the public spotlight. Late in the evening of Saturday, May 22, 1909, the Union Pacific's Overland Limited arrived in Fremont, Nebraska, about twenty-five miles northwest of Omaha.[43] The train was one of the most prominent of its era, carrying more than eighty passengers on its route between San Francisco and Chicago. Even more notably, the train regularly included a government-owned railcar formally designated as the "Ogden and Omaha Railroad Post Office," which carried a large quantity of U.S. mail, typically accompanied by a retinue of mail clerks who traveled along for administrative and security purposes. During the train's brief stop in Fremont, several men quietly slipped onto the tender car immediately behind the engine and hid themselves. As the train approached the outskirts of Omaha some thirty minutes later, the men emerged from hiding and scrambled into the cab of the locomotive. Masked by bandanas and wielding guns, they forced the engineer to stop the train at a point just west of 42nd Street where the rail line cut through a deep embankment (the location was referred to locally as the "mud cut"). Once the train was halted, the bandits turned their attention to the mail car. They demanded entry, but when the clerks inside refused, the bandits shot through a window in the metal door and forced their way in. Tossing seven large bags of mail off the train, they ordered several of the clerks to haul the bags about one hundred yards down the line, at which point they released the men to return to the train. The robbers then took off into the darkness with their loot while the train proceeded to its scheduled stop in South Omaha, where the engineer and mail clerks promptly reported the crime to the police and to railroad officials.

Predictably, the bold crime became an instant news sensation. The next day's *Omaha World-Herald* featured a front-page story with a banner headline blaring "Overland Limited Held Up by Four Masked Bandits." While the facts surrounding the crime were still quite sketchy and would be reported (in the diplomatically accurate words of one historian) "haphazardly" in the local press over the ensuing months, it was clear from the outset that both the railroad and the government were determined to catch the criminals and bring them to a harsh justice.[44] Though it was ultimately determined that only about $700 (roughly $18,000 in 2016 value) had been stolen, the Union Pacific immediately announced a reward of $5,000 per suspect for information leading to the apprehension and conviction of the robbers, and shortly thereafter the U.S. government threw an additional $5,000 into the reward pot. Meanwhile, a vast array of law enforcement officials, including Omaha police, railroad investigators, the Douglas County sheriff's office, postal inspectors, and private Pinkerton detectives hired by the Union Pacific, began to build a case against five suspects, while the local newspapers continued the daily drumbeat of feverish and often speculative coverage of the story. On May 27 authorities arrested three men—Fred Torgensen, Frank Grigware, and Donald Woods—on suspicion of their involvement in the robbery, and two weeks later a federal grand jury in Omaha indicted those three plus two others, Jack Shelton and an unidentified "John Doe" who was later determined to be William Matthews.[45] Because the elder Munger, who normally presided over cases arising in the Omaha division, was scheduled to sit temporarily on the Eighth Circuit court of appeals in Denver that fall, Tom Munger took control of the case and presided over the trial of the accused bandits, which ultimately commenced on October 25.[46]

During the five months of investigation leading up to the trial, law enforcement officials and prosecutors amassed a sizable body of both direct and circumstantial evidence against the five men. By most accounts, the case against several of the defendants was strong, while the evidence against others—most notably Grigware, according to at least one detailed analysis—amounted to little more than guilt by association.[47] Defense attorneys filed several motions seeking separate trials for their clients, but Munger overruled all of those, ensuring that the five men would stand trial together for the robbery.

Naturally, the trial drew intense press coverage, with daily front-page stories in most local and regional newspapers throughout its two-and-a-half-week duration. The scene surrounding the courthouse was described as a "party atmosphere," and news accounts indicated that Munger frequently had to demand order inside the courtroom itself.[48] U.S. District Attorney Charles A. Goss called more than eighty witnesses to testify for the prosecution in what would prove to be the last major trial of his term as federal prosecutor. (Goss stepped down from the post at the end of 1909 and served as chief justice of the Nebraska Supreme Court from 1927 to 1938.) By most accounts, Munger allowed into the record an inordinate amount of questionable testimony from alleged "eyewitnesses" who claimed to be able to recognize the defendants as the men who had robbed the train, despite the fact that the robbery had occurred in almost complete darkness and all the bandits had been masked. For example, one of the train engineers identified Grigware as one of the bandits solely on the basis of his "stature and carriage," while a mail clerk positively identified the same defendant as one of the outlaws because of "his build" and because he claimed to recognize Grigware's voice, despite his acknowledgment that the man had "not talked much" during the robbery. Moreover, there remained a good deal of uncertainty and conflict among the witnesses on many other critical issues, including even the fundamental question of how many men had taken part in the robbery. Some claimed four, as originally reported, while others now testified that five men had taken part, with at least one witness speculating that a fifth culprit had "probably" been necessary to man the signal fire that the gang used as a marker for the spot where they intended to stop the train. Despite frequent objections from defense counsel John MacFarland, an Omaha attorney appointed by the court to represent four of the defendants, Munger routinely admitted such testimony. At another point in the trial, Goss called to the stand a gun dealer from Utah who testified that he had sold a gun to the defendants at some time before the robbery. He had no invoice for the sale, nor did he know the gun's serial number, nor was there any evidence to suggest that the alleged gun had any connection whatsoever to the Omaha robbery. MacFarland vigorously objected to the testimony as wholly irrelevant and unreliable, but Munger overruled him once again, admonishing him to restrain his temper or risk a contempt charge.[49]

If the daily spectacle inside the courtroom was not dramatic enough, some of the accused men upped the ante considerably on the night before the last day of the trial. Using tools that had apparently been smuggled into the jail by unknown accomplices, one of the men sawed a hole through the roof of his cell in a futile attempt to escape. Additional saws were later discovered in the cells of some of the other defendants. Though authorities purportedly tried to suppress any news of the attempted escape, reports quickly leaked into the papers, adding even greater weight to the presumption of guilt that had seemed to permeate the trial from the outset.[50] The attempted escape also generated increased tensions over officials' ability to secure the prisoners, as rumors about friends and associates of the defendants lurking in the city made their way into the newspapers.[51]

The jury began its deliberations at about 5:00 p.m. on November 11. Though they had listened to thirteen days of testimony from more than ninety witnesses, the twelve men took less than an hour and a half to reach a verdict: all five men were found guilty as charged.[52] Defense counsel filed motions for a new trial, which Munger overruled, and on November 18 the judge sentenced all five to life imprisonment at Leavenworth Federal Penitentiary in Kansas. The very next day, they were placed on board a prison train for the 160-mile journey south to Leavenworth.[53]

If the story of the Mud Cut robbery had simply ended there, it would remain little more than a colorful but otherwise brief and unexceptional episode in the court's history. But the Mud Cut robbery story most certainly did not end with the convictions and imprisonment of the five accused bandits. Rather, the trial spawned continuing controversies that were in many ways even more intriguing than the original robbery itself. Those "aftermath" disputes evolved into lengthy and tawdry squabbles over reward money, a daring prison break by one of the convicts, a massive and decades-long international manhunt that ultimately sparked tension between the governments of the United States and Canada, and perhaps most significantly, continuing questions about the quality of justice dispensed by the Nebraska district court—questions that would ultimately make their way all the way to the White House.

Almost from the moment that the Union Pacific and the government had offered the rewards totaling $30,000 for information leading to the apprehension and convictions of the robbers, a throng of would-be claimants began jockeying for position in the race to claim the money. The competition was intense. In fact, just hours after the first of the suspects had been captured, a South Omaha policemen was fired after he assaulted his commander with a nightstick in a dispute over who deserved more credit for the arrests and thus was most deserving of the accompanying reward.[54] As the investigation continued and additional suspects were rounded up, many others claimants entered the contest, including six South Omaha schoolboys who had discovered the stolen mailbags, guns, and other evidence of the robbery near their school playground. So too, the students' principal filed a reward claim, on the grounds that she had reported the boys' discovery to police and had later testified at trial that she had seen the men in the area in the days following the robbery. Over the ensuing months and years, more than thirty additional people claimed entitlement to some or all of the reward fund, and ultimately the task of sorting out and resolving those competing claims fell squarely into Judge Munger's lap.

On November 18, just one week after the trial ended, the families of the six schoolboys launched the opening salvo in what the *Omaha World-Herald* accurately predicted would be "a long and bitter struggle," filing a lawsuit in the federal court asking Munger to award them the entirety of the reward fund.[55] Dozens of other claimants subsequently entered the lawsuit, and the case plodded on for years as attorneys wrangled over discovery and filed scores of pleadings and pretrial motions. In 1912 the Union Pacific formally disavowed any further role in the handling of the reward by filing a bill of interpleader, depositing the money with the court, and stipulating with all the parties that Judge Munger would make the final distribution. But not all of the pressure on Munger came from attorneys' formal legal arguments. In September 1913 he received several desperate handwritten notes from the wife of James Bilek, one of the "boys" who was among the leading claimants for the reward.[56] The woman begged Munger to reserve some of the money for her, as her indolent husband had abandoned her and their "dear little baby," leaving them starving and penniless. Bilek very seldom worked, she claimed, and on the rare occasions when he had any money, he gave nothing to her and the baby. "He says if he gets any reward money he will drink it all up," she continued, "so I thought that I could make use of it for the little baby and I."[57] There are no indications that Munger responded to the woman's lament. In late 1913 he entered his final order in the case, awarding $2,700 to each of the six boys who filed the original lawsuit, including James Bilek, and varying amounts to the remaining claimants.[58] Sadly, the beleaguered Mrs. Bilek and her baby do not appear further in the historical record.

But the prolonged reward litigation was only one of the stories that emerged in the aftermath of the Mud Cut robbery trial—and not even the most interesting one at that. Far more compelling were the sagas of several of the convicted robbers after they left Omaha and began their lifetime sentences at Leavenworth. Those stories began even as the investigation and trial were under way, as some of the participating law enforcement officials and prosecutors became increasingly dubious of the guilt of the defendants. In particular, postal official William Vickery, one of the lead investigators in the case, came away from the trial convinced that it had been a "botched" affair, tainted by gaping holes in the government's case, perjured testimony motivated by witnesses' desire for the reward money, erroneous rulings by Judge Munger, and a variety of other prosecutorial or evidentiary failings. He was specifically convinced that the evidence against Jack Golden and Frank Grigware was highly suspect. In short, Vickery believed that an injustice had been done to those two men in particular, and he urged his superiors in the postal service to launch an inquiry and reassess the convictions of Golden and Grigware. Vickery's bosses agreed with his recommendation, and over the next three years postal authorities conducted a massive new investigation that dwarfed the original efforts of the local police, railroad security officials, Pinkerton detectives, and other law enforcement services during the months immediately after the robbery. In August 1913 postal officials presented the results of that investigation to President Woodrow Wilson. In their report, the investigators emphasized the almost completely circumstantial nature of the evidence introduced against Golden and Grigware, and they bluntly criticized the prosecution for introducing—and Judge Munger for admitting—highly speculative, confusing, and in some cases almost certainly perjured eyewitness testimony that purported to place those two defendants at the scene of the robbery. Wilson was convinced. He promptly issued a full pardon to Golden, who walked out of Leavenworth a few days later.

Grigware too would have almost certainly received a presidential pardon but for one key factor: he was no longer under the control of the federal government. In what was certainly the most dramatic part of the Mud Cut case, on April 21, 1910, just six months after he arrived at Leavenworth, Grigware joined with five other inmates in an unprecedented escape from the notorious prison. Carving a piece of wood into the shape of a gun and using it to bluff the guards, the men hijacked a locomotive that was used to ship supplies into the prison and burst through the gates to freedom. All of the escapees were quickly rounded up except Grigware. He remained at large and eventually made his way across the northern plains and into western Canada, where he settled into a new life under the name James Fahey. Over the ensuing years, he married, raised a family, and became a respected and beloved community leader in Spirit River, Alberta. In 1916 his new friends and neighbors even elected him mayor of that small town.

Meanwhile, back in the United States, Grigware became the subject of one of the most intense and prolonged manhunts in the nation's history. The Department of Justice's Bureau of Investigation (forerunner of today's FBI) committed massive resources and scores of agents to the search, pursuing leads all over the country and around the world. The trail eventually went cold, but in 1934 FBI officials caught a break when Grigware/Fahey was arrested in Canada for illegally trapping a marten in Jasper National Forest.[59] When a records search matched his fingerprints to the now decades-old prison escape, his true identity was revealed, and U.S. officials asked the Canadian government to extradite him for return to prison. As word of the capture circulated, however, Grigware's new countrymen rallied to his cause. Thousands of Canadians besieged their elected officials with calls to reject the American extradition request, arguing that Grigware was not guilty of the crime he was charged with and that, even if he was, he had long since proven himself to be a productive and valuable member of Canadian society. Grigware even gained the support of at least one American congressman. Flamboyant and iconoclastic U.S. representative Francis Shoemaker of Minnesota, himself a former inmate at Leavenworth, urged the Canadian government to "not allow for one minute this man Fahey's Canadian home to be broken up by a travesty of justice."[60] Canadian officials heeded the outcry and formally resisted Fahey's extradition to the United States. The result was an international standoff that placed President Franklin Roosevelt on the horns of a diplomatic dilemma: should he press for Grigware's extradition and thereby alienate the Canadians, or should he let the matter drop? In the end, Roosevelt opted to drop the matter, and the Department of Justice quietly rescinded its extradition request. Nevertheless, Grigware was never formally pardoned for his role in the Mud Cut robbery, whatever it may have been, and the FBI kept tabs on him for the rest of his life. In 1977 Grigware died of natural causes at age ninety-one, bringing an end to the long and colorful story of the Nebraska Mud Cut robbery.

Continuing Progressive Controversies

While the Mud Cut robbery trial remains one of the more glamorous and well-publicized episodes of the "two Munger" era, the two Nebraska judges spent the vast majority of their time handling more mundane issues and controversies. Many, if not most, of the matters on the court's docket continued to reflect the turbulent sociopolitical dynamics of the early twentieth century. The Progressive reform movement rolled on, bringing increased government regulation of the industrial workplace and a corresponding pushback from businesses grown complacent by the preceding generations of laissez-faire government. And as always, the federal district courts served on the front lines of those conflicts, their decisions marking the cadence and rhythm of the Progressives' advance.

The Nebraska federal court, for example, handled many cases involving the interpretation and enforcement of the "twenty-eight-hour law," a Progressive measure aimed at ensuring humane treatment of livestock during transport from their grazing ranges and feedlots to the slaughterhouses. First passed in 1873 and amended numerous times thereafter, the law generally mandated that animals being transported domestically in "a rail carrier, express carrier, or common carrier" could not be confined for more than twenty-eight hours without unloading the animals for feeding, watering, and rest.[61] As enforcement of the law became more vigorous during the Roosevelt and Taft administrations, compliance proved to be a major headache for the railroads, necessitating the construction of hundreds of feeding and watering stations along the lines, and sometimes generating creative—and even humorous—new methods for meeting the law's requirements. For example, by 1910 innovative Union Pacific workers in western Nebraska had pioneered the technique of using trained billy goats to lead balky herds of sheep out of their railcars for nighttime rest, watering, and feeding breaks, without the commotion and disturbance often caused by human efforts to move the skittish animals.[62]

However sincere the railroads' efforts at compliance may have been, by 1914 government officials nationwide were collecting more than $25,000 per month from railroads for violations of the law, and litigation related to issues of compliance had become commonplace in the federal courts.[63] Given Nebraska's primacy in the cattle ranching, meatpacking, and railroad industries, it is not surprising that many such cases made their way into the Mungers' court. For example, in late May 1909, William Munger presided over a federal prosecution of Union Pacific officials before a jury in Omaha that resulted in a verdict of guilty on ten counts of violating the twenty-eight-hour law. The defense had contended that the violations were the result of "accidents and bad weather," but the jury disagreed, and Munger dutifully imposed the then-maximum fines of $500 per incident on the Union Pacific for the transgressions.[64]

A year later, Tom Munger handled a similar jury trial involving the prosecution of Chicago, Burlington, & Quincy railroad officials. In that case, the railroad argued that it had not violated the act, because the shipper of the animals in question was riding in the railcars with the livestock and had signed a contract in which he agreed that he was in sole charge of the feeding and watering of the animals. The railroad admitted that the animals were confined in the cars for more than twenty-eight consecutive hours without proper food and water, but provided evidence that the shipper had told train personnel that he was "all right" and that he could feed and water his stock. Thus, the defendants argued, they were exempt from prosecution under the language of the statute providing that "when animals are carried in cars . . . in which they can and do have proper food, water, space, and opportunity to rest, the provisions in regard to their being unloaded shall not apply." At the close of the evidence, Munger rejected that argument and directed a verdict against the railroad, writing in a short published opinion: "It is not enough to show that the animals 'can' have such supplies, as, for instance, that the one in charge may procure water and food at the stations where stops are made; but it must be shown that the animals 'do' have proper food, water, space, and opportunity to rest."[65]

In another line of cases that both reflected the Progressive trends of the era and belied the lingering perception of Tom Munger as a "railroad judge," the court consistently ruled against the railroads in cases involving the application and interpretation of the Safety Appliance Act. Enacted in 1893, the law represented a Progressive effort to improve workplace safety conditions for railroad personnel, especially brakemen, engaged in the hazardous work of coupling and uncoupling railcars by mandating the installation of airbrakes, automatic couplers, and safety grab bars on all railroad rolling stock by the year 1900. As with the twenty-eight-hour law, the years following the implementation of the safety appliance act brought an abundance of federal litigation involving the interpretation of the law, and once again the Nebraska court was tasked with resolving a substantial number of such cases. Less than six months into his tenure, Tom Munger found himself presiding over a government prosecution of the Chicago, Burlington, & Quincy railroad for hauling cars with defective couplers and missing handholds. The railroad's attorneys argued that actual knowledge of the defects and a lack of due diligence on the part of railroad officials were necessary elements of any violation under the act, but Munger disagreed. In one of the first published opinions of his judicial career, he acknowledged that there was "considerable contrariety of opinion" among the courts on the issue, but he came to the firm conclusion that actual knowledge of the defects was not an element of the offense under the statute. Offering a perspective that was more sympathetic to laboring interests than his political opponents might have expected from him, Munger directed a verdict in favor of the government: "The chief purpose of the act of Congress . . . was the protection of the lives and safety of the trainmen who have occasion to pass between the cars or to work in and about them, and the act should be construed so as to give this intent full force, if such a construction can be given to the act without doing violence to the language."[66]

Obviously concerned by Munger's enunciation of what implicitly amounted to a standard of strict liability for violations of the act, the railroad appealed, but both the Eighth Circuit and the U.S. Supreme Court ultimately affirmed Munger's ruling.[67] His firm ruling in favor of the vigorous enforcement of the Safety Appliance Act did not go unnoticed in Washington. Shortly after the Supreme Court affirmed him, Munger received a brief note from the secretary of the Interstate Commerce Commission commending him for his ruling: "The Safety Appliance Law is absolute! The Supreme Court of the United States has sustained your opinion. It must be a case of great satisfaction to you; it certainly is for me for I have unceasingly endeavored to obtain this construction of the Safety Appliance Law for years."[68]

Another matter involving the Safety Appliance Act appeared on Munger's docket soon thereafter, and once again he ruled against the railroad's position. In that case, the Chicago & Northwest Railway faced prosecution for hauling an empty car with a missing grab bar from its Omaha yards to its Council Bluffs repair shops solely for the purpose of having the necessary repairs and modifications to the car performed there. The railroad argued that the movement of the car under those circumstances did not constitute "interstate commerce" within the meaning of the statute, but Munger disagreed and entered judgment for the government. He essentially reiterated the "strict liability" standard for enforcement of the act that he had articulated several months previously; in his view, railroads were subject to compliance with the act in situations involving *any* movement of a railcar under *any* circumstances.[69] This time, however, the Eighth Circuit reversed Munger, concluding that his reasoning on that point would inevitably lead to impractical business results. The appellate court noted: "Rolling stock must necessarily become defective . . . both by use and by accident. Repair shops cannot be kept on wheels. Such shops cannot be brought to the defective vehicle. The only practical method of railroading requires that such vehicles, when out of repair, shall be taken to the shops; and if they are wholly excluded from commercial use themselves [while in such transit] they do not fall within any of the classes covered by the safety appliance acts."[70]

As the government continued its vigorous enforcement of Progressive workplace safety laws, yet another case involving the Safety Appliance Act came before Munger in February 1908, this one pitting the government against the massive Union Stock Yards Company in South Omaha. In addition to accepting delivery of livestock from at least six corporate railroad lines, the stockyard company itself maintained some thirty-five miles of internal rail lines within its sprawling complex. Government inspectors found noncompliant railcars in use on those tracks and charged the stockyards with violations of the act. Defense attorneys argued that, because all of the stockyard's internally controlled tracks were within the state of Nebraska, the business could not be considered to be a "common carrier" engaged in "interstate commerce" within the terms of the statute. Once again, however, Munger disagreed and ruled in favor of the government's regulatory intervention. In his opinion, Munger carefully assessed the evidence related to the manner in which the stockyard's internal tracks were utilized and noted that "the defendant has not built nor maintained its railway as a private track for its own use, but has devoted it to a public use." "The defendant, having chosen to devote its railroad tracks to a public use, must be held to be a common carrier."[71] The Eighth Circuit agreed with Munger's conclusion, affirming his decision some fourteen months later.[72]

A Favor for George Norris?

One of the leaders of the national Progressive movement was Nebraska's own George W. Norris. A legendary figure in Nebraska's political history, Norris served five terms in Congress representing Nebraska's Fifth District and in 1913 embarked upon an illustrious thirty-year career in the U.S. Senate. A figure of national renown, Norris was of course a powerful figure in his own state as well, and shortly after he entered the Senate, Norris flexed that muscle a bit when he made a brief foray into a judicial matter on behalf of one of his constituents. In April 1912, Tom Munger had presided over the trial of Fred A. Corbin, who served as the federal postmaster in the small western Nebraska town of Reynolds. Prosecutors had indicted Corbin for embezzlement of federal funds, a jury convicted him of the charges, and Munger promptly sentenced him to three years in prison and imposed a fine of more than $2,500.[73] On appeal, the Eighth Circuit affirmed Corbin's conviction and Munger's sentencing.[74] Shortly thereafter, Munger received a letter from Norris. Dated May 21, 1913, and written on the letterhead of the U.S. Senate, Norris's message indicated that he had been asked by Corbin's mother to "intercede in his behalf to secure for him a pardon." Norris admitted that he had no knowledge of the specific facts of the case, but stated that he had known Corbin and his family for many years and thought highly of their reputation for honesty and reliability. He claimed to be "dumbfounded" by Corbin's conviction for embezzlement and asked whether it might be possible that Corbin had been "the victim of circumstances and while being technically guilty, was not maliciously so." Norris concluded the letter with the hope that Munger would "take the time to write me your judgment in the matter."[75]

Munger did take the time to answer Norris, but his response was almost certainly not what the senator had hoped for. (Unfortunately, Munger's reply letter has not been discovered in any archival collection, but its existence, content, and effect may be clearly determined from a second letter from Norris to Munger, dated June 14, in which he makes numerous references to the judge's response.) Munger apparently told Norris that Corbin was unquestionably guilty of the crime for which he had been convicted. So too the judge must have implicitly, if not explicitly, advised the senator that a request for a pardon would not be appropriate in the case. Whatever the precise wording of Munger's reply, its effect on Norris was apparent, as he told the judge, "I am impressed of course with your viewpoint of the situation and realize that you have had a much better opportunity to hear the evidence and see it than anyone else, and I accept your conclusions without reservation. It means, of course, that it will be useless to try to get a pardon for Fred. . . . I have always made it a rule not to ask for any pardon unless I am myself convinced that the pardon ought to be granted."[76]

No other references to the Corbin matter appear in the available records or in the contemporary press. He most likely served out his prison term without any additional attention or outside intervention. Thus the brief story of Norris's pardon inquiry provides scant support for any sweeping analytical conclusions. Nevertheless, the mere fact that Norris, already a powerful political figure both nationally and locally, felt it appropriate to test the waters of a potential presidential pardon for Corbin by asking Munger for his thoughts on such a possibility offers an intriguing glimpse into the political and judicial norms of the period. Moreover, the fact that Munger felt sufficiently secure in his position and standing to reject the possibility of such a pardon, even in the face of mild pressure from a fellow Republican who wielded considerable influence throughout the state and the nation, at the very least provides some measure of perspective on the judge's strength of character and his sense of judicial independence.

Death of Judge William Munger

By September 1913 William Munger's health was in a slow but steady decline. In a letter to Eighth Circuit presiding judge Walter Sanborn asking for a visiting judge to handle his docket temporarily, Munger acknowledged that he was experiencing "serious trouble with my prostate gland" and had decided on surgery to address the problem. "If I do not," he concluded, "and conditions continue as they are now, I shall be a nervous wreck in a few months."[77] Over the ensuing months, occasional news reports indicated that Munger suffered from a series of kidney ailments and complications related to arteriosclerosis, all of which continued to impair his ability to maintain his busy court schedule.[78] His condition deteriorated throughout late 1914 and into the following year, requiring his colleague and an assortment of visiting judges to carry more and more of the court's burden in his place.[79] By the summer of 1915, Munger had become almost completely incapacitated and confined to a wheelchair. On August 12 the sixty-nine-year-old judge succumbed to his long illness, dying peacefully at his home surrounded by his family.

Praise and fond remembrances of the judge permeated the state in the aftermath of his death. Local and regional newspapers reported his passing prominently on their front pages and uniformly eulogized him as a man of integrity and distinction. The *Omaha World-Herald*, despite many years of harsh commentary on some of Munger's judicial decisions, acknowledged that he "was loved by all who knew him" and had "won renown and the esteem of his associates."[80] The rival *Omaha Daily Bee* likewise extolled Munger as a man "of most lovable disposition" who was "one of the most liked men to ever hold public office," while the *North Platte Semi-Weekly Tribune, Plattsmouth Journal*, and other papers offered similar editorial sentiments.[81]

As has become customary upon the death of federal judges, court administrators and bar association officials formed a committee to organize and host a memorial service. Those proceedings took place in the Omaha federal courthouse on October 11, 1915, and featured speeches from a multitude of the judge's friends and colleagues, including many of the state's leading legal and political figures.[82] In a mildly ironic twist, the chair of the committee and the first speaker at the memorial service was the man whom Munger had replaced on the federal bench eighteen years earlier, William D. McHugh. In his remarks, McHugh described the late judge as "transparently honest," possessing a "sense of right that was clear and strong . . . spotless integrity and high ideals."[83] Other eulogists echoed McHugh's praise. Munger's longtime friend J. J. Sullivan, former chief justice of the Nebraska Supreme Court, struck a common thematic chord for many of the day's speakers when he spoke of Munger's beneficial impact on the court's openness and the resulting rise in its standing within the state's legal culture:

> Time was when the great body of the Nebraska bar stood in awe of this court and shunned it as a place of mystery and labyrinths, of pitfalls and snares, but Judge Munger dissipated that feeling; he popularized the court. Under his genial, leveling influence it came soon to be known as a democratic tribunal, a court easy of access, where controversies were decided on their merits, after a fair hearing, before an impartial, able and courteous judge.[84]

To the same effect, O'Neill attorney Michael F. Harrington, an outspoken and sometimes controversial Populist, recalled the congenial effect that Munger brought to the relationship between the court and the "country bar" of western Nebraska:

> After the appointment of Judge Munger the country lawyers generally felt that they had a place in this court. At that time there was a general prejudice against federal courts, but after the state was cut into divisions and Judge Munger got to going about among these lawyers and jurymen and witnesses the federal court became a popular institution in Nebraska; it was found that the ordinary

man could approach that court just as easily and with just the same feeling that he would get fair play as if he approached the court in his own county; . . . and if Judge Munger did nothing else than to make popular the federal court in Nebraska and make its plain citizens believe and feel that justice was impartially and courteously administered there he would have rendered the public a great service.[85]

Sullivan and Harrington's comments serve as a fitting coda to the court's "Two Munger" era. No one could dispute that the elder Munger had played a key role in "humanizing" the court, forging it into an accessible forum for the stable and efficient administration of justice throughout the state. If his rulings had occasionally drawn the wrath of some who claimed to speak for the "common man," even the harshest of those critics could never question the man's honesty or integrity.

Yet even as the tributes to the late judge continued, the rampant speculation over the appointment of his successor was intensifying. Just three days after Munger's death, the *Plattsmouth Journal* advised its readers, "Now watch the scramble for the shoes of the late lamented Judge William Munger. They can't even wait until his body is laid to rest."[86] However unpleasant the circumstances may have been, it was both necessary and inevitable that a new judge would soon arrive. And when he did, his impact would shape the history of the state and the region for many years to come.

9

The Early Munger-Woodrough Years

The coming years will subject all of our basic institutions to tests as severe as they have ever encountered in the past. The maelstrom of war will surge about the foundations of them all.

—Judge Joseph W. Woodrough, 1918

Strikers are not above the law and they will find out that they cannot violate it with impunity.

—Judge Thomas C. Munger, 1922

A New Judge Arrives

Within two weeks of William Munger's death, five names had already been submitted to the Department of Justice for consideration as his successor. All were well-known figures in Nebraska Democratic circles, including state party chairman William H. Thompson of Grand Island. Thompson carried the strong support of William Jennings Bryan, who had only recently stepped down from service as President Woodrow Wilson's secretary of state.[1] In the weeks that followed, however, the sixty-one-year-old Thompson's age, combined perhaps with Bryan and Wilson's estrangement, removed him from consideration, and most speculation began to focus on Omaha attorney Joseph W. Woodrough.[2] He was a widely respected trial lawyer and an unabashedly enthusiastic Wilsonian Democrat, who had spearheaded the president's 1912 state primary campaign. On March 13, 1916, Wilson repaid Woodrough's loyalty and service by formally nominating him for the state's vacant judicial seat.[3] The nomination received the unanimous support of the Nebraska congressional delegation and sailed through the confirmation process with only token Republican resistance. Public reaction was similarly positive, as even Woodrough's political opponents acknowledged his legal prowess and his credentials as a sincere and dedicated Progressive. The *Omaha World-Herald* was particular effusive in its praise, calling Woodrough "a man of exceptionally high standing [in whom] the qualities of courage and independence are notably developed. . . . He is a lover of the law in its true estate as the champion and instrument of justice. Still a young man, he is nevertheless well equipped by education, by constant study, and by successful experience for the high position to which he has been named. A progressive and fearless lawyer, there is every reason to believe he will make the same kind of judge."[4]

On April 1, 1916, the forty-two-year-old Woodrough took his oath and assumed the bench. He would remain a federal judge for the next sixty-one years, becoming one of the longest-tenured federal judges in American history.

Woodrough's Colorful Background

Few jurists of his or any other era could match what Woodrough had seen and done in the years preceding his ascension to the federal bench.[5] Born in August 1873 near Cincinnati, Ohio, he grew up in a prosperous family of renowned toolmakers.[6] He received his early schooling at the Chickering Institute, an elite Cincinnati preparatory school where he excelled in his studies and graduated in 1889 at age sixteen.[7] He then embarked upon a trip to Europe, ultimately enrolling in the prestigious Annen Realschule in Dresden, where he studied law and philosophy. Famed American attorney Louis Brandeis had attended the same school twenty years earlier. Coincidentally, just as Woodrough arrived in Dresden, Brandeis was undergoing an extremely contentious Senate confirmation battle on his way to becoming the first Jewish Supreme Court justice.[8] Woodrough left Dresden after one semester and enrolled for several months at the equally prestigious Heidelberg University.[9] Soon, however, wanderlust took hold again, and the young man set out upon a months-long sojourn by foot, bicycle, and train across much of western Europe. He traversed Germany, Italy, Spain, southern France, and Switzerland, absorbing the local cultures and ultimately gaining a lifelong fluency in most of the native languages of those regions. During various portions of his travels, Woodrough was accompanied by a classmate, Richard Scovill, a nephew of future president Theodore Roosevelt.[10]

Returning once again to Dresden and reentering the Annen Realschule, Woodrough and other classmates enjoyed the heady experience of being formally "presented" to Kaiser Wilhelm II, the recently crowned ruler of the German empire.[11] It was a particularly stimulating time for a young American student to visit Germany. Twenty years earlier, chancellor Otto von Bismarck and the young Kaiser's father, Wilhelm I, had succeeded in unifying the Germanic states, creating the "2nd German Reich." Advancing their famous "blood and iron" policies, Bismarck and Wilhelm I launched a program of rapid industrialization and militarization that transformed the empire into the most powerful economic and military force in Europe. By 1888, however, Wilhelm had died and the aging "Iron Chancellor" was facing pressure to step down from the even more ambitious and territorially aggressive new emperor. In many ways, the fate of Europe and much of the rest of the world hung in the balance as the two men squared off in an epic generational showdown, and Woodrough was there to witness the drama firsthand. His exposure to European—and especially Germanic—political, legal, and cultural dynamics seemed to shape the young man's perspective for decades to come, as colleagues would later marvel at his rich understanding of European language and law.

After almost two years in Europe, Woodrough returned to the United States in 1891, celebrating his eighteenth birthday on the transatlantic crossing. He stopped only briefly in his native Cincinnati before proceeding westward to Nebraska to launch a legal career under the tutelage of his uncle, Omaha attorney William Beckett. Woodrough's interest in law had been sparked in Europe, and his arrival in Omaha coincided neatly with the opening of the Omaha Law School, which he entered with the inaugural class in 1892.[12] While attending law classes, he also continued to clerk for his uncle, who had built an impressive legal practice representing local real estate magnate Byron Reed and wealthy heirs to the Creighton family estate.[13] Life with Beckett was yet another intense learning experience for Woodrough. A skilled attorney and well-known officer of the Omaha Bar Association, Beckett also possessed a well-deserved reputation for volatility and hotheadedness. In a notorious 1895 incident, Beckett nearly found himself disbarred after he argued vehemently with a state district judge, slammed a fist on the judge's desk, and then took a swing at him, punching the face of the bailiff instead.[14]

Woodrough left Omaha after a year and headed south, following in the wake of two other uncles who had established an irrigation business in the Pecos River valley of Ward County in the panhandle region of west Texas. Within months, he gained admission to the Texas bar and began practicing law, supplementing his income by cultivating onions and attempting to raise cattle.[15] In 1894, just two months after his twenty-first birthday, he won election to the post of Ward County judge. The region he presided over was a wild and relatively lawless environment, populated by citizens who would later be described as "believing more firmly in dry powder than habeas corpus proceedings; when a blue-steel six-shooter was a more weighty instrument of the law than a writ of injunction."[16] Lamenting the "feudal wars" and pervasive gun culture that permeated the area, Woodrough set out to establish the rule of law by banning the carrying of firearms in his county. Though the details of how he could have unilaterally imposed and enforced such a policy remain murky, Woodrough reportedly had gunslingers hauled into his red sandstone courthouse, where he routinely fined them twenty-five dollars for carrying sidearms in public. However embellished the stories may have been, the legend of Woodrough as the courageous young judge who "brought peace to the Pecos" only enhanced his charismatic image in the ensuing years.[17] After serving a single two-year term as judge, Woodrough served briefly as Ward County attorney before returning to Omaha in 1897.

Back in Nebraska, Woodrough practiced once again for a short time with his uncle William Beckett before going into partnership with William Gurly and Ralph W. Breckenridge in the spring of 1899, forming the firm Breckinridge, Gurly & Woodrough.[18] Over the ensuing years, Woodrough's reputation as a trial attorney flourished.[19] He represented high-profile clients, including several of the defendants in the long-running series of cattle baron prosecutions that were winding their way through the federal court system in those years. (See chapter 6).[20] In another notable saga, Woodrough adroitly defended railroad detective Fred Hans, who was twice tried and acquitted for the murder of a Brown County man whom he was attempting to arrest.[21] And in an even more sensational case in 1908, Woodrough successfully defended a man accused of killing prominent Omaha physician Frederick Rustin in what prosecutors claimed was a bizarre double suicide pact.[22] He proved equally adept in civil and appellate litigation, most notably representing the estate of Byron Reed in a successful effort to recover $300,000 in a messy land transaction that twice made its way to the Nebraska Supreme Court.[23]

During those years of private practice, Woodrough was also becoming an ardent disciple of progressivism and an equally devoted supporter of Democratic Party causes and candidates. In 1905 he ran as the Democratic candidate for Douglas County Court judge, but lost to the Republican nominee, backed by the powerful Dennison political machine.[24] Notwithstanding that electoral defeat, Woodrough continued to develop a passionately Progressive reform agenda, philosophy, and lifestyle that would undergird the rest of his life. In a 1912 published essay, he railed against the inefficiencies of the judicial system and the inherent corruption of the political process, noting, "We have elaborate systems of courts in this state that cost the people millions of annual outlay, and they take five years to decide a dispute about a bill of goods. We have legislatures that often follow dark and devious ways, and bosses in every city that can deliver votes with unholy certainty." Just as previous generations had fought against the evils of "kingship" and "slavery," he believed that his generation needed soldiers who would fight for the reforms that society so badly needed. He contended that this new fight "will take the brain and courage of men to fire their hearts and spur them on to heroism as grand as the race has seen." He called on his peers to reject corruption, bossism, and bureaucracy, and referred to men who used their talents merely for wealth as "vulgar."[25]

Later that year, Woodrough's Progressive passions were fired to even greater heights when New Jersey governor Woodrow Wilson became the Democratic nominee for president, running on an ambitiously Progressive platform. Woodrough threw himself headlong into the campaign, creating and leading the "Wilson League of Nebraska" and working tirelessly for Wilson's election.[26] Those efforts bore fruit, in both the short and long term. Nationwide, the Republican vote was split between incumbent William Howard Taft and the insurgent "Bull Moose" candidacy of former president Theodore Roosevelt, allowing Wilson to sweep to victory in the Electoral College. Due in significant part to Woodrough's efforts, Wilson's winning total included all eight of Nebraska's electoral votes. With his devotion to the new president firmly established and his reputation as a skilled attorney on the rise, the stage was set for Woodrough's appointment to the federal bench three years later.

The Wartime Court

As Woodrough arrived on the court in April 1916, much of the world was embroiled in the mindless savagery and slaughter of World War I. Since the onset of hostilities in the fall of 1914, the Wilson administration had managed to maintain American neutrality, and the president won reelection in November 1916 campaigning in part on the slogan "He kept us out of war." Within months of that election victory, however, a multitude of complex factors combined to compel the president to ask for, and receive from Congress, a declaration of war against Germany and the other Central Powers. The impact of the war on the nation's economic, political, social, and cultural dynamics could not have been more profound, as Wilson and his administration took draconian steps to instill and maintain full and unwavering commitment to the war effort from every American. And, as always, it would not be long before many of the societal tensions arising out of that "all in" dedication to the war would be revealed in the federal court.

Among the most insidious consequences of the nation's commitment to "total war" was its chilling effect on civil liberties. All over the country, local, state, and federal authorities attempted to stifle antiwar dissent and ensure unanimous and unquestioning support for the war effort. The result was the widespread shunning of Germany and all things Germanic, often reflected in symbolic but relatively harmless gestures such as the renaming of German-based streets, towns, buildings, and even food items.[27] Far more seriously, individuals expressing opposition to the war often found themselves harassed and threatened by former friends and neighbors, while mobs throughout the country frequently attacked and forced the closing of German-language newspapers and other German-owned businesses. Universities dropped courses in German literature, orchestras stopped performing German music, and many states, including Nebraska, passed laws criminalizing "unpatriotic" activity. Other states, again including Nebraska, took steps to ban the teaching of German in the state's schools.[28]

At the national level, by far the most sinister manifestations of the desire to instill "100 percent Americanism" took the form of two pieces of notorious legislation that remain controversial to this day. The Espionage Act of 1917 outlawed words or actions intended to interfere with the operation or success of the U.S. military or to promote the success of its enemies. The act further prohibited actions that might create "insubordination, disloyalty, mutiny, [or] refusal of duty in the military or naval forces of the United States" or "obstruct the recruiting or enlistment into service of the United States."[29] The following year, Congress extended the already expansive reach of the Espionage Act by passing the Sedition Act of 1918, which forbade any expression of opinion deemed critical or abusive toward the American government, constitution, flag, or military forces.[30] Together, the two statutes led to the federal prosecution of thousands of individuals nationwide, including many in Nebraska. And in those court proceedings, the story emerges of a particularly unsettling time in the history of both the nation and the state.

Less than a month after America entered the war on April 6, 1917, the Nebraska legislature created the Nebraska State Council of Defense, charging it with the duty to ensure statewide conformity with the nation's wartime agenda. Much of the Council's work involved relatively innocuous matters such as promoting the sale of war bonds, assisting the Red Cross, allocating seed grain, or rationing food, fuel, and other consumer goods. But it was also vested with the authority to conduct investigations, subpoena witnesses and records, and punish offenders for contempt.[31] Armed with such sweeping powers, the council and its county-based subordinate units quickly evolved into an extralegal instrument of vigilantism, seeking to stamp out dissent wherever and in whatever form it might present itself. The council itself described its job as rooting out "un-American sentiments, and in some instances German propaganda, [which has] found fertile soil in the minds and the hearts of certain academic intellectuals in high places; mushroom socialists masquerading under new colors; foreign born people whose Americanization has been neglected; advocates of internationalism; clergymen of foreign soul and body; and others who fail to adjust their thoughts and actions to the standard of American citizenship."[32]

The council took that mandate very seriously. One of the most prominent "mushroom socialist" groups it targeted was the Nonpartisan League, a North Dakota–based farmers' advocacy group whose radically Progressive agenda and surging popularity in rural Nebraska made it particularly susceptible to the council's attacks.[33] Educators and intellectuals of all types were another group often scrutinized by the Council, as reflected in a series of widely publicized hearings in 1918 that ultimately forced several faculty members at the University of Nebraska–Lincoln to resign from their positions.[34] While much of the violence and harassment directed toward "disloyal" citizens was the work of individuals operating outside the government's official sanction or control, there can be little doubt that the operations of the State Council of Defense played a key role in creating the atmosphere of suspicion, intolerance, xenophobia, and paranoia that permeated the state during the war.

Woodrough and the "Slacker Cases"

From the outset, Woodrough was an ardent and vocal supporter of the Wilson administration's "all in" commitment to the war effort. Indeed, in a 1918 article published in the *Creighton Chronicle*, he once again adopted the stridently militaristic tones that he had invoked in some of his earlier writings on the Progressive "battles" of the day. Referring to himself as "a new recruit in a very important unit of democracy's far-flung battle line," Woodrough predicted that "the coming years will subject each and all of our basic institutions to tests as severe as they have ever encountered in the past. The maelstrom of war will surge about the foundations of them all." These foundations, Woodrough urged, must be defended both by "the blood of martyrs on fields of battle" as well as in "judicial tribunals [and] . . . in the quiet chambers of the courts."[35]

That soldierly philosophy was more than mere rhetoric; in his daily lifestyle and personal work habits, Woodrough steadfastly adhered to a pattern of austerity and rigid self-discipline that was remarkable to all who knew him. A later colleague on the federal bench, Richard Robinson, would memorialize him as "Spartan in his tastes and in the way he lived. He shunned luxury hotels, he spent little time in clubs . . . he disliked ostentation or pomposity in any form [and] believed in physical fitness."[36] Throughout his tenure on the district court, Woodrough routinely walked the ten miles from his Ralston-area home to the federal courthouse in downtown Omaha. He expected the same mental and physical discipline from his clerks, often assigning them after-hours readings on a wide variety of topics and peppering them with questions on what they had read. So too he regularly ordered the "whole platoon" to report to his house, where he would offer "good, if simple food" before showing them "a tree to chop down, or a fence to paint, or some other household chore requiring strong young backs."[37]

When the United States entered the war, Woodrough himself

promptly registered for the draft, despite being at the cutoff age of forty-five.[38] Unsurprisingly, the draft board's physical examiners found him perfectly fit to fight, though his offer to serve was declined. On at least one occasion, his vigorous support for the war effort even caused him to miss a court session. In 1918, as Allied air forces were bombing Cologne, Woodrough was unexpectedly absent from court, missing the plea hearing of a hotel clerk facing charges of selling whiskey to soldiers. The judge, apparently more concerned with what American soldiers were eating, was discovered at home, "doing his bit" by tilling up his lawn to make a victory garden.[39]

Woodrough's personal disdain for those who failed to heed their country's call revealed itself in other ways as well. In January 1918, as he was leaving Omaha to serve as a visiting judge in Oklahoma, he made some notably caustic public comments about the apparent lack of dedication to the war effort in that state, telling a local reporter: "Oklahoma is full of slackers and I believe the condition is due to the newspapers that circulate down there. . . . In Nebraska, now, there is no such excuse for the few slackers we have here. Take the *World-Herald*, for instance. Its editorials discuss these points of public interest so clearly that any man who reads them will know just exactly what he should do. It's too bad the *World-Herald* doesn't circulate down in that state. I am sure there would not be so many slackers there if it did."[40]

Woodrough's harsh feelings about presumed "slackers" were often (but not always) reflected in his rulings from the bench, such as when he sentenced a young farmer to twenty-four hours in jail for missing a deadline for draft registration by a few hours, despite the man's protestations that he had been delayed by a heavy rainstorm and a balky automobile. As a result of the conviction, the man's name went into the "preferred class" for conscription, and he soon found himself drafted into service.[41]

In another reflection of his ardent support for the military, Woodrough convened a special session of his court at Fort Crook in Bellevue during the summer of 1918, for the express purpose of conducting a mass naturalization ceremony for hundreds of foreign-born soldiers who had not yet become American citizens. As reported in the *Omaha World-Herald*, the ceremony included Woodrough's exhortation of the men with a series of rousing questions that were plainly designed to instill "100 percent Americanism" in each of them:

"Will you fight against your native country, if need be, for this government?" asked Judge Woodrough.

"Yes," came again, louder than before.

"Any of you believe in anarchy?"

"No."

"Any believe in polygamy—that is, having more than one wife?"

"No."

As the echo died out a single voice was heard, "One wife is enough, judge."[42]

Later that same month, Woodrough became one of the first federal judges in the country to preside over the prosecution of a defendant under the recently passed Espionage Act. The case involved a young piano tuner named C. C. Mickey, an avowed socialist and outspoken opponent of the war, who began circulating a pamphlet titled *The Price We Pay* among his neighbors in Springfield, Nebraska. The tract urged readers to resist being dragged into the "seething, heaving swamp of torn flesh and floating entrails" of the European battlefields, and warned that an "inescapable horrible death is the price you pay for your stupidity—you who have rejected Socialism."[43] A farm wife who had received the pamphlet took offense at its message and notified local authorities, who promptly arrested and indicted Mickey for violation of the Espionage Act. When the case came to trial several months later, Woodrough surprised prosecutors and other observers by dismissing the charges, commenting that a prison sentence would be a wasteful place for a young man of fighting age to spend the war. Noting that Mickey was already at the top of the draft list at the time of his trial, he set the man free, and Mickey was promptly drafted and shipped off to Europe where he served, apparently without further incident, for the duration of the war.[44] Nevertheless, he remained a dedicated socialist and went on to become the founder of an unusual cooperative "colony" in the Benson area of Omaha.[45]

Meanwhile, federal officials—often acting in concert with the State Council—were continuing their drive to stifle dissent and disloyalty, and Woodrough found himself handling additional cases arising out of those efforts. On June 1, 1918, the federal grand jury in Omaha indicted twenty-four more Nebraskans for violations of the Espionage Act. Among the accused was a Cheyenne County farmer, George W. Davis, who was charged with saying, "Germany had a right to issue the war zone proclamation. We had no business on the high seas when the *Lusitania* was sunk. The first transport carrying our troops to France ought to be sunk. This is a rich man's war. It is a war to help out the moneyed men of Wall Street." Davis's neighbor Charles McKee apparently shared those views and was indicted for proclaiming, "The Red Cross is nothing but a graft. The money is stolen and never reaches the boys. Hoover is a crook and a grafter." Lincoln County rancher John Harshfield's opposition to the war was even more defiant and menacing, as he was charged with allegedly stating, "President Wilson and the cabinet are no good. I hope the men going to France will all be killed. I am a member of the greatest league on earth, the Non-partisan League. I say what I please when and where I please. I have ammunition enough on my place to kill a regiment."[46]

Harshfield's case was the first to be heard, coming to trial in North Platte just a few weeks after the indictment was issued, with Woodrough presiding. After a short trial, the jury convicted the rancher on one count of uttering words that were defamatory to the president and hostile to the American war effort, and he promptly appealed to the Eighth Circuit court of appeals.[47] On March 3, 1919, as Harshfield's appeal was pending, the U.S. Supreme Court issued its famous decision in *Schenck v. United States*.[48] In his opinion for the court, Justice Oliver Wendell Holmes upheld the constitutionality of the Espionage and Sedition Acts, enunciating his renowned "clear and present danger test" for evaluating the limitations which government may place on free speech during wartime:

> The question in every case is whether the words used are used in such circumstances and are of such a nature as to create a clear and

present danger that they will bring about the substantive evils that Congress has a right to prevent. It is a question of proximity and degree. When a nation is at war many things that might be said in time of peace are such a hindrance to its effort that their utterance will not be endured so long as men fight and that no Court could regard them as protected by any constitutional right.[49]

Several months later, the Eighth Circuit applied the *Schenck* standard to Harshfield's circumstances and reversed his conviction, holding that however "scurrilous, improper, and disgraceful" his words had been, "taking into consideration the circumstances in which they were uttered . . . they wholly fail to sustain the purpose for which it is alleged they were uttered."[50]

Meanwhile, as Harshfield's appeal was pending, the cases of many of the other individuals named in the June indictment went to trial. By far the most prominent of the defendants in those trials was a controversial and outspoken Catholic priest in the small town of Creighton in northeastern Nebraska, Father William Windolph. Based on the testimony of government investigators as well as complaints from members of his congregation, prosecutors charged Windolph with nine counts of uttering prohibited statements. Among the more specific accusations against him, the indictment alleged that he had declared, "The majority of our soldiers are cowards. All they do is follow the crowd. They did not want to go to war, but did not have the courage to say so. War was started by a few rich men in New York. The American government is rotten and officers of the government from the president down are not honest. As a proof we have President Wilson, who promised to keep us out of war, and as soon as he was elected he declared war on Germany."

Windolph's case came to trial in Norfolk in late September, with Woodrough again presiding. The event drew a huge throng of witnesses, reporters, and spectators, including a reported 95 percent of the priest's congregation from Creighton.[51] The notoriety of the case was compounded by the fact that lurid rumors of Windolph's alleged sexual pursuits of some of the women and nuns within his parish had circulated widely throughout the region.[52] The resulting boisterous atmosphere that enveloped the trial tested Woodrough's courtroom management skills. When laughter and commotion broke out during the attorneys' opening statements, he sternly warned the gallery to refrain from such demonstrations, saying, "I will pick out those who are laughing out loud myself and throw them into jail." But the judge also softened the threat with a friendly assurance that "the court is human and smiles are permissible." That firm but affable approach proved to be effective, as no further admonitions were necessary.[53]

As the testimony and evidence began to come in, Woodrough made several procedural and evidentiary rulings that dramatically limited the scope of the government's case. In response to defense motions to dismiss many of the counts of the indictment, he held that Windolph could not be prosecuted for alleged statements he had made in the German language, since the indictment had not specified that particular "offense." Nor, he concluded, could prosecutors proceed with several other counts of the indictment, because they could not establish the precise date on which those statements had allegedly been uttered.[54] Ultimately, then, the trial proceeded on only a single count of the original nine-count indictment, charging the priest with stating to government undercover agent Werner Hanni, in English, that "the United States government is rotten," "the draft law is unconstitutional," and "the German government is better than the one here."[55]

After five days of testimony and more than three hours of closing arguments that were described in the local news as "exceptionally eloquent," the case went to the jury. In his instructions, Woodrough reportedly told the jurymen simply that if they found that the defendant "did not say what the government claimed he did he should be acquitted, otherwise convicted."[56] But the highly charged trial would have an anticlimactic conclusion. Just five hours after it began deliberations, the jury reported to Woodrough that they were hopelessly deadlocked. The judge accepted the panel's conclusion and promptly dismissed it from further service, effectively allowing the priest to stand acquitted of the one remaining charge against him.

Windolph returned to his post at Creighton, but neither the hung jury in his trial nor the armistice that ended the hostilities on the western front on November 11, 1918, were enough to cause the deep-rooted societal tensions of the era to fade away. In late December, Windolph again roiled the waters throughout the region when he resumed his practice of delivering some his homilies to his Creighton parishioners in German. The ensuing uproar culminated in a mass meeting of some five hundred townspeople, at which they produced a resolution opposing "any use of the German language being taught, preached, or spoken in any school or church, or at any public gathering in this vicinity."[57] Thus the war's chilling effect on civil liberties continued well after the shooting had stopped in Europe.

The lingering effects of the war were also reflected in two other notable cases handled by Woodrough in the immediate postwar years—cases that also happened to produce the first two published opinions of his judicial career. In *United States v. Bernstein*, the defendant was charged with violations of the 1917 Lever Act (as amended in 1919), which sought to prohibit wartime price gouging and profiteering by forbidding manufacturers and retailers from exacting "unreasonable charges for necessaries."[58] At the close of trial, the defense moved to dismiss the charges, arguing that the statute violated the Fifth Amendment by depriving defendants of their property without compensation and without due process of law. They also contended that the law violated the Sixth Amendment by failing to precisely define what was a "reasonable charge" or what was a "necessary" item, thus preventing accused individuals from being adequately informed of the nature of the charges against them. In response, Woodrough first expressed his personal "rancor and bitter resentment against the hordes of profiteers whose cold-blooded rapacity and greed multiply the burdens and sufferings of the Great War," but then found himself reluctantly compelled to agree with the defense's legal arguments. After reiterating his disgust with the "callous avarice and heartless plundering of the profiteers," he concluded, "But this law, which makes it a crime for a man to sell his private property . . . for the best price he can get in the ordinary course of trade and commerce, without coercion, without extortion . . . without wrongful combination or confederation or conspiracy, without undue influence, without misrepresentation, without any fraud recognized by law—this law cannot be sustained, while the Constitution forbids the taking of private property for public use without just compensation, and insures that no person shall be deprived of his property without due process of law." Woodrough agreed with the defendant's Sixth Amendment argument as well, holding that the language of the statute failed to adequately "prescribe a rule of conduct with [the] certainty" that the Constitution requires. Seven months later, in a case involving the same issues that Woodrough had wrestled with in *Bernstein*, the U.S. Supreme Court implicitly confirmed Woodrough's analysis and conclusions, holding that the Lever Act violated both the Fifth and Sixth Amendments.[59]

In another case that reflected the war's impact on individual Nebraskans, Woodrough considered the plight of a man, Heinrich Sinjen, who had emigrated to Nebraska from his native Germany in the years prior to the war.[60] Sinjen acquired and developed a profitable farm and became a naturalized American citizen. A few years before the war commenced, he and his wife traveled to Germany for what was expected to be a relatively short visit, leaving the Nebraska farm in the hands of his brother-in-law. An assortment of family issues, however, caused the couple's stay in Germany to be prolonged, and the war began before they could return to the United States. At that point, Sinjen found himself subject to the operation of a 1907 law called the Expatriation Act, which provided that a naturalized American citizen who resided for two years or more in the foreign state from which he originated would be presumed to have lost his American citizenship.[61] Sinjen's presumed expatriation, in turn, allowed the U.S. government to seize his Nebraska farm and other assets, through the application of a wartime statute known as the Trading with the Enemy Act.[62] Returning to Nebraska at war's end and claiming that he had continuously maintained his allegiance to the United States and had always intended to return to Nebraska as his permanent domicile, Sinjen invoked the court's equity jurisdiction to try to recover his property from the government's Office of Alien Property Custodian. He found an empathetic judge in Woodrough.

After weighing the evidence and arguments of counsel, Woodrough ruled definitively in Sinjen's favor. Noting that the 1907 law's presumption of expatriation could be overcome if the claimant could provide satisfactory rebuttal evidence, he concluded that Sinjen had done exactly that: "Having considered the circumstances in detail, I am convinced the Plaintiff is telling the exact truth when he swears that he at all times considered himself an American citizen, that he never intended to or did renounce his allegiance to this government, and that his intention to return hither for permanent domicile was fixed and abiding in his mind at all times."[63] Accordingly, Woodrough ordered the Alien Property Custodian to return Sinjen's property to his control.

These and other matters that Woodrough handled during the war suggest a sharp internal dissonance for the young judge. On the one hand, he clearly and repeatedly evinced a personal mind-set and outlook that was wholly consistent with the rigid wartime national discipline that his political hero Wilson was so determined to instill. Yet despite that palpable personal support for Wilson and the war effort, many of Woodrough's rulings during and immediately after the war ran counter to the president's goals and his administration's often overreaching approach. As his invalidation of the Lever Act in *Bernstein* and his relatively lenient handling of the defendants in the *Mickey, Windolph,* and *Sinjen* cases demonstrated, Woodrough repeatedly proved willing to make judicial decisions that were based solely on what he believed the law required, rather than what his personal sentiments might have dictated. He was a "judicial warrior" to be sure, but a decidedly measured and nuanced one.

Martial Law in Nebraska: The 1921–22 Meatpackers' Strike

As Woodrough dealt with these and other repercussions of the war, his colleague Thomas Munger faced a postwar challenge of his own: the resumption of intense labor-management conflicts that would once again bring those volatile issues to the court for handling. The war years were good for the state's economy generally, with farm prices at an all-time high and meatpacking plants and other industries running at full throttle to meet the needs of millions of American and Allied soldiers.[64] Labor shortages during the war temporarily provided union organizers with the leverage necessary to spur collective bargaining efforts in some industries, but those wartime gains for organized labor were short-lived. When the fighting in Europe ended, the process of "reconversion" from a wartime to a peacetime economy, along with the return of millions of soldiers from the fighting, produced a nationwide labor surplus and an economic recession, which, in turn, resulted in wage cuts and widespread efforts to destroy the recently revived union movement.

All of these dynamics were particularly notable in the meatpacking industry, making eastern Nebraska one of the flashpoints for postwar labor unrest. As had been the case during the labor wars handled by William Munger a generation earlier (see chapter 6), union workers in South Omaha and in Nebraska City joined with thousands of others at meatpacking centers across the nation to launch a massive strike in early December 1921. In South Omaha, the struggle pitted four of the largest packing companies of the day—Morris and Dold, Armour, Swift, and Cudahy—against the Amalgamated Meat Cutters and Butcher Workmen of North America–AFL, which represented a large majority of the thousands of workers employed in those companies' slaughterhouse and packing center operations. In the small town of Nebraska City about forty miles to the south, the fifth of the "Big Five" packers, Wilson, operated a plant that employed about four hundred workers, most of whom were also members of the Amalgamated union. Wilson operated the Nebraska City plant through a subsidiary company called Morton-Gregson.

On December 5, 1921, thousands of workers in South Omaha and at least three hundred in Nebraska City went on strike, joining tens of thousands of their fellow union members in cities across the nation.[65] The strikers quickly established picket lines along and across the entrances to the stockyards and packinghouses, but news reports during the first few days of the strike indicated that few confrontations or incidents of harassment had occurred.[66] The calm would not last long. As production at the plants dwindled, company managers responded with the familiar and time-tested strikebreaking tactic of hiring new employees to take the place of strikers. Given the labor surplus throughout the region and the nation, replacement workers were not difficult to find. On just the second night of the strike, tensions began to rise on the picket lines in Nebraska City when Morton-Gregson officials attempted to bring in ten Mexican workers as strikebreakers. Seventy-five striking workers went to the railroad station to confront the replacements, but the initial flare-up quickly dissipated when both the county attorney and the sheriff took custody of the Mexicans and sent them away, explaining that "there was enough trouble here now without permitting Mexican strike-breakers to [get involved in] the situation."[67]

Meanwhile, the state of affairs in South Omaha was deteriorating rapidly. As labor historian William Pratt described the scene:

Strikers and their supporters swarmed the entrances of the South Side plants, first harassing strikebreakers and sometimes attacking police when one or more from their ranks had been arrested. On occasion, Omaha police fixed bayonets to disperse crowds. . . . The police also arrested strikebreakers for assaulting pickets or other strikers with knives and guns, or for carrying concealed weapons. On December 26, 1921, a Cudahy strikebreaker fired into a group of striking workers who attempted to keep him out of the plant. He himself was shot by a policeman and arrested.[68]

The ugliness and violence was not confined to the packing district itself; it spread into the surrounding communities as well, often pitting friend against friend and neighbor against neighbor. Strikers sometimes stopped streetcars in downtown Omaha, yanked would-be replacement employees onto the street, and beat them severely. Workers who refused to join in the strike found themselves and their families threatened in their homes, in neighborhood stores, and even occasionally in their churches. In one of the nastiest incidents of the entire strike, shots were fired into the home of a nonstriking Armour employee, narrowly missing his wife and severely wounding his fifteen-month-old son. Police later arrested three young strikers for the shooting.[69]

Women played an active role in virtually every aspect of the 1921–22 Nebraska strike, both as strikers themselves and as supporters of their husbands, fathers, brothers, or friends. In one of the most dramatic episodes of the entire ten-week-long ordeal, more than three hundred women marched through downtown Omaha to the chambers of the Omaha City Council in a demonstration of mass support for the strike. A raucous encounter with the council members ensued, as the group dubbed the "Amazon Army" by the local press vigorously voiced their grievances, complaining that the police had showed favoritism toward the companies by insulting and harassing strikers and their supporters on the picket lines. More specifically, they charged the companies with purposefully hiring and housing "diseased strikebreakers," thereby exacerbating the already woeful sanitary conditions in the plants.[70] One of the leaders of the Amazons, Anna Papek, summarized the women's concerns.

> We have been insulted, called nasty names, and otherwise mistreated by the special police who don't do anything but carry big clubs around . . . we have husbands, brothers, and fathers on strike. We pay taxes. WE have rights, and we are going to have them. . . . We gave our sons up in the war . . . they were no slackers. Now they can't be scabs. [But] what shall we do to feed our children? We can't let them starve. . . . We'll break the packers! We've got 'em licked now. All we want is a fair deal and we'll whip 'em.[71]

As the strike dragged on into the following weeks, women became even more prominent in the struggle, especially in and around the Wilson plant where, on December 31, some forty women attempted to stop carloads of female strikebreakers from entering the plant. Ten of the women were arrested for assault and other charges. When the picketers attempted to use a large American flag as a barrier to the plant entrance, one of the cars refused to stop, dragging the flag a considerable distance along the ground. Authorities responded by charging two of the picketing women with flag desecration.[72]

Despite the violence in and around South Omaha, none of the participants there sought judicial intervention, and the court remained on the sidelines as the drama played itself out. In the Nebraska City situation, however, Judge Munger soon found himself thrust into a leading role. With tensions escalating during the second week of the strike, city officials dispatched a formal request to Governor Samuel McKelvie for the assignment of National Guard troops to "patrol the district near the plant, protect men who declare their intention to work, and stop assaults on Mr. Common Citizen."[73] McKelvie was out of the state and unavailable to respond, leaving Lieutenant Governor Pell Barrows to act in his place. Barrows refused to provide the requested troops, deciding instead to send investigators to the scene and await further developments.[74] Just a few hours after Barrows's decision, however, more violence occurred as picketers stopped a bus carrying strikebreakers as it approached the plant and proceeded to force one man off the bus and assault him. At about the same time, the plant superintendent reported that a brick had been thrown through the top of his car and that a shot had been fired into the body of the car, causing broken glass to cut his cheek and ear.[75]

The continuing harassment apparently convinced Morton-Gregson officials that federal judicial intervention was needed. On December 16, 1921, the company filed a petition in the Lincoln division of the federal district court, seeking a temporary restraining order and then a permanent injunction to prevent strikers from "interfering with the employees of the company or acting in any way detrimental to the company's work or property in Nebraska City."[76] Union attorneys strenuously opposed the petition, arguing that the environment surrounding the strike was not as dire as company officials claimed and that the sheriff and other local officials had full control of the situation.

Hovering over the impending legal battle was a very recent decision of the U.S. Supreme Court. In *American Steel Foundries v. Tri-City Central Trades Council*, handed down just eleven days earlier, Chief Justice William Howard Taft held that the practice of picketing by large groups was "inconsistent with [the notion of permissible] peaceful persuasion." Proceeding from that premise, he went on to conclude that, under the particular circumstances of that case, striking picketers should be "limited to one representative for each point of ingress and egress in the plant or place of business, and that all others [would] be enjoined from congregating or loitering at the plant or in the neighboring streets by which access is had to the plant."[77] While Taft specifically disavowed any intention of establishing a rigid rule limiting the number of picketers in all strike situations, most federal courts took the court's ruling at face value and interpreted it as doing precisely that.[78] Munger was no exception. He granted the restraining order sought by the company and specifically invoked the Supreme Court's ruling in *American Steel Foundries*, directing that the union would be limited to only a single picketer at each entrance and exit to the Morton-Gregson plant.[79] He further prohibited the striking workers from threatening, importuning, or acting abusively toward any of the company's employees or customers. Munger scheduled the hearing on the company's request for a permanent injunction for December 26 and directed that the hearing would be conducted primarily on the basis of affidavits to be submitted by the parties prior to that date.

Despite the temporary restraining order, tensions continued to escalate, exacerbated by the racial hostility that permeated the nation, region, and state during that era. Although there were only about sixty black residents of Nebraska City at the time of the 1921 strike, racism was nevertheless, in the words of historian William Pratt, a "way of life" in the area, as reflected in the fact that the portion of the city where most African Americans lived was referred to locally as "Nigger Ridge." The importation of black and Mexican strikebreakers inflamed local prejudices, prompting local authorities to speak out against the company's employment of people of color. Shortly after the strike began, local newspapers reported that "Mayor Thomas said he bitterly opposes the use of Mexicans or Negroes here as strike-breakers and said their arrival would probably cause trouble quicker than any other strike factor."[80] Still, as Pratt has noted, the racial aspects of the turmoil surrounding the strike were not always as linear and consistent as one might expect. Much of the violence, of course, did involve whites attacking blacks, but many other incidents were considerably more nuanced in their racial dynamics. One of the most notorious examples of that reality involved James Estes, a black strikebreaker who was kidnapped by a mob made up of both white and black strikers, driven across the river to Iowa, and then brutally beaten. In the subsequent prosecutions of several of his assailants, a local jury ultimately convicted a white man named Martin Mullaney for his part in the atrocity, and he died seven months later in prison. In contrast, when a local black striker named Dan Smith was tried for his participation in the Estes kidnapping and assault, the jury acquitted him, despite the fact that Estes offered the identical testimony against Smith that he had given against Mullaney. The only apparent difference: Smith was a local football star and a decorated World War I veteran, while Mullaney had only recently arrived in Nebraska from Chicago and had developed a reputation at the plant as a union rabble-rouser in the weeks leading up to the strike.[81]

As the December 26 injunction hearing approached, both sides in the dispute filed voluminous affidavits supporting their positions. Company officials produced dozens of sworn statements describing the many acts of harassment and violence against their employees and customers that had occurred during the three weeks the strike had been under way.[82] Union officials countered with affidavits showing that their policy from the outset had been to conduct a peaceful and orderly strike and argued that the actions of a few troublemakers, many of whom were not even members of the union itself, did not warrant a broad prohibition of nonviolent collective action by the union's members. In addition to their disclaimers related to the disputed facts surrounding the strike, the union's attorneys also raised an intriguing jurisdictional issue as part of their defense. They contended that the federal court did not have the authority to intervene in the matter because, in a labor dispute back in 1902, the same parties—Morton-Gregson and Local 122 of the Amalgamated Meat Cutters and Butcher Workmen—had been involved in an action for injunctive relief in state court. In that proceeding, the district court of Otoe County had issued a permanent injunction that, the union claimed, remained in effect as *res judicata* and therefore still controlled the relationship between the company and the union.[83] Morton-Gregson's attorneys responded by arguing that, while the name of the company remained the same, the current operator of the plant was actually a new corporate entity and not the one that had managed the plant in 1902. On a lighter note, they also pointed out that there could no legitimate legal identity among the parties in the two cases, since most of the current striking employees "were wearing knee length trousers nineteen years ago."[84]

The available records do not reveal Munger's specific reaction to the jurisdictional argument, but it can be safely assumed that he brushed it aside rather easily, inasmuch as he did proceed to issue a preliminary injunction of his own on January 4, 1922. The new injunction essentially extended the terms of his existing restraining order, prohibiting strikers from "interfering in any way . . . by use of threats or personal injury, intimidation or otherwise with the employees of the company at Nebraska City and from maintaining more than one picket at each point of ingress and egress to the plant." The order further prohibited union members from "loitering near the plant, entering it in any manner, or in any manner impeding the business of the company."[85]

If any of the parties believed that Munger's order might bring greater stability to the situation, they were sorely disappointed. Over the ensuing weeks, the judge spent a great deal of his time hearing contempt of court cases brought by federal prosecutors against striking workers who were alleged to have violated the letter or spirit of the court's injunction. His treatment of the strikers seemed admirably evenhanded. For example, after first convicting ten men for violation of his restrictions on the number of picketers that could be posted at each plant gate, Munger reversed himself several days later and dismissed those same charges, following a long day of testimony and evidence that convinced him that prosecutors had failed to meet their burden of proof.[86] Acknowledging that his order may not have been as precise as the situation called for, Munger noted that it was apparent that "the strikers in Nebraska City do not exactly understand the full import of the order against them." He promised to rectify the situation by sending union officials and their attorneys "a carefully written interpretation of the order so that in the future there may be no more misunderstandings on the subject."[87]

Despite those good intentions, contempt cases continued to roll in to the court. Three days later, Munger presided over the trial of another large group of strikers and their supporters who were charged with illegal picketing. The long hearing extended almost until midnight, and Munger's exhaustion and frustration were palpable as he dismissed the charges against most of the defendants while convicting three others and sentencing them to sixty-day jail terms. As he sentenced the men, the judge delivered a stern lecture and perhaps also attempted to send an ominous message to other would-be violators of his order, saying:

> The defendants . . . were picketing, the evidence shows. It is true that the evidence doesn't show that they were actually talking [to] or stopping cars, but they were participating in it by backing the women. They were there, one might say, to enjoy the show, and their presence there back of the women served as an intimidation, as if they were saying "we are here to support the women, just dare to touch them." Strikers are not safe in deciding the meaning of the law for themselves. They cannot even rely completely on their counsel's advice. A court order is the only thing they can rely on. Strikers are not above the law and they will find out that they cannot violate it with impunity.[88]

By the end of that late-night hearing, Munger also seemed to recognize the limits of what even he could do to end the violence. After sentencing the three men for their illegal picketing, Munger went on to express in open court his belief that only military force could reestablish stability and order in the Nebraska City area. In a tone that the press described as "unsparing," the judge declared that troops must eventually be sent to Nebraska City to stop the ongoing disturbances. "It was only a question of time," he stated, "until the National Guard would be called in."[89]

The events of the ensuing weeks seemed to confirm Munger's opinion. Over the next several weeks, increasingly desperate strikers, beset by financial distress in the midst of a harsh winter, seemed to increase their pressure on the strikebreakers and company managers.

The headlines in the local *Nebraska Daily Press* reveal the grim story: January 11: "Lincoln Men Tell of Beating They Received in City"; January 12: "Pitched Battle with Strikers on Third Street"; January 13: "Man Assaulted Files Action against Railway; Says He Was Beaten by Strikebreakers and Missouri Pacific Neglected to Protect Him"; January 18: "Home Owners Will Use Buckshot on Marauders"; January 24: "Pitched Battle at Cemetery Bridge"; January 26: "Street Battle Staged between Strike Factions."

By the end of the month, local officials had seen enough. On the evening of Friday, January 27, they once again asked Governor Samuel McKelvie to dispatch state militia forces to the area to restore order.[90] This time the request was granted. On Saturday morning, McKelvie dispatched five companies of National Guard troops to Nebraska City and imposed martial law in a geographic subdivision of the county called "Four Mile Precinct," which included Nebraska City and all of its subdivisions.[91] McKelvie's proclamation declared:

> Whereas, it appears that a state of lawlessness and disorder is now prevalent in Nebraska City, Neb., and territory adjacent thereto, and
>
> Whereas, it appears that such condition of lawlessness and disorder have existed for some time, and is now rapidly becoming more pronounced and is out of and beyond the control of the civil authorities of said territory, and
>
> Whereas, the county attorney and the Sheriff of Otoe County, Nebraska, and the mayor of Nebraska City, Nebraska, have applied for assistance from the state of Nebraska, requesting that the National Guard of the state of Nebraska be dispatched to and placed in control of said territory for the restoration and maintenance of law and order, and the proper execution of the laws of the state of Nebraska, now in said state of lawlessness and disorder, Now therefore
>
> I, Samuel R. McKelvie, governor of the state of Nebraska, by virtue of my office, and the powers vested in me by the constitution and laws of the state of Nebraska, do hereby order, announce and declare all the territory comprising and including in four mile

precinct, in Otoe county, Neb., including the city of Nebraska City, and all its subdivisions to be now subject to and under martial law, and order such portion of the national guard of the state of Nebraska, as may be necessary for said purpose of restoring and maintaining law and order and properly executing the laws of the state of Nebraska in said territory.[92]

Later that day, five companies of National Guard troops, mustered out of Falls City, Auburn, Lincoln, Seward, and Hastings, began to arrive in Nebraska City. The soldiers immediately took up positions surrounding the Morton-Gregson plant and began patrolling streets, roads, and highways throughout the area. That same evening, the Guard commander issued a proclamation that specified, in stark and dramatic terms, the limitations on public activity that his soldiers would be enforcing and the extent of the authority that they would be exercising. Among the more notable provisions, the order required all residents within the martial law zone to surrender their "arms, equipment, and munitions of war" to the military by 6:00 p.m. the following day. It also banned the publication or distribution of material "commenting in any way on the work or action of the military authorities" or "reflecting in any way upon the United States or the state of Nebraska or their officers, or tending to influence the public mind against the United States or the State of Nebraska or their officers." Other provisions prohibited all "assemblages in the street, either by day or night," and warned that all persons "who appear to be habitually idle and without visible means of support" would be arrested.[93] The final layer of martial law infrastructure took form on Monday, January 30, when McKelvie issued an additional proclamation establishing a "Military Commission or Provost Court, or both, to take cognizance and jurisdiction of such violations of the civil law and the ordinances in force in said district as the Commanding Officer in his discretion may prescribe."[94]

The imposition of martial law in Nebraska City served its intended purpose, as confrontations and violence in the area virtually ceased in the days immediately following the soldiers' arrival.[95] So too the military occupation seemed to sap whatever was left of the union's willingness and ability to continue its struggle. On February 2, the two-month-old strike collapsed. Tacitly acknowledging their defeat, union members decided to return to work, while Morton-Gregson officials promised only to rehire the strikers "as the need arose."[96] Many of the recently hired strikebreaking employees drifted away over the ensuing days and weeks, significantly reducing the tension that still pervaded the plant and surrounding community.[97] Meanwhile, in the South Omaha meatpacking district, the same story unfolded, absent the military intervention. There too, striking workers returned to work by early February without gaining any significant concessions from management.[98] Back in Nebraska City, the military presence remained in place for several more weeks to ensure stability and an orderly transition back to civilian authority. During that time, the use of military tribunals to enforce law and order proved to be much more than an empty threat. In the three weeks that martial law was in effect, dozens of area residents were tried before the military commission for a variety of offenses, usually involving weapons possession or liquor violations.[99] Most were convicted, with several of the defendants receiving startlingly severe punishment—so severe, in fact, that the governor almost immediately reduced several of the sentences.[100] On February 16 McKelvie formally ended martial law in the area, and the story of the Nebraska City meatpackers' strike wobbled toward an uneasy conclusion.[101]

Munger's involvement in the matter, however, was not yet finished. Shortly after the rescission of martial law, two of the men convicted by the military tribunal in Nebraska City, Ernest Watson and Hugh Seymour, filed a federal habeas corpus action, claiming that the governor's declaration of martial law had been unwarranted and unconstitutional. Attorneys C. J. Southard and W. M. Jamison contended that martial law could only be invoked "to repel an invasion or to suppress an insurrection and execute the laws of the state," and neither condition existed in Nebraska City during the period of the strike. Moreover, they contended, even if the imposition of martial law had been valid, the military court's punishment of their clients could not legally extend beyond the duration of the martial law period.[102]

After a lengthy hearing, Munger rejected those arguments and upheld the sentences imposed by the military commission. In a published opinion issued on February 27, 1922, he acknowledged that McKelvie's proclamation of martial law had not specifically used the word "insurrection," but he held that the omission of that word did not affect the legitimacy of the order. Munger concluded that the governor's declarations described conditions "of lawlessness and disorder beyond the control of civil authorities [that were] equivalent to a declaration of the existence of that organized resistance to authority known as an insurrection."[103] Responding to the petitioners' argument that their jail sentences could not outlast the period of martial law, Munger held that their position would lead to absurd results. Referring to precedent from other jurisdictions, he noted:

> The power [of military authorities during martial law] to punish serious offenses by imposition of the death penalty is well understood and the lesser punishment of imprisonment for life has been sustained. . . . In case of serious offenses, it is not doubted the sentence of imprisonment may continue during the war or insurrection. If the punishment is inflicted but a few days before the establishment of peace, it would seem absurd that sentences, otherwise just, should at once expire. While the necessity for crushing of further resistance may have passed, the reason for continuance of sentences theretofore given has not ceased.[104]

Watson and Seymour appealed the decision to the Eighth Circuit, which affirmed Munger's ruling without an opinion two years later, long after the two men's sentences had expired.[105]

In the final analysis, the 1921–22 strike was nothing short of a disaster for the Amalgamated union and, indeed, for organized labor throughout the meatpacking industry nationwide. In the words of historian William Pratt, the failed strike "marked the end of an era" and "added to the momentum of the open shop drive by inflicting a mortal blow to a large union." Collective bargaining never returned to the Nebraska City plant, which closed in 1932 during the Depression. In the meantime, alarmed and aroused by the violence surrounding the 1921–22 strike, Nebraska citizens pushed through the legislature a referendum to enact a strict antipicketing law that remained in effect until 1949.[106] The strike also proved to be tragically divisive in the communities where it occurred. In Otoe County and Nebraska City, both the county sheriff and the entire city police force were discharged from office in the aftermath of the strike for their alleged failure to work more vigorously to end the violence and turmoil that the strike had unleashed.[107] And, of course, bitter internecine tensions produced by the strike between neighbors, and even within families, continued to fester well into the future.

Throughout the ordeal, the federal court, in the person of Judge Munger, played a pivotal role in the story. From his issuance of the original restraining order, through the numerous contempt proceedings, his public call for military intervention, and his handling of the Seymour and Watson habeas proceedings, Munger's rulings in the case evinced a decidedly pro-management tilt. Modern observers more sympathetic to labor's concerns, however, should understand that there was nothing unusual or unexpected in Munger's actions during the strike, given the prevailing legal currents and his own staunchly conservative pedigree. However one evaluates Munger's handling of the strike, what cannot be disputed is that the court proved once again to be a powerful echo of its time, reverberating with the tumultuous ebb and flow of the nation's and the state's political, social, economic, and military dynamics.

Docket Management, a World Tour, and Looming Challenges

Obviously the wartime civil liberties cases and the litigation related to postwar labor unrest were not the only matters that Munger and Woodrough dealt with during the late 1910s and early 1920s. Cases involving railroad rate regulation, antitrust, public utilities, interstate commerce, patents, bankruptcy, insurance, and many other prosaic topics continued to pass through the court with metronomic regularity.[108] So too, both judges seemed to be favorite targets of Eighth Circuit Administrative Judge Walter Sanborn during those years for fill-in assignments in other districts and on appellate panels, which necessitated a good deal of schedule-juggling and cooperation between the two men in order to maintain control over their own crowded dockets. For example, while serving as a visiting judge in Denver in late September 1917, Munger wrote to Woodrough to report on his status and discuss the available options for covering their respective Nebraska caseloads. He began by observing that "it seems quite evident that some [Nebraska] attorneys will have to defer the trial of their cases for a period," inasmuch as he had more than forty "slacker, bootleg, and white slave cases," as well as numerous potential jury trials on other issues, to deal with in Colorado.[109] He acknowledged that Woodrough too was dealing with an extremely full schedule and would himself soon be serving out of state, saying, "With your engagements for October and the Oklahoma court to begin the first of November, you will be very busy also." He concluded by asking Woodrough to "let me know just what your view is of the situation" and ruefully noted, "As Emerson says, 'We are on the knees of the Gods.'"[110]

Two years later, as Munger was away from Nebraska sitting on the Eighth Circuit, the judges again commiserated over the problem of covering their dockets. Munger asked for Woodrough's assistance, writing, "I hope you will not be surprised if I ask you to hold court for me a couple of weeks at Lincoln, say early in November. As nearly as I can estimate it will take me all of October and perhaps a good part of November to finish my Court of Appeals work."[111] The same problem resurfaced in March 1921, as Munger wrote to Woodrough reporting:

I must bear some bad news. Judge Sanborn has seen me personally and kept up a fusillade of letters to me—insisting, in his polite way, that I sit in the Court of Appeals in May, for three weeks. I tried to beg off and estop with one week but he won't accede. I told him of the large docket here and he said he could send in Judge Dyer to hear law cases. Judge Dyer is over eighty and would be quite unsatisfactory to lawyers. . . . I fear I may have to call on you again. . . . I have finished my last Court of Appeals case after putting in the last two nights till 10:00 p.m. . . . On my return I hope we can meet and confer on the state of affairs in Nebraska.[112]

In 1923 Munger enjoyed a temporary respite from the demands of his caseload when he embarked with his wife on a world tour that lasted almost two months. During the journey he met with judicial officials and witnessed court operations in a host of nations, beginning in Japan and proceeding westward through India, Italy, Austria, Germany, France, and England. The trip was a stimulating experience for Munger, and upon his return to Nebraska, he shared his insights with colleagues across the nation by delivering talks and writing an account of his observations that was published in both the *American Bar Association Journal* and the *Nebraska Law Bulletin*.[113] Among many other topics he addressed in the article, Munger commented on the unique problems facing the Japanese courts as they struggled to adopt modern western-style legal processes, noting that the Japanese judges he spoke with "were quite frank in expressing doubts if the Japanese were fit for jury service." With perhaps just a hint of envy, he noted the way in which French and Italian judges controlled their courtrooms almost to the complete exclusion of the parties' attorneys, having the sole power to ask questions of witnesses, and without the restrictions imposed by "any provision by which the accused shall not bear witness against himself." And he seemed particularly enamored with the speed and efficiency of the English judicial system, noting that *voir dire* and juror challenge procedures were dramatically less extensive than in American practice. Thus, he reported, "impaneling a jury ordinarily takes less than five minutes" and a single jury could "often try five or six cases in a day." Yet despite the intriguing detail with which he recounted his experiences abroad, Munger's conclusion was disappointingly bland. Rather than offering specific suggestions for the enhancement of American procedures gleaned from his overseas observations, he opted instead to close his article with the rather empty statement that "we have learned much, but there is still very much that we can learn."[114]

However enjoyable and enlightening Munger's world tour may have been, and as significant and abundant as all the other matters on the court's docket were, the overwhelmingly dominant issue before the court throughout the 1920s was Prohibition. And on that issue, and in the handling of those voluminous cases, a sharp rift between the two judges on the Nebraska federal court would soon emerge.

10

Prohibition and the Dennison Trial

It is probable that no greater hindrance to the effective and successful enforcement of the National Prohibition Act could arise than a persistent ignoring of the limitation put by law upon searches and seizures.
—Judge Joseph Woodrough, *U.S. v. Musgrave* (1923)

The Omaha idea doesn't prevail here. You can't do as you please in Lincoln and get away with it.
—Judge Thomas Munger, May 3, 1924

Laws that people don't believe in can't be enforced if whole armies tried it.
—Tom Dennison

Among the many aftereffects of the Great War in the United States, none had a more profound impact on the nation—and on the Nebraska district court—than the advent of Prohibition. Within the state, political, social, religious, and economic battles between "wets" and "drys" had raged for generations, culminating in the prohibition of liquor production and distribution at the state level effective May 1, 1917.[1] Two years later, the ratification of the Eighteenth Amendment and the ensuing enactment of the Volstead Act made Prohibition a nationwide reality. The "Noble Experiment" lasted fourteen years and produced a host of unintended consequences that have been exhaustively analyzed by historians, sociologists, and other scholars over the ensuing decades. In 1933 the Nineteenth Amendment ended that controversial chapter in the nation's history, but in the meantime, the already bulging docket of the Nebraska district court, like that of other federal courts across the country, swelled to overflowing with thousands of criminal prosecutions of alleged bootleggers, moonshiners, and speakeasy operators. From 1920 to 1933, close to two-thirds of all criminal cases handled annually by the federal courts involved liquor violations.[2] By 1927 the volume of liquor cases was so heavy in Nebraska that Woodrough publicly called for the creation of a third federal judgeship for the district, devoted solely to the processing of liquor violations.[3] Moreover, the massive influx of Prohibition cases began to reveal a sharp division between the two Nebraska judges on the question of how the federal laws should be interpreted and enforced.

The Munger-Woodrough Relationship

By most outward appearances, the relationship between the two Nebraska judges was cordial from the moment of Woodrough's arrival in 1916, and it remained so throughout their seventeen years together on the district court. They worked together harmoniously in dealing with the myriad administrative details and scheduling complications that their duties entailed and seemed genuinely respectful and kind to one another in all of their interactions. In many ways, that rapport was natural and predictable, for the two men had much in common. Both loved the outdoor life and were avid golfers. So too they shared wide-ranging intellectual interests and enjoyed traveling, as reflected in Munger's frequent sojourns around the nation and the world and Woodrough's lifelong "wayfaring" tendencies. Perhaps most important, they both possessed a rigorous sense of self-restraint and personal discipline, as well as a deep passion for the law and the judicial process.

Beyond those surface similarities, however, Munger and Woodrough possessed quite distinct personalities, political views, and judicial philosophies, and those differences became increasingly apparent as the court entered the 1920s. The contrast was particularly visible in their respective attitudes toward Prohibition. Simply put, Munger was a conservative Republican "dry," while Woodrough was a liberal Democratic "wet." Munger firmly supported the moral reformist philosophy underlying Prohibition and adopted a consistently stern approach to the trial and punishment of most of the violators who appeared in his courtroom throughout the era. Moreover, he was himself a teetotaler, abstaining from the use of alcohol or tobacco throughout his life.[4] His personal views on the topic were perhaps best revealed in a 1926 case in which a prominent attorney appeared before him to appeal his disbarment for brewing batches of wine, brandy, and beer for his own use. Munger firmly rejected the man's contention that his crime involved "no moral turpitude," declaring "in the court's opinion, the violation is a matter of moral turpitude when done by a leading attorney of many years' experience and is an act of depravity in his social and personal relations."[5]

In contrast, Woodrough saw no "depravity" in the moderate use of alcohol and was dubious about the merits of legislating morality, preferring to "put his faith in the honesty and wisdom of the human race."[6] He felt that federal judges had far better ways to spend their time than presiding over the trials of thousands of small-time liquor offenders, and he began to develop a well-deserved reputation—admired in some circles, vilified in others—for his tendency toward leniency in Prohibition prosecutions. "I wouldn't say he was soft on anybody, but he was not a headhunter," recalled a longtime friend and colleague, Harold Rock. "He had a great affection for the little fellow. He looked around and saw what the times were. He didn't consider brewing a mortal sin." Moreover, Woodrough did not share Munger's steadfast personal aversion to alcohol. "He wasn't a rouster," Rock noted, "but he would have a scotch now and then." Robert Van Pelt, a later colleague of Woodrough's on the federal bench, succinctly summarized the two men's differences on the Prohibition issue, saying, "[Judge] Munger believed in the National Prohibition Act prosecutions. Judge Woodrough did not. Judge Woodrough believed in prosecuting intoxicating liquor violators through the Internal Revenue Act for failure to pay taxes. Judge Munger did not."[7]

The two judges' courtroom demeanor also set them apart. Woodrough became widely known for his warmth, humor, and gentle "human touch" in managing his docket. Those personal traits, coupled with his distaste for the exclusive social clubs where many of his contemporaries spent much of their free time, seemed to allow him to remain grounded and empathetic to working-class Nebraskans. Indeed, Van Pelt eulogized Woodrough as "probably the most human judge the District Court of Nebraska has ever had."[8] In 1924 an Omaha attorney who practiced frequently in Woodrough's court expressed his admiration much more passionately, publishing an ode to the judge's virtues that must have brought a blush to his judicial cheeks:

> The United States has many judges of whom they must be proud,
> That wear that noble, well earned judicial shroud.
> But there's one upon the bench now in Omaha,
> The one that surely can be called the best they ever saw,
> He sits upon that bench, just like you and me,
> And the office does not swell his head in the slightest degree,
> For he belongs to the people they call the Common Herd,
> For degrees of self importance to him they are absurd,
> He cares for no one in so far as their success,
> For he treats the wealthy just like the widow in distress,
> And while upon the bench he is patient all the while,
> And carries with him a nice and lovely smile,
> Oh? What a great blessing President Wilson did bestow,
> On Nebraska when he appointed us our beloved Judge Woodrough,
> And Oh, that God his grace would give us,
> To see ourselves as he does us,
> It is the prayer of all the people both high and low,
> That God will spare us our beloved Judge Woodrough.[9]

Even defendants who were punished in Woodrough's court could be charmed by his geniality. On one occasion, despite receiving a $50 fine for a minor liquor violation, a repentant haberdasher blurted out: "Judge, any time you want your hats cleaned or reblocked it won't cost you a cent."[10] As Woodrough's reputation as a firm but compassionate jurist ascended, the *Omaha World-Herald*'s love affair with him soared to new heights. In a 1929 editorial, it urged his appointment to the Supreme Court, gushing:

> The next time some chief executive of this favored nation lifts his presidential eyes and begins scanning the wide horizon for an associate justice of the supreme court of the United States he can shift his gaze to Omaha and save himself a lot of time. We have the man right here in town. . . . Give us a judge who understands! That's what we ask and it is practically all that we ask. What are books and weighty tomes? Give us a judge who knows and loves human beings, individually and in the mass. That understanding trait has characterized the great men of the world. It makes us almost sad that we can't stand up before Judge Woodrough to be sentenced.[11]

Perhaps unfairly, Munger inspired no such public acclaim. To be sure, he was by all accounts courteous to those who appeared before him, and his integrity and honesty were beyond reproach. He most certainly enjoyed the respect and admiration of most of his contemporaries. But there can also be little doubt that, as one of the two most prominent human "faces" of the federal court in the state, his appeal to everyday Nebraskans paled in comparison with Woodrough's. His was a more imposing and intimidating presence in the courtroom, and the differences in the two men's styles were never more apparent than in their handling of the hundreds of Prohibition cases that came before them.

Woodrough vs. "Raiding Bob"

During the 1920s, the man chiefly responsible for the enforcement of the Prohibition laws in Nebraska was Robert Samardick. An immigrant from Montenegro in the Balkans, he worked in the iron mines of northern Minnesota in his youth before making his way to South Omaha's growing Serbian community. He was a "spy chaser" in the counterintelligence service during the war and then returned to Nebraska in 1919, where he joined the Omaha Police Department and "quickly gained a reputation as a tough officer on the morals squad" before resigning to become a federal Prohibition agent in 1920.[12] With a teetotaler's zeal for punishing immorality and an apparently sincere belief in the need to vigorously and impartially enforce the nation's new liquor laws, Samardick quickly gained renown as "Raiding Bob," both admired and feared for his aggressive and frequent raids against bootleggers, still operators, and retailers of illicit liquor. His calling cards were a swinging ax and rubber boots, as he and his agents frequently burst through doors and chopped up stills, before pouring thousands of gallons of whiskey, beer, and wine into streets, sewers, or creeks.[13] Samardick's investigations and raids often tested the limits of the Fourth and Fifth Amendments, as he routinely smashed his way into suspects' homes and businesses, often without warrants and armed only with debatable degrees of "probable cause." These and other volatile issues, combined with the massive numbers of his arrests, made Samardick a familiar figure in both Munger's and Woodrough's courtrooms throughout the Prohibition years.

Tales of "Raiding Bob's" exploits are endless. Not only was he often arrested himself for injuring suspects during his raids, but he was also frequently shot at, bribed, or otherwise threatened by his adversaries.[14] Still, he and his team of agents kept raiding, and the charges brought both by and against him continued to mount. In 1925 alone, Samardick and his men faced prosecution by state and county authorities for more than a dozen alleged assaults. The Douglas County attorney claimed that he was "trying to keep federal officers from beating up our citizens," but Samardick remained unbowed and unrepentant. He admitted that he and his agents occasionally "smacked the noses of bootleggers who resist us," but then vowed that "we're going to continue smacking them when they resist. . . . This won't stop us from enforcing the law fearlessly as we have in the past."[15] In one of those 1925 cases, he was acquitted by a jury in Woodrough's court for punching a cab driver in the face and was then hauled into court a few months later for allegedly assaulting a female suspect named Lillian Laux, who happened to be a friend of Nebraska senator Robert Howell. After smashing through the front door at the home of Laux's grandmother, Samardick allegedly pinned the young woman to the ground, twisting her arm while questioning her about possible liquor in the house.[16] In yet another incident a few years later, he pleaded guilty to assaulting a postal worker who he claimed had made disparaging comments about one of his former agents and received a $150 fine from Munger.[17] Despite the controversy that his methods produced, Samardick became one of the favorites of federal law enforcement leaders, who often praised his work and brought him to Washington and other eastern cities to train other Prohibition agents.[18] Meanwhile, the "wet" and progressive *Omaha World-Herald* began to refer routinely to the targets of Samardick's raids as his "victims."[19]

Given their opposing viewpoints on both the merits of Prohibition and the limits of police power, Samardick and Woodrough seemed destined for conflict. It was not long in coming. One of their most prominent clashes came in 1923, when Samardick obtained a warrant and raided an Omaha pharmacy, finding clear evidence of liquor violations. At trial, however, Woodrough sustained the defendants' motion to dismiss the charges. In a pathbreaking decision styled *United States v. Musgrave* that prompted banner headlines in local newspapers and alarmed law enforcement officials nationwide, he held that Prohibition agents like Samardick, operating under the auspices of the U.S. Treasury Department, were not "civil officers" authorized to execute federal search warrants.[20] After first deciding that "the Prohibition officer in question [Samardick] is clearly not a civil officer in any strict or constitutional sense," Woodrough observed that "the real question here is whether the term 'civil officer' may be given a popular and less strict meaning." He acknowledged that federal courts in other states had in fact adopted a less technical meaning of the phrase, but nevertheless he concluded, "I find myself unable to concur." Using language that endeared him to civil libertarians and "wets" all over the country, he declared:

> I am persuaded that a strict and literal observance of all limitations incorporated in the law concerning the issuance of search warrants is not only in accordance with the historical tradition and spirit of our law, but it appears equally clear that Congress, in the Volstead

Act itself, imperatively commands the maintenance of the specified limitations. . . . It is probable that no greater hindrance to the effective and successful enforcement of the National Prohibition Act could arise than a persistent ignoring of the limitation put by law upon searches and seizures.[21]

Despite the notoriety of Woodrough's ruling, it had little practical effect on the specific parties involved in the case. The bootlegging pharmacist who had escaped conviction continued selling moonshine from his drugstore, and Samardick went right back after him, this time bringing along a federal marshal to formally serve the warrant. Woodrough once again presided over the trial, and a jury convicted the pharmacist on thirteen counts.[22]

Another clash between Samardick and the judge arose out of the Prohibition forces' aggressive use of section 22 of the Volstead Act, popularly dubbed the "padlock provision." In essence, the law gave federal authorities the power to obtain court injunctions to close ("padlock") for up to one year places where liquor was manufactured or sold.[23] The provision proved to be one of the most effective tools in the federal enforcement arsenal, and Samardick and other local officials used it repeatedly and effectively. In early 1923, enforcement officials in Washington encouraged their subordinates to be even more aggressive in their use of the padlock law, prompting Samardick's regional supervisor to vow to do precisely that. "If we are successful," he said, "we will close them all up for a year and a day."[24]

Samardick and his men needed no such encouragement. On the very day that national authorities announced their desire for more aggressive padlocking efforts by local officers, Raiding Bob's undercover agents discovered a handful of entrepreneurial bellboys at the Fontenelle Hotel in downtown Omaha selling whiskey to patrons, apparently without the knowledge or complicity of the hotel's management. Samardick promptly raided the building. Despite failing to find a drop of liquor on the premises, the agents arrested two of the bellboys and immediately petitioned Woodrough for an injunction allowing them to padlock the entire hotel. Woodrough was skeptical of

Samardick's case, but he agreed to issue a temporary restraining order against the hotel, pending an evidentiary hearing on the injunction request. In the days leading to the hearing, prosecutors negotiated favorable plea bargains with several of the bellboys in exchange for their testimony against the hotel's owner, Eugene Eppley. Eppley, meanwhile, vigorously denied any knowledge of the bellhops' actions and declared his belief that there was "something sinister about the raid," and vowed "to find out what it is."[25]

At the injunction hearing in early March, Woodrough listened to and took part in extensive questioning of the hotel's managers and the accused bellmen.[26] In the end, he determined that management had no knowledge of or involvement in the illicit liquor sales, and he denied the government's request for an injunction closing the hotel. Predictably, Samardick was angered by Woodrough's decision and did little to hide his belief that the outcome had been dictated by the hotel owner's wealth and prominence. "This decision is not going to discourage me in my efforts to bring bootleggers to justice," he declared, "no matter what their ratings might be in Dun and Bradstreet."[27]

Whatever Samardick may have believed about Woodrough's motives, as Omaha attorney and writer Nick Batter has pointed out, his ruling in the case provides fodder for one of the great "what ifs" in Omaha's history. The Fontenelle Hotel was one of Eppley's earliest business ventures, and he would go on to make it into the flagship property of a large chain of upscale hotels. The fortune he amassed allowed him to eventually become one of the greatest philanthropists in Omaha's history. Had Woodrough allowed the government to shutter Eppley's fledgling business in 1923, it likely would have snuffed out one of the brightest lights of Omaha's midcentury growth, quite possibly changing the future of the city and the region.[28]

Despite the ruling in the Fontenelle case, authorities were not significantly deterred, and they continued to apply for padlock injunctions in dozens of cases. Woodrough occasionally acceded, granting two such injunctions in late 1923 against businesses that had been charged and convicted several times before.[29] But in early 1924, his tolerance for the government's tactics reached its limit. Authorities sought a padlock order on the home of an elderly Omaha couple who had pled guilty and been fined for selling a small amount of wine from their house during the previous year. Prosecutors alleged no new sales or violations, but nevertheless sought to seal the home and its contents for a year—effectively throwing the pair out into the streets without their belongings.[30]

This time Woodrough did not merely deny the government's requested injunction. He boldly declared that the "padlock provision" of the Volstead Act was unconstitutional in its entirety. In a thoughtfully constructed opinion published as *United States v. Lot 29, Block 16, Highland Place, City of Omaha, Neb.*, Woodrough analyzed the statutory language that purported to vest a court of equity with the power to try a defendant for a crime without benefit of a jury. He concluded that only courts of law—not chancellors in equity exercising the power of injunction—have such power, and the statute therefore violated the clear mandate of Article III of the Constitution that "trial of all crimes shall be by jury." Woodrough declared:

> The federal government cannot put offenders against its criminal laws on trial, except before a jury. This is a very fundamental feature of the federal institution and must be scrupulously safeguarded by the court. . . . I feel it my duty to put the decision of this case upon the constitutional provision, and to decide, as the ground of dismissal of the case, that the act which attempts to confer such powers on the chancellor is contrary to the constitutional requirement that the trial of all crimes shall be by jury, and hence is null and void. . . . As to the present case, the petition is dismissed, because the particular provision of the law on which it is based is unconstitutional and void.[31]

As with *Musgrave*, Woodrough's decision in *Lot 29* created a stir throughout the country. In Illinois, where courts were routinely issuing padlock orders against hundreds of homes and businesses, a reporter excitedly (and certainly hyperbolically) called it "the most important court ruling affecting personal liberties since the famous *Dred Scott* case."[32] In his opinion, Woodrough explicitly invited a Supreme Court ruling on the issue, and most observers expected the high court to step in and bring closure to the question. An editorial in the *Detroit News*, for example, commended Woodrough for the clarity of his opinion, but concluded that "the opinion of the highest tribunal in the land on the fundamental principles involved should be procured without loss of time."[33] But no appeal was taken, and the Supreme Court remained silent. Unfettered, Woodrough applied his own precedent to reject more petitions for padlock orders in the ensuing years.[34]

While Woodrough became increasingly well known for his leniency in Volstead prosecutions, his colleague in Lincoln, Judge Munger, generally took a much firmer and harsher line. Woodrough's decision in *Lot 29* invalidating the padlock law struck Munger as particularly egregious, and he soon took a subtle but unmistakable jab at his younger colleague that made its way into the local press. As he was handing out stiff penalties to some two dozen liquor violators just a few weeks after Woodrough's *Lot 29* decision was announced, Munger said to the defendants in open court, "The Omaha idea doesn't prevail here. You can't do as you please in Lincoln and get away with it."[35] The comments drew a stinging rebuke from Woodrough's longtime champion, the *Omaha World-Herald*, which promptly issued an editorial that asked, "Can he mean to imply that it is his associate, Judge Woodrough, who waives the law and its enforcement and so allows Omaha to become a sink of iniquity?"[36] The writer then challenged Munger to either prove or retract his statement, which it called "an indictment of a whole people" made all the more offensive because it was "delivered not by a prosecuting attorney or a scandalmonger or a tin horn politician, but by a distinguished jurist." Munger did not respond further at that time, but he also proceeded to routinely ignore Woodrough's ruling in his own courtroom. Indeed, in a prominent 1929 case, Munger implicitly but clearly expressed his disdain for Woodrough's *Lot 29* opinion, as he declared that there were no constitutional defects in the padlock provisions of the national statute.[37]

As Woodrough continued to chip away at the government's Prohibition powers on constitutional grounds, authorities began "judge shopping" by manipulating the timing of their actions to try to avoid

Woodrough's court. Samardick and other officials would wait until Woodrough left town to sit in the western divisions of the district or was on assignment in other states, and then dump their backlog of cases onto the docket of a replacement judge who they hoped would prove tougher on their targets. For several years, that tactic proved successful, because one of Woodrough's most frequent substitutes from 1923 to 1925 was Judge John McGee of the Minnesota district court. McGee, a recent Harding appointee, quickly gained a reputation for "striking fear into the hearts of Omaha bootleggers," as his record of imposing extremely harsh sentences for minor liquor offenses won him the nickname "Ten-Year McGee."[38] In cases where defendants were found guilty despite their protestations of innocence, McGee was even known to lengthen their sentences, since they had presumably committed perjury by denying their guilt. The Minnesota judge was also truly exceptional in the efficiency with which he disposed of his caseload. He held court in the evenings and on Saturdays and became known for his "sentence a minute" operations, on one remarkable occasion imposing 112 sentences in 130 minutes.[39] But McGee's manic efficiency may also have been his undoing, as his career and his life came to an early end. After completing a stint as Woodrough's substitute in 1925, McGee returned to his chambers in Minneapolis and killed himself with a gunshot to the head. He left behind a suicide note that poignantly highlighted the crushing burden that Prohibition was placing on the federal courts, while also offering cautionary guidance for any and all judges who may feel overburdened by their dockets:

I have, against the advice of my associates and others, held court since I went on the bench in March, 1923, six days in the week instead of five, and seven and one half hours a day instead of five, winter and summer without vacations, the matters heard and submitted piling up except when taken home nights and Sundays and worked on there. . . . The fact is that the United States District Court has become a police court for the trial of whiskey and narcotic cases which the state courts should look after. Those cases occupy 80 per cent of the court's time and are exciting and trying on the nerves, with the end not in sight. I started work in March 1923, to rush that branch of the litigation and thought I would end it, but it has ended me.[40]

Despite Woodrough's growing reputation for leniency toward liquor violators, by no means were all of his rulings in Prohibition cases adverse to prosecutors. During most of the 1920s, for example, he remained relatively tolerant of the often scanty quantity and quality of federal agents' "probable cause" used to obtain warrants or, even more regularly, to justify warrantless searches. In one notable 1928 case, federal agents raided a downtown Omaha distillery after obtaining a warrant based on their claims of smelling hints of fermenting mash in the air. They found and confiscated truckloads of equipment and supplies—clearly the tools of a large-scale operation—but they ultimately discovered only four small containers of actual mash. The well-financed defendants introduced affidavits from both a meteorologist and a chemist to dispute the possibility that any such fumes could have been detected by a human nose, and argued that the warrant for the search of the premises has been issued without adequate probable cause.[41] Nevertheless, Woodrough sided firmly with the prosecution and upheld the validity of the search, issuing a published opinion in which he reasoned that "officers must go where their senses tell them a crime is being committed."[42]

Over the ensuing months, however, Woodrough seemed to become thoroughly disenchanted with what he perceived to be increasingly aggressive warrantless searches, based upon increasingly flimsy probable cause. He responded with a decision in late 1929 that would prove to be his most resounding salvo yet in the Prohibition wars. The case began when agents raided a farmhouse without a warrant after claiming to smell fermenting mash from two hundred yards away, despite a strong wind at their backs.[43] When the case came to trial, Woodrough expressed "sickening doubt" that agents had smelled anything at all and invalidated the search.[44] Seeing the raids as symptomatic of the government's escalating abuse of power, Woodrough then proceeded to carve out a "bright line" rule, declaring that "the mere odor of fermenting mash would not justify a raid" in any case. The "protection of the inalienable rights of the American citizen is of more importance than easy enforcement of the Prohibition law."[45] Applying the rule he had just enunciated, Woodrough promptly dismissed a dozen more pending cases, each of which involved searches based on agents' sense of smell.[46]

Once again, Woodrough found himself lauded in some quarters and sharply criticized in others. Recognizing the notoriety and controversy that the judge's "sniff search" ruling would generate, one Omaha reporter mailed photographs of Woodrough to his colleagues across the country, predicting that "Woodrough's pictures will be in good demand."[47] He was correct. National praise poured in, led by a *New York Herald Tribune* editorial that declared: "[Woodrough] is expressing a philosophy of government that lies at the foundation of American institutions. Needless to say, the vast majority of his fellow countrymen will agree with him; they will applaud his refreshing reassertion of a principle which in the last 10 years has been made to yield right and left to enforcement expediency. . . . The confidence of the people in the federal bench as a bulwark of their rights would be greatly strengthened were it graced with more men of the caliber and fearlessness of this Omaha jurist."[48]

On the other hand, local and national law enforcement officials were aghast at the ruling. Nebraska U.S. district attorney James Kinsler epitomized those views, complaining that Woodrough's decision was "equivalent to saying that a man cannot break into a house without a warrant, even if he can see or hear a felony—even a murder—being committed."[49] The issue also exacerbated the growing, but still largely private, rift between Woodrough and Munger. Munger had for years routinely admitted evidence seized during sniff searches, and just a few days after issuing his "bright line" ruling, Woodrough agitated his senior colleague considerably when he dismissed charges against a defendant that were based on a search that Munger had previously held to be valid. The *Omaha World-Herald* did its part to fan the flames of controversy, running a huge front-page headline reading, "2 Federal Judges Clash on Arrests without Warrant; Woodrough Frees Man after

Munger Refuses to Suppress Evidence."[50] Woodrough's "bright line" ruling was implicitly reversed by the Eighth Circuit later that year in *Day v. U.S.*, but he continued to invalidate overreaching searches on a case-by-case basis for the remainder of the Prohibition years.[51] The relationship between the Fourth Amendment's privacy protections and the olfactory senses of law enforcement officers has continued to vex courts and legal scholars ever since.[52]

Through all the controversy and backlash, Woodrough remained unfazed. He viewed his relatively lenient approach to liquor cases as not only legally correct but also necessary for the efficient handling of his massive caseload. He felt that his light sentencing tendencies, particularly for minor and first time violators, encouraged more defendants to enter guilty pleas, avoiding lengthy trials. Woodrough also allowed prosecutors wide berth in striking plea deals. When criticized for these practices, he responded that "he knew of no other way in which the hundreds of liquor cases could be disposed of," and he reaffirmed his belief that "no real injustice is [being] done."[53] Perhaps just as significantly, Woodrough was not at all averse to serving as a catalyst for changes that he felt necessary, both in life and in the law. To him, the march of public progress was more compelling than the maintenance of a hoary status quo, and as Prohibition agents repeatedly learned, he had no qualms about striking down existing law in order to foster liberties he deemed more important to the public. As Harold Rock recalled, "He didn't mind causing a stir . . . he probably got a bang out of it. Seeing those Prohibition [agents] staggering around in their underwear would be kind of entertaining [to him]."[54]

In contrast, Munger remained committed to strict and rigorous enforcement of the liquor laws. Throughout Prohibition, and without the concerns that Woodrough frequently expressed, he issued scores of "padlock injunctions" and routinely validated warrantless "sniff searches." He also made it clear that the overwhelming number of liquor cases on his docket would not affect his sentencing of convicted defendants. In 1921, for example, after imposing a fine of $400 and a six-month jail sentence on a repeat offender, he told the man, "Congress didn't mean the law for a joke, and Congress put it up to the courts to enforce the law . . . when sentences for violation of the law become serious, the violators will take the law seriously."[55] A few weeks later, he repeated his message while sentencing five more men, saying: "If necessary, I can fill the jails and penitentiaries so full that those on the outside won't believe the liquor business to be very profitable. You five Seward boys are like a lot of others who make the mistake of not taking the Prohibition law seriously. You make a lark out of this . . . but the law must be obeyed like any other, and nobody can forever evade the consequences."[56]

At least one of Munger's assertions, however, was wrong. For some people, the liquor business was in fact "very profitable," and one of those who was profiting the most was Omaha crime boss Tom Dennison.

The Dennison Trial

The culminating event of the Prohibition era in Nebraska—and one of the most prominent trials in the history of the Nebraska court—came in 1932, when Omaha crime boss Tom Dennison and almost sixty of his associates stood trial in Woodrough's courtroom for a wide array of liquor, racketeering, and tax evasion charges. Many skilled historians and other writers have told the story of the Dennison trial, and a full recitation of that narrative is neither possible nor necessary here.[57] But an appreciation of the trial and its impact does require some contextual "table-setting," as well as a brief introduction to some of the protagonists in the drama. Those leading characters include not only Woodrough and Dennison and a few of Dennison's most unsavory associates, but also both the father and grandfather of the current chief U.S. district judge for the district of Nebraska.

In the late 1890s, at about the same time that Woodrough was returning to Omaha after his stint as a county judge in Texas (see chapter 9), Tom Dennison was taking his initial steps toward becoming the unchallenged king of the Omaha underworld. He settled in the city to stay in 1892 at age thirty-four, after spending his younger years prospecting, gambling, running saloons, and engaging in petty thievery throughout the West.[58] Within a decade, however, the former small-time criminal had consolidated his control over a massive gambling, prostitution, racketeering, vice, and bootlegging empire by leveraging corrupt police officials and routing his rivals. While Omaha and the rest of Nebraska had much to be proud of during those years, including the glamour of the city's Trans-Mississippi Exposition in 1898, Dennison's growing power and the criminal/political machine that he controlled did nothing to improve the city's reputation for lawlessness and vice. Indeed, to many observers at the turn of the century, Omaha's long-standing notoriety as a "dirty, wicked town" seemed to be as accurate as it had ever been, as the city continued to garner national infamy for brazen kidnappings, racial violence, and xenophobia.[59]

Meanwhile, inefficiencies in the judicial system slowed adjudication to a crawl. As a young practicing attorney, Woodrough complained that new cases were simply left "mouldering, like John Brown's body," and he longed to do his part to combat organized crime as well as the disorganized legal system.[60] Woodrough's partner and mentor, William Gurley, was a prominent enemy of Edward Rosewater, publisher of the *Omaha Daily Bee* and a man who was widely perceived to be one of Dennison's foremost "bought and paid for" patrons. The perpetual feud between Gurley and Rosewater was highlighted in 1902, when they squared off against one another for a public debate on the issues of the day. A huge crowd filled the Orpheum Theater to witness the spectacle, and it proved to be a show "well worth the price of admission." Gurley attacked Rosewater for his shadowy alliance with Dennison and their use of bribery and cronyism to build a corrupt political machine. Predictably, the progressive *Omaha World-Herald* praised Gurley's eloquence, while mocking Rosewater for "teetering on tiptoe as he shrieked in high falsetto." Rosewater's own *Bee*, of course, painted a vastly different picture of the debate, claiming that he had "cleaned up" against Gurley, but the *World-Herald* got in the final word on the event, wryly observing that Rosewater had only "cleaned up" against Gurley "like the man cleaned up the packing house when he was dragged through it by the heels."[61]

The Gurley-Rosewater rivalry soon affected Woodrough directly. In 1905 he ran as the Democratic candidate for county judge. Although his opponent was "not as well versed in the law," Rosewater and his paper campaigned strongly against Woodrough, contributing to his defeat in the general election.[62] Disappointed by the defeat, Woodrough continued his successful practice with Gurley until his appointment to the federal court eleven years later.

Meanwhile, as Dennison's machine continued its domination of the city and its infrastructure, a nucleus of anti-Dennison voices began to emerge, calling for a purge of the machine's corrupt influences from the city's government. Among the leaders of that reform movement were U.S. senator R. B. Howell, state attorney general C. A. Sorensen, city commissioner Roy Towl, and the longtime clerk of the Douglas County district court, Robert Smith.[63] The reformers' efforts came to fruition in 1918, when their candidate Edward Smith (no relation to Robert) unseated multi-term Omaha mayor "Cowboy" Jim Dahlman, long considered a Dennison crony. Dennison was not impressed by the temporary setback. In the aftermath of Dahlman's defeat, he suppos- edly remarked, "I think we better let the bastards have it their way for a while. Let's just lie low for the next election . . . they'll be glad to see us back."[64] Woodrough was well acquainted with the new mayor. While in private practice, he and Smith had shared neighboring offices, and both served as adjunct instructors at Creighton Law School.[65]

The years immediately following World War I, which coincided with the Smith administration's efforts to "clean up" Omaha, were partic- ularly turbulent ones for the city and the state, marked by economic distress and violence in labor relations, among many other travails. Racial tensions were one of the most troubling elements of those years, and Dennison's operatives took advantage of the situation to try to discredit and bring down Smith and his reformers. The *Omaha Bee*, now managed by Edward Rosewater's son, Victor, "printed whatever [Dennison] wanted" and repeatedly ran provocative stories of crimes against whites at the hands of blacks.[66]

The racial tensions in the city reached a boiling point in the early fall of 1919, when a black man named Will Brown was arrested for allegedly raping a white woman. Rosewater's *Bee* inflamed local passions with a series of incendiary articles, and on September 19 a massive throng of enraged whites stormed the Douglas County Courthouse intent on seizing and lynching Brown. The tragedy that ensued has been aptly called "the darkest day in Omaha history," as the mob besieged the building and set it on fire. Mayor Smith was inside the courthouse when the riot began, and as the intensity of the threat mounted, he strode out of the burning courthouse, telling the crowd, "I will not give up the man. I'm going to enforce the law even with my own life. If you must hang somebody, then let it be me."[67] He fought as the angry crowd closed in on him, but was knocked unconscious and, with a noose placed around his neck, was dragged behind a car and strung up from a traffic pole before he was rescued by a city policeman. Meanwhile, the police defending the courthouse succumbed to the mob and surrendered their prisoner. The crazed rioters shot Brown repeatedly, then hung his body from a telephone pole, then dragged him around the city behind a stolen police car, and ultimately set his remains on fire, all while news photographers took photos and bystanders stood by, either unable or unwilling to intercede. Mayor Smith survived the melee, but remained hospitalized, drifting in and out of consciousness for days thereafter.

In the midst of all this turmoil, Prohibition arrived. Predictably, Dennison and his minions quickly took control of most of the illicit liquor trade throughout the region, using the massive profits to reestablish their control of the city from behind the scenes. Upstart allies of the machine, among them a twenty-two-year-old immigrant named Louise Vinciquerra, helped to fuel the Dennison machine's resurgence. Dubbed "Queen Louise" by the press and her fellow bootleggers, the exotically beautiful young woman quickly accumulated a vast fortune and an accompanying taste for extravagance and self-indulgence. "Her home oozed opulence," recorded the *Omaha World-Herald*, and she drove a Packard high-luxury sedan. Unlike Dennison, who shunned the limelight and operated behind intricate layers of intermediaries, Vinciquerra worked in plain sight, treating Prohibition fines as if they were merely the business expenses of a legitimate enterprise. She routinely appeared in Woodrough's court, pled guilty to whatever offense she was charged with, paid her fine, and then immediately returned to her distilleries. Her cavalier approach attracted a tremendous amount of legal and media attention, which Dennison always sought to avoid. But despite their opposing methods and the fact that they were ostensibly competitors, Dennison seemed fascinated by Vinciquerra, and he reportedly bankrolled some of the legal expenses arising out of her numerous and colorful court appearances.[68]

Much of Vinciquerra's success was also attributable to a number of bribed "moles" that she employed within law enforcement agencies. On multiple occasions, Prohibition agents raided her facilities only to find the lingering smell of mash and signs of recently moved equipment. But her insiders aided her with more than tip-offs about impending raids. Prohibition agent Earl Haning fell in love with Vinciquerra and sought to win her favor by specifically targeting her rivals, confiscating their supplies and equipment and sometimes funneling them directly to his paramour. Whereas some suitors might have sent boxes of chocolates, Haning sent Vinciquerra hundred-pound sacks of distilling sugar. Haning's boss, "Raiding Bob" Samardick, eventually uncovered his scheme and, true to form, left Haning "badly beaten" before stripping him of his badge and sending him to the federal penitentiary. Federal officials continued to attack Vinciquerra's operations with fines and raids, but with little impact.[69]

Watching these developments from his courtroom, Woodrough grew increasingly frustrated and disgusted with the endless stream of working-class Nebraskans who were dragged before him facing all sorts of punishments for minor liquor offenses, while major operators like Vinciquerra and Dennison thrived with impunity, seemingly beyond the reach of the law. He was not alone in those sentiments. By the mid-1920s, federal prosecutors elsewhere in the country were beginning to win some of their battles with major crime bosses, using creative new tactics pioneered in part by Assistant Attorney General Mabel Walker Willebrandt. Like Woodrough, Willebrandt was something of an iconoclast among her contemporaries, seeing little reason to waste valuable time and resources in going after minor liquor offenders. "I have no patience with this policy of going after the hip-pocket and speakeasy cases," she declared. "That's like trying to dry up the Atlantic Ocean with a blotter."[70]

An expert in both Prohibition and tax law, Willebrandt's foremost contribution to the fight against crime bosses was to use the tax code against them, with indictments alleging not only liquor violations but also tax evasion and conspiracy charges that allowed prosecutors to place significant new pressures on their well-protected targets. Willebrandt gained some notable victories with these new tactics, including the successful prosecution of George Remus, a major bootlegging kingpin in Woodrough's hometown of Cincinnati.[71]

Woodrough became an enthusiastic advocate of Willebrandt's approach. While sitting on an Eighth Circuit panel in 1929, he wrote a dissent that agreed with her position regarding the aggressive use of the tax code, albeit in a non-Prohibition case.[72] Ultimately, in an opinion written by Louis Brandeis the following year, the Supreme Court agreed with Willebrandt and Woodrough's reasoning and reversed the Eighth Circuit's decision.[73] By then, however, Willebrandt had left the Justice Department, after failing to receive an expected appointment as attorney general from newly elected president Herbert Hoover.[74]

In Omaha, however, a new twenty-four-year-old assistant U.S. attorney, Edson Smith, eagerly and aggressively adopted many of Willebrandt's ideas and techniques. Smith was the son of Douglas County district court clerk Robert Smith, one of the long-standing leaders of the anti-Dennison forces in Omaha. Within just four months of his graduation from Harvard Law School in 1929, Smith had been appointed to his new post and returned to his native Nebraska, where he was assigned responsibility for spearheading all bootlegging prosecutions in the state. During those waning years of Prohibition, Smith prosecuted more than a hundred cases against some of Omaha's most infamous criminals. One of his most notorious targets was Gene Livingston, a violent figure in the Omaha underworld who was reputed to be an associate of legendary Chicago gangster John Dillinger. Dubbed by the press as "the man of many rackets," Livingston's fingers were indeed in many pots, and he had been in and out of countless scrapes with police, always escaping serious punishment. After a winter raid on

Livingston's operations by Prohibition agents in 1929, Smith charged him with both liquor offenses and tax evasion, taking a page directly from the Willebrandt playbook. Smith used inventory lists and even empty grain sacks to calculate the amount of illicit business Livingston had failed to pay taxes on, and he sought back taxes and penalties that exceeded a quarter of a million dollars.[75]

Accustomed to favorable treatment, light penalties, and a protective network of bribed public officials, Livingston received a rude awakening in Woodrough's court. His attorneys sought an expedited trial, but Woodrough denied all their requests, while Smith gave notice that Livingston's days of special treatment were over, saying, "In view of the fact that there are more than one hundred defendants now awaiting trial, it will be necessary for Livingston to wait his turn."[76] When the trial eventually took place, Livingston took the stand in his own defense and offered a far-fetched tale for the jury, recounting in detail how he had run from the police on the night of the raid in a burst of excitement, accidentally fallen into a hiding spot, and failed to respond to officers due to "dizziness." Smith wisely opted to let the ludicrous account speak for itself and quickly rested his case. The jury promptly convicted Livingston, and Woodrough imposed a stiff fine and lengthy prison term.[77]

Despite the conviction, Livingston never saw the inside of a federal prison, as it quickly became clear why he had been so eager to have his trial schedule accelerated: he was trying to leave town. He had apparently borrowed his expensive distilling equipment from two of Al Capone's Chicago lieutenants. With that equipment in government possession, and with his cash and other assets frozen by Smith's tax charges, Livingston found himself unable to pay his debts to his mobster financiers. Shortly after the trial, as he remained free on bond, a car with Chicago license plates pulled up beside him in traffic and fired a hail of bullets into his vehicle. Livingston miraculously survived and took refuge in a local speakeasy. As he sat in the back of the bar, an assassin thrust a shotgun through a nearby window and killed Livingston instantly with a shot that nearly cut him in half.[78]

This and similar episodes of violence, all rooted in organized crime, only bolstered Smith's determination to focus his efforts primarily on major crime bosses rather than low-level offenders. Woodrough agreed. He had always been sympathetic to that position and lenient toward minor bootleggers, and he was consistently much harsher in his treatment of the lieutenants and leaders of the bigger criminal enterprises. Smith's tax evasion cases, however, also produced a new wedge in the growing schism between Woodrough and Munger, as the latter did not approve of prosecutors' use of the tax code as an instrument for enforcing the Prohibition laws. This led Smith to do some "judge shopping" of his own, preferring to bring his "hybrid" liquor/tax cases to Woodrough's court whenever possible.

Throughout the late 1920s, Louise Vinciquerra remained a leading figure in the Omaha bootlegging market, and she too became one of Smith's primary targets. After divorcing her first husband (following a heavy exchange of gunfire in their bedroom) in 1928, she had married the disgraced former Prohibition agent Earl Haning, who had recently been released from prison. The couple celebrated their reunion with a string of small crimes and continued to enjoy the lavish lifestyle for which Vinciquerra had always been known.[79] Their ongoing operations represented the classic scenario that so frustrated officials like Woodrough and Smith. Unlike small offenders, who were regularly stripped of their savings for enjoying a single bottle of wine, Vinciquerra and Haning lived in luxury while publicly flouting the laws.

On an early September evening in 1930, Prohibition agents crept into the overgrown weeds along Blondo Street, near the criminal couple's home. Already tipped off about the impending raid, Vinciquerra was outside, directing a team of men hauling casks of whiskey down the sidewalk into waiting trucks. Agents rushed into the garage, dodging a jug of whiskey lobbed at them by Vinciquerra's young son. Both Vinciquerra and Haning were arrested, and Vinciquerra calmly called an associate to arrange her release. She even asked an officer to escort her to jail in her Packard so she could return home more easily later that day. But this time Queen Louise would not be allowed to return home so easily. Again, Smith used both the liquor statutes and the tax code to bury Vinciquerra in a deluge of charges against her entire enterprise, and he ultimately won multiple convictions in Woodrough's court. With Queen Louise and most of her major associates behind bars, her operation came to a crashing end.[80]

Buoyed by his victories over Livingston and Vinciquerra, Smith now set his sights on the ultimate target—the aging kingpin himself, Tom Dennison. In December 1931 the brutal execution of respected local businessman Harry Lapidus gave Smith and other anti-Dennison forces the opening and the political traction they needed. Lapidus had been an outspoken critic of the Dennison machine, and the likelihood that he had been silenced on the order of the "Old Man" was an obvious and immediate conclusion for many to reach. Still, in the weeks following his murder, police investigated a dizzying array of alternate theories concerning other potential suspects and their possible motives.[81] In the end, no arrests were made and the murder remained officially unsolved, but deep suspicions remained about Dennison's involvement, and sworn testimony would ultimately confirm those suspicions. Longtime Dennison henchman and former Omaha police officer Tom Crawford would eventually testify that Dennison ordered the execution because Lapidus had been at the forefront of efforts to return "Raiding Bob" Samardick to a prominent position in the drive to bring down Dennison. "We can't control Samardick," Crawford recalled Dennison saying. His return "would mean our ruination." Crawford also claimed that Dennison admired what he called the "Capone System" of maintaining a "killer squad" to eliminate opponents. "He [Dennison] went on to tell me we should have such a squad in this organization," Crawford recalled, "and that his system was to have such a squad get rid of such as Lapidus and Bob Smith."[82] It is difficult to imagine how prosecutor Edson Smith must have felt as he elicited that chilling reference to the potential murder of his own father. And that father himself, Robert Smith, may well have been present in the courtroom—perhaps even at the counsel table with his son—at that moment.

In early 1932, however, Crawford's sensational testimony was still ten months away. In the meantime, as speculation about Dennison's involvement in the Lapidus murder spread throughout the region, the notoriety of the tragedy provided Smith and other federal officials with the political capital they needed to launch a massive investigation into the dozens of speakeasies, brothels, gambling dens, and other businesses that Dennison controlled. The result of that investigation would be the indictment of Dennison and fifty-eight of his associates on 168 counts of conspiracy to violate the National Prohibition Act. As political scientist Orville Menard, the leading scholar on the Dennison machine, has written, the anti-Dennison forces were "determined to bring Tom Dennison to trial, not for the Lapidus murder for which there was no evidence, but on other charges. Their goal was not a guilty verdict in the conventional sense—they sought the publicity of a lengthy and public courtroom contest, the means they adopted to weaken and finally destroy the "Old Man' politically. . . . Those political reformers and Dennison enemies were willing to resort to whatever means within the law they perceived as likely to bring defeat to their opponent. The instrument they decided upon was a court of law turned to blatant political purpose."[83] Judge Joseph Woodrough would preside over that court of law, and young Edson Smith would be the lead prosecutor.

The Dennison trial commenced on October 10, 1932, and lasted two months. Like most long and celebrated trials, it was often tedious but sometimes spectacular. Exhaustively covered by all of the local newspapers as well as many national publications, the trial ultimately provided the public with a detailed exposé of Dennison's four-decade reign as king of the Omaha underworld, and it revealed the astonishing level of behind-the-scenes political influence he exercised in order to preserve that empire. Day by day and week by week, Smith and his team of prosecutors painstakingly elicited testimony from almost one hundred witnesses and introduced scores of documents detailing the machine's operations: bootlegging, protection rackets, jury-rigging, hijackings, gambling, prostitution, and bribery of police and other public officials, all of which were often accomplished through strong-arm intimidation and brutal violence.[84]

The prosecution's star witness was the aforementioned Crawford. During his three days on the stand, he not only linked Dennison directly to the Lapidus killing but also explained in meticulous detail the inner workings of the machine's operations. Describing "how he and the organization protected bootleggers who paid their protection money and raided those who were remiss, how signatures were forged on bail bonds, how juries were fixed—the gamut of machine underworld activities," Crawford left the massive throng in the courtroom gallery "in stunned silence."[85] Vinciquerra also testified for the government, describing how, as a retailer, she would be required to pay a $200 monthly fee and a fixed price of $3 per gallon for the whiskey that she purchased from the syndicate. Any product she made on her own had to be sold to the syndicate at $2 per gallon. If she failed to comply with those terms, she declared, Dennison's thugs would "make it hot for her."[86] Another government witness, Clifford Hill, who was then serving a four-year sentence for manslaughter related to the killing of a still operator, told the jury about the "150 to 200 hijackings he had participated in." In virtually every case, he said, he had delivered the stolen goods directly to one of the defendants in the case, Dennison's top henchmen, William Maher.[87]

With ample justification, Smith went to great lengths to maintain security for his witnesses, often bringing them into and out of the courthouse surrounded by a cordon of police and federal agents. Crawford, in particular, was "guarded like the rajah's ruby," and during part of the trial he lived in a makeshift "apartment" in the grand jury room at the courthouse, where he was surrounded around the clock by armed guards who slept on cots that Smith had ordered into the room for that purpose.[88]

By all accounts, Woodrough conducted the trial in an admirably evenhanded manner, usually ruling in favor of the government on evidentiary disputes, but also occasionally sustaining objections when government witnesses strayed too far from the specifics of the indictments. A hotly contested issue that recurred frequently during the early stages of the trial was the admissibility of evidence and testimony related to violent acts that some witnesses attributed to the defendants, including most notably the Lapidus murder. Defense counsel repeatedly raised strenuous objections to such material, arguing that it was beyond the scope of the indictments, which were limited to liquor violations and related conspiracy charges. Woodrough seemed genuinely conflicted on the question and entertained a great deal of argument on the point by attorneys on both sides. Ultimately he allowed the disputed testimony to come in, declaring that "while he concurred very sincerely" with the defense's concerns, he could not preclude testimony in which a witness was relating conversations he or she had taken part in or overheard, if those conversations also pertained to the conspiracy that was the centerpiece of the government's case. Woodrough offered an analogy to explain his reasoning: "It is undoubtedly the law that if a man is being inquired of as to whether he stole a horse, if the evidence shows that while he was stealing the horse he killed the owner and jumped on the horse and ran away, he cannot object that the killing of the owner is brought into evidence before the jury."[89] In the same way, Woodrough stated, Dennison and his co-defendants could not object if evidence relating to matters outside of liquor violations emerged from conversations that were otherwise relevant to the conspiracy. The only remedy for such problems, he concluded, would be to later admonish the jury to disregard those extraneous portions of the testimony.

While that evidentiary ruling was obviously adverse to many of the defendants, Woodrough tipped the scales in the other direction as the trial went on. When the prosecution rested its case in early November, he dismissed the charges against several of the defendants for lack of evidence. Several weeks later, when the remaining defendants rested, most of their attorneys filed routine motions to dismiss, making the same claim. In an unusual act of judicial humility, Woodrough freely acknowledged that he was "unable to remember what the evidence was as it applied to this or that individual" and concluded that "he would be remiss in his duties if he turned an individual over to the jury where such doubts existed in his own mind."[90] He therefore dismissed the charges against thirty-two more of the defendants, leaving only sixteen of the original conspirators to face the jury. Those remaining defendants, however, included all of the major figures, including Dennison himself.

The closing days of the trial brought more indications of Woodrough's neutral or even pro-defense handling of the case. During closing arguments, he chastened Smith's associate counsel, Lawrence Shaw, after he talked for more than an hour without saying a word about the specific charges in the indictment. "I would like to know," Woodrough demanded, "what evidence there is to connect these defendants with violations of the liquor law." Similarly, his final charge to the jury on December 5 seemed quite favorable to the defense. To find the defendants guilty of a conspiracy, he told the jurors, they had to specifically find that money had changed hands in pursuit of that conspiracy. Woodrough then told the panel directly, and rather inexplicably, that "there was no testimony of money paid to any defendant," and he reminded them that the prosecution carried the burden of proving that essential element of the case. The judge proceeded to direct blunt commentary toward the government's star witness, Tom Crawford, warning the jury that they should evaluate his testimony with "caution and hesitancy." Crawford's credibility deserved "exacting analysis," he said, since much of his own testimony "exemplified to us an abnormally deceitful bent of mind, unscrupulous in concocting falsehoods."[91]

Several explanations for Woodrough's pro-defense statements and rulings at the end of the trial seem plausible. First, it may have simply reflected Occam's razor, that is, the simplest explanation might well be the most accurate: Woodrough may just have been doing his duty and interpreting the law as he felt it was, rather than as he might have wished it to be. He had certainly proven himself willing to do that in the wartime sedition cases years before, and he may have held sincere doubts about whether the prosecution had in fact met its burden of proof on the conspiracy charges. Alternatively, he may have bent over backward to be "fair" to the defense in order to demonstrate his judicial impartiality and insulate himself and his court from any posttrial accusations of "railroading" the defendants into prison. Finally, if one accepts Orville Menard's conclusion that the trial was primarily an act of political theater designed to expose and discredit the Dennison machine in the court of public opinion, then Woodrough may have felt that the trial had already achieved that purpose. Thus it made little difference whether he dismissed many of the minor defendants or gave particularly harsh instructions to the jury regarding one of the government's most important witnesses.

In the end, the trial concluded with a thud rather than a bang. After five days of deliberation, the jury notified Woodrough that it was hopelessly deadlocked. The judge urged the panel to continue its deliberations, and they complied for several more days. Finally, after jurors again reported the hopelessness of their situation, Woodrough acknowledged the hung jury and declared a mistrial, saying, "While a verdict is obviously highly desirable, it seems to be futile to keep the jury any longer."[92] Within a week, news reports indicated that most of the twelve jurors had voted immediately and repeatedly to convict, while one or perhaps two others stubbornly held out for acquittal. Evidence uncovered decades later strongly suggests that at least one of those holdouts had been bribed or intimidated to ensure his refusal to convict.[93] Alternatively, as at least one scholar and some of the contemporary news coverage suggests, the jury's deadlock could have been attributable to legitimate doubts about the credibility of Tom Crawford's testimony, and Woodrough's charge to the jury could certainly have led some jurors in that direction.[94] Whatever the case, prosecutors initially vowed to refile the case, but within months the momentum for a retrial had died away, and Dennison and his associates walked free.

As numerous commentators have observed, however unsatisfying the mistrial may have been, that legal result was largely irrelevant, at least in terms of Dennison's ultimate fate. If the goal of the trial had been to publicly and graphically expose the sins of the machine and break its grip on the city, then it clearly succeeded. Anti-Dennison forces led by Roy Towl, Bob Smith, and others coalesced under the banner of the "Independent Voter's League" in the spring 1933 elections and swept incumbent Dennison cronies out of most city offices, with Towl himself becoming the city's next mayor.[95] The incorruptible "Raiding Bob" Samardick soon became Omaha police chief, adding a significant new layer to the transformation of the city's political and legal culture.[96] The old regime was dead and gone, and it would never return. With his machine dismantled, his personal reputation in tatters, and his health failing, Dennison moved to San Diego, where he died of a cerebral hemorrhage the following year.[97]

The Dennison trial emerges as a watershed event in the history of both the state of Nebraska and the U.S. District Court of Nebraska, marking not only the demise of the Dennison machine but also the end of two other distinct eras. At a symbolic level, it represented the closing days of the Prohibition years, with their colorful but endless and often bloody confrontations between mobsters, bootleggers, and the law enforcement officials who doggedly tried to stop their operations. Less than a year after the trial concluded, the ratification of the Nineteenth Amendment officially ended the "Noble Experiment," and Nebraskans, like the rest of the country, moved on to other challenges, struggling to escape the grip of the Great Depression at home and confronting ominous new threats abroad.

Finally, and most important for this study, the Dennison trial marked the end of the era of the Munger/Woodrough court. Just a few months after the trial's conclusion, newly inaugurated president Franklin D. Roosevelt nominated Woodrough to the Eighth Circuit court of appeals. The Senate quickly confirmed his selection, and he assumed his new post on April 12, 1933. His service on the circuit court continued for the next forty-four years, as he took senior status in 1961 but never officially retired before his death in 1977 at the age of 104.[98] Thomas Munger remained on the court another eight years, until his death in 1941.[99]

As current Nebraska district judge Robert F. Rossiter Jr. and DC circuit chief judge Merrick Garland can both attest, the nomination and confirmation of federal judges is a much more "extended"—and more bitterly partisan—process today than it was in the 1930s. Within just weeks of Woodrough's departure for the circuit court, he was replaced on the district bench by Fremont attorney James A. Donohoe.[100] Together, Munger and Donohoe would lead the court into the New Deal years and beyond. But those stories must wait for another day.

NOTES

INTRODUCTION

1. Tocqueville, *Democracy in America*.
2. Holmes's phrase, in turn, has become more widely disseminated and popularized as the title of historian Kermit Hall's classic text in American legal history, *The Magic Mirror*. Hall cites Oliver Wendell Holmes Jr., *Speeches by Oliver Wendell Holmes* (1891), 17.

1. IN THE BEGINNING

1. Pound, *An Introduction to the Philosophy of Law*, 28.
2. Tachau, *Federal Courts*, 14; Friedman, *A History of American Law*, 139.
3. Tachau, *Federal Courts*, 15–16.
4. Tachau, *Federal Courts*, 14–15.
5. Surrency, *History of the Federal District Courts*, 61.
6. "An Act to Establish the Judicial Courts of the United States [hereinafter Judiciary Act of 1789]," *U.S. Statutes at Large* 1 (September 24, 1789): 73–93. See particularly Sections 2–5, 9–13, and 21–24.
7. Carter, "United States District Courts," 1943.
8. McGowan, "United States Courts of Appeals."
9. Judiciary Act of 1789, Section 25, 1:85–87.
10. Judiciary Act of 1789, Section 34, 1:92.
11. Hall and Karsten, *Magic Mirror*, 75.
12. Frankfurter and Landis, *The Business of the Supreme Court*, 17, quoted in Friedman, *A History of American Law*, 143.
13. Friedman, *A History of American Law*, 142.

14. "An Act to Provide for the More Convenient Organization of the Courts of the United States," *U.S. Statutes at Large* 2 (February 13, 1801): 89–100.

15. Friedman, *A History of American Law*, 128; Hall and Karsten, *Magic Mirror*, 76–79.

16. "An Act to Amend the Judicial System of the United States," *U.S. Statutes at Large* 2 (April 29, 1802): 156–67.

17. Ellis, *The Jeffersonian Crisis*, 69.

18. Ellis, *The Jeffersonian Crisis*, 70, quoting *Message from the President Enclosing Documents Relative to John Pickering.*

19. Ellis, *The Jeffersonian Crisis*, 72–81.

20. "An Act in Addition to the Act for the Punishment of Certain Crimes against the United States," *U.S. Statutes at Large* 1 (June 5, 1794): 381–90.

21. *U.S. Statutes at Large* 2 (May 10, 1800): 70–71.

22. "An Act Further to Provide for the Collection of Duties on Imports and Tonnage," *U.S. Statutes at Large* 3 (March 3, 1815): 231–35.

23. "An Act in Addition to the 'Act for the Punishment of Certain Crimes against the United States,' and to Repeal the Acts Therein Mentioned," *U.S. Statutes at Large* 3 (April 20, 1818): 447–50; "An Act Respecting the Punishment of Piracy," *U.S. Statutes at Large* 3 (March 3, 1823): 789.

24. "An Act Providing for the Better Organization of the Treasury Department," *U.S. Statutes at Large* 3 (May 15, 1820): 592–96.

25. "An Act Establishing Circuit Courts, and Abridging the Jurisdiction of the District Courts in the Districts of Kentucky, Tennessee, and Ohio," *U.S. Statutes at Large* 2 (February 24, 1807): 420–21.

26. "An Act to Extend the Power of Granting Writs of Injunctions to the Judges of the District Courts of the United States," *U.S. Statutes at Large* 2 (February 13, 1807): 418. So that the balance was not tipped too far, in 1815 Congress allowed some sharing of jurisdiction between U.S. district courts and state courts. See "An Act to Vest More Effectually in the State Courts and in the District Courts of the United States Jurisdiction in the Cases Therein Mentioned," *U.S. Statutes at Large* 3 (March 3, 1815): 244–45.

27. Surrency, *History of the Federal District Courts*, 62; "An Act to Divide the State of Pennsylvania into Two Judicial Districts," *U.S. Statutes at Large* 3 (April 20, 1818): 462–63.

28. Surrency, *History of the Federal District Courts*, 62–63.

29. Shirley, *Law West of Fort Smith*, 12–14; Surrency, *History of the Federal District Courts*, 64; Chase et al., *Biographical Dictionary of the Federal Judiciary*, 235.

30. Shirley, *Law West of Fort Smith*, 14–16, 25–40.

31. Chase et al., *Biographical Dictionary*, 79, 293; Zelden, *Justice Lies in the District*, 15–21.

32. Zelden, *Justice Lies in the District*, 21–22.
33. The story of Nebraska statehood relies upon Naugle, Montag, and Olson, *History of Nebraska*, 111–30.
34. U.S. Congress, Office of the Historian, *Biographical Directory of the United States Congress, 1774–Present*, "Richard Yates," at http://bioguide.congress .gov/scripts/biodisplay.pl?index=Y000011 [hereinafter *Biographical Directory*].
35. *Congressional Globe*, 40th Cong., sess. 1, Senate 38 (March 13, 1867): 77.
36. *Congressional Globe*, 40th Cong., sess. 1, Senate 38 (March 16, 1867): 133; *Biographical Directory*, "George Franklin Edmunds," at http://bioguide .congress.gov/scripts/biodisplay.pl?index=E000056.
37. The latest configuration of the Eighth Circuit came in 1866 when Congress approved the following districts: Minnesota, Iowa, Missouri, Kansas, and Arkansas. "An Act to Fix the Number of Judges of the Supreme Court of the United States, and to Change Certain Judicial Circuits," *U.S. Statutes at Large* 14 (July 23, 1866): 209.
38. *U.S. Statutes at Large* 14 (July 23, 1866): 209.
39. *Congressional Globe*, 40th Cong., sess. 1, House 38 (March 19, 1867): 187, 214; *Biographical Directory*, "James Falconer Wilson," at http://bioguide.congress .gov/scripts/biodisplay.pl?index=W000594.
40. *Congressional Globe*, 40th Cong., sess. 1, House 38 (March 21, 1867): 252–53.
41. *Congressional Globe*, 40th Cong., sess. 1, House 38 (March 21, 1867): 253.
42. *Biographical Directory*, "George Servel Boutwell," at http://bioguide.congress .gov/scripts/biodisplay.pl?index=B000674.
43. *Congressional Globe*, 40th Cong., sess. 1, House 38 (March 21, 1867): 253.
44. *Congressional Globe*, 40th Cong., sess. 1, House 38 (March 21, 1867): 253; *Biographical Directory*, "Charles Augustus Eldredge," at http://bioguide .congress.gov/scripts/biodisplay.pl?index=E000103, and *Biographical Directory*, "Rufus Paine Spalding," at http://bioguide.congress.gov/scripts/biodisplay .pl?index=S000697. Note: Representative Eldredge's name is misspelled throughout the *Congressional Globe* as Eldridge.
45. *Congressional Globe*, 40th Cong., sess. 1, Senate 38 (March 22, 1867): 268, 328; House 38 (March 22, 1867): 285; "An Act to Provide for a District and a Circuit Court of the United States for the District of Nebraska, and for Other Purposes," *U.S. Statutes at Large* 15 (March 25, 1867): 5–6.
46. Dockstader, *Great North American Indians*, 204–6.
47. *Omaha Daily Herald*, March 12, 1867.
48. *Omaha Daily Herald*, March 14, 1867; March 25, 1867.
49. *Omaha Daily Herald*, March 27 and 29, 1867.
50. Mills and Peterson, *"No One Is above the Law,"* 21.
51. Chase et al., *Biographical Dictionary*, 168.

52. *Omaha Daily Herald,* May 9, 1867.

53. *Omaha Daily Herald,* May 9, 1867; May 10, 1867.

54. *Omaha Daily Herald,* November 13, 1867.

55. Zelden, *Justice Lies in the District,* 4.

56. See Hall, *The Politics of Justice;* Zelden, *Justice Lies in the District,* particularly his very thoughtful introductory remarks, 3–14; Tachau, *Federal Courts;* Freyer, *Forums of Order* and *Harmony and Dissonance.* For phrase quotation, see Zelden, *Justice Lies in the District,* 4.

2. THE DUNDY YEARS

1. Price, "Public Life of Elmer S. Dundy," 2–5.

2. Price, "Public Life," 7–10; Johansen, "'To Make Some Provision for Their Half-Breeds.'"

3. Price, "Public Life," 11–12.

4. Isham Reavis, "Reminiscences," *Falls City Tribune,* April 9, 1909, 2, quoted in Price, "Public Life," 13.

5. Price, "Public Life," 13–15.

6. Price, "Public Life," 30.

7. Price, "Public Life," 16–29.

8. Nebraska Territory, House, 5th sess., November 1, 1858, *Journal,* 199. For a thorough discussion of slavery and Nebraska Territory, see Price, "Public Life," 38–42; Morton and Watkins, *Illustrated History,* 2:39–55; and Rich, "Slavery in Nebraska."

9. Nebraska Territory, Council, 6th sess., January 3, 1860, *Journal,* 139; January 9, 1860, *Journal,* 160–66; Nebraska Territory, "An Act to Prohibit Slavery," pt. 1, 43–44; Price, "Public Life," 38–41.

10. The history of Dundy's family contains some startling highlights. Dundy's namesake son, "Skip" as he was known, attended the relatively new University of Nebraska, served eventually as a clerk in his father's federal court, and enjoyed the public arts, in particular amusement shows. In 1898 he presented a concession at the Trans-Mississippi Exposition in Omaha, and this led to a partnership with Frederic Thompson. Skip soon moved to New York where the partners invested in amusements for the Pan American Exposition in 1901, and then they built the largest amusement park in the world at that time, opening Coney Island in 1903. The park was named Luna Park after Skip's sister. After her husband died, Mary Dundy moved to New York City, relocating her family in an apartment on Broadway. Skip died in her apartment in February 1907. Luna Dundy moved with her mother and became the wife of Henry Newman of Bayonne, New Jersey. She died, perhaps in childbirth, in January 1906. Elmer Dundy's wife survived all but

one of her children, Mary Mae. Her namesake attended Brownell Hall School in Omaha, was elected as a Queen of Quivira by Ak-Sar-Ben at the Nebraska State Fair in 1896, the year of her father's death, and married George Lee. Mary Mae survived until 1944. The relocation to New York City by the Dundy family included moving the graves of Elmer and the infant daughter Enid to New York. Dundy's political biographer concluded that no children were born to the children of Elmer Dundy and that it is improbable that any family survive today. See Price, "Public Life," 101–2 and appendix, 143–46.

11. U.S., Congress, House, *Evidence and Other Papers Submitted in the Contested Election of Samuel G. Daily versus J. Sterling Morton as Delegate from the Territory of Nebraska in the Thirty-Seventh Congress*, Misc. Doc. No. 4, 37th Cong., 18th sess., 1861, House Miscellaneous Documents, 40–49, quoted in Price, "Public Life," 54.

12. *Daily Omaha Nebraskian*, November 1, 1860; *Nebraska Tri-Weekly Republican* [Omaha], August 20, 1862.

13. Pomeroy, *Territories and the United States*, 124. Price mistakenly believes Judge Street died in February 1863 and was replaced directly by Judge Dundy. Price, "Public Life," 59.

14. Price, "Public Life," 55–59.

15. *Nebraska Daily Press* [Nebraska City, Nebraska Territory], November 12, 1863; Price, "Public Life," 59–62.

16. Homer, "Territorial Judiciary"; Price, "Public Life," 59–60.

17. Homer, "Territorial Judiciary," 356, 361–63, 378–79, specifically notes 22, 35, and 38; Nebraska Territory, Nebraska Territory Supreme Court, Second District, Judge's Docket, RG 58 Territorial Courts, Series 3, Subseries 4, October term, 1863, Nebraska State Historical Society, Lincoln [hereinafter Dundy Docket].

18. Dundy Docket, cases #1–36 U.S. code violations, cases #1–8 territorial criminal actions, cases #1–59 territorial civil actions; U.S. v. Pe-to-ke-mah [otherwise called Hard Fish], #17.

19. Dundy Docket, U.S. v. James Kough [otherwise called James Crow], #30 and #31. See also #32 for a third involvement of James Kough.

20. Dundy Docket #34 considered a photographer without a license, U.S. v. Henry Garbanat; #35 involved a peddler without a license, U.S. v. Marquis Johnson; and #36 involved an auctioneer without a license, U.S. v. Joseph M. Longfellow.

21. Dundy Docket, Territory of Nebraska v. George W. Boulware, William Schallinger, Nicholas Stubbs, and Reese Steel, #2.

22. Dundy Docket, J. Sterling Morton v. Samuel W. Black, #21.

23. See Woolworth, "Judges of the Supreme Court of the Territory of Nebraska." See also Homer, "The Territorial Judiciary," table 3, 370, and 379n38.

24. Woolworth, "Judges of the Supreme Court," 415–16.

25. Woolworth, "Judges of the Supreme Court," 432; italics in quotation added.

26. "Black letter law" is a phrase typically used to denote basic principles of law that are generally known and applied and are free from doubt or dispute.

27. *Omaha Weekly Herald,* July 13, 1866; *Nebraska City News,* April 5, 1867; *Omaha Weekly Republican,* May 31, 1867; *Nebraska Commonwealth* [Lincoln], January 11, 1868; Price, "Public Life," 63–68.

28. Price, "Public Life," 71.

29. *Omaha Weekly Republican,* April 15, 1868.

30. *Nebraska City News,* April 17, 1868.

31. *Omaha Weekly Herald,* April 8, 1868; Price, "Public Life," 69–70.

32. "An Act to Amend the Judicial System of the United States," *U.S. Statutes at Large* 16 (April 10, 1869): 44–45.

33. "An Act to Amend the Judicial System of the United States," 44–45. The movement to eliminate circuit riding for the U.S. Supreme Court justices was officially jumpstarted with passage of a reform no longer requiring the justices to sit on every term of the circuit court. They needed after 1844 to attend only one term per year. See "An Act Concerning the Supreme Court of the United States," *U.S. Statutes at Large* 5 (June 17, 1844): 676–77.

34. Mills and Peterson, *"No One Is above the Law,"* 24–30; Chase et al., *Biographical Dictionary of the Federal Judiciary,* 72–73.

35. "An act to Provide for the Holding of a Term of the District and Circuit Courts of the United States at Lincoln, Nebraska," *U.S. Statutes at Large* 20 (June 19, 1878): 169.

36. Mills and Peterson, *"No One Is above the Law,"* 31–34; Chase et al., *Biographical Directory,* 184.

37. Chase et al., *Biographical Directory,* 30.

38. Chase et al., *Biographical Directory,* 40–41.

3. NATIVE AMERICANS AND JUDGE DUNDY

1. See Price, "Public Life," chapters 1–3.

2. Price, "Public Life," 6–11.

3. Price, "Public Life," 59–60. Dundy's district covered all of the area south of the Platte River. Once a year, the three justices heard appeals in Omaha.

4. See U.S. District Court of Nebraska Territory, 2nd Judicial District, 1862–1867. See also *Complete and Final Record Book,* criminal case numbers 1–4, 13–19, 22–36 (1863) and civil case numbers 17–18 (1863). See also Woolworth,

Reports of Cases of the Supreme Court of Nebraska [Territory], 415–16, 432, 460, 472–73; and Pomeroy, *Territories of the United States, 1861–1890*, 123–24.

5. See Ponca Tribe of Nebraska, "Historical Overview," at https://www.poncatribe -ne.org/culture/history/.

6. Starita, *"I Am a Man,"* 6, 14. See also Rollings, *The Osage*.

7. Rollings, *The Osage*, 96–100.

8. Starita, *"I Am a Man,"* 14–15.

9. Starita, *"I Am a Man,"* 4–5, 17.

10. Starita, *"I Am a Man,"* 17; "U.S.-Ponca Treaty of 1817," Oklahoma State University Digital Collections, at http://dc.library.okstate.edu/digital/collection /kapplers/id/17521/rec/1.

11. Starita, *"I Am a Man,"* 17–18; "U.S.-Ponca Treaty of 1825," Oklahoma State University Digital Collections, at http://dc.library.okstate.edu/digital/collection /kapplers/id/17836/rec/1.

12. Starita, *"I Am a Man,"* 23.

13. Starita, *"I Am a Man,"* 17, 24.

14. "U.S.-Ponca Treaty of 1858," Oklahoma State University Digital Collections, at http://dc.library.okstate.edu/digital/collection/kapplers/id/19802/rec /1; Starita, *"I Am a Man,"* 28.

15. "U.S.-Ponca Treaty of 1865," Oklahoma State University Digital Collections, at http://dc.library.okstate.edu/digital/collection/kapplers/id/20143/rec/1.

16. Starita, *"I Am a Man,"* 28–36.

17. Starita, *"I Am a Man,"* 36–40.

18. Starita, *"I Am a Man,"* 40–46. See also Rollings, *The Osage*.

19. Starita, *"I Am a Man,"* 48–49, 87.

20. Starita, *"I Am a Man,"* 79; Standing Bear v. Crook in *New York Times*, May 14, 1879, 1; Price, "Public Life," 99.

21. Starita, *"I Am a Man,"* 105–8.

22. Starita, *"I Am a Man,"* 107, 110.

23. Starita, *"I Am a Man,"* 110–11, 113, 116.

24. Starita, *"I Am a Man,"* 133–39, 158.

25. Starita, *"I Am a Man,"* 139; King, "'A Better Way.'"

26. Starita, *"I Am a Man,"* 139–40.

27. Starita, *"I Am a Man,"* 140.

28. Starita, *"I Am a Man,"* 142–44.

29. Starita, *"I Am a Man,"* 144–47.

30. Starita, *"I Am a Man,"* 149–51.

31. Starita, *"I Am a Man,"* 151. Tom Tibbles reported that Dundy and Crook both cried, as did many in the audience. King, "A Better Way," 244.

32. Starita, *"I Am a Man,"* 150.

33. Starita, *"I Am a Man,"* 152.

34. Starita, *"I Am a Man,"* 152–53, 155.

35. Starita, *"I Am a Man,"* 156.

36. Starita, *"I Am a Man,"* 157.

37. Starita, *"I Am a Man,"* 158, 160.

38. Price, "Public Life," 100. For example, see *Omaha Herald,* May 15, 1879.

39. Price, "Public Life," 108–9.

40. *New York Times,* May 20, 1879. See Price, "Public Life," 100–101.

41. *U.S. Statutes at Large* 16 (1871): 566; Wunder, "No More Treaties."

42. Price, "Public Life," 110–12.

43. Elk v. Wilkins, 112 U.S. 94 (1884); Price, "Public Life," 118–19n2.

44. Price, "Public Life," 118–20; Stephen D. Bodayla, "Can an Indian Vote?" See also the many works of Wilcomb E. Washburn.

45. George W. McCrary, biographical entry on Wikipedia, at https://en.wikipedia.org/wiki/George_W._McCrary.

46. Price, "Public Life," 118–19; Lambertson, "Indian Citizenship."

47. Bodayla, "Can an Indian Vote?" 375; Price, "Public Life," 119–20.

48. Felix v. Patrick 145 U.S. 317 (1892); Price, "Public Life," 120–23.

49. Felix v. Patrick; Price, "Public Life," 122.

50. Price, "Public Life," 122.

4. RAILROADS AND THE ERMINE OF THE BENCH

1. Summers, *Railroads, Reconstruction, and the Gospel of Prosperity,* 47. See also Jay, "General N. B. Forrest as a Railroad Builder in Alabama."

2. U.S., "An Act to Aid in the Construction of a Railroad and Telegraph Line from the Missouri River to the Pacific Ocean, and to Secure to the Government the Use of the Same for Postal, Military, and Other Purposes," *U.S. Statutes at Large* 12 (July 1, 1862): 489–98.

3. U.S., "An Act to Amend an Act Entitled 'An Act to Aid in the Construction of a Railroad and Telegraphy Line from the Missouri River to the Pacific Ocean, and to Secure to the Government the Use of the Same for Postal, Military, and Other Purposes,' approved July first, eighteen hundred and sixty-two," *U.S. Statutes at Large* 13 (July 2, 1864): 356–65

4. See, e.g., Mercer, *Railroads and Land Grant Policy* and Decker, *Railroads, Lands, and Politics.*

5. *U.S. Statutes at Large* 13 (July 2, 1864): 365.

6. Decker, *Railroads, Lands, and Politics,* 14–15.

7. Decker, *Railroads, Lands, and Politics,* 6–7, 193.

8. Mercer, *Railroads and Land Grant Policy,* 6; White, *"It's Your Misfortune and None of My Own,"* 145–47, 246–47. Mercer conservatively estimates the amount

of land involved in land grants, basing his analysis on an exact total of 179,187,040 acres, approximately 60 million acres less than figures used by other scholars.

9. Decker, *Railroads, Lands, and Politics*, 119, 131.

10. Decker, *Railroads, Lands, and Politics*, 87–90.

11. Hine, *Letters from an Old Railway Official to His Son, a Division Superintendent*, 45.

12. Haines, *Restrictive Railway Legislation*, 330.

13. Beard and Beard, *The Rise of American Civilization*, 129, quoted in Mercer, *Railroads and Land Grant Policy*, 10. The Beards are specifically referring to the Union Pacific Railroad Company.

14. Decker, *Railroads, Lands, and Politics*, 6–7, 26; White, *"It's Your Misfortune,"* 116. For an overview and general history of torts and railroads, see Friedman, *A History of American Law*, 467–87.

15. Decker, *Railroads, Lands, and Politics*, 33, 42–43; Hewitt, "'The Public Be Damned,'" 26; Price, "Public Life," 110–14.

16. White, *"It's Your Misfortune,"* 252–57; Mercer, *Railroads and Land Grant Policy*, 41; Kolko, *Railroads and Regulation, 1877–1916*, 3–5.

17. Hewitt, "'The Public Be Damned,'" 19–20, 26; White, *"It's Your Misfortune,"* 367.

18. Hewitt, "'The Public Be Damned,'" 26, 45–46.

19. Quoted in White, *"It's Your Misfortune,"* 373.

20. "Populist Party Platform, July 4, 1892," with preamble reproduced in Commager, *Documents of American History*, 593.

21. Mercer, *Railroads and Land Grant Policy*, 39–40, and see also table A-3, "Total Current Dollar Value of Construction and Equipment Cost of Individual Railroads in the Union Pacific System (1864–1889) and Information on Their Entrance into the System," 162–63.

22. Decker, *Railroads, Lands, and Politics*, 189–93. See also Overton, *Burlington West*; Spencer, "The Union Pacific's Utilization of Its Land Grant, with Emphasis on Its Colonization Program"; Mattison, "The Burlington Tax Controversy in Nebraska over the Federal Land Grants"; and Davis, "Building the Burlington through Nebraska."

23. Decker, *Railroads, Lands, and Politics*, 193.

24. Kraenzel, *The Great Plains in Transition*, 127.

25. White, *"It's Your Misfortune,"* 246. See also Kraenzel, *The Great Plains in Transition*, 246–49, 257.

26. Kraenzel, *The Great Plains in Transition*, 128; Licht, *Ecology and Economics of the Great Plains*, 109–13; White, *"It's Your Misfortune,"* 125–27.

27. Decker, *Railroads, Lands, and Politics*, 229, 234–39.

28. Dundy's issuance of an injunction here is a guess, because the circuit

court's opinion alludes to an injunction, but Dundy rarely (only on seven known occasions) provided a written opinion of his U.S. district or circuit court orders.

29. Union Pacific Railroad Company v. Lincoln County, 24 Fed. Cases 631–36 (1871), Case No. 14,378.

30. Union Pacific Railroad Company v. Lincoln County, 634.

31. Union Pacific Railroad Company v. Lincoln County, 635 quoting Judge George F. Shepley, U.S. district court judge in Maine (1869–78), from a recent decision involving a railroad bankruptcy case.

32. Union Pacific Railroad Company v. Lincoln County, 24 Fed. Cases 636–37, Case No. 14,379. Quotation at 636, italics added.

33. Union Pacific Railroad Company v. Lincoln County, 24 Fed. Cases 637–38, Case No. 14,380.

34. Union Pacific Railroad Company v. William S. Peniston, Treasurer of Lincoln County, Nebraska, 85 U.S. 787–98 (1873).

35. Abraham, *Justices and Presidents*, 112–23. See also Kens, *Justice Stephen Field*, 129–68, 218–27, 236–64 for a discussion of Field's close connection to the railroad industry.

36. Abraham, *Justices and Presidents*, 119.

37. Union Pacific Railroad Company v. Peniston, 85 U.S. 787 at 791 (1873).

38. Union Pacific Railroad Company v. Peniston, 793–94.

39. Union Pacific Railroad Company v. Peniston, 794–98.

40. *Union Pacific Railroad Company v. McShane*, 24 Fed. Cases 638–40 (1873), Case No. 14381.

41. Union Pacific Railroad Company v. McShane, 638.

42. Union Pacific Railroad Company v. McShane, 639.

43. Union Pacific Railroad Company v. McShane, 24 Fed. Cases 640–44 (1874), Case No. 14382.

44. Hagenbuck v. Alexander Reed, Treasurer of Washington County, 3 Neb. 17 (1873).

45. Union Pacific Railroad Company v. McShane, 24 Fed. Case 642 (1874).

46. Union Pacific Railroad Company v. Edward C. McShane, Treasurer, et al. and Edward C. McShane, Treasurer, etc., et al., v. Union Pacific Railroad, 89 U.S. 747 (1875).

47. Union Pacific Railroad Company v. McShane, 89 U.S. 747 at 750 (1875).

48. Abraham, *Justices and Presidents*, 122.

49. Union Pacific Railroad Company v. McShane, 89 U.S. 747 at 752 (1875).

50. *Omaha Bee*, August 6 and September 3, 1873.

51. *Beatrice* [NE] *Express*, August 21, 1873, quoted in Decker, *Railroads, Lands, and Politics*, 26.

52. *Grand Island* [NE] *Times,* August 20, 1873, quoted in Decker, *Railroads, Lands, and Politics,* 27.

53. *Congressional Record,* 44th Cong., sess. 1 (March 7, 1876): 1521–22, quoted in Decker, *Railroads, Lands, and Politics,* 125.

54. Decker, *Railroads, Lands, and Politics,* 27.

55. Decker, *Railroads, Lands, and Politics,* 24–26; William H. Platt v. Union Pacific Railroad Company and Frederick L. Ames, 99 U.S. 424–30 (1879).

56. Union Pacific Railroad Company v. Merrick County, 24 Fed. Cases 644–45 (1874), Case No. 14383.

57. Union Pacific Railroad Company v. James R. Watts, 24 Fed. Case 648 (1872), Case No. 14385.

58. Horatio H. Hunnewell v. Burlington & Missouri Railroad Company et al., 12 Fed. Cases 893–95 (1874), Case No. 6879.

59. Horatio H. Hunnewell v. County of Cass et al., 89 U.S. 752–55 (1875). See also William H. Platt v. Union Pacific Railroad Company and Frederick L. Ames, 99 U.S. 424–30 (1879) and United States v. Burlington and Missouri River Railroad Company in Nebraska, 98 U.S. 198–201 (1879) for other Supreme Court actions based on railroad litigation in Nebraska's lower federal courts.

60. Union Pacific Railroad Company v. Board of County Commissioners of the County of Dodge [Nebraska], 98 U.S. 196–98 (1879).

61. McMurry, *Great Burlington Strike,* 4–5; Heskett, "The Burlington Strike in Nebraska, 1888," 1–4, 20–21.

62. Heskett, "The Burlington Strike in Nebraska," 5.

63. McMurry, *Great Burlington Strike,* 30–40.

64. McMurry, *Great Burlington Strike,* 8–15, phrase quotation on 15.

65. McMurry, *Great Burlington Strike,* 23–25; Heskett, "The Burlington Strike in Nebraska," 22.

66. McMurray, *Great Burlington Strike,* 42–52, 70.

67. McMurry, *Great Burlington Strike,* 161; Heskett, "The Burlington Strike in Nebraska," 23, 27, 38–49.

68. McMurry, *Great Burlington Strike,* 177–79; Heskett, "The Burlington Strike in Nebraska," 59–60, 63–64, 74–80.

69. Heskett, "The Burlington Strike in Nebraska," 11–12, 110–12.

70. McMurry, "The Legal Ancestry of the Pullman Strike Injunctions"; Eggert, "A Missed Alternative," 289.

71. *Omaha Daily Herald,* March 10, 1888, italics added.

72. *Omaha Daily Herald,* March 10, 1888.

73. McMurry, *Great Burlington Strike,* 115.

74. McMurry, *Great Burlington Strike,* 121.

75. Eggert, *Railroad Labor Disputes,* 125. See also McMurry, *Great Burlington Strike,* 123.

76. *Omaha Daily Bee,* March 10, 1888.

77. *New York Times,* March 11, 1888.

78. See, e.g., *Omaha Daily Bee,* March 9–10 and 12–13, 1888; *Omaha Daily Herald,* March 11–13, 1888.

79. Chase et al., *Biographical Dictionary of the Federal Judiciary,* 109.

80. McMurry, "Legal Ancestry of Pullman Strike Injunctions," 241–42.

81. *Omaha Daily Bee,* March 13, 1888.

82. *Omaha Republican,* March 18, 1888. See also McMurry, "Legal Ancestry of Pullman Strike Injunctions," 241.

83. Eggert, *Railroad Labor Disputes,* 87.

84. *Omaha Daily Bee,* March 12, 1888.

85. *New York Times,* March 18, 1888.

86. *Omaha Republican,* March 20, 1888.

87. *Omaha Daily Herald,* March 18, 1888.

88. *Omaha Daily Bee,* March 19, 1888.

89. McMurry, *Great Burlington Strike,* 16–17.

90. The Chicago, Burlington, and Quincy Railroad Company v. George Hastings, Atty. Gen., et al., Case No. 55q; Oliver Ames v. Union Pacific Railway Company, et al., Case No. 59q; and George Smith, et al. v. Chicago and Northwestern Railway Company, et al., Case No. 60q, U.S. 8th Circuit Court of Appeals (1893). See also Price, Public Life," 126–27.

91. Price, "Public Life," 127.

92. Constantine J. Smith, Attorney General, et al., Constituting the Board of Transportation of Nebraska, et al., v. Oliver Ames, et al., 169 U.S. 466 (1898), quoted in Price, "Public Life," 128.

93. Trottman, *History of the Union Pacific: A Financial and Economic Survey,* 249–50; Athearn, *Union Pacific Country,* 367; Eggert, "A Missed Alternative," 294–96.

94. McMurry, "Legal Ancestry of Pullman Strike Injunctions," 249. See also Eggert, "A Missed Alternative," 296; Eggert, *Railroad Labor Disputes,* 120; *Omaha Evening Bee,* January 29, 1894; and *Omaha World Herald,* January 29, 1894.

95. *Omaha World Herald,* January 30, 1894.

96. McMurry, "Legal Ancestry of Pullman Strike Injunctions," 249; Eggert, "A Missed Alternative," 297.

97. Ames et al. v. Union Pacific Railway Company et al., 62 F. 12 (1894).

98. Ames et al. v. Union Pacific Railway Company et al., 15, 13, 14–15.

99. *Omaha Evening Bee,* April 14, 1894. See also *New York Times,* April 14, 1894.

100. David Reavis, "Falls City," *Falls City Journal,* June 25, 1934; Price, "Public Life," 131–32.

101. "The Late Judge Dundy's Ways"; Price, "Public Life," 133.

5. THE POLITICS OF TRANSITION

1. The literature devoted to the turbulent political dynamics of the Gilded Age is extensive. Useful overviews include Cherny, *American Politics in the Gilded Age*, Summers, *Party Games*, and Calhoun, *From Bloody Shirt to Full Dinner Pail*.

2. For insights on the origins, development, and impact of the Populists, see McMath, *American Populism: A Social History, 1877–1898*, Postel, *The Populist Vision*, and Naugle, Montag, and Olson, *History of Nebraska*, chap. 16, "Power to the People: Populism." See also Stock, *Rural Radicals*, placing the Populists within a broader tradition of American agrarian radicalism.

3. The Omaha Platform is available in dozens of published document collections and online databases. See, for example, "Populist Party Platform, July 4, 1892," with a preamble reproduced in Commager, *Documents of American History*, 593; Tindall, *A Populist Reader*, 90–96; and George Mason University, History Matters, "The Omaha Platform: Launching the Populist Party."

4. More specifically, the act allowed the U.S. Treasury to purchase 4.5 million ounces of silver each month and to issue treasury notes backed by that silver, which would be deemed full legal tender redeemable in gold or silver at the government's option. Morton, like Cleveland, supported the gold standard and sought the repeal of the act. See Naugle, Montag, and Olson, *History of Nebraska*, 273–75. See also McIntyre, "The Morton-Bryan Controversy," 17–18. Kenneth McIntyre makes no mention of the rift between Morton and Bryan over the McHugh nomination.

5. Bryan has been the subject of numerous biographical treatments, all of which offer analysis of his "Cross of Gold" speech. The definitive biography remains Coletta, *William Jennings Bryan*. See also Cherny, *A Righteous Cause*, and Kazin, *A Godly Hero*.

6. Bryan ran again as the Democratic nominee for president in both 1900 and 1908, but he never came closer to victory than he did in 1896.

7. Woolson was the U.S. district judge for the Southern District of Iowa, while Shiras held the same position in the Northern District. Woolson handled the Nebraska judicial duties for the first several weeks after Dundy's death, and Shiras relieved him for the last several weeks of the interim period. See "Dundy's Bench," *Omaha World-Herald*, November 10, 1896. For a colorful account of Woolson's service in the Civil War, see "Judge's Friends in Omaha," *Omaha World Herald*, November 16, 1896.

8. "In the United States Court," *Omaha Evening Bee*, November 17, 1896.

9. "In the United States Court," *Omaha Evening Bee*, November 25, 1896.

10. Recess appointments are authorized by Article 1, section 2 of the U.S. Constitution.

11. "Takes the Oath of Office," *Omaha Evening Bee*, November 30, 1896.

12. "It's Judge McHugh," *Omaha World Herald,* November 22, 1896, and "M'Hugh to Succeed Dundy," *Nebraska State Journal,* November 22, 1896.

13. Bryan, *The First Battle,* 122.

14. "McHugh and His Prize," *Omaha World Herald,* November 22, 1896.

15. "Mr. McHugh and His Friends," *Omaha World Herald,* November 29, 1896.

16. "Mr. McHugh as a 'Tagger,'" *Omaha World Herald,* December 4, 1896.

17. Quoted in "Judge McHugh's Appointment," *Omaha Evening Bee,* November 30, 1896.

18. *Omaha Bee News,* November 30, 1896, 4.

19. "M'Hugh to Succeed Dundy," *Nebraska State Journal,* November 22, 1896, and "Had the Best of Backing," *Nebraska State Journal,* November 24, 1896.

20. "Had the Best of Backing," *Nebraska State Journal,* November 24, 1896.

21. "Should Be a Republican," *Nebraska State Journal,* December 11, 1896.

22. "Holds Up McHugh," *Omaha World Herald,* December 15, 1896.

23. "The Mask Torn Off," *Nebraska State Journal,* January 12, 1897.

24. "The Mask Torn Off." See also "Because He Bolted Bryan," *Omaha Evening Bee,* January 13, 1987.

25. "McHugh Has a Chance," *Nebraska State Journal,* January 20, 1897. See also "Whole Senate May Decide," *Nebraska State Journal,* January 21, 1897, and "M'Hugh May Be Confirmed," *Omaha Evening Bee,* January 19, 1897.

26. "Munger May Be the Man," *Nebraska State Journal,* January 31, 1897.

27. "Munger Named for Judge," *Omaha Evening Bee,* February 1, 1897.

28. "May Suffer McHugh's Fate," *Nebraska State Journal,* February 8, 1897.

29. "Allen Approves of Munger," *Omaha World Herald,* February 2, 1897. See also "Munger May Pass Muster," *Nebraska State Journal,* February 2, 1897.

30. "Munger May Be Confirmed," *Nebraska State Journal,* February 16, 1897.

31. "Senate Confirms Munger," *Omaha World Herald,* February 19, 1897.

32. Charles F. Manderson to William V. Allen, February 23, 1897, Nebraska State Historical Society, Allen Papers, RG 2632.AM, box 1.

6. THE "ONE MUNGER" COURT

1. For biographical sketches of Munger, see "Munger, William Henry," in Morton and Watkins, *Illustrated History,* 2:733, and Dolezai, "History of the Dodge County Bar," 91–98.

2. "William H. Munger," in Wakely, *Omaha: The Gate City.*

3. Woolworth was one of the leading figures in Omaha's early legal community and achieved national prominence as president of the American Bar Association, 1896–97. See, e.g., Savage, "The Bar of Omaha—Woolworth."

4. For more on the controversy between the "silverites" and the "sound money" advocates, see chapter 5.

5. "Names Munger for Judge," *Omaha Daily Bee*, February 2, 1897.
6. For discussion of the Progressive Era generally, see McGerr, *A Fierce Discontent* and Cooper, *Pivotal Decades*. For useful insights on the impact of progressivism in Nebraska, see Cherny, *Populism, Progressivism, and the Transformation of Nebraska Politics, 1885–1915* and Folsom, *No More Free Markets or Free Beer*.
7. For examples of some of Munger's earliest reported decisions, involving routine topics such as real estate, probate, bankruptcy, insurance, debt collection, or pleading technicalities, see Gombert v. Lyon, 80 F. 305 (D. Neb. 1897); Chilton v. Town of Gratton, 82 F. 873 (D. Neb. 1897); Tracy v. Morel, 88 F. 801 (D. Neb. 1898); State of Nebraska v. First Nat. Bank of Orleans, 88 F. 947 (D. Neb. 1898); State of Nebraska v. Hayden, 89 F. 46 (D. Neb. 1898); In re Boston, 98 F. 587 (D. Neb. 1899); and In re Appel, 103 F. 931 (D. Neb. 1900).
8. Hall and Karsten, *Magic Mirror*, 226.
9. Morris, *Establishing Justice in Middle America*, 84.
10. "Boiler Makers to Ask for an Increase in Pay," *Omaha World-Herald*, June 18, 1902; "Union Pacific in Labor War," *Omaha Daily Bee*, June 19, 1902; "Walk Out All Along the Line," *Omaha World-Herald*, June 19, 1902; "Gompers Sends Men to Help in Strike Matters," *Omaha World-Herald*, June 21, 1902.
11. As the size and impact of the strike grew, newspapers across the country began to report on the story. See "Machinists Quit Railroad Shops," *San Francisco Call*, July 1, 1902; "The Union Pacific Strike," *New York Times*, July 2, 1902; "Union Pacific Strike," *Los Angeles Herald*, July 2 and July 24, 1902.
12. "Increase Armed Guards," *Omaha World-Herald*, July 26, 1902.
13. *Nebraska: A Guidebook to the Cornhusker State*, 214. See also Pratt, "Workers, Unions, and Historians on the Northern Plains."
14. "Kill a Nonunionist," *Omaha Sunday Bee*, September 14, 1902; "Kill a Non-Union Man," *New York Times*, September 15, 1902.
15. McPherson and Munger often substituted for one another during the years when their judicial careers overlapped.
16. "Union Pacific Secures a Restraining Order," *Omaha World-Herald*, September 16, 1902; and "Court Enjoins Men; Judge McPherson of Iowa Signs Order Drawn by Railroad Lawyers," *Omaha Daily Bee*, September 16, 1902.
17. "Someone Has Abused Guards and Breakers," *Omaha World-Herald*, September 28, 1902.
18. "Injunction Case Argument," *Omaha Daily Bee*, October 14, 1902.
19. At the time, Smith was a promising young attorney and aspiring Progressive politician who would go on to be elected mayor of Omaha on a reform agenda in 1916. He gained lasting historical prominence during the infamous Omaha Riot of 1919, when black criminal suspect Will Brown was shot, lynched, and

burned by an Omaha mob. Mayor Smith himself was lynched when he tried to intercede with the rioters. He narrowly escaped death when he was cut down from the noose by an Omaha policeman. For more on the riot and Smith's role in it, see Menard, *River City Empire*, 248–51.

20. "Baldwin Attacks Pickets," *Omaha World-Herald*, October 13, 1902.

21. "Defense of the Pickets; Attorney Smith for Strikers Makes a Good Showing of Their Conduct," *Omaha World-Herald*, October 14, 1902. See also "Injunction Case Argument; Judges McPherson and Munger Listen to Lawyers for Ten Hours," *Omaha Daily Bee*, October 14, 1902; and "Injunction Hearing Ends in Federal Court," *Omaha World-Herald*, October 15, 1902.

22. "Two Judges Are Thinking; Several Days to Elapse before They Decide as to UP Strike Injunction," *Omaha World-Herald*, October 22, 1902.

23. Union Pacific R. Co. v. Ruef, 120 F. 102 (Cir. Ct., D. Neb 1902). For local reporting of the decision, see "Makes Order Permanent; Judge Munger Decides the Union Pacific Injunction Case against the Men, Injunction Is Less Radical than Original Order and Falls Far Short of Ideal Sought by Baldwin," *Omaha Daily Bee*, November 9, 1902; and "Must Keep Off the Grounds; Former Restraining Order Is Now Modified in Some of the Essential Particulars," *Omaha World-Herald*, November 9, 1902.

24. *Ruef*, 109, 119.

25. *Ruef*, 128, 124.

26. "Must Keep Off the Grounds."

27. *Ruef*, 129.

28. "UP Strikers' Pickets Allowed; Do Not Violate Court Order," *Omaha World-Herald*, December 15, 1902.

29. "Pickets Do Not Violate Court's Order," *Omaha World-Herald*, December 16, 1902.

30. "Union Pacific Strike Settled in New York," *Omaha World-Herald*, May 23, 1903, and "Boiler Makers Go to Work; Machinists and Blacksmiths Will Meet with President Burt on Monday and Make Their Final Adjustments," *Omaha Daily Bee*, May 28, 1903.

31. "Judge Munger Strikes Out Drastic Measures; Injunction Prepared against Strikers Modified in Important Particulars; Organization May Be Continued, and Peaceful Concert of Action Is Not Interfered With," *Omaha World-Herald*, May 7, 1903.

32. Quoted in "Will Allow Picketing and Mild Persuasion," *Omaha World-Herald*, July 26, 1904.

33. Northwestern Mut. Life Ins. Co. v. Seaman, 80 F. 357 (D. Neb. 1897).

34. Seaman v. Northwestern Mut. Life Ins. Co., 86 F. 493 (8th Cir. 1898); see also Elgutter v. Northwestern Mut. Life Ins. Co., 86 F. 500 (8th Cir. 1898),

rejecting similar arguments regarding Dundy Jr.'s role and upholding another foreclosure sale he had conducted.

35. "Dundy Hands in His Resignation," *Omaha Daily Bee*, April 24, 1897.

36. "Hillis Will Succeed Dundy, Judge Munger Consolidates the Two United States Clerkships," *Omaha Daily Bee*, June 17, 1897.

37. Hoyt was reported to be a relative of Grover Cleveland, who had, of course, appointed Munger to the bench.

38. For more details on the colorful post-Nebraska life and career of Skip Dundy, see his obituary in the *New York Times*, "Elmer S. Dundy Is Dead; Won a Fortune in Shows," February 6, 1907. See also "Skip Dundy Dies Suddenly," *Omaha Daily Bee*, February 6, 1907; "Skip Dundy's Funeral Held in New York," *Omaha World-Herald*, February 8, 1907; and "Skip Dundy Dead," *Falls City Tribune*, February 8, 1907.

39. See "U.S. Senator Dietrich Has Been Indicted," *Omaha World-Herald*, November 17, 1903; "Brings in the Bills; District Attorney Summers Secures Grand Jury Indictment against Dietrich," *Omaha Daily Bee*, November 17, 1903; and "Did He Sell Office?" *Nebraska Advertiser* [Nemaha], November 20, 1903.

40. The relevant statute was, and remains, 18 U.S.C. sec. 431. See "Dietrich and Colby in List of Indictments," *Omaha World-Herald*, December 17, 1903; "Windup of Grand Jury," *Omaha Daily Bee*, December 17, 1903; and "Grand Jurywork; Senator Dietrich among the Indicted," *Columbus Journal*, December 23, 1903.

41. The Dietrich case marked only the second time in the nation's history that a sitting U.S. senator had faced a federal criminal indictment. See *Time Magazine*, "A Brief History of Indicted Senators." For samples of the national press coverage, see "United States Senator Indicted for Bribery," *Los Angeles Herald*, November 17, 1903; "Dietrich Again Indicted," *New York Times*, December 18, 1903; "Did He Try to Bribe Dietrich?" *St. Paul Globe*, December 11, 1903.

42. *Omaha Daily Bee*, November 18, 1903, 6.

43. "The Dietrich Inquiry," *Omaha World-Herald*, November 20, 1903.

44. "Senator Dietrich among Them," *Columbus Leader*, November 25, 1903.

45. United States v. Dietrich, 126 F. 659 (Cir. Ct., D. Neb 1904). As explained in chapter 1, from 1789 until 1911, federal district judges essentially wore two hats: they presided over their own district court dockets, and they also served as judges on the federal "circuit courts," where they sat on panels with Supreme Court justices and later with judges who were appointed specifically to seats on those circuit courts. For most of the nineteenth century, the circuit courts not only exercised appellate jurisdiction over decisions rendered in the district courts but also served as the federal trial courts of general jurisdiction, handling serious federal crimes and exercising concurrent jurisdiction with

the state courts in other types of cases involving more than $500 in controversy. In 1891 Congress enacted a major organizational reform of the federal judiciary, creating the Circuit Courts of Appeal and empowering those new tribunals to assume the appellate jurisdiction previously exercised by the circuit courts. The circuit courts continued to exist, however, until they were finally abolished in 1911. Thus for all but the last few years of his tenure on the federal bench, William Munger served in both capacities. He was the sole judge of the U.S. District Court of Nebraska, and he also frequently assumed the mantle of judge on the U.S. Circuit Court for the District of Nebraska. It was in the latter capacity that he heard and rendered decisions in some of the most noteworthy cases of his tenure, including the criminal prosecution of Senator Dietrich.

46. "Van Derventer [*sic*] Writes He Will Be Here Monday," *Omaha World-Herald*, December 30, 1903. Van Devanter would be appointed to the Supreme Court in 1911 by President William Taft and would ultimately prove to be one of the most conservative justices in the court's history. Along with Justices George Sutherland, Pierce Butler, and James McReynolds, he remains best remembered in the historiography of the court as one of the "Four Horsemen of Reaction," so named because of the four jurists' steadfast opposition to much of Franklin Roosevelt's liberal New Deal programming of the 1930s. See, e.g., Hall and Karsten, *Magic Mirror*, 277; Schwartz, *A History of the Supreme Court*, 214; and Irons, *A People's History of the Supreme Court*, 264.

47. United States v. Dietrich, 126 F. 664 (Cir. Ct., D. Neb 1904). See also "Point for Dietrich," *Omaha Daily Bee*, January 4, 1904.

48. The chronology of events related to Dietrich's appointment to the Senate is as follows: On March 28, 1901, the Nebraska legislature selected him to fill the vacant Senate seat previously held by M. L. Hayward, who had died in office. On May 1, 1901, Dietrich resigned as governor in order to accept the Senate appointment. He did not, however, take the oath of office, assume the duties, or begin to receive the salary of a senator until December 2, 1901. (The Senate was not in session at any time between March 28 and December 2 of that year.) The parties stipulated at the trial that all of Dietrich's actions related to the alleged bribery and the lease agreement that were the subjects of the indictments took place between March 28 and December 2, 1901.

49. United States v. Dietrich, 126 F. 676 (Cir. Ct., D. Neb 1904). Other reported opinions in the case, dealing with an assortment of ancillary procedural issues, may be found at 126 F. 659 and 126 F. 671.

50. "Current Topics," *Commoner*, January 22, 1904.

51. *Omaha Daily Bee*, January 9, 1904.

52. *Omaha World-Herald*, January 8, 1904.

53. *Alliance Herald*, January 15, 1904.
54. "Current Topics," *Commoner*, January 22, 1904.
55. "Dockets and Briefs Are Forgotten for the Time," *Omaha World-Herald*, January 8, 1904.
56. Like the judicial proceedings in Omaha, the Senate's investigation of the charges against Dietrich attracted extensive news coverage not only in the Nebraska press but also in newspapers across the country. See, e.g., "Senatorial Committee Commences Inquiry into Dietrich Charges," *San Francisco Call*, March 12, 1904, and "Hearing Charges against Dietrich," *Salt Lake Tribune*, March 13, 1904.
57. "Charges Affecting the Hon. Charles H. Dietrich," Serial Set Vol. 4575, Session Vol. No. 6, 58th Congress, 2nd sess., S. Rept. 2152. This report provides the most complete published description of the facts and evidence surrounding the allegations against Dietrich, including the complete record of the proceedings in the Nebraska district and circuit courts.
58. Summers was replaced as U.S. attorney by Douglas County district judge Irving F. Baxter of Omaha. See "Judge Baxter Agreed On for District Attorney," *Omaha World-Herald*, April 1, 1904, and "Judge Baxter Succeeds Prosecutor of Dietrich; Senator's Friends Forced United States Attorney Summers Out of the Nebraska Berth," *St. Louis Republic*, April 17, 1904.
59. "There Are Others, Merciful Judge," *Omaha World-Herald*, January 17, 1904.
60. See also "Oleson Gets Off with Fine," *Omaha Daily Bee*, January 15, 1904.
61. "Paid a Fine of $2000," *Red Cloud Chief*, January 22, 1904. The specific "fraternal order" that Oleson belonged to and which reportedly paid part of his fine is not identified in the news coverage. Current research, however, reveals that Oleson was a Mason, and Judge Munger was quite active in the Nebraska Masonic Order himself. See *Proceedings of the Grand Chapter of Royal Arch Masons of Nebraska at Its Thirty-Sixth Annual Convocation, Held at Omaha, December 10 and 1, 1902*, listing an Alfred M. Oleson as "Grand Master, Third Vail" in the roster of Office-Bearers shown on the back cover.
62. "There Are Others."
63. "There Are Others."

7. THE CATTLE BARONS CASES

1. For more on the Homestead Act and its effects in Nebraska, see Naugle, Montag, and Olson, *History of Nebraska*, 189–94.
2. For astute and intriguing analysis of the way in which the development of courts and other legal institutions on the Great Plains in the late nineteenth century belied the later Wild West imagery, see Ellis, *Law and Order in Buffalo Bill's Country*, and Anderson and Hill, *The Not So Wild, Wild West*.

3. One of the more notable episodes in the Nebraska "range wars" was the gruesome lynching and burning of two homesteaders in 1878 by a gang led by one of the richest and most prominent ranchers of the day, I. P. "Print" Olive. Olive and the other men involved in the grisly affair were convicted of second degree murder in state court, but their convictions were later overturned on jurisdictional grounds by the Nebraska Supreme Court. *Olive v. State*, 11 Neb. 1, 7 N.W. 444 (1881). For more on the notorious case, see Chrisman, *Ladder of Rivers*; Butcher, *Pioneer History of Custer County*, 43–62; and Paine, "Decisions Which Have Changed Nebraska History."

4. *U.S. Statutes at Large*, 23:231, February 25, 1885.

5. Theodore Roosevelt, "Seventh Annual Message," December 3, 1907. Online by Gerhard Peters and John T. Woolley, *American Presidency Project.*

6. Reynolds, "Land Frauds and Illegal Fencing in Western Nebraska."

7. Quoted in "The Stockgrowers' Meeting," *Alliance Herald*, February 21, 1902.

8. Reynolds, "Land Frauds and Illegal Fencing," 174, citing U.S. Department of the Interior, *Report of the Secretary, 1904*, 20.

9. "Cattlemen Next on Trial; Rangers Indicted for Illegal Land Fencing to Come before Court," *Omaha Sunday Bee*, May 14, 1905. The 1905 prosecutions arose out of indictments that had been issued in 1903. The cases had been deferred for several years as the cattlemen lobbied for legislative relief and the Interior Department continued its efforts to persuade the ranchers to voluntarily take down their fences. See "Richards and Lowe Indicted," *Omaha World-Herald*, December 11, 1903, and "Richest Ranchmen in Nebraska Are under Indictment," *St. Louis Republican*, December 11, 1903.

10. "Cattlemen Next on Trial," *Omaha Sunday Bee*, May 14, 1905.

11. For biographical information on Baxter, see Morton and Watkins, *Illustrated History*, 2:529, and for more on Rush, see Morton and Watkins, *Illustrated History*, 3:575–76.

12. "Homesteaders Tell Story; Osborn and Wife Testify in Federal Court against Krause Brothers," *Omaha Daily Bee*, June 3, 1905. See also "Krause Land Case; Sensational Testimony in Case Now in Federal Court in Omaha," *Alliance Herald*, June 8, 1905.

13. "Krause Admits the Killing; Cattleman on Witness Stand Says He Shot in Self-Defense," *Kearney Daily Hub*, June 9, 1905.

14. *Kearney Daily Hub*, June 6, 1905.

15. "Land Fencers Are on Trial," *Omaha Daily Bee*, June 1, 1905.

16. "Homesteaders Tell Story," *Omaha Daily Bee*, June 3, 1905.

17. "Krause Brothers Are Fined," *Omaha Daily Bee*, September 29, 1905.

18. "Krause Brothers Are Fined."

19. "Krauses Are Found Guilty," *Omaha Daily Bee*, June 10, 1905.

20. *Kearney Daily Hub*, June 10, 1905.

21. "Land Fence Trials Stop," *Red Cloud Chief*, June 23, 1905.

22. Richards and Van Ackeren, *Bartlett Richards*, 69.

23. According to the Spade's own records, as of 1903 the company owned outright about 28,000 acres in Sheridan and Cherry Counties, and leased another 35,000 to 40,000 acres from the state of Nebraska or private individuals. See Richards and Van Ackeren, *Bartlett Richards*, 268n16. Presumably, all the rest of the acreage used by the Spade was public domain.

24. Quoted in Richards and Van Ackeren, *Bartlett Richards*, 108. For the full transcript of the congressional hearing on the leasing bill, containing hundreds of pages of testimony on both sides of the issue, see *Hearings before the Committee on Public Land of the House of Representatives on the Question of Leasing of the Public Lands for Grazing Purposes, January 29–June 4, 1902.*

25. "Big Rangers Plead Guilty," *Omaha Daily Bee*, November 14, 1905; "Cattle Barons Plead Guilty," *Omaha World-Herald*, November 14, 1905; "Cattlemen Plead Guilty," *Red Cloud Chief*, November 17, 1905.

26. Judge William Munger, "Docket Entry," U.S. v. Bartlett Richards et al., November 13, 1905. See also "Big Rangers Plead Guilty." For brief discussions of the famous six-hour sentence in the secondary literature, see Reynolds, "Land Frauds and Illegal Fencing in Western Nebraska"; Naugle, Montag, and Olson, *History of Nebraska*, 235–36; Paine, "Decisions Which Have Shaped Nebraska History," 202–4; and Richards and Van Ackeren, *Bartlett Richards*, 143–53.

27. Richards and Van Ackeren, *Bartlett Richards*, 147.

28. Richards and Van Ackeren, *Bartlett Richards*, 149.

29. "Sentence Disgusts Secretary Hitchcock," *Omaha World-Herald*, November 17, 1905. For similar reports of Hitchcock's anger, see also "Sore over Richards Case," *Omaha Daily Bee*, November 15, 1905; "Outcome of Nebraska Cattle Cases Displeasing," *Nebraska State Journal*, November 17, 1905; "Hitchcock Indignant," *Bemidji Daily Pioneer*, November 17, 1905; "Baxter Placed under Fire," *Nebraska State Journal*, November 19, 1905; and "Special Agent Criticizes Judgment in Richards Case," *Omaha World-Herald*, November 20, 1905.

30. "Result Pleases Uncle Sam," *Omaha Daily Bee*, November 15, 1905.

31. "Head of Mr. Baxter May Fall into Basket," *Lincoln Evening News*, November 17, 1905. See also "Secretary Hitchcock Will Make an Investigation," *Omaha World-Herald*, November 19, 1905.

32. "Penalty Too Light," *Omaha Daily Bee*, November 17, 1905.

33. "Hitchcock Complains of Attorney at Omaha," *Washington Times*, November 19, 1905.

34. For more details on Baxter's public responses to the criticism and the subtle

shifts over time in his points of emphasis, see "No Word from Hitchcock," *Omaha Daily Bee*, November 19, 1905; "Baxter Doubts Rumor Inspector Will Be Sent," *Omaha World-Herald*, November 19, 1905; "Baxter's Side of the Case," *Omaha Daily Bee*, November 22, 1905; "Baxter's Worried Look since Hitchcock Wired," *Omaha World-Herald*, November 26, 1905; and "Baxter Lays All Blame on Judge Munger," *Lincoln Evening News*, December 20, 1905.

35. "Judge Munger Answers Secretary Hitchcock," *Omaha World-Herald*, November 17, 1905. See also "Federal Judge Munger Replies to Hitchcock," *Lincoln Daily Star*, November 17, 1905; "Hitchcock Angers Judge," *New York Times*, November 17, 1905.

36. The full text of Matthews's letter to Moody is printed in "Mathews Loses Job," *Omaha Daily Bee*, December 9, 1905. For other coverage of the firing, see "Head in Basket; President Orders Dismissal of Marshal Matthews," *Nebraska State Journal*, December 9, 1905; "United States Marshal Matthews Out of Office," *Omaha World-Herald*, December 9, 1905.

37. "Vigorous Protest to Moody; Entire Nebraska Delegation Demands That Matthews Be Heard," *Omaha Daily Bee*, December 10, 1905.

38. "Plea for Matthews," *Nebraska State Journal*, December 15, 1905. See also "Schneider Is Not Hopeful; Nebraska Republican Visits Washington to Intercede for Mr. Matthews," *Omaha World-Herald*, December 14, 1905.

39. "Will Not Get Back; Marshal Matthews' Plea for Reinstatement Denied," *Nebraska State Journal*, December 19, 1905.

40. "Baxter Lays All Blame upon Judge Munger," *Lincoln Evening News*, December 20. 1905.

41. "Baxter Told to Go; Official Wrath over Cattle Cases Not Appeased," *Nebraska State Journal*, December 20, 1905.

42. Reynolds, "Land Frauds and Illegal Fencing," 176.

43. Reynolds, "Land Frauds and Illegal Fencing," 178.

44. Ware v. United States, 154 F. 577 (8th Cir., 1907).

45. Ware v. United States, 207 U.S. 588 (1907).

46. Details of the trial testimony and evidence are available in multiple sources, including the official district court docket and records, U.S. District Court, District of Nebraska, Case No. 101, NARA RG 21, Subgroup 3; the Eighth Circuit's opinion on appeal, Richards v. U.S., 175 F. 911 (8th Cir., 1909); Richards and Van Ackeren, *Bartlett Richards*; Reynolds, "Land Frauds and Illegal Fencing"; McIntosh, "Patterns from Land Alienation Maps"; and of course dozens of contemporary newspaper articles.

47. Quoted in Hall, *Life and Letters of Richard Smith Hall*, 84.

48. Hall, *Life and Letters*, 84.

49. Hall, *Life and Letters*, 85.

50. Hall, *Life and Letters*, 84.
51. Richards and Van Ackeren, *Bartlett Richards*, 171.
52. Richards and Van Ackeren, *Bartlett Richards*, 172.
53. Oddly, the full text of Munger's lengthy charge to the jury is published at United States v. Richards, 149 F. 443 (D. Neb 1906).
54. Richards v. U.S., 175 F. 911 (8th Cir., 1909).
55. Richards v. U.S., Philips's dissent, 933, 950.
56. *North Platte Semi-Weekly Tribune*, December 2, 1910.
57. Quoted in *Hastings Daily Republican*, December 8, 1910.
58. See, e.g., "Rich Convict at Resort," *New York Times*, June 19, 1911.
59. Richards and Van Ackeren, *Bartlett Richards*, 215.
60. "Cattle Man Dies in Jail," *New York Times*, September 5, 1911.

8. THE "TWO MUNGER" COURT

1. *Annual Report of the Attorney General of the United States for the Year 1896*, Washington: Department of Justice, Office of the Attorney General, Serial Set Vol. No. 3499, Session Vol. No. 23, 54th Cong., 2nd sess., H. Doc. 9 pt. 1 & 2.
2. *Annual Report of the Attorney General of the United States for the Year 1906*, Washington: Department of Justice, Office of the Attorney General, Serial Set Vol. No. 5129, Session Vol. No. 26, 59th Cong., 2nd sess., H. Doc. 10.
3. "Burkett Ready with His New Federal Court Bill," *Omaha World-Herald*, January 5, 1906.
4. In the early twentieth century, Nebraska enjoyed six congressional districts, giving it a congressional delegation of eight members. In addition to Burkett and Norris, the rest of the Nebraska contingent in 1905–6 included Senator Joseph Millard and Representatives Moses Kinkaid, Edmund Hinshaw, John McCarthy, John L. Kennedy, and Ernest Pollard. All were Republicans.
5. *U.S. Statutes at Large*, 34: 997–99.
6. For details on the debates over the qualifications of various potential nominees for the new judicial seat, see "Nice Plum to Pick; Possible Candidates for Federal Judgeship," *Nebraska State Journal*, February 19, 1907; "Burkett Busy for Munger; Senator Fights Hard for Appointment of His Political Manager," *Omaha Evening Bee*, February 26, 1907; "Both Want Munger; Nebraska Senators Favorable to Lincoln Man," *Nebraska State Journal*, February 26, 1907; and "Munger Shy on Practice; Reasons Advanced for Bar Association's Opposition," *Omaha Evening Bee*, February 26, 1907.
7. For accounts of the machinations within the Nebraska caucus and reactions to the Munger nomination, see "Munger Is Chosen New Federal Judge; 'Easy' Victory of Senator Burkett Came Near to a Deadlock—Congressman Norris Dangerous," *Omaha World-Herald*, February 28, 1907; "Tom Munger Is

Named; Burkett's Friend Wins Out; Two Mungers on Same Bench," *Norfolk Weekly News-Journal,* March 1, 1907; "Tom Munger Is Endorsed; Majority of Nebraska Delegation Asks President to Name Judge; Action Taken in Secret Meeting," *Omaha Evening Bee,* February 27, 1907; and "Named as Judge; Thomas C. Munger Selected for Federal Position," *Nebraska State Journal,* February 28, 1907.

8. Quoted in "Named as Judge; Thomas C. Munger Selected for Federal Position," *Nebraska State Journal,* February 28, 1907.

9. The account of Munger's meeting with Roosevelt is drawn from his brother's recollections, as recorded in the memorial proceedings in the judge's honor following his death in 1941. See "In Memoriam, Honorable Thomas Charles Munger (1861–1941)," 22 *Neb. L. Rev.* 146 (June 1943) [hereinafter T. C. Munger Memorial Proceedings].

10. Surprisingly, there seemed to be little commentary in the contemporary press on the shared surname of the two Nebraska judges. One of the most direct references to the odd coincidence appeared in the *Norfolk Weekly News,* which predicted that "now, with two federal judges each named Munger, confusion will be in the air." The story went on to report that "somebody at Omaha has suggested that since the newly named judge is 'Tom' Munger, the other one might be called 'Jerry.'" See "Tom Munger Is Named; Burkett's Friend Wins Out; Two Mungers on Same Bench," *Norfolk Weekly News-Journal,* March 1, 1907.

11. Published biographical information on the new judge is relatively scarce. Many of the details of his early life and career may be found in the aforementioned memorial proceedings in his honor following his death in 1941. See also "Named as Judge; Thomas C. Munger Selected for Federal Position," *Nebraska State Journal,* February 28, 1907, which describes the new judge's biographical background in some detail.

12. T. C. Munger Memorial Proceedings, 159.

13. Quoted in Schroeder, *The Snowball: Warren Buffett and the Business of Life,* 223. For more on the Munger family's history, see also Lowe, *Damn Right!*

14. "Named as Judge; Thomas C. Munger Selected for Federal Position," *Nebraska State Journal,* February 28, 1907.

15. "The Public Pulse; 'My Judge,' Says Mr. Burkett," *Omaha World-Herald,* June 2, 1910.

16. Fortunately for historians, the new Judge Munger proved to be a meticulous record keeper. His judicial files, including a vast collection of his personal correspondence, memoranda, and notes as well as all other historical records of the Nebraska District Court, are housed in RG 21 of the Central Plains Regional Records Center of the National Archives and Records Administration

(NARA) in Kansas City, Missouri. The Thomas C. Munger collection is particularly notable for its extensive breadth and depth, offering rare insights into some of the judge's relationships with his colleagues and staff, his thoughts on specific cases, and his generalized jurisprudential development (cited hereafter as T. C. Munger Papers).

17. T. C. Munger to W. H. Munger, March 21, 1907, T. C. Munger Papers, RG 21, box 31.

18. T. C. Munger to W. H. Munger, February 27, 1909, T. C. Munger Papers, RG 21, box 32.

19. T. C. Munger to W. H. Munger, April 5, 1909, T. C. Munger Papers, RG 21, box 32.

20. T. C. Munger to J. C. Nelson, Western Union Telegraph Co., March 27, 1907, T. C. Munger Papers, RG 21, box 31.

21. T. C. Munger to the Attorney General, March 22, 1907, T. C. Munger Papers, RG 21, box 31.

22. Acting Attorney General to T. C. Munger, June 23, 1907, T. C. Munger Papers, RG 21, box 32.

23. Assistant Secretary of the Interior to Hon. Thomas C. Munger, December 11, 1907, T. C. Munger Papers, RG 21, box 32. The incident referred to in the letter, in which the publishing plates had been destroyed, was the great San Francisco earthquake of April 1906 and the resulting massive fire that engulfed the city.

24. T. C. Munger to W. H. Munger, July 22, 1909, T. C. Munger Papers, RG 21, box 32.

25. "Old Soldier Entrymen Testify in Huntington Land Case," *Omaha World-Herald*, April 12, 1907.

26. "Jail Term and Fine for Land Barons," *Omaha World-Herald*, June 20, 1907.

27. "Babcock Falls from His Chair; Defendant in Land Fraud Case Has Nervous Seizure While Undergoing Trial," *Omaha World-Herald*, October 21, 1907.

28. "Babcock and Others Convicted of Land Fraud; Sentencing to Follow," *Omaha Daily Bee*, July 18, 1908.

29. See, e.g., "Spectacular Land Grabbing by Ranchmen; Perry Yeast and Eight Associates Are Indicted; Remarkable Story Is Told by Victims," *Omaha World-Herald*, November 4, 1910; and "Indictments Are Returned; Ranchers Charged with Driving Out Homesteaders; Settlers Were Persecuted," *Nebraska State Journal*, November 4, 1910.

30. The *World-Herald*'s only reference to the verdict was a tiny five-line article buried on page 3. "Perry Yeast and Others Are Found Not Guilty," *Omaha World-Herald*, November 14, 1910.

31. For more on the fight to enact the Newberry law, see Naugle, Montag, and

Olson, *History of Nebraska*, 266–67, and Breitzer, "Newberry Railroad Rate Bill (1894)," 463.

32. Smyth v. Ames, 171 U.S. 361 (1898). For detailed analysis of the decision and its impact, see Eric Monkkonen, "Can Nebraska or Any State Regulate Railroads? *Smyth v. Ames*, 1898."

33. Naugle, Montag, and Olson, *History of Nebraska*, 287–89.

34. "Is It War with Nebraska?" *Omaha World-Herald*, June 3, 1907.

35. "Railway Commission Can't Mail Out Notices; Railroad Gets Injunction Stopping Them from Giving Notification of Reduced Freight Rates," *Omaha World-Herald*, September 11, 1907.

36. "Big Fight in Prospect over Railroad Injunctions; Governor Sheldon Announces He Will Give Roads All the Fight They Want in Matter," *Omaha World-Herald*, September 12, 1907.

37. "Face to Face with the Issue," *Omaha World-Herald*, September 12, 1907.

38. "Protests Too Much, and Too Soon," *Nebraska State Journal*, September 12, 1907.

39. "Not Harmless," *Omaha World-Herald*, September 14, 1907.

40. Powell and Nilsson to T. C. Munger, September 12, 1907, T. C. Munger Papers, RG 21, box 33.

41. No transcript of the hearing is available. The account given here is from contemporary press reports, including "Argue Grain Case; Railroad Commission Rights in Federal Court; Matter under Advisement," *Nebraska State Journal*, September 24, 1907; "State Says Roads Are Too Quick; Attorney General Thompson Insists They Can't Ask Rate Enjoined Until in Effect," *Chicago Tribune*, September 24, 1907, reprinted same date *Omaha World-Herald*.

42. Munger's opinion was not published in the *Federal Reporter*, nor is it found in the archived court files. But it was widely reported, with excerpting, in newspapers. See "Railway Commission May Lower Grain Freight Rates; Judge Munger Gives Decision Late Last Night, Dissolving Order Secured by Railroads," *Omaha World-Herald*, September 27, 1907.

43. For a thorough and entertaining account of the train robbery of 1909 and the ensuing federal prosecutions of the men charged with the crime, see Thompson, "The Great Omaha Train Robbery." The case is also discussed in some detail in Jackson, *The Leavenworth Train* and in Folsom, *The Money Trail*. The most "official" recitation of the facts leading to the convictions of the accused robbers may be found in the Eighth Circuit's published opinion in the case (with Judge William H. Munger sitting on the panel), Matthews v. United States, 192 F. 490 (8th Cir., 1911). The narrative provided here is taken largely from those sources, as well as from archived court files and contemporary newspaper accounts.

44. Thompson, "The Great Omaha Train Robbery," fn1.
45. "Three Suspects Arrested as Bandits; Fourth Alleged Train Robber Escapes," *Omaha World-Herald*, May 28, 1909.
46. "Try Train Bandit Suspects Together; Judge T. C. Munger Will Try Them about October 1—Elder Judge to Denver," *Omaha World-Herald*, September 4, 1909.
47. For detailed analysis of the evidence amassed by authorities against the accused men, see Thompson, "The Great Omaha Train Robbery" and Jackson, *The Leavenworth Train*, 111–56. Jackson's book is a sympathetic account of Grigware's colorful life before and after his involvement in the train robbery and is highly critical of the prosecution's case against Grigware as well as Munger's handling of the trial in general.
48. Jackson, *The Leavenworth Train*, 146. For representative samples of the press coverage of the trial, see "Jury Secured to Try Bandit Suspects; Will Determine Whether Five Prisoners Go to Penitentiary for Life or Go Free," *Omaha World-Herald*, October 26, 1909; "Seven Point Out Bandits; Woods and Torgenson Positively Identified by Many Witnesses," *Omaha Daily Bee*, October 28, 1909; "School Principal Is Star Witness," *Omaha World-Herald*, October 30, 1909; "Kansas City Day in Trial; Witnesses from Kawville Testify to Show Prisoners Were There," *Omaha Daily Bee*, November 3, 1909; and "Arrest of Matthews Is Related by May; Trial of Alleged Head of Union Pacific Train Robbers Reached in Cases," *Omaha World-Herald*, November 6, 1909.
49. Jackson, *The Leavenworth Train*, 146, 148.
50. "Daring Dash for Liberty; Alleged Mail Robbers Foiled in Effort to Break from Jail; Saws and Weapons Smuggled," *Omaha Daily Bee*, November 11, 1909; and "Accused Train Robbers, Armed with Iron Bars, Almost Saw Their Way Out of New County Jail," *Omaha World-Herald*, November 10, 1909.
51. See, e.g., "'Bad Men' in City Cause Officers to Redouble Vigilance; Officials Having Bandits in Custody Are Uneasy over Possible Repetition of Attempt to Escape," *Omaha World-Herald*, November 11, 1909. Note the absence of "Accused" or "Alleged" before the word "Bandits" in the headline.
52. "Verdict of Guilty in Case of the Union Pacific Train Robbers; Jury Decides the Matter in Just One Hour and a Quarter," *Omaha World-Herald*, November 12, 1909; and "Five Robbers Found Guilty; Jury in Federal Court Convicts Overland Limited Train Holdups after Two Hours of Deliberation," *Omaha Daily Bee*, November 12, 1909.
53. "Marshal Glad to Be Rid of Bandits; Lodges Them Safely in Federal Prison at Leavenworth to Stay for Life," *Omaha World-Herald*, November 20, 1909.
54. "Police Captain Is Assaulted: Jealousy over the Arrest of the Train Robbers Alleged as the Cause," *Omaha World-Herald*, June 1, 1909.

55. "Boys File Suit for $25,000 Reward," *Omaha World-Herald,* November 19, 1909. See also "Many Seek Bandit Reward," *Omaha Daily Bee,* November 18, 1909, and Thompson, "The Great Omaha Train Robbery," 228.

56. Although newspaper accounts and the reported opinion in the case refer to the claimant's name as "Belek," his wife's notes to Judge Munger clearly spell the name "Bilek." Assuming the woman was who she claimed to be, one would think she would know the spelling of her own married surname, so the case name may well be erroneous.

57. Mrs. Josephine Bilek to Judge Thomas Munger, September 8 and September 13, 1913, T. C. Munger Papers, RG 21, box 41.

58. Union Pac. R. Co. v. Belek, 211 F. 699 (D. Neb., 1913).

59. See Chris Zdeb, "Escaped Lifer Hid His Past for Almost a Quarter Century in Alberta," *Edmonton Journal,* April 1, 2015.

60. Quoted in Jackson, *The Leavenworth Train,* 210. See also "U.S. May Drop Fahey Extradition Claim" and "Travesty to Return Fahey to Cell, Says Ex-Convict Now in Congress, Declares U.S. Cannot Claim Man," *Edmonton Journal,* April 4, 1934. For more on the colorful career of Francis Shoemaker, see Johnson, "From Leavenworth to Congress."

61. The statute remains in effect today and is codified as 49 USC sec. 80502. While it retains the original twenty-eight-hour limit, the current law is still criticized by animal rights advocates for containing far too many exceptions and loopholes. See Sheley, "Live Animals: Toward Protection for Pets and Livestock in Contracts for Carriage."

62. See "How Bill Goat Helps a Great Railway System," *Omaha World-Herald,* March 20, 1910, and "Goats Assist Railroad," *North Platte Semi-Weekly Tribune,* June 10, 1910.

63. See "Railroads Fined over $25,000," *Lincoln Commoner,* October 1, 1914, and "Fined for Law Violations; Railroads Have Been Fined Large Sums Lately for Violation of Quarantine and 28 Hour," *Alliance Herald,* July 2, 1914.

64. "Guilty of Violating the 28 Hour Law; Jury Returns Verdict against Union Pacific on Ten Counts in Federal Court," *Omaha World-Herald,* May 27, 1909.

65. United States v. Chicago, B. & Q. R. Co., 184 F. 984 (D. Neb., 1910). For references to other cases involving the twenty-eight-hour law during the "two Munger" era, see "Four Suits against Road: Action Brought to Punish Northwestern for Alleged Violation of Twenty-Eight-Hour Law," *Omaha Daily Bee,* November 13, 1907; "Charge Burlington with Violating 28-Hour Law," *Omaha Daily Bee,* May 16, 1915; and "Railroad Pleads Guilty to Law Violations," *Omaha World-Herald,* November 20, 1915.

66. United States v. Chicago, B. & Q. Ry. Co., 156 F. 180 (D. Neb., 1907).

67. Chicago, B. & Q. Ry. Co. v. U.S., 170 F. 556 (8th Cir., 1908); and Chicago, B.

& Q. Ry. Co. v. U.S., 220 U.S. 559 (1911). See also "Higher Court Upholds Safety Appliance Law," *Omaha World-Herald*, April 27, 1908.

68. Interstate Commerce Commission Secretary Edward A. Mosely to Hon. Thomas C. Munger, May 22, 1908, T. C. Munger Papers, RG 21, box 34.

69. United States v. Chicago & N. W. Ry. Co., 157 F. 616 (D. Neb., 1907).

70. Chicago & N.W. Ry. Co. v. U.S., 168 F. 236 (8th Cir. 1909). See also "Decision against Railway Company Reversed," *Omaha World-Herald*, March 12, 1909.

71. United State v. Union Stock Yards Co. of Omaha, 161 F. 919 (D. Neb. 1908). See also "Stock Yards Guilty of Violating Safety Appliance Law," *Omaha World-Herald*, February 22, 1908.

72. Union Stockyards Co. of Omaha v. U.S., 169 F. 404 (8th Cir., 1909). See also "Union Stock Yards Held to Be Common Carrier; Circuit Court of Appeals Decides It Is Subject to Safety Appliance Act," *Omaha World-Herald*, April 2, 1909.

73. United States v. Fred A. Corbin, Case No. 3789, U.S. District Court for District of Nebraska, Lincoln Division (unreported). See also "Judge Munger Sentences Postmaster Corbin," *Plattsmouth Journal*, April 8, 1912; and "Postmaster Sentenced," *Dakota County Herald*, April 19, 1912.

74. Corbin v. United States, 205 F. 278 (8th Cir., 1913).

75. Senator George W. Norris to Honorable T. C. Munger, May 21, 1913, T. C. Munger Papers, RG 21, box 34.

76. Norris to Munger, June 14, 1913, T. C. Munger Papers, RG 21, box 34.

77. W. H. Munger to Hon. Walter H. Sanborn, September 22, 1913, T. C. Munger Papers, RG 21, box 34.

78. See, e.g., "Judge Munger Confined to Home by Illness," *Omaha World-Herald*, August 13, 1914, describing Munger as "seriously ill"; and "Judge Munger Is Ill," *Omaha Daily Bee*, October 23, 1914, reporting that the judge remained at home and was "not quite so well."

79. See, e.g., "Federal Court Opens," *Omaha World-Herald*, September 29, 1914, reporting that Munger was unavailable to preside over the opening of the court's fall term and that he had been temporarily replaced by Judge Paige Morris of Minneapolis; and "Judge Youmans Assigned to Nebraska Division," *Omaha World-Herald*, January 9, 1915, reporting that Judge Munger remained confined to his home and that Judge Frank A. Youmans from the Eastern District of Arkansas had been temporarily assigned to handle his docket.

80. "Federal Judge Munger Dead after an Illness of Two Years; Veteran Nebraska Jurist Passes Away at Age of 69—Had Been Unable to Occupy Bench for Past Year," *Omaha World-Herald*, August 12, 1915.

81. See "Munger Funeral to Be Saturday," *Omaha Daily Bee*, August 13, 1915, and "The Passing of Judge Munger," *North Platte Semi-Weekly Tribune*, August 13, 1915.

82. A transcript of the memorial ceremony for Judge Munger may be found at http://www.ned.uscourts.gov/internetDocs/judicialArchive/*whm* _Memoriam.pdf. [hereinafter W. H. Munger Memorial Proceedings].
83. W. H. Munger Memorial Proceedings, 2–3.
84. W. H. Munger Memorial Proceedings, 5.
85. W. H. Munger Memorial Proceedings, 18–19.
86. *Plattsmouth Journal,* August 15, 1915.

9. THE EARLY MUNGER-WOODROUGH YEARS

1. Bryan served as Wilson's secretary of state until June 1915, when he resigned in protest of what he perceived to be the president's increasingly belligerent attitude toward Germany, which Bryan believed threatened to bring the United States into World War I. See also "Five Candidates for Judge Munger's Place," *Omaha World-Herald,* August 23, 1915.
2. "Consider Successor to Munger This Week; Age Limit Thought Bar to Appointment of W. H. Thompson," *Omaha World-Herald,* September 19, 1915. See also "Bryan Presents the Little Giant; Former Secretary of State and W. H. Thompson Hold Interview with Gregory," *Omaha Daily Bee,* September 17, 1915, and "Stated in Washington Thompson Not the Choice," *Omaha World-Herald,* September 22, 1915.
3. "Woodrough Is Named New Federal Judge," *Omaha World-Herald,* March 14, 1916.
4. Editorial, "Judge Woodrough," *Omaha World-Herald,* March 14, 1916.
5. The most recent—and by far the best—overview of Woodrough's early life may be found in the work of Omaha attorney and writer Nick Batter, who has served as an invaluable research aide and draftsman in the preparation of portions of this book. Some of his work has been previously published as Batter, "The Wayfaring Judge." Batter's sourcing for the Woodrough family history is derived in part from his correspondence with the judge's descendent and family genealogist, Margot Woodrough. An additional fertile source of information on Woodrough's background is the lengthy illustrated feature story "On the Bench at 21, Federal Judge at 42; Unusual Career of Young Lawyer Appointed Successor of Late Judge Munger," *Omaha World-Herald,* March 26, 1916.
6. Woodrough's uncle James was a particularly innovative toolmaker, procuring a multitude of patents for new and improved designs and manufacturing processes. His most famous patented design would prove to be an ornamental wooden saw handle featuring the carved head of a panther. Today, "Woodrough Panther" saws are highly sought after by collectors. See, e.g., http://www.popularwoodworking.com/article/the-painted-panther.

7. "Judge Met King, Lived amid Guns," *Omaha World-Herald*, October 4, 1977.
8. See National Constitution Center, "Louis Brandeis Confirmed as Justice 100 Years Ago Today."
9. Some sources erroneously indicate that Woodrough studied at Heidelberg University in Ohio. While an understandable mistake—the college was and remains a well-regarded institution located in Woodrough's native state— the fact is that he was never a student there. Batter, correspondence with Heidelberg (Ohio) University archivist, summer 2014.
10. "On the Bench at 21," *Omaha World-Herald*, March 26, 1916.
11. "On the Bench at 21."
12. "Omaha Law School Opened; A Red Letter Occasion with the Legal Fraternity of the City," *Omaha World-Herald*, September 14, 1892.
13. Batter, "The Wayfaring Judge," 75.
14. See "Tried to Whip Judge Scott; Attorney Beckett Got Riled at the Criminal Court and Went after Blood," *Omaha World-Herald*, August 12, 1895.
15. Woodrough's foray into cattle ranching proved to be a disaster. After he had nearly exhausted the county's grain supply in an unsuccessful attempt to fatten his herd for market, all of his livestock broke free and stampeded into Mexico. He never recovered them. He later considered it to be a blessing, as the cost of continued feed for the cattle would have bankrupted him.
16. "On the Bench at 21."
17. "Judge Met King, Lived amid Guns."
18. See Morearty, *Omaha Memories*.
19. Sadly, however, as Woodrough's reputation was on the rise, his uncle William Beckett's promising but checkered career was descending into tragedy. In late 1902 Beckett's much younger wife, Ella, divorced him on grounds of "habitual drunkenness." Several weeks later Beckett's body was discovered frozen stiff in a snowbank near Benson, where he had apparently wandered aimlessly before succumbing to the bitter cold. The story received extensive local and national news coverage. See, e.g., "Lawyer Beckett Found Frozen in Snow Drift," *Omaha World-Herald*, January 12, 1903, and "W. D. Beckett Found Dead," *Omaha Daily Bee*, January 12, 1903. The *New York Times* picked up the story and was more lurid in its coverage. See "Insane, He Froze to Death," *New York Times*, January 12, 1903. Adding an additional enigmatic layer to the story, Woodrough himself married Ella later that year and eventually adopted her two children—Woodrough's cousins—and raised them as his own children. He and Ella remained married for the rest of their lives, but never had children of their own.
20. Woodrough and Gurley successfully defended several of the cattlemen accused of procuring fraudulent homestead claims in what were known

as the Modisett Cattle Land case in early 1907, which was presided over by his future colleague on the bench, Thomas Munger. It was the first of the cattle baron cases in which the defendants were acquitted of the charges. See "Cattlemen Win Out in Modisett Trial," *Omaha World-Herald,* January 11, 1907.

21. See "Hans Arrested for Murder; Northwestern Detective Must Answer for Killing of D. O. Luce; Story of Self-Defense Is Doubted," *Omaha Daily Bee,* May 24, 1903, and "Arguing Hans Case," *Norfolk Weekly News-Journal,* May 19, 1905.

22. The case was front-page news throughout the state and region, and it remains a macabre and still-unsolved episode in Nebraska legal history. See, e.g., "Murder in the First Degree; Gravest Charge Will Be Preferred against Charles E. Davis; Magnifies Importance of Davis and Rice Story of Death Pact," *Omaha Daily Bee,* September 11, 1908, and Nebraska State Historical Society, "Dr. Rustin's Mysterious Death."

23. Drexel v. Rochester Loan & Banking Co., 65 Neb. 231, 91 N.W. 254 (1902), and Drexel v. Reed, 69 Neb. 468, 95 N.W. 873 (1903).

24. For much more on Dennison and his later battles with Woodrough, see chapter 10.

25. Woodrough, "The Game You Can't Lose," 309.

26. Morearty, *Omaha Memories,* 201.

27. The literature describing anti-German animus in Nebraska and elsewhere during the war is abundant. For a fine example, see Luebke, *Bonds of Loyalty.*

28. The Nebraska statute related to the banning of German in the schools ultimately became the subject of an important Supreme Court decision, Meyer v. Nebraska, 262 U.S. 390 (1923). For an excellent analysis of the case, see Ross, "Meyer v. Nebraska."

29. Espionage Act of 1917, Pub. L. 65–24, 40 Stat. 217 (65th Congress, June 15, 1917).

30. Sedition Act of 1918, Pub. L. 65–150, 40 Stat. 553 (65th Congress, May 16, 1918).

31. For details on the Nebraska Council of Defense and its activities, see Naugle, Montag, and Olson, *History of Nebraska,* 297–308.

32. Nebraska State Historical Society, RG 23, "Nebraska. State Council of Defense, Historic Note," http://www.nebraskahistory.org/lib-arch/research/public/state_finding_aids/council_of_defense.pdf.

33. For more on the Nonpartisan League's battles with the State Council, see Manley, "The Nebraska State Council of Defense and the Nonpartisan League, 1917–1918."

34. For more on the UNL faculty hearings, see Naugle, Montag, and Olson, *History*

of *Nebraska*, 302–5, and "University of Nebraska Loyalty Trials," University of Nebraska-Lincoln Digital Archives, at http://unlhistory.unl.edu/exhibits /show/schillerlinden/uprootingthetree/nebraskacouncilofdefense.

35. Woodrough, "Beginning My Work on the Federal Bench."

36. Quoted in Batter, "The Wayfaring Judge," 77.

37. Batter, "The Wayfaring Judge."

38. Batter, "The Wayfaring Judge."

39. "Judge Making War Garden; Clerk Couldn't Make Plea," *Omaha World-Herald,* May 17, 1918.

40. "Judge Says Paper Like the World-Herald Would Prevent 'Slackers' in Oklahoma," *Omaha World-Herald,* January 29, 1918.

41. "Combination of Mishaps Results in Jail Sentence," *Omaha World-Herald,* January 29, 1918.

42. "Foreign-Born Soldiers Make Good Americans; Seven Hundred Fighters at Fort Crook Take Naturalization Oath," *Omaha World-Herald,* June 7, 1918.

43. "Say Hindered Army; Piano Tuner Is Held," *Omaha World-Herald,* January 20, 1918. See also "Held under Espionage Law" and "Socialist with Country Place Held for Jury," *Omaha World-Herald,* January 23, 1918.

44. "Slacker Charges Dismissed," *Omaha World-Herald,* June 2, 1918.

45. For more on Mickey's odd, and ultimately short-lived, experiment in creating a socialist society that he called the "Commonwealth Co-Operators," see "Mickey Plans Adding to Scope of Society; Founder Sees Hope of World in Applying Co-Operative Principles," *Omaha World-Herald,* June 2, 1925, and "Commonwealth Has 'Court' over Dispute," *Omaha World-Herald,* October 28, 1925.

46. "The Rev. William Windolph Indicted for Alleged Violation of Espionage Act," *Omaha World-Herald,* June 2, 1918.McKee's mention of "Hoover" referred to future president Herbert Hoover, who served as director of the U.S. Food Administration during the war. James Gerard was the ambassador to Germany prior to American entry in the war and thereafter became notorious for his strident advocacy of strong measures to suppress antiwar dissent among German Americans.

47. "Harshfield Case Today," *North Platte Semi-Weekly Tribune,* June 28, 1918.

48. Schenck v. United States, 249 U.S. 47 (1919).

49. *Schenck,* at 52.

50. Harshfield v. United States, 260 F. 659 (8th Cir., 1919).

51. "Crowd Here for Windolph Case; Over 200 Creighton People Arrive for Trial of Priest for Alleged Sedition," *Norfolk Daily News,* September 24, 1918.

52. For details on some of the more titillating aspects of the Windolph trial, see "Thrills in Plenty in Windolph Case; Widow Paints Her Priest as an Ardent

Wooer," *Nebraska State Journal,* October 1, 1918; and "Woman Accuses Priest of Improper Conduct; Mrs. Mary Green Says Father Windolph Made Wrongful Suggestions," *Omaha World-Herald,* September 27, 1918.

53. "Crowd at Trial of Fr. Windolph Warned by Court," *Norfolk Daily News,* September 25, 1918.

54. "Court's Ruling Limits Counts against Pastor," *Norfolk Daily News,* September 27, 1918. See also "Sedition in His Sermons; Not in Evidence—Witnesses Couldn't Fix Date," *Nebraska State Journal,* October 1, 1918.

55. "Windolph Case Halts as Government Rests," *Omaha World-Herald,* September 28, 1918. See also "Prosecution in Windolph Case Ends Testimony; Throwing Out of Eight of Nine Counts Limits Government to Single Witness," *Norfolk Daily News,* September 28, 1918. For intriguing insights into secret service agent Werner Hanni's investigation of Windolph and many other midwestern clergymen suspected of disloyalty, see Thomas, *Unsafe for Democracy.*

56. "Windolph Jury Disagrees after 5-Hours' Session," *Norfolk Daily News,* October 2, 1918.

57. "Creighton Opposed to Any Use of the Hun Tongue; Father W. W. Windolph Said to Have Resumed Preaching in German," *Omaha World-Herald,* December 30, 1918.

58. United States v. Bernstein, 267 F. 295 (D. Neb. 1920).

59. United States v. L. Cohen Grocery Co., 255 U.S. 81 (1921). The *Cohen* court did not cite Woodrough's opinion in *Bernstein,* most likely because it had not yet been published in the *Federal Reports,* but the majority's reasoning coincided precisely with Woodrough's.

60. Sinjen v. Miller, 281 F. 889 (D. Neb., 1922).

61. Expatriation Act of 1907, Pub. L. 59–193, 34 Stat. 1228 (59th Cong., March 12, 1907).

62. Trading with the Enemy Act of 1917, Pub. L. 65–91, 40 Stat. 411 (65th Cong., October 6, 1917).

63. *Sinjen,* at 891.

64. For discussion of the general impact of World War I on the Nebraska economy, see Naugle, Montag, and Olson, *History of Nebraska,* 291–97.

65. For the definitive account of the 1921–22 meatpackers' strike in Omaha and Nebraska City by the foremost labor historian in the region, see Pratt, "Divided Workers, Divided Communities." For additional background and context, see Brody, *The Butcher Workmen,* and Pratt, "Advancing Packinghouse Unionism in South Omaha, 1917–1920."

66. "Strikers Claim Nearly 100 Per Cent Out Locally; Situation Was Quiet; Pickets on All Approaches but No Intimidations or Threats Made," *Nebraska Daily*

Press, December 6, 1921. See also "Both Sides Predict Packer Strike Victory," *Omaha World-Herald*, December 7, 1921.

67. "Strike Continues at Local Plant; Mexicans Stopped; Strike-Breakers Who Arrived Last Night Not Permitted to Go to Plant," *Nebraska Daily Press*, December 7, 1921.

68. Pratt, "Divided Workers, Divided Communities," 53–54.

69. See "Watching over Her Wounded Baby," *Omaha World-Herald*, December 9, 1921.

70. "Three Hundred Women at Council on Packing Strike; Demand Medical Examination of Workers, Accuse Police of Using Insulting Language to Striking Women," *Omaha World-Herald*, December 20, 1921. See also Pratt, "Divided Workers, Divided Communities," 54.

71. Quoted in Pratt, "Divided Workers, Divided Communities," 57–58. See also "Protest to City Council," *Omaha World-Herald*, December 21, 1921.

72. Pratt, "Divided Workers, Divided Communities," 58.

73. "National Guard Company Asked for Local Duty; Application Signed by Mayor Thomas and County Authorities Yesterday; Request Sent by Wire," *Nebraska Daily Press*, December 13, 1921.

74. "Declines to Call Militia; Acting Governor Decided Not Needed," *Lincoln State Journal*, December 13, 1921.

75. "Put Guards on Buses Today to Protect Workers; Mayor Thomas and County Attorney Heinke Say Assaults Must Stop," *Nebraska Daily Press*, December 14, 1921.

76. "Petition," Morton-Gregson Company v. Local Union No. 122 of Amalgamated Meat Cutters and Butcher Workmen of North America, et al., Equity Case No. 164, December 16, 1921, RG 21, Records of the U.S. District Court for the District of Nebraska, Lincoln Division, Equity and Law Final Records Book (October 29, 1907–February 27, 1924), 2 [hereinafter Records of the District Court]. See also "Packing Company Asks Injunction against Union," *Nebraska Daily Press*, December 16, 1921, and "Ask Order in Strike," *Lincoln Star*, December 16, 1921.

77. American Steel Foundries v. Tri-City Trades Council, 257 U.S. 184, 205 (1921), at 206.

78. For detailed analysis of the impact of the court's ruling, see Hellerstein, "Picketing Legislation and the Courts," and Frankfurter and Greene, *The Labor Injunction*.

79. "Restraining Order," Morton-Gregson Company v. Local Union No. 122 of Amalgamated Meat Cutters and Butcher Workmen of North America, et al., Equity Case No. 164, "Records of the District Court." See also "Judge Munger Issues Order," *Nebraska Daily Press*, December 17, 1921, and "Pickets

to Work Singly; Judge Munger Applies Supreme Court Decision to Nebraska City Strike Case," *Lincoln State Journal,* December 17, 1921.

80. Pratt, "Divided Workers, Divided Communities," 56. See also "Strike Continues at Local Plant; Mexicans Stopped," *Nebraska Daily Press,* December 7, 1921.

81. Pratt, "Divided Workers, Divided Communities," 56–57. See also "Strike Sympathizers Held; Four Men Named in Complaint as Abductors of James Estes, Who Was Taken from State," *Lincoln State Journal,* December 22, 1921, "Negroes Refused Carte Blanche to Packing District," *Nebraska Daily Press,* December 20, 1921, and "Two Strikers Are Bound Over on Kidnapping Charge," *Nebraska Daily Press,* December 30, 1921.

82. "Packers File Statements," *Lincoln State Journal,* December 23, 1921; "Hearing of Morton-Gregson Company's Application for Restraining Order Held before Judge Munger," *Lincoln State Journal,* December 27, 1921; and "Munger to Hand Down Opinion in Strike Situation," *Nebraska Daily Press,* December 28, 1921.

83. "Defendant's Answer to Plaintiff's Petition," Morton-Gregson Company v. Local Union No. 122 of Amalgamated Meat Cutters and Butcher Workmen of North America, et al., Equity Case No. 164, Records of the District Court.

84. "Jurisdiction of Court Attacked by the Strikers; Judge Munger Hears Argument on Question Raised by Union," *Lincoln Star,* December 26, 1921.

85. "Temporary Injunction," Morton-Gregson Company v. Local Union No. 122 of Amalgamated Meat Cutters and Butcher Workmen of North America, et al., Equity Case No. 164, Records of the District Court. See also "Copies of Munger Injunction Are Received Locally," *Nebraska Daily Press,* January 6, 1922.

86. "Memorandum Opinion," Morton-Gregson Company v. Local Union No. 122 of Amalgamated Meat Cutters and Butcher Workmen of North America, et al., Equity Case No. 164, Records of the District Court. See also "Strikers Win Over Packers," *Nebraska Daily Press,* January 4, 1922; "Strikers Are Discharged; Will Not Be Punished on Contempt Charge; Packing House Employees Convince Judge They Have Not Picketed in Groups," *Lincoln State Journal,* January 4, 1922; and "Judge Declares Evidence Did Not Prove Violation," *Nebraska Daily Press,* January 5, 1922.

87. "Make Order More Plain; Judge Munger Says Written Explanation Will Be Furnished Strikers," *Nebraska Daily Press,* January 5, 1922.

88. "Strikers to Jail; Judge T. C. Munger Holds Three Nebraska City Men for Contempt after Hearing in Federal Court Saturday Night," *Lincoln Star,* January 8, 1922. See also "Three Guilty of Contempt; Nebraska City Strikers Are Given Jail Terms," *Lincoln State Journal,* January 8, 1922, and "Three

Defendants Found Guilty of Contempt of Court," *Nebraska Daily Press,* January 8, 1922.

89. "Munger's Talk about Militia Arouses Interest; Federal Judge Says Troops Must Be Sent Here to Stop Disturbances," *Nebraska Daily Press,* January 10, 1922.

90. "Nebraska City Asks for National Guard," *Lincoln State Journal,* January 28, 1922, and "Troops Have Been Called," *Nebraska Daily Press,* January 28, 1922.

91. "Martial Law Is Declared" and "Troops Are Now on Duty," *Nebraska Daily Press,* January 29, 1922; "Martial Law at Nebraska City," *Lincoln Star,* January 28, 1922; and "City Guarded by Soldiers; Nebraska City Is Now under Martial Law," *Lincoln State Journal,* January 29, 1922.

92. "Martial Law Is Declared," *Nebraska Daily Press,* January 29, 1922.

93. "Proclamation of Nebraska National Guard, January 28, 1922," *Nebraska Daily Press,* January 28, 1922.

94. "Proclamation of Governor Samuel McKelvie, January 30, 1922," *Nebraska Daily Press,* January 30, 1922.

95. "Quiet Reigns in Strike Town; Militia Is in Control," *Lincoln Star,* January 29, 1922; "Quiet at Nebraska City," *Lincoln State Journal,* January 30, 1922; and "Military Forces Say Situation Is Very Satisfactory; No Disturbances Reported to Headquarters Yesterday," *Nebraska Daily Press,* February 1, 1922.

96. "Strike Over at the Plant; Packing Company Will Take Back Men as Needed," *Nebraska Daily Press,* February 2, 1922; "Declare the Strike Over; Nebraska City Workers Decide to Seek Former Jobs," *Lincoln State Journal,* February 2, 1922. See also "Crowds Thronged to Plant Seeking Return to Places; Many Were Disappointed; No Further Dealings with a Union, Officials Said to a Reporter," *Nebraska Daily Press,* February 3, 1922.

97. See, e.g., "Strike-Breakers Leaving; Tension Being Relieved by Exodus of Men at Nebraska City Who Helped Packers," *Lincoln Daily Journal,* February 4, 1922, reporting that about sixty replacement workers had already left town.

98. Pratt, "Divided Workers, Divided Communities," 61–62.

99. For details on some of the cases handled by the military tribunal during the period of martial law, see "Military Court Holds Session for First Time," *Nebraska Daily Press,* February 4, 1922; "Cases Heard by Provost Court Took Entire Day," *Nebraska Daily Press,* February 5, 1922; "Military Court Takes Evidence in Seven Cases" and "Military Court Passes Judgment on Six Accused," *Nebraska Daily Press,* February 7, 1922; "Heavy Sentence by Military for Hugh H. Seymour," *Nebraska Daily Press,* February 8, 1922; "Ernie Watson Gets Six Months in County Jail; Pleaded Guilty before Military Court to Having Fire Arms in Possession," *Nebraska Daily Press,* February 9, 1992; "Another Session of Military Court Held Yesterday," *Nebraska Daily Press,* February 10, 1922;

and "Ben Case Gets Five Months in the County Jail; Charles Logan Who Attacked Strike-Breaker Received Six Months in Jail," *Nebraska Daily Press,* February 12, 1922.

100. See "Military Court Cases Taken Up before Governor," *Nebraska Daily Press,* February 15, 1922, and "Governor Finds Two Sentences Were Excessive," *Nebraska Daily Press,* February 19, 1922.

101. "Governor Ends Military Rule in Strike Town," *Lincoln Star,* February 16, 1922, and "Proclamation of Governor Samuel McKelvie Terminating Martial Law," *Nebraska Daily Press,* February 16, 1922.

102. "Question the Right to Declare Martial Law," *Omaha World-Herald,* February 25, 1922, and "Two Nebraska City Men Declare They Are Held Illegally," *Nebraska Daily Press,* February 23, 1922.

103. U.S. ex rel. Seymour v. Fischer, 280 F. 208 (D. Neb. 1922), at 210.

104. Fischer, at 211–12.

105. "Appeals Court Affirms Local Men's Conviction by Military Court," *Nebraska Daily Press,* February 29, 1924.

106. Pratt, "Divided Workers, Divided Communities," 62.

107. "Sheriff Fischer Is Shorn of His Power," *Lincoln State Journal,* February 13, 1922.

108. For samples of published opinions by the court between 1916 and 1925 dealing with matters that were not directly related to the war or labor unrest, see Flas v. Illinois Cent. R. Co., 229 F. 319 (D. Neb. 1916); Crews v. Illinois Commercial Men's Ass'n., 256 F. 268 (D. Neb 1916); Luten v. Wilson Reinforced Concrete Co., 254 F. 107 (D. Neb. 1917), aff'd, 263 F. 983 (8th Cir. 1920); Friesen v. Chicago, R.I. & P. Ry. Co., 254 F. 875 (D. Neb. 1918); Rutherford v. Union Pac. R. Co., 254 F. 880 (D. Neb. 1919); Shukert v. Allen, 300 F. 754 (D. Neb. 1924), aff'd 6 F.2d 551 (8th Cir. 1925), rev'd 273 U.S. 545 (1927); U.S. v. Updike, 1 F.2d 550 (D. Neb. 1924), aff'd 8 F.2d 913 (1925); Munroe v. United States, 10 F.2d 230 (D. Neb. 1925); Mutual Oil v. Zehrung, 11 F.2d 887 (D. Neb. 1925); and Northwestern Bell Telephone Co. v. Spillman, 6 F.2d 663 (D. Neb. 1925).

109. T. C. Munger to J. W. Woodrough, September 28, 1917, T. C. Munger Papers, RG 21, box 35.

110. The expression was a fairly common idiom of the early twentieth century, roughly meaning "outside of human control," but Munger's reference to Emerson is puzzling, since the phrase is not typically attributed to him.

111. Munger to Woodrough, September 26, 1919, T. C. Munger Papers, RG 21, box 35.

112. Munger to Woodrough, March 4, 1921, T. C. Munger Papers, RG 21, box 36.

113. Munger, "An American Visitor's Impressions of Foreign Courts" and "A

Visitor's Impression of Foreign Courts." See also "Judge Munger Will Speak at Bar Meet," *Omaha World-Herald*, November 15, 1923, reporting that Munger would be the featured speaker at the upcoming Nebraska State Bar Association annual meeting.

114. Munger, "An American Visitor's Impression," 178, 179, 180, 183.

10. PROHIBITION AND THE DENNISON TRIAL

1. Useful information on the impact of Prohibition in Nebraska may be found in a number of well-constructed digital exhibits, including nebraskastudies. org, "Nebraska Prohibits Alcohol," at http://www.nebraskastudies.org/0700 /frameset.html, and Nebraska State Historical Society, "Bootlegger's Carnival."

2. For more on the impact of Prohibition on the federal courts generally, see Federal Judicial Center, "History of the Federal Judiciary, *Olmstead v. United States.*"

3. "Over a Hundred Are Indicted on Federal Liquor Charges," *Omaha World-Herald*, January 13, 1927.

4. "In Memoriam, Honorable Thomas Charles Munger (1861–1941)," 146, 159.

5. "Finds Moral Turpitude in Bartos' Act," *Lincoln Star*, June 2, 1926.

6. Editorial, "The People Have Good Sense Too," *Omaha World-Herald*, March 7, 1924.

7. Batter, "The Wayfaring Judge," 80, 84.

8. Batter, "The Wayfaring Judge," 77.

9. Ed F. Morearty, "Judge Woodrough," *Omaha World-Herald*, May 21, 1924. Morearty also praised Woodrough in his earlier memoir, *Omaha Memories*, 201.

10. "Man Fined $50 Offers to Clean Judge Woodrough's Hats Free," *Omaha World-Herald*, November 19, 1929.

11. Editorial, "We Have the Man," *Omaha World-Herald*, November 18, 1929.

12. "Bob Samardick, Ex-Police Chief, Dies after Stroke; Raiding Bob a Prohibition Era Legend," *Omaha World-Herald*, June 26, 1964. Following his federal service, Samardick went on to serve several colorful and often controversial terms as Omaha's police chief.

13. "Dry Raiders Wore Boots; Agent's Men Found Booze to Dump," *Omaha World-Herald*, June 26, 1964.

14. "Bob Samardick Ignored the Odds," *Omaha World-Herald*, June 26, 1964.

15. See "Raiders Charged with Oppression, Violence; Samardick, Schmitt, Deputy Sheriffs Fee, Graham, and Phillips Named," *Omaha World-Herald*, January 7, 1925.

16. "Samardick Freed in Assault Case by Federal Jury," *Omaha World-Herald*, April 29, 1925. See also Batter, "The Wayfaring Judge," 79.

17. "Samardick Fined $150 for Assault on Postal Clerk," *Omaha World-Herald*, January 3, 1929.

18. "Bob Samardick Ignored the Odds," *Omaha World-Herald,* June 26, 1964.

19. For a representative example of the paper's references to Samardick's "victims," see "Admits Selling Hooch in Branch Post Office," *Omaha World-Herald,* July 14, 1923.

20. United States v. Musgrave, 293 F. 203 (D. Neb. 1923). The *Omaha World-Herald*'s huge headline on December 4, 1923, read, "Bars Dry Agents from Search; Woodrough Rules Rum Sleuths Not 'Civil Officers.'" For samples of the national reaction, see "U.S. Judge Rules Dry Agents Lack Right to Serve Search Warrants," *San Francisco Chronicle,* December 5, 1923; "Search Warrant Service Barred to Dry Agents," *Chicago Daily Tribune,* December 5, 1923; and "Not Civil Officers," *Little Rock Arkansas Gazette,* December 5, 1923.

21. *United States v. Musgrave,* 293 F. 203, 207.

22. Batter, "The Wayfaring Judge," 80.

23. National Prohibition (Volstead) Act, Pub. L. 66–66, 41 Stat. 305 (66th Cong., October 28, 1919).

24. "Haynes Proposes an Extensive Use of the 'Padlock,'" *Omaha World-Herald,* February 1, 1923.

25. "Temporary Order, Fontenelle Hotel," *Omaha World-Herald,* February 1, 1923.

26. "Government to Call Bellhops against Hotel; Woodrough Decision on Closing Held Up," *Omaha World-Herald,* March 7, 1923.

27. "Judge Woodrough Denies Petition to Padlock Hotel," *Omaha World-Herald,* March 8, 1923.

28. Batter, "The Wayfaring Judge," 80. Batter noted that, at the time of the Prohibition case, Eppley was only leasing the Fontenelle and was struggling to obtain title from its bankrupt owners. He ultimately succeeded and spent the rest of his life living in the Fontenelle, from which he ran his multistate enterprise.

29. "Issue 'Padlock Orders' against Two Places," *Omaha World-Herald,* December 21, 1923.

30. Batter, "The Wayfaring Judge," 80.

31. United States v. Lot 29, Block 16, Highland Place, City of Omaha, Neb., 296 F. 729, 735, 738 (D. Neb. 1924).

32. Batter, "The Wayfaring Judge," 81, citing *Daily Register Gazette* (Rockford IL), May 27, 1924.

33. "Let's Have This Decided," *Detroit News,* reprinted in "Gleaned from Many Fields," *Omaha World-Herald,* May 31, 1924.

34. See U.S. v. Cunningham, 21 F.2d 800 (D. Neb. 1927) and U.S. v. Cunningham, 37 F.2d 349 (D. Neb. 1929).

35. "Omaha Idea Doesn't Go Here," *Lincoln Journal,* May 6, 1924.

36. Editorial, "Judge Munger on Omaha," *Omaha World-Herald*, May 7, 1924.
37. See "Injunction Act Is Held Valid; Munger Holds Liquor Law Violator May Be Enjoined," *Lincoln Star*, June 19, 1929, and "Liquor Injunction Upheld by Munger," *Lincoln State Journal*, June 20, 1929.
38. Batter, "The Wayfaring Judge," 81. See also "'Ten Year' McGee in Woodrough's Court," *Omaha World-Herald*, July 21, 1924.
39. Boyd, "The Life and Career of the Honorable John B. Sanborn Jr." Sanborn replaced McGee on the Minnesota District Court.
40. Boyd, "The Life and Career of the Honorable John B. Sanborn, Jr.," fn 136.
41. Batter, "The Wayfaring Judge," 81–82.
42. United States v. White, 29 F.2d 294, 295 (D. Neb. 1928).
43. Batter, "The Wayfaring Judge," 82.
44. "Doubts Agents' Noses," *Omaha World-Herald*, January 4, 1930.
45. Batter, "The Wayfaring Judge," 82.
46. "Sight, Hearing, Smell Don't Form Warrant," *Omaha World-Herald*, November 28, 1929.
47. Batter, "The Wayfaring Judge," 82.
48. "A Rock in a Weary Land," *New York Herald Tribune*, reprinted *Omaha World-Herald*, December 3, 1929.
49. "Prosecutor Dismayed with Ruling," *Omaha World-Herald*, November 28, 1929.
50. *Omaha World-Herald*, December 3, 1929.
51. Day v. U.S., 37 F.2d 80 (8th Cir. 1929).
52. See, e.g., Simon, "Dog Sniffs, Robot Spiders, and the Contraband Exception to the Fourth Amendment," 111.
53. "Woodrough on Critics," *Omaha World-Herald*, May 4, 1928.
54. Batter, "The Wayfaring Judge," 83.
55. "A Serious Business," *Nebraska State Journal*, December 17, 1921.
56. "Seward Men Sentenced," *Nebraska State Journal*, January 14, 1922.
57. The most authoritative and thorough analysis of Dennison and his Omaha criminal empire is Menard, *River City Empire*. Other valuable references include Davis, "The Gray Wolf: Tom Dennison of Omaha," and relevant portions of Larsen et al., *Upstream Metropolis*. For a fascinating examination of the story, told by an objective but "interested" relative of two of the key figures in the Dennison trial, see Smith Camp, "When Clerks of the District Court Had Real Power."
58. Menard, *River City Empire*, 4–11.
59. For more on the city's unsavory reputation, see Bristow, *A Dirty Wicked Town*, as well as Larsen et al., *Upstream Metropolis*, and Liz Rea, *History at a Glance*, Douglas County Historical Society, http://www.omahahistory.org/History%20at%20a%20glance%209–2007.pdf.

60. Woodrough, "Reform of Legal Procedure," 167. The judicial backlog is evident by the fact that cases brought by Woodrough and Beckett, who ended their practice together in 1899, were still caught up in the courts as late as 1905. Batter, "The Wayfaring Judge," fn 10.

61. The story of the debate between Gurley and Rosewater and all related quotes are from Batter, "The Wayfaring Judge," 75.

62. Morearty, *Omaha Memories*, 201. Morearty incorrectly recalls the race as being in 1902.

63. Smith was the grandfather of current chief judge of the Nebraska Federal District Court, Laurie Smith Camp. For more on the anti-Dennison forces, see generally Menard, *River City Empire*, and Smith Camp, "When Clerks of the District Court Had Real Power."

64. Menard, *River City Empire*, 113.

65. Batter, "The Wayfaring Judge," 77.

66. Menard, *River City Empire*, 245–48.

67. Menard, "Lest We Forget, 159.

68. Batter, "The Wayfaring Judge," 83.

69. Batter, "The Wayfaring Judge."

70. O'Donnell, "Can This Woman Make America Dry?"

71. O'Donnell, "Can This Woman Make America Dry?"

72. Kansas City Structural Steel Co. v. Com'r of Int. Revenue, 33 F.2d 53 (8th Cir. 1929).

73. Lucas v. Kansas City Structural Steel Co., 281 U.S. 264 (1930).

74. Batter, "The Wayfaring Judge," fn 76.

75. Batter, "The Wayfaring Judge," 83–84.

76. "Alleged Bootlegger Will Wait," *Omaha World-Herald*, April 22, 1930.

77. Batter, "The Wayfaring Judge," 84.

78. Batter, "The Wayfaring Judge," 84.

79. Batter, "The Wayfaring Judge," 84–85.

80. Batter, "The Wayfaring Judge," 84–85.

81. For a thorough review of the police investigation of all the theories related to Lapidus's murder, see Menard, *River City Empire*, 267–81.

82. "Crawford Says a 'Killer Squad' Was Suggested; Names of Lapidus and Smith Mentioned; Testifies Dennison Sought Lapidus Death," *Omaha World-Herald*, October 28, 1932.

83. Menard, *River City Empire*, 281.

84. Again, many able scholars and writers have studied Dennison's trial, but by far the most thorough recounting of the testimony and evidence is Menard, *River City Empire*, 299–310.

85. Menard, *River City Empire*, 301.

86. "Louise Says Warned Where to Buy Liquor; Ex-Bootleg 'Queen' Is Witness at Rum Trial," *Omaha World-Herald*, October 15, 1932.

87. Menard, *River City Empire*, 302.

88. Menard, *River City Empire*, 300.

89. Woodrough's evidentiary ruling was published verbatim in "The Court's Ruling," *Omaha World-Herald*, October 18, 1932.

90. Menard, *River City Empire*, 305.

91. Menard, *River City Empire*, 305, 307.

92. "Say 'Syndicate' Jury Was Never Near Agreement," *Omaha World-Herald*, December 13, 1932.

93. Menard, *River City Empire*, 308–9. See also Smith Camp, "When Clerks of the District Court Had Real Power," 21.

94. For support of this view, see Davis, "The Gray Wolf," 47, and sources cited therein.

95. Menard, *River City Empire*, 310–13. See also Davis, "The Gray Wolf," 47–48; Smith Camp, "When Clerks of the District Court Had Real Power," 22; and Batter, "The Wayfaring Judge," 86–87.

96. "Raiding Bob a Prohibition Era Legend," *Omaha World-Herald*, June 26, 1964.

97. Davis, "The Gray Wolf," 47–48; see also "Tom Dennison, Political Figure, Dies," *Omaha World-Herald*, February 15, 1934.

98. "Judicial Archive," United States District Court for the District of Nebraska, http://www.ned.uscourts.gov/public/judicial-archive/woodrough-j-w

99. Judicial Archive, United States District Court for the District of Nebraska, http://www.ned.uscourts.gov/public/judicial-archive/munger-t-c

100. Judicial Archive, United States District Court for the District of Nebraska, http://www.ned.uscourts.gov/public/judicial-archive/donohoe-j-a.

BIBLIOGRAPHY

MANUSCRIPTS AND ARCHIVES

National Archives and Records Administration, Central Plains Region, Kansas City MO (NARA):

Records of the U.S. Territorial Court, Nebraska, RG 21, Subgroup 29.1.

Records of the U.S. District Court for Nebraska:

Papers of Hon. Thomas C. Munger, RG 21, Subgroup 29.2, boxes 31–36, 41.

Voluminous Assorted Case Files, RG 21, Subgroup 29.2.

Records of the U.S. Circuit Court for Nebraska, RG 21, Subgroup 29.3.

Nebraska State Historical Society, Lincoln (NSHS):

Records of the Nebraska Territorial Courts, RG 58, Subgroup 1, Series 1–3; Subgroup 2, Series 1–5; Subgroup 3, Series 1–3; and Subgroup 4, Series 1–6.

William V. Allen Papers, RG 2632.AM, boxes 1–2.

National Archives and Records Administration, Central Plains Region, Kansas City MO (NARA):

Records of the U.S. Territorial Court, Nebraska, RG 21, Subgroup 29.1.

Records of the U.S. District Court for Nebraska:

Papers of Hon. Thomas C. Munger, RG 21, Subgroup 29.2, boxes 31–36, 41.

Voluminous Assorted Case Files, RG 21, Subgroup 29.2.

Records of the U.S. Circuit Court for Nebraska, RG 21, Subgroup 29.3.

Nebraska State Historical Society, Lincoln (NSHS):

Records of the Nebraska Territorial Courts, RG 58, Subgroup 1, Series 1–3; Subgroup 2, Series 1–5; Subgroup 3, Series 1–3; and Subgroup 4, Series 1–6.

William V. Allen Papers, RG 2632.AM, boxes 1–2.

PUBLISHED WORKS

Abraham, Henry J. *Justices and Presidents: A Political History of Appointments to the Supreme Court.* New York: Oxford University Press, 1974.

Anderson, Terry L., and Peter J. Hill. *The Not So Wild, Wild West.* Stanford CA: Stanford University Press, 2004.

Athearn, Robert G. *Union Pacific Country.* Lincoln: University of Nebraska Press, 1971.

Batter, Nick. "The Wayfaring Judge: Woodrough and Organized Crime in the U.S. District Court." *Nebraska History* 97, no. 2 (Summer 2016): 73–92.

Beard, Charles A., and Mary R. Beard. *The Rise of American Civilization.* New York: Macmillan, 1927.

Bodayla, Stephen D. "Can an Indian Vote?" *Elk v. Wilkins,* a Setback for Indian Citizenship." *Nebraska History* 67 (Winter 1986): 372–80.

Boyd, Thomas H. "The Life and Career of the Honorable John B. Sanborn Jr." *William Mitchell Law Review* 23, no. 2 (1997): 203–312.

Breitzer, Susan Roth. "Newberry Railroad Rate Bill (1894)." In *Encyclopedia of Populism in America,* edited by Alexandra Kindell and Elizabeth S. Demers, 463–64. New York: ABC-CLIO, 2014.

Bristow, David. *A Dirty Wicked Town: Tales of 19th Century Omaha.* Caldwell ID: Caxton, 2000.

Brody, David. *The Butcher Workmen: A Study of Unionization.* Cambridge: Harvard University Press, 1964.

Bryan, William Jennings. *The First Battle.* New York: Sampson Low, 1897.

Butcher, Solomon D. *Pioneer History of Custer County.* Broken Bow NE: Merchants, 1901.

Calhoun, Charles W. *From Bloody Shirt to Full Dinner Pail: The Transformation of Politics and Governance in the Gilded Age.* New York: Hill and Wang, 2010.

Carter, Robert L. "United States District Courts." In *Encyclopedia of the American Constitution,* 4 vols., edited by Leonard W. Levy, Kenneth L. Karst, and Dennis J. Mahoney, 4:1943. New York: Macmillan, 1986.

Chase, Harold, Samuel Krislov, Keith G. Boyum, and Jerry N. Clark, comps. *Biographical Dictionary of the Federal Judiciary.* Detroit: Gale Research, 1976.

Cherny, Robert W. *American Politics in the Gilded Age, 1868–1900.* Wheeling IL: Harlan Davidson, 1997.

———. *Populism, Progressivism, and the Transformation of Nebraska Politics, 1885–1915.* Lincoln: University of Nebraska Press, 1981.

———. *A Righteous Cause: The Life of William Jennings Bryan.* Norman: University of Oklahoma Press, 1994.

Chrisman, Harry E. *Ladder of Rivers: The Story of I. P. (Print) Olive.* Denver: Sage, 1962.

Coletta, Paolo E. *William Jennings Bryan*. Lincoln: University of Nebraska Press, 1969.

Commager, Henry Steele, ed. *Documents of American History*. 8th ed. New York: Appleton-Century-Crofts, 1968.

Cooper, John M., Jr. *Pivotal Decades: The United States, 1900–1920*. New York: Norton, 1990.

Davis, John Kyle. "The Gray Wolf: Tom Dennison of Omaha." *Nebraska History* 58 (1977): 25–52.

Davis, Thomas M. "Building the Burlington through Nebraska: A Summary View." *Nebraska History* 30 (December 1949): 317–47.

Decker, Leslie E. *Railroads, Lands, and Politics: The Taxation of the Railroad Land Grants, 1864–1897*. Providence RI: Brown University Press, 1964.

Dockstader, Frederick J. *Great North American Indians: Profiles in Life and Leadership*. New York: Van Nostrand Reinhold, 1977.

Dolezai, Frank. "History of the Dodge County Bar." In *History of Dodge and Washington Counties, Nebraska, and Their People*, edited by William H. Buss and Thomas T. Osterman, 91–98. Chicago: American Historical Society, 1921.

Eggert, Gerald G. "A Missed Alternative: Federal Courts as Arbiters of Railway Labor Disputes, 1877–1895." *Labor History* 17 (Fall 1966): 287–94.

———. *Railroad Labor Disputes: The Beginnings of Federal Strike Policy*. Ann Arbor: University of Michigan Press, 1967.

Ellis, Mark R. *Law and Order in Buffalo Bill's Country: Legal Culture and Community on the Great Plains, 1867–1910*. Lincoln: University of Nebraska Press, 2007.

Ellis, Richard E. *The Jeffersonian Crisis: Courts and Politics in the Young Republic*. New York: W. W. Norton, 1971.

Federal Judicial Center. "History of the Federal Judiciary, *Olmstead v. United States*: The Constitutional Challenges of Prohibition Enforcement—Historical Background and Documents." http://www.fjc.gov/history/home.nsf/page /tu_olmstead_narrative.html.

Folsom, Burton W., Jr. *No More Free Markets or Free Beer: The Progressive Era in Nebraska, 1900–1924*. Lanham MD: Lexington, 1999.

Folsom, Robert G. *The Money Trail: How Elmer Irey and His T-Men Brought Down America's Criminal Elite*. Washington DC: Potomac 2010.

Frankfurter, Felix, and Nathan Greene. *The Labor Injunction*. New York: Macmillan, 1930.

Frankfurter, Felix, and James Landis. *The Business of the Supreme Court: A Study of the Federal Judicial System*. New York: Macmillan, 1928.

Freyer, Tony. *Forums of Order: The Federal Courts and Business in American History*. Greenwich CT: Jai, 1979.

———. *Harmony and Dissonance: The Swift and Eric Cases in American Federalism*. New York: New York University Press, 1981.

Friedman, Lawrence M. *A History of American Law.* 2nd ed. New York: Simon & Schuster, 1985.

George Mason University, History Matters. "The Omaha Platform: Launching the Populist Party." http://historymatters.gmu.edu/d/5361.

Haines, Henry S. *Restrictive Railway Legislation.* New York: Macmillan, 1905.

Hall, Dorothy M. *Life and Letters of Richard Smith Hall.* New York: Comet, 1965.

Hall, Kermit L. *The Politics of Justice: Lower Federal Judicial Selection and the Second Party System, 1829–1861.* Lincoln: University of Nebraska Press, 1979.

Hall, Kermit L., and Peter Karsten. *The Magic Mirror: Law in American History.* 2nd ed. New York: Oxford University Press, 2008.

Hellerstein, Jerome R. "Picketing Legislation and the Courts." 10 *N.C. L. Rev.* (1932): 158–88.

Heskett, Jesse Theodore. "The Burlington Strike in Nebraska, 1888." Master's thesis, University of Nebraska–Lincoln, 1933.

Hewitt, James W. "'The Public Be Damned': Railroads, the Free Pass System, and the Nebraska Supreme Court, 1875–1911." Master's thesis, University of Nebraska–Lincoln, 1994.

Hine, Charles DeLano. *Letters from an Old Railway Official to His Son, a Division Superintendent.* Chicago: Railway Age, 1904.

Holmes, Oliver Wendell, Jr. *Speeches by Oliver Wendell Holmes* Boston: Little, Brown, 1891.

Homer, Michael W. "The Territory Judiciary: An Overview of the Nebraska Experience, 1854–1867." *Nebraska History* 63 (Fall 1982): 349–80.

Irons, Peter. *A People's History of the Supreme Court.* New York: Penguin, 2006.

Jackson, Joe. *The Leavenworth Train: A Fugitive's Search for Justice in the Vanishing West.* New York: Carroll & Graf, 2001.

Jay, John C. "General N. B. Forrest as a Railroad Builder in Alabama." *Alabama Historical Quarterly* 24 (Spring 1962): 16–31.

Johansen, Gregory J. "'To Make Some Provision for Their Half-Breeds': The Nemaha Half-Breed Reserve, 1830–1866." *Nebraska History* 67 (Spring 1986): 8–29.

Johnson, Frederick L. "From Leavenworth to Congress: The Improbable Journey of Frances H. Shoemaker." *Minnesota History* 51, no. 5 (Spring 1989): 166–77.

Kazin, Michael. *A Godly Hero: The Life of William Jennings Bryan.* New York: Anchor, 2007.

Kens, Paul. *Justice Stephen Field: Shaping Liberty from the Gold Rush to the Gilded Age.* Lawrence: University Press of Kansas, 1997.

King, James T. "'A Better Way': General George Crook and the Ponca Indians." *Nebraska History* 50 (Fall 1969): 239–56.

Kolko, Gabriel. *Railroads and Regulation, 1877–1916.* Princeton NJ: Princeton University Press, 1965.

Kraenzel, Karl Frederick. *The Great Plains in Transition*. Norman: University of Oklahoma Press, 1955.

Lambertson, G. M. "Indian Citizenship." *American Law Review* 20 (March–April 1886): 183–93.

Larsen, Lawrence H., Barbara J. Cottrell, Harl A. Dalstrom, and Kay Calame. *Upstream Metropolis: An Urban Biography of Omaha and Council Bluffs*. Lincoln: University of Nebraska Press, 2103.

"The Late Judge Dundy's Ways." *American Lawyer* 5 (1897): 123.

Licht, Daniel S. *Ecology and Economics of the Great Plains*. Lincoln: University of Nebraska Press, 1997.

Lowe, Janet. *Damn Right! Behind the Scenes with Berkshire Hathaway Billionaire Charlie Munger*. New York: John Wiley, 2000.

Luebke, Frederick C. *Bonds of Loyalty: German Americans and the First World War*. Urbana: University of Illinois Press, 1974.

Manley, Robert N. "The Nebraska State Council of Defense and the Nonpartisan League, 1917–1918." *Nebraska History* 43 (1962): 229–52.

Mattison, Ray H. "The Burlington Tax Controversy in Nebraska over the Federal Land Grants." *Nebraska History* 28 (April 1947): 110–31.

McGerr, Michael. *A Fierce Discontent: The Rise and Fall of the Progressive Movement in America, 1870–1920*. New York: Oxford University Press, 2005.

McGowan, Carl. "United States Courts of Appeals." In *Encyclopedia of the American Constitution*, 4 vols., edited by Leonard W. Levy, Kenneth L. Karst, and Dennis J. Mahoney, 4:1939–42. New York: Macmillan, 1986.

McIntosh, C. Barron. "Patterns from Land Alienation Maps." *Annals of the Association of American Geographers* 66, no. 4 (December 1976): 570–82.

McIntyre, Kenneth E. "The Morton-Bryan Controversy." Master's thesis, University of Nebraska–Lincoln, 1934.

McMath, Robert C., Jr. *American Populism: A Social History, 1877–1898*. New York: Hill and Wang, 1990.

McMurry, Donald L. *The Great Burlington Strike of 1888: A Case History in Labor Relations*. New York: Cambridge University Press, 1956.

———. "The Legal Ancestry of the Pullman Strike Injunctions." *Industrial and Labor Relations Review* 14 (January 1961): 235–45.

Menard, Orville D. "Lest We Forget: The Lynching of Will Brown, Omaha's 1919 Race Riot." *Nebraska History* 91 (2010): 152–65.

———. *River City Empire: Tom Dennison's Omaha*. Lincoln: University of Nebraska Press, 2013.

Mercer, Lloyd J. *Railroads and Land Grant Policy: A Study in Government Intervention*. New York: Academic Press, 1982.

Message from the President Enclosing Documents Relative to John Pickering. Washington DC: Government Printing Office, 1803.

Mills, George, and Richard W. Peterson. *"No One Is Above the Law": The Story of Southern Iowa's Federal Court*. Des Moines: Southern District of Iowa Branch of the Historical Society of the United States Courts in the Eighth Circuit, 1994.

Monkkonen, Eric. "Can Nebraska or Any State Regulate Railroads? *Smyth v. Ames*, 1898." *Nebraska History* 54 (1973): 364–82.

Morearty, Edward F. *Omaha Memories: Recollections of Events, Men, and Affairs in Omaha, Nebraska, from 1879 to 1917*. Omaha: Swartz, 1917.

Morris, Jeffrey Brandon. *Establishing Justice in Middle America: A History of the United States Court of Appeals for the Eighth Circuit*. Minneapolis: University of Minnesota Press, 2007.

Morton, J. Sterling, and Albert Watkins. *Illustrated History of Nebraska: A History of Nebraska from the Earliest Explorations of the Trans-Mississippi Region with Steel Engravings, Photogravures, Copper Plates, Maps, and Tables*. 3 vols. Lincoln: Jacob North, 1907.

Munger, Thomas C. "An American Visitor's Impressions of Foreign Courts." *American Bar Association Journal* 10 (1924): 178–83.

———. "A Visitor's Impression of Foreign Courts." *Nebraska Law Bulletin* 3 (1924): 68–82.

National Constitution Center. "Louis Brandeis Confirmed as Justice 100 Years Ago Today." *Constitution Daily*, June 1, 2016. http://blog.constitutioncenter .org/2016/06/louis-brandeis-confirmed-as-justice-100-year-ago-today/.

Naugle, Ronald C., John J. Montag, and James C. Olson. *History of Nebraska*. 4th ed. Lincoln: University of Nebraska Press, 2014.

Nebraska: A Guidebook to the Cornhusker State. New York: Hastings House, 1947.

Nebraska Bar Association. "In Memoriam, Honorable Thomas Charles Munger (1861–1941)." *Neb. L. Rev.* 22 (June 1943): 146–68.

Nebraska State Historical Society. "Bootlegger's Carnival." *Nebraska Timeline* (May 2012). https://history.nebraska.gov/blog/bootleggers%e2%80%99-carnival.

———. "Dr. Rustin's Mysterious Death." https://history.nebraska.gov/publications /dr-rustins-mysterious-death.

nebraskastudies.org. "Nebraska Prohibits Alcohol." http://www.nebraskastudies .org/0700/frameset.html.

Nebraska Territorial Legislature. "An Act to Prohibit Slavery." *Laws of Nebraska*, January 15, 1861.

Nebraska Territory *Journal*. Council, 6th sess. January 9, 1860.

———. House, 5th sess., November 1, 1858.

O'Donnell, Jack. "Can This Woman Make America Dry?" *Collier's Magazine*, August 6, 1924, 23–29.

Overton, Richard C. *Burlington West: A Colonization History of the Burlington Railroad*. Cambridge MA: Harvard University Press, 1941.

Paine, Bayard H. "Decisions Which Have Changed Nebraska History." *Nebraska History Magazine* 16 (October–December 1935): 195–219.

Pomeroy, Earl S. *Territories of the United States, 1861–1890: Studies in Colonial Administration*. Seattle: University of Washington Press, 1947.

Postel, Charles. *The Populist Vision*. New York: Oxford University Press, 2009.

Pound, Roscoe. *An Introduction to the Philosophy of Law*. New Haven CT: Yale University Press, 1922.

Pratt, William C. "Advancing Packinghouse Unionism in South Omaha, 1917–1920." *Journal of the West* 35 (April 1996): 42–49.

———. "Divided Workers, Divided Communities: The 1921–22 Packinghouse Strike in Omaha and Nebraska City." *Labor's Heritage* 5 (Winter 1994): 50–65.

———. "Workers, Unions, and Historians on the Northern Plains." *Great Plains Quarterly* 16 (Fall 1996): 229–50.

Price, David H. "The Public Life of Elmer S. Dundy, 1857–1896." Master's thesis, University of Nebraska–Omaha, 1971.

Proceedings of the Grand Chapter of Royal Arch Masons of Nebraska at Its Thirty-Sixth Annual Convocation, Held at Omaha, December 10 and 11, 1902. Omaha: Omaha Printing, 1902.

Reynolds, Arthur R. "Land Frauds and Illegal Fencing in Western Nebraska." *Agricultural History* 23, no. 9 (July 1949): 173–79.

Rich, Edson P. "Slavery in Nebraska." *Transactions and Reports of the Nebraska State Historical Society* 2 (1897): 92–108.

Richards, Bartlett, Jr., and Ruth Van Ackeren. *Bartlett Richards: Nebraska Sandhills Cattleman*. Lincoln: Nebraska State Historical Society, 1980.

Rollings, Willard H. *The Osage: An Ethnohistorical Study of Hegemony on the Prairie-Plains*. Columbia: University of Missouri Press, 1995.

Roosevelt, Theodore. "Seventh Annual Message," December 3, 1907. *The American Presidency Project*, ed. Gerhard Peters and John T. Woolley. http://www.presidency.ucsb.edu/ws/?pid=29548.

Ross, William G. "Meyer v. Nebraska." In *The History of Nebraska Law*, edited by Alan Gless, 271–88. Athens: Ohio University Press, 2008.

Savage, James W. "The Bar of Omaha—Woolworth." *Magazine of Western History Illustrated* 9 (November 1888–April 1889): 281–86.

Schroeder, Alice. *The Snowball: Warren Buffett and the Business of Life*. New York: Bantam, 2008.

Schwartz, Bernard. *A History of the Supreme Court*. New York: Oxford University Press, 1993.

Time Magazine. "A Brief History of Indicted Senators." http://content.time
.com/time/specials/packages/article/0,28804,1827969_1827972_1828024
,00.html.

Sheley, Erin. "Live Animals: Toward Protection for Pets and Livestock in Contracts for Carriage." 3 *J. Animal L.* 59 (2007): 168–82.

Shirley, Glenn. *Law West of Fort Smith: A History of Frontier Justice in the Indian Territory, 1834–1896.* Lincoln: University of Nebraska Press, 1968.

Simon, Stephen A. "Dog Sniffs, Robot Spiders, and the Contraband Exception to the Fourth Amendment." *Charleston Law Review* 7 (2012): 111–23.

Smith Camp, Laurie. "When Clerks of the District Court Had Real Power: Robert Smith's Omaha, 1908–1950." *Nebraska Lawyer*, April 2001, 18–23.

Spencer, Morris Nelson. "The Union Pacific's Utilization of Its Land Grant, with Emphasis on Its Colonization Program." PhD diss., University of Nebraska–Lincoln, 1950.

Starita, Joe. *"I Am a Man": Chief Standing Bear's Journey for Justice.* New York: St. Martin's Griffin, 2008.

Stock, Catherine McNicol. *Rural Radicals: A History of Political Extremism in America.* Ithaca NY: Cornell University Press, 1996.

Summers, Mark W. *Party Games: Getting, Keeping, and Using Power in the Gilded Age.* Chapel Hill: University of North Carolina Press, 2004.

———. *Railroads, Reconstruction, and the Gospel of Prosperity: Aid under the Radical Republicans, 1865–1877.* Princeton NJ: Princeton University Press, 1984.

Surrency, Erwin C. *History of the Federal District Courts.* New York: Oceana, 1987.

Tachau, Mary K. Bonsteel. *Federal Courts in the Early Republic: Kentucky, 1789–1816.* Princeton NJ: Princeton University Press, 1978.

Thomas, William H., Jr. *Unsafe for Democracy: World War I and the U.S. Justice Department's Covert Campaign to Suppress Dissent.* Madison: University of Wisconsin Press, 2008.

Thompson, Tommy R. "The Great Omaha Train Robbery." *Nebraska History* 63 (1982): 216–31.

Tindall, George Brown, ed. *A Populist Reader: Selections from the Works of American Populist Leaders.* New York: Harper & Row, 1966.

Tocqueville, Alexis de. *Democracy in America.* Edited by J. P. Mayer. Translated by George Lawrence. 1835. Garden City NY: Doubleday, 1969.

Trottman, Nelson. *History of the Union Pacific: A Financial and Economic Survey.* New York: Ronald, 1923.

"University of Nebraska Loyalty Trials." University of Nebraska–Lincoln Digital Archives. http://unlhistory.unl.edu/exhibits/show/schillerlinden /uprootingthetree/nebraskacouncilofdefense. U.S. Congress. An Act Concerning the Supreme Court of the United States. 5 Stat. 676. June 17, 1844.

————. An Act Establishing Circuit Courts, and Abridging the Jurisdiction of the District Courts in the Districts of Kentucky, Tennessee, and Ohio. 2 Stat. 420. February 24, 1807.

————. An Act to Amend an Act Entitled 'An Act to Aid in the Construction of a Railroad and Telegraphy Line from the Missouri River to the Pacific Ocean, and to Secure to the Government the Use of the Same for Postal, Military, and Other Purposes, Approved July First, Eighteen Hundred and Sixty-Two. 13 Stat. 356. July 2, 1864.

————. An Act to Amend the Judicial System of the United States. 16 Stat. 44. April 10, 1869.

————. An Act to Amend the Judicial System of the United States. 2 Stat.156. April 29, 1802.

————. An Act to Divide the Judicial District of Nebraska into Divisions and to Provide for an Additional District Judge in Said District. 34 Stat. 997. February 27, 1907.

————. An Act to Establish the Judicial Courts of the United States (Judiciary Act of 1789). 1 Stat. 73. September 24, 1789.

————. An Act to Extend the Power of Granting Writs of Injunctions to the Judges of the District Courts of the United States. 2 Stat. 418. February 13, 1807.

————. An Act to Fix the Number of Judges of the Supreme Court of the United States, and to Change Certain Judicial Circuits. 14 Stat. 209. July 23, 1866.

————. An Act to Prevent Unlawful Occupancy of the Public Lands (Van Wyck Law). 23 Stat. 231. February 25, 1885.

————. An Act to Provide for a District and a Circuit Court of the United States for the District of Nebraska, and for Other Purposes. 15 Stat. 5. March 25, 1867.

————. An Act to Provide for the Holding of a Term of the District and Circuit Courts of the United States at Lincoln, Nebraska. 20 Stat. 169. June 19, 1878.

————. An Act to Provide for the More Convenient Organization of the Courts of the United States. 2 Stat. 89. February 13, 1801.

————. An Act to Vest More Effectually in the State Courts and in the District Courts of the United States Jurisdiction in the Cases Therein Mentioned. 3 Stat. 244. March 3, 1815.

————. "Charges Affecting the Hon. Charles H. Dietrich." Serial Set Vol. 4575, Session Vol. No. 6, 58th Cong., 2nd sess., S. Rep. 2152.

————. Espionage Act of 1917. 40 Stat. 217. June 15, 1917.

————. Evidence and Other Papers Submitted in the Contested Election of Samuel G. Daily versus J. Sterling Morton as Delegate from the Territory of Nebraska. 37th Cong., 18th sess., 1861. H. Misc. Docs., 40–49.

————. Expatriation Act of 1907. 34 Stat. 1228. March 12, 1907.

————. *Hearings before the Committee on Public Land of the House of Representatives on* the Question of Leasing of the Public Lands for Grazing Purposes, January 29–June 4, 1902. Washington DC: Government Printing Office, 1902.

———. National Prohibition (Volstead) Act. 41 Stat. 305. October 28, 1919.

———. Pacific Railway Act. 12 Stat. 489. July 1, 1862.

———. Sedition Act of 1918. 40 Stat. 553. May 16, 1918.

———. Trading with the Enemy Act of 1917. 40 Stat. 411. October 6, 1917.

U.S. Congress. Office of the Historian. Biographical Directory of the United States Congress, 1774–Present. http://bioguide.congress.gov/biosearch/biosearch.asp.

U.S. Department of the Interior. Report of the Secretary, 1904. 58th Cong., 3rd sess., H. Doc. 5, serial 4797, 20.

U.S. Department of Justice. Annual Report of the Attorney General of the United States for the Year 1896. Washington DC: Office of the Attorney General, Serial Set Vol. No. 3499, Session Vol. No. 23, 54th Cong., 2nd sess., H. Doc. 9 pt. 1 & 2.

———. Annual Report of the Attorney General of the United States for the Year 1906. Washington DC: Office of the Attorney General, Serial Set Vol. No. 5129, Session Vol. No. 26, 59th Cong., 2nd sess., H. Doc. 10.

U.S. District Court, District of Nebraska. "William H. Munger Memorial Proceedings." Judicial Archive. http://www.ned.uscourts.gov/internetDocs/judicialArchive/whm_Memoriam.pdf.

Wakely, Arthur C., ed., Omaha: The Gate City, and Douglas County, Nebraska: A Record of Settlement, Organization, Progress, and Achievement. Chicago: S. J. Clarke, 1917.

White, Richard. "It's Your Misfortune and None of My Own": A New History of the American West. Norman: University of Oklahoma Press, 1991.

Woodrough, Joseph W. "Beginning My Work on the Federal Bench." Creighton Chronicle 9, no. 7 (April 20, 1918): 409–15.

———. "The Game You Can't Lose." Creighton Chronicle 3, no. 7 (April 1, 1912): 309–13.

———. "Reform of Legal Procedure." Creighton Chronicle 4, no. 3 (December 1, 1912): 167–79.

Woolworth, James. "Judges of the Supreme Court of the Territory of Nebraska." In Reports of Cases in the Supreme Court of Nebraska [Territory]. Chicago: Callaghan & Cockcroft, 1871.

Wunder, John R. "No More Treaties: The Resolution of 1871 and the Alteration of Indian Rights to Their Homelands." In Working the Range: Essays on the History of Western Land Management and the Environment, edited by John R. Wunder, 39–56. Westport CT: Greenwood, 1985.

Zelden, Charles L. Justice Lies in the District: The U.S. District Court, Southern District Of Texas, 1902–1960. College Station: Texas A&M University Press, 1993.

JUDICIAL DECISIONS

American Steel Foundries v. Tri-City Trades Council, 257 U.S. 184, 205 (1921)

Chicago & N.W. Ry. Co. v. U.S., 168 F. 236 (8th Cir. 1909)

Chicago, B. & Q. Ry. Co. v. U.S., 170 F. 556 (8th Cir. 1908)

Chicago, B. & Q. Ry. Co. v. U.S., 220 U.S. 559 (1911)

Chilton v. Town of Gratton, 82 F. 873 (D. Neb. 1897)

Corbin v. United States, 205 F. 278 (8th Cir. 1913)

Crews v. Illinois Commercial Men's Ass'n., 256 F. 268 (D. Neb 1916)

Day v. U.S., 37 F.2d 80 (8th Cir. 1929)

Drexel v. Reed, 69 Neb. 468, 95 N.W. 873 (1903)

Drexel v. Rochester Loan & Banking Co., 65 Neb. 231, 91 N.W. 254 (1902)

Elgutter v. Northwestern Mut. Life Ins. Co., 86 F. 500 (8th Cir. 1898)

Flas v. Illinois Cent. R. Co., 229 F. 319 (D. Neb. 1916)

Friesen v. Chicago, R.I. & P. Ry. Co., 254 F. 875 (D. Neb. 1918)

Hagenbuck v. Reed, 3 Neb. 17 (1873)

Harshfield v. United States, 260 F. 659 (8th Cir. 1919)

Hunnewell v. County of Cass, 89 U.S. 752 (1875)

In re Appel, 103 F. 931 (D. Neb. 1900)

In re Boston, 98 F. 587 (D. Neb. 1899)

Kansas City Structural Steel Co. v. Com'r of Int. Revenue, 33 F.2d 53 (8th Cir. 1929)

Lucas v. Kansas City Structural Steel Co., 281 U.S. 264 (1930)

Luten v. Wilson Reinforced Concrete Co., 254 F. 107 (D. Neb. 1917), *aff'd,* 263 F. 983
    (8th Cir. 1920)

Matthews v. United States, 192 F. 490 (8th Cir. 1911)

Meyer v. Nebraska, 262 U.S. 390 (1923)

Munroe v. United States, 10 F.2d 230 (D. Neb. 1925)

Mutual Oil v. Zehrung, 11 F.2d 887 (D. Neb. 1925)

Northwestern Bell Telephone Co. v. Spillman, 6 F.2d 663 (D. Neb. 1925)

Northwestern Mut. Life Ins. Co. v. Seaman, 80 F. 357 (D. Neb. 1897)

Olive v. State, 11 Neb. 1, 7 N.W. 444 (1881)

Platt v. Union Pacific Railroad Co., 99 U.S. 424 (1879)

Richards v. U.S., 175 F. 911 (8th Cir. 1909)

Rutherford v. Union Pac. R. Co., 254 F. 880 (D. Neb. 1919)

Schenck v. United States, 249 U.S. 47 (1919)

Seaman v. Northwestern Mut. Life Ins. Co., 86 F. 493 (8th Cir. 1898)

Shukert v. Allen, 300 F. 754 (D. Neb. 1924), *aff'd* 6 F.2d 551 (8th Cir. 1925), *rev'd*
    273 U.S. 545 (1927)

Sinjen v. Miller, 281 F. 889 (D. Neb., 1922)

Smyth v. Ames, 171 U.S. 361 (1898)

State of Nebraska v. First Nat. Bank of Orleans, 88 F. 947 (D. Neb. 1898)

State of Nebraska v. Hayden, 89 F. 46 (D. Neb. 1898)

Tracy v. Morel, 88 F. 801 (D. Neb. 1898)

U.S. ex rel. Seymour v. Fischer, 280 F. 208 (D. Neb. 1922)

U.S. v. Updike, 1 F.2d 550 (D. Neb. 1924), *aff'd* 8 F.2d 913 (1925)

Union Pacific Railroad Co. v. Belek, 211 F. 699 (D. Neb., 1913)

Union Pacific Railroad Co v. Board of County Commissioners, 98 U.S. 196 (1879)

Union Pacific Railroad Co. v. Ruef, 120 F. 102 (Cir. Ct., D. Neb 1902)

Union Pacific Railroad Co. v. Peniston, 85 U.S. 787 (1873).

Union Pacific Railroad Co. v. McShane, 89 U.S. 747 (1875).

Union Stockyards Co. of Omaha v. U.S., 169 F. 404 (8th Cir. 1909)

United State v. Union Stock Yards Co. of Omaha, 161 F. 919 (D. Neb. 1908)

United States v. Bernstein, 267 F. 295 (D. Neb. 1920)

United States v. Burlington and Missouri River Railroad Co, 98 U.S. 198 (1879)

United States v. Chicago & N. W. Ry. Co., 157 F. 616 (D. Neb., 1907)

United States v. Chicago, B. & Q. R. Co., 184 F. 984 (D. Neb., 1910)

United States v. Chicago, B. & Q. Ry. Co., 156 F. 180 (D. Neb., 1907)

United States v. Cunningham, 21 F.2d 800 (D. Neb. 1927)

United States v. Cunningham, 37 F.2d 349 (D. Neb. 1929)

United States v. Dietrich, 126 F. 659 (Cir. Ct., D. Neb 1904)

United States v. Dietrich, 126 F. 664 (Cir. Ct., D. Neb 1904)

United States v. Dietrich, 126 F. 676 (Cir. Ct., D. Neb 1904)

United States v. L. Cohen Grocery Co., 255 U.S. 81 (1921)

United States v. Lot 29, Block 16, Highland Place, City of Omaha, Neb., 296 F. 729 (D. Neb. 1924)

United States v. Musgrave, 293 F. 203 (D. Neb. 1923)

United States v. Richards, 149 F. 443 (D. Neb 1906)

United States v. White, 29 F.2d 294 (D. Neb. 1928)

Ware v. United States, 154 F. 577 (8th Cir. 1907)

Ware v. United States, 207 U.S. 588 (1907)

INDEX